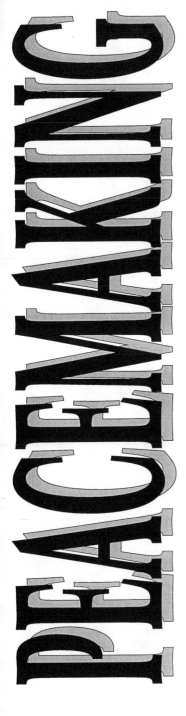

PEACEMAKING

Moral and Policy Challenges for a New World

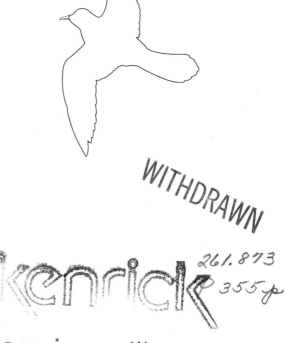

Edited by

Gerard F. Powers, Drew Christiansen, SJ, and Robert T. Hennemeyer

From November 1992 to November 1993, the bishops' ad hoc subcommittee on the tenth anniversary of *The Challenge of Peace* undertook a process of consultation in preparation for a statement on the moral dimensions of the post-Cold War world entitled *The Harvest of Justice Is Sown in Peace.* In order to share some of the contributions the bishops received during this process as well as to place the bishops' statement in a wider theological and policy context, the ad hoc subcommittee commissioned this collection of essays and authorized staff of the Office of International Justice and Peace to serve as editors. This book, *Peacemaking: Moral and Policy Challenges for a New World*, is authorized for publication by the undersigned.

Monsignor Robert N. Lynch
General Secretary
NCCB/USCC

June 1, 1994

ISBN 1-55586-682-4

Contents

Appendix

Preface

Most Reverend Daniel P. Reilly

The end of the Cold War has radically altered the way we think about the world, forcing us to discard old ideas and challenging us to consider new ways to shape our world that only a few years ago would have been dismissed as naive utopianism. The challenge today is to build a new international order that will be more just and more peaceful than the Cold War order it replaces. What this new order means, how it should be achieved, and what the role of the United States should be in it are questions which have generated much debate but little consensus. Many Americans, like people throughout the world, are groping for answers when few can even agree on the questions.

This exciting, challenging, and often frustrating search for new directions invites the Church to take seriously two aspects of its role in the modern world. First, according to the Second Vatican Council, the Church has a responsibility to read "the signs of the times" and interpret them in light of the Gospel. Second, the method for doing this is respectful dialogue with the world. In short, the Church has something to learn and something to teach about the shape of the post-Cold War world.

This book is part of a larger effort of the bishops in the United States to engage in a dialogue within the Church and with the wider community about the signs of these historic times and how to interpret them in light of our faith. This effort began in January 1990 when the bishops' International Policy Committee began reflecting on the implications of the liberation of Eastern Europe. The magnitude of the task led us to form an ad hoc subcommittee to examine in depth the challenge of peacemaking in a new world. Over the course of a year, this subcommittee consulted with dozens of theologians, policymakers, military strategists, scientists, academics, and peace advocates. The subcommittee also solicited written input from hundreds of others, including bishops' conferences from around the world and other religious bodies.

The bishops' statement, *The Harvest of Justice Is Sown in Peace*, which is published in this volume, is the fruit of this subcommittee's work. *The Harvest of Justice* is a modest document compared to the documents whose anniversaries it commemorates: The bishops' 1983 peace pastoral, *The Challenge of Peace: God's Promise and Our Response*, and Pope John XXIII's 1963 encyclical, *Pacem in Terris*. Nevertheless, it represents the most comprehensive reflection by the U.S. bishops to date of the moral and religious dimensions of peacemaking after the Cold War. It looks back to some of the unfinished business of the peace pastoral, namely, the validity of the just-war tradition and the issue of nuclear weapons. It also looks ahead at issues that were not among the primary concerns of a decade ago, such as the more central role of the United Nations and other multilateral institutions, the problem of religious and nationalist violence, and the moral dimensions of economic sanctions and humanitarian intervention.

This collection of essays enables us to share with a wider audience both *The Harvest of Justice* and some of the many excellent contributions we received during our process of consultation. It also places our own reflections in a much wider theological and policy context by providing background and analysis that could not be included in a relatively short and wide-ranging bishops' statement. Since we have sought to include a spectrum of views on a range of critical issues, we include essays by those who might not share our faith perspective or necessarily subscribe to our judgments about many important issues. We do so in a spirit of dialogue and in the hope that we and the reader will benefit from the diverse points of view expressed here.

Finally and most importantly, like the much more extensive process surrounding *The Challenge of Peace*, we hope this present volume, together with *The Harvest of Justice*, will contribute to the interdisciplinary dialogue about the moral and religious dimensions of the challenges and opportunities involved in shaping a just and peaceful post-Cold War world. We are convinced that religion and morality must be a prominent part of the debate about the decisions our country and the international community are making about the shape of this new order. At the same time, religious and moral reflection must be joined with and be refined by the insights of political scientists, economists, military strategists, and policy-makers, like those who have entered into dialogue with us here.

This book would not have been possible without the generous contributions of the distinguished authors of these essays, who were so willing to devote their time and expertise to this project. The idea of this book became a reality only with the hard work of Rev. Drew Christiansen, SJ, Gerard Powers, and Ambassador (ret.) Robert Hennemeyer of the U.S.

Catholic Conference's Office of International Justice and Peace, Ann Zimmerman and Tim Delaney of the Office for Publishing and Promotion Services, and Monica Theis Huber, who helped in the editing process.

Finally, I would like to express my special thanks to the members of the ad hoc subcommittee charged with drafting *The Harvest of Justice*: Bishop John J. Glynn (Military Archdiocese), Cardinal Roger Mahony (Los Angeles), Bishop James Malone (Youngstown), Bishop Ricardo Ramirez (Las Cruces), Bishop Walter Sullivan (Richmond), and Bishop Donald Wuerl (Pittsburgh).

We are especially indebted to two ad hoc committee members. As chairman of the bishops' International Policy Committee, Archbishop John R. Roach (Saint Paul and Minneapolis) played an invaluable leadership role in the work of the drafting committee. And as chairman of the committees that drafted the 1983 peace pastoral and the 1988 follow-up statement on nuclear deterrence, Cardinal Joseph Bernardin (Chicago) has made a singular contribution to the bishops' efforts to address the pressing issues of war and peace.

Introduction

Drew Christiansen, SJ

"How many divisions has the pope?" Stalin's gibe rang hollow in 1989 with the destruction of the Berlin Wall and the retreat of communism from Eastern Europe. A decade and a half after the election of a Polish pope and nearly as long since the ascendancy of Poland's Solidarity labor movement, a movement which drew both inspiration and guidance from Pope John Paul II, the influence of religion in international affairs has become undeniable.

The respected British journalist Timothy Garton Ash, one of the most acute Western commentators on the Eastern European revolutions of 1989, has noted the special role the Holy Father played in the delegitimation of communist rule in Eastern Europe and the mentoring of Christian opponents to the military regime in Poland.[1]

The Holy Father himself, in the encyclical *Centesimus Annus*, commented on the events of that momentous year: "An important, even decisive, contribution was made by *the Church's commitment to defend and promote human rights*. In situations strongly influenced by ideology, in which polarization obscured the awareness of a human dignity common to all, the Church affirmed clearly and forcefully that every individual . . . bears the image of God and therefore deserves respect." He continued, "Often, the vast majority of people identified themselves with this kind of affirmation, and this led to a search for forms of protest and for political solutions more respectful of the dignity of the human person."[2]

---

1 Timothy Garton Ash, *The Uses of Adversity: Essays on the Fate of Central Europe* (New York: Random House, 1989), 47-60; see also C. Bernstein, "The Holy Alliance," *Time*, February 24, 1992, 28-35.

Underlying the pontiff's analysis lay a transformation of the Church's approach to politics with roots in the papacy of Pope John XXIII and the Second Vatican Council. Pope John XXIII's much acclaimed encyclical letter *Pacem in Terris* reconceptualized Catholic social thinking, including its vision of international order, in human rights terms.[3] This move was ratified by the council which declared that "by virtue of the Gospel committed to her, the Church proclaims the rights of man."[4] At the same time, the council set in motion a process which led to the growth of a transnational justice and peace network with the Pontifical Council for Justice and Peace at its heart "for the worldwide promotion of justice for the poor."[5]

It quickly became apparent that while church leaders intended the Church itself to remain apart from politics, they still looked to the faithful to heed their "call to action." As Pope Paul VI wrote in his apostolic letter *Octagesima Adveniens*, "It is not enough to recall principles, state intentions, point to crying injustices, and utter prophetic denunciations; these words will lack real weight unless they are accompanied for each individual by a livelier awareness of personal responsibility and by effective action."[6] Pope John Paul II has made the same plea for action in his 1987 encyclical *Sollicitudo Rei Socialis.* "Every individual is called upon to play his part or her part in this peaceful campaign . . . in order to secure development in peace, in order to safeguard nature itself and the world around us."[7]

I

What was then the National Catholic Welfare Conference, the social policy agency of the U.S. Catholic bishops, had been instrumental in the Second Vatican Council's adoption of the proposal for the establishment

---

2 John Paul II, *On the Hundredth Anniversary of* Rerum Novarum *(Centesimus Annus)*, papal encyclical (Washington, D.C.: USCC Office for Publishing and Promotion Services, 1991), no. 22.

3 John XXIII, *Peace on Earth (Pacem in Terris)*, papal encyclical (Washington, D.C.: USCC Office for Publishing and Promotion Services, 1963).

4 Second Vatican Council, *Pastoral Constitution on the Church in the Modern World (Gaudium et Spes)*, no. 41.

5 Ibid., no. 90.

6 *Octagesima Adveniens*, no. 48.

7 John Paul II, *On Social Concern (Sollicitudo Rei Socialis)*, papal encyclical (Washington, D.C.: USCC Office for Publishing and Promotion Services, 1987), no. 47.

of an international justice and peace network. Due to the distinctive situation of U.S. Catholics as citizens in one of the superpowers of the Cold War era, the NCWC's successor agency, the United States Catholic Conference, managed a full agenda not only in bipolar affairs but especially in mediating the human rights, justice, and peace concerns of Third World countries to the U.S. government and American public.

While other religious communities have sometimes been heavily and directly involved in politics, the Catholic Church in the United States has generally walked a narrow line, championing social action while endeavoring to refrain from partisan politics. Like the Catholic Church elsewhere, the U.S. Church has recognized the autonomy of secular life, including political activity, and repeatedly affirmed that in practice a variety of options could satisfy the standards of social justice expounded in Catholic social teaching.

As Pope Paul VI wrote in *Octagesima Adveniens*, a diversity of political goals is possible because the Christian faith entails wider commitments and deeper resources than politics can provide. Thus, from believers with different political agendas, the Church, Pope Paul wrote, asked for "an effort at mutual understanding of the other's positions and motives; a loyal examination of one's behavior and its correctness will suggest to each one an attitude of more profound charity which, while recognizing differences, believes nonetheless in the possibility of convergence and unity. 'The bonds which unite the faithful are mightier than anything which divides them.'"[8]

In their own work, therefore, the Catholic bishops of the United States have carefully distinguished between the social teaching itself and positions they might take on particular public policy issues. In a formula which has become a conventional disclaimer, the bishops distinguish between "universally binding moral principles found in the teaching of the Church" and "specific applications, observations, and recommendations which allow for diversity of opinion."[9] While endorsing a charitable pluralism in the social agenda, the bishops have nonetheless themselves been advocates for particular policies consistent with the Church's social teaching on human rights, war and peace issues, and matters of justice.

---

8 *Octagesima Adveniens*, no. 50.
9 *The Challenge of Peace: God's Promise and Our Response* (Washington, D.C.: USCC Office for Publishing and Promotion Services, 1983), i-ii.

II

The essays gathered in this volume are an effort to expand and deepen understanding of the international issues treated in the bishops' November 1993 statement on moral dimensions of the post-Cold War world, *The Harvest of Justice Is Sown in Peace*. They are grouped under five broad themes: (1) theology, morality, and foreign policy in a new world, (2) human rights, self-determination, and sustainable development, (3) global institutions, (4) the use of force, and (5) education and action for peace.

1. Theology, Morality, and Foreign Policy. *The Harvest of Justice* opened with a retrieval of the theological underpinnings of peacemaking, a reassessment made possible in some measure by the changed strategic relations between the former Soviet Union and the West. The contributors to this section attempt to lay out both the theological and strategic considerations which affect international morality in our new era.

Cardinal Joseph Bernardin, who in 1983 chaired the committee that drafted *The Challenge of Peace* and in 1988 oversaw a five-year review of developments in nuclear policy for the bishops' conference, also played an active role in the 1993 Tenth Anniversary Committee. In "The New Challenge of Peace," Cardinal Bernardin sketches a three-part effort to construct a political ethic to guide U.S. foreign policy. It includes: (1) a vision of the future rooted in human rights and dignity, social and economic justice, and cooperation between peoples and nations; (2) active collaboration in building the institutions of peace, and (3) development of an ethic of collective security.

To those who may object that he sets too demanding an agenda for a nation with diminished expectations, the cardinal replies, "The unimaginable changes that have taken place in the years since we wrote *The Challenge of Peace* confirm our confidence that we can shape a better future and begin to overcome today's daunting and seemingly irresolvable problems."

Zbigniew Brzezinski served as National Security advisor in the Carter administration. Dr. Brzezinski, who helped implement President Carter's human rights policy, has long been concerned with the moral underpinnings of U.S. foreign policy. Making the case that, for its own coherence and effectiveness, U.S. foreign policy must serve moral goals, he worries that our domestic political culture may be too tainted by materialism and even hedonism to provide the moral purpose needed to guide the United States in world affairs.

"The needed correction," Brzezinski writes, "will not come from a catalog of policy recommendations. It can only emerge as a consequence of a new historical tide that induces a change both in values and in conduct; in effect, out of a prolonged process of cultural self-reexamination and philosophical reevaluation. . . ."

Drawing on Pope John XXIII's *Pacem in Terris* and Pope John Paul II's *Sollicitudo Rei Socialis* and *Centesimus Annus*, Georgetown University's Professor *Marilyn McMorrow, RSCJ*, sketches the positive vision for a world at peace as found in official Catholic teaching. Peacemaking, according to McMorrow, is "working to institute conditions which protect and promote human rights." She also makes the case for individual responsibility in peacemaking. "[T]he entire citizenry," she writes, "is responsible to make peace, not just the elected officials."

George Weigel, president of the Ethics and Public Policy Center, makes a case that the cardinal sin of international affairs today is isolationism. "[T]he most important thing the bishops' conference, and indeed the Church as a whole, must teach about peacemaking 'ten years after *The Challenge of Peace*,'" he writes, "is the moral impossibility of isolationism in its Old Right, New Left, or libertarian forms." Weigel argues for an internationalism in which America's "duties are not infinite in number." Like Zbigniew Brzezinski, he argues for a foreign policy with "purpose," reminding readers that in the classic Catholic tradition, "there is only one human universe of reflection and action: a universe that is at once moral and political."

2. A second set of contributions deals with some of the substantive issues that vex the post-Cold War order. It includes: (1) human rights, (2) religious nationalism, (3) self-determination, (4) democracy, (5) ecology, and (6) sustainable development.

As Senior Deputy Assistant Secretary of State for Human Rights and Humanitarian Affairs in the Bush and early Clinton administrations, *James K. Bishop* was in the forefront of U.S. government policy to defend human rights in China, Bosnia-Herzegovina, Guatemala, and Africa. His review of developments in human rights policymaking shows how much progress has been made in making human rights a standard component of U.S. foreign policy.

In a trenchant and noteworthy analysis, Bishop, who served with some heroism as U.S. ambassador to Somalia, reflects on the failures of the United States and the international community to defend the rights of civilians in that country's civil war. He also sets out a challenge to human rights activists to find ways to improve their collaboration with government agencies in advancing the human rights agenda.

Senior scholar in the Religion, Ethics, and Human Rights Program of the United States Institute for Peace, *David Little* reflects on religious nationalism as a fact of contemporary international life. Endorsing a human rights approach to religious conflict, Little proposes applying a "radical" solution to problems of religioethnic conflict that differentiates sharply between the legitimation of political authority and religious belief of any kind. While favoring such "a 'secular' or 'neutral' reference point" for arbitrating religious conflicts, he urges that just such a move "is an important step toward civil peace."

Many of the nations divided by religious conflict have experienced autonomy movements on the part of ethnic minorities. Vanderbilt University political philosopher *Jean Bethke Elshtain* argues that contrary to the model of nineteenth-century nationalisms, national identity need not inevitably require sovereignty and independence, but can be sustained in a variety of forms of group association. "[E]thical space can be created or expanded," she writes, "for a form of civic identification *sans* irredentist or chauvinist aspirations."

One trend in U.S. foreign policy that men and women of every political stripe are ready to support is the promotion of democracy. Even though exporting democracy has sometimes led to morally dubious actions on the part of the U.S. government and the specific policies which comprise democracy promotion are left vague, people agree that the U.S. government ought to aid the growth of democracy abroad.

Bruce Russett, Dean Acheson Professor of International Relations and Chair of the Political Science Department at Yale University, contends that promoting democracy abroad will serve the interests of peace. Russett reviews empirical studies demonstrating that democracies rarely fight each other and identifies the conditions necessary for democracy to take root. In the 1990s, he concludes, "A[n international] system created by autocracies centuries ago might now be re-created by a critical mass of democratic states."

Dianne Bergant, CSA, of Chicago's Catholic Theological Union takes up the global, as distinguished from international, problem of environment. Drawing on her research as an Old Testament scholar, Sr. Bergant argues that peace can no longer be regarded in narrow terms of human concord but rather in terms of the overall "integrity of creation." "The covenant with its promise of *shalom* was made with all of creation," she writes, "not merely with humankind in the person of Noah." On this analysis, she reasons, the principle of proportionality in moral theology needs to be expanded to apply to calculations of harm done the environment.

A key component of the Catholic idea of peace has been that of "integral" or "authentic development." Notre Dame economist *Charles K. Wilber*, a consultant to the committee which drafted the bishops' 1986 pastoral *Economic Justice for All*, examines humane development as a component of peace in the post-Cold War world. In a world where markets dominate, Wilber notes, development economics has also learned that "all good things do not go together. . . . Rapid growth and economic development may be accompanied by severe social and political problems." Wilber contends, "a strategy that softens the destructive aspects of free market capitalism is essential for humane development" and for sustained civil and international peace. As part of this strategy, Wilber proposes three goals for genuine development: (1) life sustenance, (2) esteem and fellowship, and (3) freedom.

3. Global Institutions. Since *Pacem in Terris* in 1963, Catholic social teaching has advocated the strengthening of global institutions, a call the U.S. bishops renew in *The Harvest of Justice*. In this section, two veteran diplomats, well acquainted with the United Nations system, reflect on how the United Nations can be strengthened. *Alvaro de Soto*, a Peruvian diplomat, is senior political advisor to the secretary-general of the United Nations. Ambassador de Soto has played a leading role in several UN peacemaking operations, most notably in El Salvador. *Edward Joseph Perkins* was U.S. ambassador to the United Nations in the Bush administration and now serves as ambassador to Australia.

Beginning with Secretary-General Boutros Boutros-Ghali's June 1992 report, *Agenda for Peace*, Alvaro de Soto reviews the United Nations' recent experience with peacekeeping and humanitarian intervention in three especially difficult situations: the former Yugoslavia, Somalia, and Haiti. Unlike traditional peacekeeping operations and like other less noticed and successful operations in Namibia, Cambodia, El Salvador, and Mozambique, these are multidisciplinary endeavors with a wide variety of overlapping and sometimes conflicting tasks: peacekeeping, human rights monitoring, humanitarian aid, refugee resettlement, and so on. Success in the growing number of tasks set before the United Nations will demand, according to de Soto, better coordination and integration of activities, a far greater degree of support from member states, and decisiveness on the part of policymakers.

Ambassador Edward Perkins contends that today's global institutions, whether they choose to be or not, are "conflict resolution activist(s)." The existing set of institutions, he maintains, forms a workable system, but it needs to be strengthened and supplemented by greater activity on the part of regional organizations, religious groups, and businesses. In addition, Perkins proposes, the conflict resolution tasks of international organizations can be improved with the use of up-to-date communications technology, new theories of public administration, and the adoption of an evolving view of citizenship on the part of global institutions.

4. Contrary to expectation, the end of the Cold War and the superpower rivalry did not lead to a disappearance of armed conflict. Indeed, the 1990s have been marked by a multiplication of civil wars and ethnic conflicts. The international community has been divided on how to ad-

dress these conflicts, and international intervention in civil conflict has become a leading policy and moral problem. The essays in this section seek to shed some light on the use of force today, particularly with respect to humanitarian intervention.

Notre Dame peace studies professor *George A. Lopez* addresses the startling rise in civilian deaths in recent conflicts. In the 1980s, defense doctrines focused on constraining internal insurgents and nonstate terrorists contributed to a serious growth in the number of noncombatant casualties. Even calls for international intervention in ethnic conflicts, Lopez warns, need to be received cautiously, lest in the absence of other political and diplomatic conditions they lead to increased killing.

John Langan, SJ, the Rose Kennedy Professor of Christian Ethics at Georgetown University, has written widely on just war. Reflecting on events in the Gulf War, he examines, with his characteristic judiciousness, the bombing of civilian infrastructure in Iraq, concluding that "the right thing for the coalition in the circumstances was to refrain from bombing those parts of the infrastructure needed to sustain civilian society."

Langan uses the case of infrastructure bombing, however, to illustrate some general principles about the application of just-war norms and argue for the usefulness of the just-war tradition in a culturally pluralist world. "In a multicultural world," he writes, "the just-war tradition with its commitments to reason, history, and the values of both individual life and community order, is an intellectual and moral resource that is needed both by those called to exercise power and by those who may be the objects and victims of power."

Indiana University professor *Richard B. Miller* begins his essay with an acknowledgment that the end of the Cold War greatly weakens the self-defense argument for military preparedness and the use of force, thereby permitting greater assertiveness on the part of pacifists in policy debates at the same time that just-war theorists attempt "to clarify other possible causes that might justify recourse to lethal force." For just-war thinkers, he suggests, there are two key issues: the grounds for intervention (when national interest is not involved) and the extent to which sanctions must be tried before resorting to force. With increased resistance to using force, pacifists for their part, reasons Miller, will have to think more carefully about the relation of nonviolence to coercive diplomacy and particularly to economic sanctions. He predicts that, "In the post-Cold War era, one should not be at all surprised to find some pacifists approving the use of force (as a police action) more readily than the use of various forms of economic coercion (understood as structural violence)."

Kenneth R. Himes, OFM, of the Washington Theological Union brings some master themes of Catholic social teaching to bear on the issue of humanitarian intervention. These include: (1) the qualified nature of sovereignty in Catholic thought, (2) the principle and virtue of solidarity as expressions of Catholic universalism, (3) the intimate connection between political order and justice in modern Catholic thought, (4) the evolving conversation between pacifists and just-war thinkers, and (5) the primacy of human rights in Catholic thought and practice. All these, Himes argues, create a moral context in which intervention for the protection of human rights is a morally justifiable undertaking. At the same time, Himes admonishes, humanitarian intervention is a measure which must be undertaken cautiously with care to observe traditional just-war limits.

Charles William Maynes, editor of *Foreign Policy*, recognizes that an evolving international human rights policy will be limited by the reality that few "young men and women will be willing to die for humanitarian intervention on a significant scale." To be successful in the future, Maynes argues, interventions by the international community must be accompanied by: (1) transparency, i.e., accurate and creditable reporting on human rights situations worldwide; (2) a volunteer force made up of a small independent UN unit with additional volunteers from the militaries of member states; (3) greater discrimination in intervening through the use of regional forces; and (4) an increase in financial resources through some automatic UN fundraising mechanism, such as fees on the use of space or on arms transfers.

Catherine M. Kelleher of the Brookings Institution is a member of the USCC Committee on International Policy and an expert on European security questions. With *Rachel A. Epstein*, also of Brookings, Dr. Kelleher provides a wide-ranging rethinking of security issues in the post-Cold War era. Among the issues they discuss are: nonproliferation, a new force structure consisting of a minimal deterrent, advanced conventional forces and new defensive options, and new cooperative security arrangements which would include Russia.

A distinctive contribution is the Kelleher-Epstein reappraisal of nuclear deterrence. While arguing for a nuclear retaliatory capability "at lower numbers and levels of alert," they pose sharp questions about the desirability of the strategy of "mutual nuclear deterrence" when weighted against the overall costs paid by both U.S. and Soviet society. They also counsel that the threat of nuclear weapons will prove an ineffective tool for the testy problems of this transitional era.

5. Education and Action for Peace. *The Harvest of Justice* declared that "our peacemaking vocation is not a passing priority, a cause for one decade, but an essential part of our mission to proclaim the Gospel and renew the earth." The three essays in this last section share the experience of educators and activists on how to realize the vocation to peacemaking.

Rev. Theodore M. Hesburgh, CSC, president emeritus of the University of Notre Dame, tells the story of his efforts to contribute to peace in founding such institutions as the Ecumenical Institute for Theological

Studies in Jerusalem (Tantur), the Kellogg Institute for International Studies, and the Kroc Institute for International Peace Studies. One of the unique programs of the latter is an international scholars program in which 15 master's-level students from around the world live and pursue peace studies together in a yearlong course of studies.

The dean of American Catholic pacifists, *Gordon C. Zahn,* has worked tirelessly for many years in the cause of nonviolence and to educate the Catholic community and the American public about conscientious objection. Professor Zahn reviews *The Harvest of Justice* from the perspective of a sociologist and committed pacifist. His "most serious note of disappointment and disapproval" concerns the bishops' continued acceptance of "the tortured moral reasoning" justifying "'strictly conditioned acceptance' of nuclear deterrence." While commending the bishops' call in *The Harvest of Justice* for an openly declared "no first use policy" and other stipulated restrictions on nuclear policy, he concludes "the new document still does not face the ultimate question": If the use of nuclear weapons is so morally flawed that the bishops "abhor" them, "how can they justify mounting and maintaining the *credible* threat to use them?"

Dr. Mary L. Heidkamp heads the Campaign for Human Development for the Archdiocese of Chicago and *James R. Lund* directs the Office for the Ministry of Peace and Justice for the archdiocese. Drawing on experiences since the 1983 peace pastoral, they offer a survey of pastoral responses to today's challenges of peace. These include: convenings, ministry to the military, international networking, and local initiatives in refugee resettlement, conflict resolution, and advocacy. They also review the role of liturgy and preaching in nurturing the Church as a community of peacemakers.

In commissioning these articles, as in issuing *The Harvest of Justice*, the Committee on International Policy hoped to serve as "a catalyst and resource in the larger national debate over issues of war and peace." It is our hope that in a time of considerable confusion about the U.S. role in the world and of the practicability of international collaboration, this volume may contribute to an appreciation, in keeping with the classical tradition of Catholic political thought, that world politics must be an arena of great purposes.

I.

Theology, Morality, and Foreign Policy in a New World

The New Challenge of Peace

Cardinal Joseph Bernardin

We live in a remarkable period of transformation from one era to a yet-undefined new era. This watershed in world affairs is reflected in the contrast between the Catholic bishops' 1983 pastoral letter, *The Challenge of Peace*, and our ten-year follow-up, *The Harvest of Justice Is Sown in Peace*. In 1983, we focused on the moral dangers of nuclear weapons, a problem of strategic ethics. Today, we are concerned about questions of political ethics: the moral dangers of anarchy, resurgent nationalism, and underdevelopment; and the moral responsibility of the United States and other nations to avoid the illusion of isolationism and to make a sustained commitment to building a more just and integrated international order. While the two documents are grounded in the same theological and moral tradition and deal with some of the same issues, notably nuclear arms, they clearly are documents of and for different eras.

The bishops are not alone in trying to assess the significance of this new time of transition. Like many others, we do not want to miss this historic opportunity to help shape a new world that we hope will be a significant advance, in human and moral terms, over the one we have left behind. Our role in this effort is to help raise the moral and religious aspects of this task. We do not think there is a purely moral blueprint for the post-Cold War world, but we are equally sure of the inadequacy of any blueprint bereft of moral concerns.

Our reflections on the moral and religious dimensions of the new world order are inspired and shaped by the life of Jesus, the Gospel call to be peacemakers, and a rich tradition of church teaching on the moral foundations of the social order and questions of war and peace. We are also impelled to address the many pressing issues of the day by our participation in a universal church. Pope John Paul II has been a consistent voice for a fundamental reordering of values, relationships, and structures in order to better protect human dignity and deepen unity among peoples and nations. Because of our relationships with the Catholic Church and other religious bodies around the world, we are moved to support those struggling for democracy in South Africa and Eastern Europe, and those aiding refugees and breaking down walls of hatred in Bosnia-Herzegovina. We are moved to be in solidarity with those healing the wounds of war in Central America, those suffering religious persecution in China, and those suffering under predatory government in Haiti. We are also moved by what we encounter in our own dioceses. My diocese — Chicago — is, in many ways, a microcosm of the hopes, dreams, and possibilities, as well as the violence, injustice, and alienation, that are replicated many times over throughout the world. It is not only our beliefs and traditions, then, but also our relationships and experiences, that shaped our pastoral letter of 1983 and shape our reflections on the new challenges of today.

In 1983, our theological and moral vision called for what few of us imagined could be realized in our lifetime: that we would be freed from the prison of the Cold War and what Pope John Paul II has called its "structures of sin."[1] It was hard to imagine how we could escape an insane arms race and extricate the superpowers from their proxy wars in the developing world. We hoped and prayed for, but did not foresee, a time when nuclear weapons and the threat of global nuclear war would cease to be central to international affairs. We spoke out against injustices in many countries, but did not anticipate that the massive denial of human rights by dictatorial regimes, sustained by the rigid ideologies of Marxist-Leninism or the national security state, would be alleviated so quickly by the nonviolent overthrow of many of these regimes.

Today, our surprise and celebration at the end of the Cold War are already giving way to new pessimism about our ability to build a more just and peaceful international order. Fears generated by the clash of the superpowers have been replaced by concerns about a clash of cultures and nationalisms. The threat of global nuclear war has been replaced by the threat of global nuclear proliferation. Qualms about superpower inter-ventions have been replaced by frustration at the international commu-nity's inability or unwillingness to intervene effectively to save threatened populations in Bosnia-Herzegovina. In the developing world, the end of

---

1 John Paul II, *On Social Concern (Sollicitudo Rei Socialis)*, papal encyclical (Washington, D.C.: USCC Office for Publishing and Promotion Services, 1987), no. 36.

the Cold War rationale for intervention might have the perverse effect of exacerbating the intolerable misery of millions of people, as isolationist sentiments and a growing indifference to the world's poor contribute to an ever-widening — and morally intolerable — gap between the haves and have-nots. The deplorable human rights records of dictatorships around the world are now matched, even exceeded, by the atrocities unleashed by anarchy in failed states such as Somalia and Rwanda. Intolerance of religion has ended in Eastern Europe but not in China and elsewhere, while a secularist and materialist mentality that would privatize or marginalize religion remains pervasive worldwide. As religious believers, we are challenged in a special way by the disturbing way religion is being manipulated to serve the cause of virulent nationalism and ethnic conflict in many countries.

A New Religious and Moral Agenda for Peacemaking

The dramatic changes we are living through and the vexing problems of the post-Cold War world are forcing a fundamental reexamination of our basic assumptions about international affairs and the role of the United States in the world. The Cold War political stalemate understandably led policymakers and ethicists to concentrate on the appropriate means to deal with the superpower conflict, a question of a strategic ethic of means.

As new possibilities as well as new problems force a reconsideration of basic assumptions about international affairs and the U.S. role in the world, what is most needed is a political ethic of international order. From self-determination to sanctions, from multilateral institutions to minority rights, from proliferation to pollution, peacemaking requires that the United States help build a new international order in service of the common good. To do that, our nation needs to strengthen its own moral fabric and discern a clearer moral vision of a just and peaceful world and the U.S. role in that world. This reexamination of the moral basis for U.S. involvement in the world does not preclude our usual preoccupation with more specific questions of means but rather shifts our focus. The critical means questions no longer revolve around the role and limits of military force, as important as these remain. Rather, the focus must be on what institutions, structures, and forms of collaboration are necessary to achieve our vision of a new order.

The task ahead may be seen as a three-dimensional effort to construct and implement a political ethic to guide U.S. foreign policy in the post-Cold War world. This political ethic should include: (1) a moral benchmark and a moral vision of a future rooted in peace and justice, (2) active collaboration to build institutions and structures that can bring about this vision, and (3) development of an ethic of cooperative security.

A Peaceful World: A Vision

The starting point for a political ethic to guide U.S. involvement in constructing a new world order is a positive vision of peace. In line with a century of modern Catholic social teaching, Pope John Paul II's recent encyclicals, *Sollicitudo Rei Socialis* (1987) and *Centesimus Annus* (1991), call for a world order in which peace is measured not only in terms of the absence of war but also in broader terms of human rights and dignity, social and economic justice, and cooperation between peoples and nations. This broader, positive approach to peace should shape America's moral vision of a new world order in four ways.

First, drawing on the theological principle that the suffering of one member of the human family is of vital concern to all of us, security is defined broadly to include not only U.S. national interests but also the interests of the international community. America's common good and the global common good are intertwined. U.S. power and values can bring tremendous good as well as much suffering to people around the world. With this power to shape events and lives comes a corresponding obligation to contribute positively to the welfare of the wider world community.

Second, a U.S. vision of a new world order should include protection of basic human rights. A new world order should protect the spectrum of both political and civil rights as well as economic, social, and cultural rights. This human rights agenda includes the promotion of authentic democracy and minority rights in countries torn by civil strife. It includes a sustainable and equitable development that can overcome the "intolerable extremes of misery" and the gross inequities that afflict the developing world.[2]

A third moral objective of U.S. policy should be furthering the unity of the human family. The world is becoming at once both more interdependent and more fractured. In the name of solidarity, the United States should promote an international order which can overcome the economic, political, and social divisions that plague today's world and which

---

2 Fourth General Conference of Latin American Bishops, October 12-28, 1992, *Santo Domingo Conclusions: New Evangelization, Human Development, Christian Culture* (Washington, D.C.: USCC Office for Publishing and Promotion Services, 1993), no. 179.

can transform the fact of interdependence into a firm basis for international cooperation. Of special urgency is the need for the United States to support international arrangements that rectify the gross inequalities between the poor nations and the rich nations, and that uphold a vision of a pluralistic nation-state free of chauvinist or exclusivist tendencies.

Finally, in pursuing this moral vision, the United States must rediscover and readjust its own moral compass. The best of America's values and actions continue to inspire other peoples' struggles for justice and freedom. Our democratic ideals, in particular, have inspired political progress in many parts of the world. But our country is not a uniformly positive example for the world. As the bishops said in *The Harvest of Justice*:

> Our society's excessive individualism and materialism, pervasive violence, and tendency to denigrate moral and religious values, however, can be harmful. A practical materialism and a militant secular mentality undermine cultural and moral values here and abroad, generate expectations that cannot and should not necessarily be fulfilled, and inhibit efforts to strengthen international order.[3]

The task of defining a political ethic in support of a new international order must include, therefore, a careful examination of the basic values, both positive and negative, that define our own experience as a nation.

Peacebuilding: Structures of Justice and Peace

This moral vision of the U.S. role in a new international order — a commitment to the global common good, human rights and sustainable development, solidarity, and a redirection of our nation's moral compass — will remain merely a set of ideals unless the United States does its part to build corresponding structures of justice and peace. In the post-Cold War world, the arduous, complex, and often unheralded work of institution-building has new moral significance. The breakdown of political order in Somalia and Rwanda, the emergence of new states out of the remnants of Yugoslavia and the Soviet Union, the unsteady steps toward democracy in Central America, Cambodia, South Africa, and Eastern Europe, the increasing demands for UN peacekeeping around the world, the seemingly intractable problem of underdevelopment in the Third

---

3 National Conference of Catholic Bishops, *The Harvest of Justice Is Sown in Peace* (Washington, D.C.: USCC Office for Publishing and Promotion Services, 1993), 18.

World, and the protection of minority rights all require attention to institution-building: legal, political, economic, social, and cultural.

This institution-building must first take place at the local and national levels, based on a commitment to authentic democracy, basic human rights, and a thriving civil society. It must simultaneously take place at the regional and global levels. The United Nations, in particular, should be a central focus. In Catholic social teaching, a worldwide public authority is necessary, not to limit or replace the authority of individual states, but rather to address problems beyond their control. As we said in *The Harvest of Justice*, "Just as the United Nations should not be asked to solve problems it has neither the competence nor the resources to solve, neither should it be prevented from taking the bold steps necessary to fulfill the promise of its charter to save 'succeeding generations from the scourge of war.'"[4]

Somalia, Haiti, Bosnia, and Rwanda show how difficult it will be to achieve this promise. The halting and ineffectual response of the United Nations to these and other crises reinforces the need for a reformed and strengthened United Nations. This requires, in turn, a sustained, consistent, and full commitment on the part of the United States and other nations to collaborate with one another and sacrifice in order to improve the ability of the United Nations and other multilateral institutions to resolve conflicts, promote economic and political development, and protect human rights.

Along with responsible and responsive multilateral institutions, a strong international system, like a strong nation, requires a strong civil society. Human rights groups, humanitarian aid organizations, businesses, labor unions, and religious bodies can play an invaluable role in building bridges of understanding and respect between cultures, and in contributing to positive social change and a sense of global community. Much more attention should be given to the importance of this international civil society in promoting justice and peace.

Peacemaking: An Ethic of Cooperative Security

The third theme of *The Harvest of Justice*, the need for an ethic of cooperative security, links the vision of a peaceful world, structures ani-

---

4 Ibid., 8.

mated by this vision, and a strategic ethic that delimits the means that may be used to achieve this vision.

Cooperative security begins with the broad definition of peace described earlier: the primacy of the common good, defined in terms of human dignity and human rights; social and economic development; and solidarity between diverse peoples and nations. This broad definition of security does not mean that the United States should conceive its interests so broadly that it feels compelled to act as the world's policeman. But neither should the United States define its interests so narrowly that indifference, inaction, and isolationism become the hallmarks of U.S. foreign policy.

In our conception of cooperative security, the role of military force is not the primary focus. The primary concern is the development of structures and ways to achieve a broad, positive vision of peace. Cooperative security involves finding effective means to anticipate and resolve problems before they erupt into violence, to mediate conflicts that break out, and to use nonmilitary options, such as economic and political sanctions at the international level, and nonviolent means of civilian resistance and protest at the local level, in response to manifest injustice and aggression. When these means fail, cooperative security entails improving international peacekeeping to ensure the delivery of humanitarian aid, establish safe havens, disarm conflicting parties, and enforce political settlements.

Finally, cooperative security entails a presumption in favor of broad collaboration and shared sacrifice on the part of the international community, especially through the United Nations and other multi- lateral organizations. International cooperation is not a panacea, for it can sometimes make decisive action difficult and can become a victim of political stalemate. But cooperation among nations also can ensure that peacemaking is an authentic act of international solidarity and not a new form of domination by the powerful.

An ethic of cooperative security cannot escape wrestling with difficult issues of strategic ethics, but the context for considering these issues has changed. Events of the last decade have had an impact on the continuing debate over the traditions of just war and nonviolence. On the one hand, the power of nonviolence in Eastern Europe and elsewhere suggests that nonviolence should not be restricted to personal commitments but should have a greater role in the political order. On the other hand, the human tragedies in Somalia and Bosnia remind us of the sad necessity of using force, as a last resort, to defend innocent life and basic values.

These tragedies have forced us to reflect anew on the legitimacy and limits of what Pope John Paul II has said is the international community's right and duty of humanitarian intervention "where the survival of populations and entire ethnic groups is seriously compromised."[5] In *The Harvest of Justice*, the bishops offer a framework for evaluating when humanitarian intervention may be justified. These exceptional cases must be more clearly defined in international law, political philosophy, and ethics, so that humanitarian intervention does not open the door to new forms of imperialism or endless wars of altruism.

As with the use of force generally, the context for our moral judgments regarding nuclear weapons has also changed. Nuclear weapons are no longer at the center of international affairs, but they remain of vital political and moral significance, particularly given the problem of nuclear proliferation. In reviewing the status of nuclear weapons, we have reaffirmed our earlier judgment that nuclear deterrence may be morally justified (1) so long as it is limited to deterring nuclear use by others; (2) so long as sufficiency, not nuclear superiority, is its goal; and (3) so long as deterrence is used as a step on the way toward progressive disarmament.

Our analysis differs in two respects from that of 1983, however. First, our emphasis has changed. In the early 1980s, the first task was to restart the arms control process so as to blunt the growth of already-bloated nuclear arsenals and to eliminate the most threatening of these weapons. In the 1990s, new prospects for arms control and new threats of proliferation lead us to focus much more than we did previously on the third condition for the moral acceptability of deterrence: progressive disarmament. The bishops believe that the eventual elimination of nuclear weapons should be "more than a moral ideal; it should be a policy goal."[6] The moral credibility of nonproliferation efforts will be greatly enhanced if the United States and the other nuclear powers commit themselves to disarmament by example, beginning with a comprehensive test ban and deeper cuts in nuclear weapons. The second difference in our approach is to link more explicitly the morality of deterrence to the responsibility of the nuclear powers to use their power and resources to take the lead in building an effective system of cooperative security and a more just and stable international order, as I have outlined above.

Peace: A Realistic Hope

The bishops are both hopeful and realistic about prospects for achieving this admittedly ambitious vision of a peaceful post-Cold War world. We are hopeful because, with Pope John Paul II, we are convinced that "[w]ar is not inevitable; peace is possible."[7] Peace is possible because we are

---

5 John Paul II, "Address to the International Conference on Nutrition," *Origins* 22:28 (December 24, 1992), 475.

6 *The Harvest of Justice Is Sown in Peace*, 13.

loved and sustained by God and, by God's grace, we are able to participate in the transformative work of witnessing to the kingdom here on earth. We are realistic, however, in that we know that we are scarred by sin and that the kingdom may be realized only partially within history.

For peacemakers, hope is the indispensable virtue. Ten years ago, hope was what convinced us that it was possible to break out of the seemingly intractable dynamic of the Cold War:

> To believe we are condemned in the future only to what has been the past of United States-Soviet relations is to underestimate both our human potential for creative diplomacy and God's action in our midst which can open the way to changes we could barely imagine.[8]

The unimaginable changes that have taken place in the years since we wrote this confirm our confidence that we can shape a better future and begin to overcome today's daunting and seemingly irresolvable problems.

At the same time, our realism guards against the misdirected hope of excessive idealism or utopianism. We cannot witness the "ethnic cleansing" in Bosnia-Herzegovina without reflecting anew on our human capacity for evil. It is hope in our capacity for good that keeps our realism from sliding into a pragmatic acceptance of aggression in places like Bosnia, an overreliance on military force to solve these agonizing problems or a new form of isolationism which would distance ourselves from such evil.

In our five-year report on *The Challenge of Peace*, we said: "To contain the nuclear danger of our time is itself an awesome undertaking. To reshape the political fabric of an increasingly interdependent world is an even larger and more complicated challenge."[9] We must be wary not to retreat from this challenge due to an understandable but dangerous temptation to turn inward, focus only on domestic needs, and ignore global responsibilities. This is not an option for believers in a universal church or for citizens of a powerful nation.

What the United States can offer the world — and what the world desperately needs — is creative engagement, a willingness to collaborate, and a commitment to values that can build up the global community through an ethic of cooperative security. "Liberty and justice for all" is not only a profound national pledge; it is also a worthy goal for a world leader.

---

7 John Paul II, "Address to the Diplomatic Corps," *Origins* 23:33 (February 3, 1994), 582.

8 National Conference of Catholic Bishops, *The Challenge of Peace: God's Promise and Our Response* (Washington, D.C.: USCC Office for Publishing and Promotion Services, 1983), no. 258.

9 U.S. Catholic Conference, "A Report on *The Challenge of Peace* and Policy Developments 1983-1988" (Washington D.C.: USCC Office for Publishing and Promotion Services, 1988), no. 129.

Peace is not merely a pious hope; it is a realistic objective for a new world order.

The Illusion of Control

Zbigniew Brzezinski

The twentieth century — the century of metamyths and of mega-deaths — spawned false notions of total control, derived from arrogant assertions of total righteousness. The religious man of premodern times, who accepted reality as God-ordained, gave way to the secular fanatic, increasingly inclined to usurp God in the effort to construct heaven on earth, subordinating not only nature but humanity itself to his own utopian vision.

In the course of the present century, this vision was perverted into the most costly exercise of political hubris in mankind's history: the totalitarian attempt to create coercive utopias. In these utopias, all of reality — on the objective level of social organization and on the subjective level of personal beliefs — was to be subject to doctrinal control emanating from a single political center. The price paid in human lives for this excess is beyond the scope of comprehension.

The manifest failure of that endeavor has given way in the West to the current antithesis, which is essentially that of minimal control over personal and collective desires, sexual appetites, and social conduct. But inherent in the almost total rejection of any control is the notion that all values are subjective and relative. In brief, this century has seen mankind move from experimentation with coercive utopia to the enjoyment of permissive cornucopia, from a passionate embrace of absolutist metamyths to careless toying with relativistic agnosticism.

In that philosophic context, global political conditions are characterized by a dynamic and interactive expansion in:

physical power — over nature, over humanity's life and death, and even over the human being itself through the expanding capacity for scientific self-manipulation;

political activism — with humanity more politically conscious, hence also more susceptible to mass mobilization, and insistent on enhanced participation in decision making;

personal expectations — with both individual and collective ones rising rapidly, especially as the world's rich want more of everything and the poor desire what the rich already have;

pace of societal change — with every generation growing up in a world whose culture, lifestyle, and social infrastructure tend to be increasingly different from those of its predecessor.

It is an illusion, however, to think that change in any of the above dimensions is truly controlled by mankind. Each is expanding and altering at a pace that is determined by its own momentum. Man does not control or even determine the basic directions of his ever-expanding physical powers. The plunge into space, the acquisition of new weapons, the breakthroughs in medical and other sciences are shaped largely by their internal dynamics. Each innovation breeds another; every expansion of knowledge, skill, or capability is but a step forward, not just in opening ever new doors to the future but actually in leading mankind into that future. The human being, while the inventor, is simultaneously the prisoner of the process of invention.

Much the same is true of the other two major dimensions of our changing reality. Political activism is not necessarily tantamount to the establishment of an effectively functioning democracy. It is, however, a process that involves ever-increasing social demands for participation in decision making, for human rights, and for limits on the unequal distribution not only of power but also of privilege. It transforms a politically passive humanity into an activist mass yearning for a sense of direction.

Personal expectations are being transformed by the accelerating pace with which new products are being introduced — with every new product then generating its own demand — by the consumerist culture of the West that places special emphasis on instant self-gratification, and by the examples that are thereby set for the vast majorities that still mostly watch and envy the lifestyles of the fortunate few.

Finally, societal change dramatically alters within the life span of a single generation both the prevailing culture and the socioeconomic infrastructure, and does so at a pace that is at least equivalent to what used to transpire within the time span of a century. The interaction of technology, education, travel, and modern communications has redefined totally the meaning of time and distance and has generated rapid alterations — on the subjective level — in the social mores and — on the objective level — in the social context.

However, the expansion and the exercise of humanity's powers are not subject to choices influenced by a widely shared moral consensus. In the absence of some shared philosophical criteria that help to define the choices on behalf of which power is exercised, the sheer acquisition and then exercise of power thus become haphazard, motivated mostly by self-interest and expediency, and driven by their own inner logic. What appears to be exuberant human liberation consequently becomes dangerous submission to historical forces dominated by the dynamic interaction between technological capabilities and philosophical sophistry.

These broad trends bear very directly on the likely shape of world affairs in the decades to come. A politically activated world, driven by rising social frustrations, even if not soon likely to be infected by a new metamyth, could quite easily become vulnerable to massive instability and violence in the absence of tangible progress, both on the level of political conduct and applied political values, toward an increasingly cooperative and just global system. New spasms of political irrationality would then be likely to manifest themselves.

In such a setting, even though America will remain for some time to come the peerless superpower, its effective global sway may lack authority. American power by itself will be insufficient to impose the American concept of "a new world order." Just as important, the inclination toward cultural hedonism may make it more difficult for America to develop a shared language with those major portions of mankind that will feel they are excluded from meaningful participation in world affairs. As a consequence, they are likely to be on the lookout for some mobilizing message and some relevant example around which to rally in a comprehensive challenge to the global status quo. . . .

[T]he world's ideological discourse in the foreseeable future is likely to be surprisingly uniform, with most governments and with most political actors paying public lip service to the same verities and relying on the same cliches. The failure of the totalitarian challenge, and especially the collapse of the communist model, has meant that almost the entire global dialogue is suffused with ostentatious references and fervent proclamations of fidelity to the democratic ideal. Only very fringe groups dare to profess openly their contempt for or rejection of democracy. Even authoritarian regimes these days tend to define themselves as democracies and espouse democratic sloganeering. This uniformity in expression reflects the waning in doctrinal passions and is mute testimony to the current supremacy — to repeat, on the level of lip service — of the democratic ideal.

It would be a mistake, however, to see the above as a sign of a universal surge in the appeal and staying power of democracy as such. It would be an even more egregious error to confuse the rhetorical uniformity with philosophical consensus. Though the notions of "democracy" are fashionable, in much of the world the practice of democracy is still quite superficial and democratic institutions remain vulnerable. There is no shared global understanding of the real meaning of democracy, and especially to what degree democracy should go beyond the political realm and also entail at least minimum guarantees for individual material well-being. Confusion is even more evident in the case of the concept of "the free market." Today, it is also triumphant — with "Thatcherism" held in higher repute than Marxism. But in many parts of the world the understanding of its inner workings, and of its cultural mainsprings, is quite shallow. Moreover, unless democratic practice, and especially the economic performance of the free market system, leads to a demonstrable improvement in social conditions, it is only a question of time before a negative reaction to these concepts sets in.

The massive failure of totalitarian metamyths, the extraordinary scale of the megadeaths exacted in the name of dogmas, and the currently more pervasive intellectual skepticism regarding the practicality of utopias make it unlikely that a self-destructive political wave will replicate the tragic errors of the twentieth century. But a spasm of irrationality, probably reminiscent of the Fascist abomination in style and content — with emotions generated by deep instincts of national identity, ethnic passions, religious beliefs, as well as social and racial resentments, all tapping the hidden wells of mankind's hatreds — could sweep some portions of the globe. Not only are the masses of the poorest countries potentially susceptible; the Fascistic skinheads of Western Europe and their counterparts in other advanced democracies are a reminder that even established democracies nurture their own antibodies. However, the strongest outbursts would most probably take place within those countries that — following the overthrow of totalitarianism — embraced, with naive enthusiasm, the democratic vision and then felt betrayed by it.

It will, therefore, be incumbent on the democratic, more stable, and richer West to promote global conditions that reduce the likelihood of such political regression. This will not be easy, in part because of the West's attitudes toward much of the rest of the world. The West considers itself to be inherently superior, not only on the level of economic development but in political maturity. Much of the West's political rhetoric about the world reflects that attitude: the less developed countries are viewed as politically primitive, economically backward, and religiously fanatic. And while there may be some justification for such feelings, they also tend to betray a patronizing and parochial attitude, insensitive to the historical and cultural factors that prevented other societies from pursuing the same path of development as the West. Moreover, inherent in that attitude is the assumption that historical development is unilinear, and that imitation of the West is the only positive option open to others.

The West's contempt for religion is also part and parcel of this mindset. Though it focuses most overtly on Islam, it is more generalized. As N. J. Demerath argued in the summer 1991 issue of the journal *Dœdalus* dedicated to "Religion and Politics":

> Few conceits have been more enduring in the West than the notion that other societies will inevitably "evolve," "develop," or "modernize." One critical element of this perspective for Western intellectuals involves the secularization motif. Whether defined as the demystification of the sacred, the diminishment of sacred salience, or the sacred's retreat from the societal core, the process denotes a cultural change that many regard as the inevitable result of such basic developmental processes as Weberian rationalization and Durkheimian differentiation.

Stated more simply, the prevailing orthodoxy among intellectuals in the West is that religion is a waning, irrational, and dysfunctional aberration.

Yet in fact, religion not only persists but in some parts of the developing world is staging a comeback. In addition to the proselytizing efforts of the Catholic Church in Africa and Asia, and to the spread also of Islam, evangelical and charismatic Protestantism has been gaining adherents, especially in Latin America and lately in the former Soviet Union. However, the religious revival is often marked by theological confusion and may lack institutional staying power, particularly in the case of the evangelical sects that are dependent on individual and highly charismatic preachers. Nonetheless, it is important to note that the source of the moral sinews of many societies has been established religion, and its heralded decay — especially in the more advanced countries — is not necessarily a sign of human progress.

The absence in the West of any binding moral imperatives perpetuates passivity, if not lack of compassion, regarding the dilemmas of inequality. It is no longer possible for anyone in the West to pretend a lack of awareness of the massive hunger that decimates hundreds of thousands of people each year, and in some years even millions (as recently has been the case in Africa) nor to plead ignorance regarding the appalling poverty and the diseases that characterize the life of large portions of the populations not living either in Western Europe, North America, or the newly prosperous countries of the Far East. Within the much more intimate setting of Europe itself, such selfish indifference has characterized the reaction of the West Europeans to the painful struggles of their Eastern brothers with the difficult legacies of communism, and much the same could be said about the attitude of many in America to the plight of America's urban blacks. Knowledge combined with passivity raises a troubling moral issue (with a disturbing, though admittedly somewhat remote, parallel to the question that was often put to the Germans who had lived during the Nazi times), that the West at some point may find it painful to have to answer.

In the meantime, the gulf in the texture of life — that is to say, both in its material and in its spiritual dimensions — may widen between those who increasingly will be able to exploit humanity's enhanced powers both to gratify and to redefine themselves, and those for whom life remains dominated by the struggle for survival in an essentially threatening external world. Immanuel Kant once defined the end of history as the realization of human freedom in the context of "a perfectly just civic constitution," at which point mankind would have fulfilled itself. But what Kant did not and could not have anticipated was the enhancement of human capabilities both for material self-gratification and for increasingly far-reaching scientific self-engineering, thereby refocusing man's preoccupation from the externalities of life — such as the struggle with nature — toward what might be called the internalities of life — such as gratification of personal desires (and not just needs) and even capricious self-alteration. The explosive popularity in the West of cosmetic surgery is a striking, though superficial, example of the latter phenomenon.

A significant portion of humanity thus finds itself on the brink of an entirely new era in human affairs. The philosophical implications of human history being on the edge of a new and mysterious age are almost mind-boggling. Ultimately, they raise the question of what is the essence of the human being. But the more immediate and practical implications are also complex. They augur a potential dichotomy in global outlook and human identity that is not only unprecedented but that stands in sharp — indeed, paradoxical — conflict with our age's compression of space and time.

It is ironical that when the world was enormous, separated by weeks and even months of sailing time, the human condition in terms of man's relationship to nature and in terms of man's self-comprehension was in fact much more uniform than it is today, when distance is now only a matter of hours and an instant global perception of events is possible through television. Any further widening of the gulf in the texture of life, though that gulf may be currently somewhat obscured by the universal adoption of democratic rhetoric, will certainly make it more difficult to cope with the world's tangible socioeconomic problems and political dilemmas.

Moreover, it must be recognized that in any case, even under the best of circumstances, progress toward a more genuinely global cooperation — one that begins also to bridge these existential differences — will develop through long stages, will be piecemeal, and at most will be only partial. Slogans about one world, about global justice, or even about a new world order to the contrary, the enhancement of practical cooperation on the global scale, imposing thereby some degree of control over the dynamics of historical change, will be a very slow process, at best minimally ahead of tendencies toward fragmentation and doctrines of irrational escapism. And a positive response will have to manifest itself both on the political as well as the philosophical levels, transforming gradually both the world's distribution of power and its cultural mores.

However, global political dilemmas which are heavily influenced by cultural and philosophical factors cannot be quickly remedied by a few specific prescriptions. Indeed, it must be recognized that the expectation of instant solutions to complex and deeply rooted problems is itself a characteristic of our modern age, with its mind-set heavily conditioned by ideological expectations and technological capabilities. These have induced a reductionist mode of thought, with its inclination to evade sensitive moral and attitudinal problems by imposing on them doctrinal or technical solutions. *The needed correction will not come from a catalog of policy recommendations. It can only emerge as a consequence of a new historical tide that induces a change both in values and in conduct; in effect, out of a prolonged process of cultural self-reexamination and philosophical reevaluation, which over time influences the political outlook both of the West and of the non-Western world. That process can be encouraged by an enlightened dialogue but it cannot be politically imposed.*

In the course of any such process, the West will have to shed its parochial blinders to its own cultural malaise, not only because its spiritual emptiness deprives it of the ability to empathize but also because it would be physically impossible to duplicate on a global scale the West's consumerist society, with its limitless appetite for self-gratification beyond personal need. The non-Western world will have to recognize that the advocacy of confiscatory egalitarianism — propounded quite hypocritically by its often corrupt elites — is not the solution, not only because it frightens and alienates the West but also because the recent communist experience demonstrates that as a policy it is a prescription for coercive poverty. And all will have to seek a more explicitly defined balance in the modern world between the material and the spiritual dimensions of life, especially if the purpose of global politics is increasingly defined as the progressive shaping of a common global community, with gradually equalizing opportunities for human fulfillment.

In our age the profoundest problems that humanity faces have become too great for the nation-state, the traditional unity of international affairs, to handle. This does not mean that the nation-state has outlived its usefulness or that one should seek to create a world of supranational cartels. The nation-state will remain, for quite some time, the primary focus of civic loyalty, the basic source of historical and cultural diversity, and the prime force for mobilizing the individual's commitment. However, the world today needs more than the nation-state to organize global peace, to promote global welfare, to diffuse globally the fruits of science and technology, and to cope with global environmental problems. All of these things can be done more effectively and rationally if nation-states are encouraged to cooperate in the setting of a larger community that reflects what unites them and submerges what has traditionally divided them.

Accordingly, to institutionalize the progressive emergence of such a common global community, new forms of enhanced cooperation will have to evolve along two major axes: the trilateral relationship among the world's richest and democratic states of Europe, America, and East Asia (notably Japan); and through the United Nations as the wider and more representative framework of global politics. This will require a redefinition not only of America's world role but also the adoption by Europe as well as Japan of a broader outlook; and it will require the deliberate enhancement of the UN's political role, even at some cost to the unilateral power of some presently dominant states.

The gradual redistribution of responsibilities within the trilateral relationship is needed in order to stimulate a wider appreciation within the more advanced and prosperous portions of the world of a common and shared responsibility both for peace and for peaceful change. As long as that responsibility is wielded, however imperfectly, in the main by the United States alone, both Europe and Japan can feel absolved from having to assume political and moral obligations outside the more immediate areas of their national interest. That self-absolution reinforces their parochialism even as it intensifies American resentments over unequal burden sharing, overstretches American power, and tempts the American public with escapist isolationism.

Thus each of the three will have to alter its predominant mind-set if trilateral cooperation is to be further enhanced. America will have to restrain its missionary impulses and recognize the limits of its power; Japan will have to shed its monopolistic proclivities in world trade and accept limitations on its high-tech ambitions; Europe will have to move beyond its inward preoccupations and be willing to assume larger outside burdens, especially in order to assimilate into Europe some of the former communist states.

As a practical matter, the translation into political reality of the notion of a truly balanced trilateral cooperation will have to mean some devolution of American power to the advantage of Europe and Japan. Some of that devolution has already taken place in financial and economic matters, with the United States compelled to defer more to the views of Japan and Germany in particular. But in time, it should also involve greater European and Japanese participation in political and security decision making, if Europe and Japan are to assume enhanced roles in an increasingly cooperative global political process. There is bound to be some understandable American reluctance to move in that direction. However, without such devolution, trilateral cooperation will remain unbalanced, with self-serving European and Japanese parochialism conveniently perpetuated by one-sided American interventionism.

The central purpose of trilateral cooperation should not be just to preserve existing privileges but rather to promote more basic progress in the human condition. That more ambitious goal will also require — in addition to changes in their respective mind-sets — significant changes within each of the three trilateral partners, but especially within America and Europe. America remains, and will remain for some time to come, the world's catalytic nation. Europe is also, though to a lesser extent, especially given the continued worldwide cultural influence of both France and Great Britain. The fact that much of the world looks particularly to America for a preview of its own future imposes a special burden on America to espouse a domestic transformation in its social mores and culture that in turn can provide a meaningful example for others. *The American society cannot be the model for the world — both morally and as a matter of practical economics — if a predominantly cornucopian ethic defines its essence, while a sizable but impoverished minority is simultaneously excluded from meaningful social participation. Preoccupation with the satisfaction of material desires that are growing more and more out of control can only perpetuate and deepen the objective and subjective gulf that is already dividing mankind.*

For Europe to play a more active world role, especially as America's coequal, the decisive precondition is continued unification. Only a more united Europe — the very scale of which defines Europe as a genuine global power — is likely to infuse into the European outlook a more generous global vision. Short of that, Europe will run the risk of reverting to ancient feuds, of remaining selfishly absorbed by its internal problems, and of again becoming preoccupied by its traditional concern with the power of Germany. That is why the promotion of a genuinely united Europe is in the fundamental interest of the world at large. Only such a Europe can undertake, and is likely to be inclined to assume, the larger burdens of participation in the building of a global community.

The renewal of America and the unification of Europe are hence the two basic preconditions for a globally more responsible and historically more effective trilateralism. In that context, Japan will have to follow suit, joining its two occidental partners in a global policy designed to maintain political stability while also promoting social change. Japan — like Europe — suffers from a parochialism that fortifies its selfishness, but — unlike Europe — it is a single national community, and as such its sense of national interest can be more easily reoriented toward wider global concerns both by the example and the pressures emanating from a renewed America and a more united Europe.

Such historically responsive trilateral cooperation can also help to infuse into the United Nations a more constructive sense of direction. *The UN's time has finally come. It is only within the framework of that global organization that the common problems of mankind can be collectively addressed.* In the years to come, the UN will have to be gradually reformed in order to make its structure more consistent with global power realities. As already noted, it is unlikely that in the near future it will prove possible to enlarge the number of states which are permanently represented on the UN's Security Council since any such enlargement would jeopardize the special status of the five powers which enjoy the veto-wielding permanent membership. However, perhaps it might prove possible to arrive at a formula for the enlargement of the council by creating a new category of members with permanent seats but without the right to cast the veto. Such an arrangement might prove more palatable, and thus open the doors for the addition of Japan, Germany, India, Nigeria, and Brazil — thereby also meeting the need for a greater political role in the management of world affairs by some of the key non-Western powers.

The fact that in the course of 1992 the UN was able to mount a major peacekeeping initiative in Cambodia and to provide legitimacy for the humanitarian — though predominantly American — mission in Somalia may justify cautious optimism regarding prospects of UN-sponsored international peacekeeping. But the prolonged failure both of the UN and of the European community to respond to the bloody crisis in the former Yugoslavia is also a reminder that such international cooperation is still very much constrained by national fears, suspicions, and selfishness. Moreover, one cannot discount the possibility that, before too long, progress toward wider cooperation might be derailed by UN vetoes cast either by a Russian or by a Chinese government that at some point may be tempted by great power ambitions to opt out of the Western-led UN consensus.

This is why the enhancement of the role of the UN is likely to be more significant in such less political areas of central concern to human survival as assuring global habitability, environmental lawmaking, a worldwide consensus on population policy, and the encouragement of increased flows of overseas development aid to the poorer states. It is the current cliche to say that these problems represent the new agenda of the world, replacing earlier concerns with the struggle for power. In fact, security threats and power struggles within, and perhaps between, the likely global clusters will persist and will remain a major danger to global stability. The new problems, mentioned above, will not displace the more traditional ones — but will be in addition to them, making the global agenda more complex than ever.

Though efforts to address the new problems are bound to make tangible progress very slowly — given the persisting absence of global consensus — one can still expect that a step-by-step increase in international cooperation will occur. Despite existing global cleavages, an incipient global consciousness of a common destiny, inherent in the growing awareness of the finite nature of resources and the vulnerability of the world's ecosystem, is maturing. That awareness offsets to some degree the tendencies toward the polarization of global outlooks and creates the basis for at least some limited but joint responses, especially in regard to ecological problems.

The UN's growing role is also abetted by the increase in the number of those who are acquiring a vested interest in a cooperative effort to change the status quo gradually and not violently. The world, in the broadest sense, can be seen as divided into two mankinds, living in two distinct cultures: the rich minority and the poor majority. By the end of the century, the first might number somewhere around one billion and the second account for the remaining five or so. But the five billion are also becoming increasingly differentiated, with perhaps as many as one billion of them during the last two decades enjoying a manifest improvement in their material condition as a result of successful economic growth. Their stake in reformist and increasingly cooperative policies is thus likely to grow. That, in and of itself, may not be enough to bridge the deep philosophical and material gulfs dividing mankind — with a resentful majority pitted against a privileged minority — but it might somewhat mitigate the risk that the UN could become paralyzed by a struggle between hostile coalitions and dominated by a new wave of irrational escapism.

Ultimately, however, the effort to gain control over the collective destiny of mankind will succeed or flounder on the critically important philosophical/cultural dimension. It is this dimension that shapes the critical ideas that guide political conduct. And to the extent that the West is still the spearhead of social progress and of political democratization worldwide, it will need to undertake a difficult philosophical and cultural reorientation. It is crucially important that the West's — and especially America's — crisis of the spirit does not vitiate and undo the West's potential for exercising a constructive influence on world affairs, at a stage when for the first time ever a truly global political process makes feasible a common attempt to shape mankind's future.

To reiterate a point made earlier: cultural and philosophical change is a matter of historical waves and not of disparate policy decisions. That change can be influenced by a heightened moral and ethical awareness but it cannot be directed politically. Change can only come out of a fundamental reevaluation of the core beliefs that guide social conduct and from a recognition of the need for a globally shared concept of the meaning of the good life, with the latter based on notions of self-restraint in social self-gratification. The West's ecological movement — whatever may be said about some of its specific advocacy — may be the first step toward such self-limitation. That may prove to be the movement's greatest philosophical contribution, auguring the emergence of a broader acceptance of the principle of self-denial as the point of departure for a globally shared moral consensus.

Any such consensus has to be derived from the recognition that humanity's control over its destiny requires a moral compass as well as a sense of balance. The exercise of control must be infused with an awareness of the consequences of choice, both in practical and in moral terms, which also implies the need for conscious self-restraint. Being able to alter the environment, or to alter oneself genetically, or to consume more because there is more to consume, or to compound the capacity to inflict mass destruction is not the exercise of control if the expanding human ability to do so automatically becomes the dominant motive for doing so. *The real alternative to total control is not minimal control or, even worse, the absence of any self-restraint, but public self-control that is derived from some internalized and self-restraining notions as to what is appropriate and what is not.*

The imperative of self-restraint has to apply to all the four major dimensions of change in the character of contemporary world politics. It has to apply to physical power, which has to be deliberately restrained through international agreements and voluntary moral codes, because power now can destroy all of humanity directly as well as indirectly through mindless exploitation of the environment and human self-alteration. It has to apply to political activism, which has to be channeled within defined and respected constitutional frames, lest society become increasingly ungovernable, with the quest for meaningful political participation degenerating into demagogic mobilization. It has to apply to personal expectations, because unlimited self-gratification by the relatively few will not only intensify global inequality for the many but will altogether demoralize both the self-indulgent and the deprived. It has to apply also to societal change, particularly in terms of enhanced educational efforts to inculcate in the public the understanding that long-enduring values need not be abandoned simply because of the onrush of new gadgets and new technologies that alter the external dimensions of social life. In the final analysis, taken together, all of the above mean respect for guidelines inspired by more than expediency.

It is noteworthy that the need for an enhanced moral consciousness is not only advocated by religious authorities but also by more reflective political leaders. Even disillusioned Marxist ideologues are recognizing that life cannot be defined meaningfully only on the basis of material criteria. Note, for example, what Alexander Yakovlev, a former Soviet Politburo member and a close associate of Mikhail Gorbachev, had to say in a major address in 1991 to professors and students at Columbia University about mankind's options:

> Social alternative presupposes choice of the quality of *social development*, and by the same token, the qualities of the human potential being formed through the natural course of new social relations. But what does it mean to speak of *a new quality of society?* A political system? Economic effectiveness? Scientific achievements? Wealth?
>
> No, the new quality of society means elevating man through his morality. (Italics in the original.)

Yakovlev's conclusion was a striking echo of the powerful statement of Pope John Paul II, who in his encyclical *Centesimus Annus* proclaimed that:

> Of itself, an economic system does not possess criteria for correctly distinguishing new and higher forms of satisfying human needs from artificial new needs which hinder the formation of a mature personality. . . . It is therefore necessary to create lifestyles in which the quest for truth, beauty, goodness, and communion with others for the sake of common growth are the factors that determine consumer choices, savings, and investments. Even the decision to invest in one place rather than another, in one productive sector rather than another, is always *a moral and cultural choice*. (Italics in the original.)

Moral guidance ultimately has to come from within. The modern age, initiated by the French Revolution, placed a premium on the certainties of the so-called objective truth, spurning subjectivity as irrational. The failure of the most extreme perversion of that mode of political thought — namely, of the totalitarian metamyth — has lately prompted an extreme swing in the pendulum of fashionable post- modern thought: from the intellectuals' fascination with "scientific" Marxism as the epitome of "objective truth" to their currently antithetical embrace of uninhibited relativism. But neither response is likely to provide the framework for a world that has become politically awakened and active. The alternative to total control cannot be amoral confusion out of control.

The global crisis of the spirit has to be overcome if humanity is to assert command over its destiny. The point of departure for such self- assertion must be awareness that social life is both objectively and subjectively too complex to be periodically redesigned according to utopian blueprints. The dogmatic certainties of the modern age must yield to the recognition of the inherent uncertainty of the human condition. In a world of fanatical certitudes, morality could be seen as redundant; but in a world of contingency, moral imperatives then become the central, and even the only, source of reassurance. Recognition both of the complexity and the contingency of the human condition thus underlines the *political* need for shared moral consensus in the increasingly congested and intimate world of the twenty-first century.

Creating Conditions of Peace

A Theological Framework

Marilyn McMorrow, RSCJ

Matthew's Gospel has Jesus proclaim: "How blest are the peacemakers; God calls them his own."[1] We readily agree. Intuitively, we understand authentic peacemakers deserve to be called "blessed." We stand in amazement and gratitude before persons who find — or create — a way (sometimes miraculous) to break through long-standing relations of estrangement, injustice, violence, or war. It is easy to conclude that such persons enact God's own design.

In contrast, it is bitterly demoralizing when individuals lay false claim to the mantle of peacemaker. The world community has repeatedly witnessed, often courtesy of videotape, leaders who procure "peace for our time" by ratifying aggression or by crushing under the heel of the boot those who "disturb" the peace.[2] Even so, hearts still expand when persons widely perceived to be authentic peacemakers receive the Nobel Peace

---

1 Matthew 5:9.
2 References in this sentence are to: (1) Neville Chamberlain's infamous claim, in September 1938, when the Western powers ceded to Hitler's demand to annex the Sudetenland; and (2) George Orwell's depiction of tyranny, in *1984* (New York: Harcourt Brace, 1949), 271.

Prize or some comparable form of universal acclaim. We honor the peacemaker.

Holding the peacemaker in such high regard, however, might lead us, at least unconsciously, to consider peacemaking the special vocation of a chosen few. In marked contrast, recent writings on Catholic social thought[3] insist that every human being is called to be a peacemaker. These texts address this conviction not just to Catholics, but to all people of good will. Proposing an explicitly *"religious* vision of peace among peoples and nations,"* these documents contend that this vision "has an objective basis and is capable of progressive realization."[4]

This vision is not whole cloth, given once and for all. Interaction among practitioners and pastors, jointly engaged in reading and responding to the signs of the times, shapes both its substance and its realization. If it is the role of pastors to enunciate a vision of peacemaking, practitioners help construct and fill in the contours of that vision through their concrete efforts to institute peace in the actual and changing circumstances of our country and the world. The project of creating conditions of peace is properly the "work of the entire community of faith and of all people of good will."[5] All participants in this project who are willing to "become learners in the kingdom of heaven" may draw from a storehouse of resources, "both the new and the old," that can assist in the task.[6]

A striking example of this interaction between practitioners and pastors is the extent to which Pope John XXIII shapes his vision of "peace on earth" by fusing the relatively "new" understanding of universal and basic human rights with the "old," received, revelation of the human person as worthy of dignity, having been created in God's image and redeemed by God's action, in history, through Christ. The belief that human beings are created in the image of God is as ancient as Genesis itself. The claims of the international human rights movement — for example, the idea that all persons have certain basic human rights which it is the *purpose* of the international political order to guarantee and promote — are of more recent origin.[7] The *Universal Declaration of Human Rights* was not

---

3 This article discusses: *Pacem in Terris* (1963), *Populorum Progressio* (1967), *Sollicitudo Rei Socialis* (1987), *Centesimus Annus* (1991), *The Challenge of Peace* (1983), *The Harvest of Justice* (1994).

4 National Conference of Catholic Bishops, *The Challenge of Peace: God's Promise and Our Response* (Washington, D.C.: USCC Office for Publishing and Promotion Services, 1983), no. 20. Emphasis mine.

5 National Conference of Catholic Bishops, *The Harvest of Justice Is Sown in Peace* (Washington, D.C.: USCC Office for Publishing and Promotion Services, 1994), 2.

6 Matthew 13:52.

7 See, for example, Article 28 in *The Universal Declaration of Human Rights*: "Everyone is entitled to a social and international order in which the rights and

adopted until 1948, a scant 15 years before the publication of *Pacem in Terris*; the texts of the international human rights covenants would not be completed until 1966, three years after the encyclical was published. Discerning the signs of the times, Pope John XXIII recognized that the worldwide defense and promotion of human rights — arguably, the most important social movement of our time — is integral to the work of building peace. So he incorporated human rights doctrine, along with the teachings of Scripture and tradition, into his articulation of the "immense task" incumbent upon all persons of good will of bringing about "true peace in the order established by God."[8] For instance, Pope John XXIII situates the duties to combat racism and discrimination, improve the status of women, and protect refugees with the human rights framework.[9]

When the American Catholic bishops reflect on this immense task, they emphasize that the work of peacemaking is "not an optional commitment" for the Christian; rather, it is a "requirement," an "essential dimension" of faith. "We are called to be peacemakers, not by some movement of the moment but by our Lord Jesus."[10] Speaking of the particular case of defending peace, the bishops state this duty in even stronger terms. "The Christian has no choice but to defend peace, properly understood, against aggression. This is an inalienable obligation."[11]

Carrying out this obligation presupposes a clear idea of the meaning of peace and peacemaking, "properly understood." What does peacemaking entail at this juncture of time, culture, and historical circumstance? More fundamentally, what is peace? The word is utterly familiar. What exactly does it signify?

The purpose of this article is to argue that the texts cited above provide important guidance in devising responses for these questions. As *The Challenge of Peace* observes, the community of faith needs but has not as yet developed a comprehensive theology of peace. Such a theology would be a central resource in illuminating peacemaking as an essential dimension of Christian faith.[12] While important, the long-standing emphasis in traditional Catholic theology on the obligation to limit resort to force is not in itself sufficient to:

> . . . ground the task of peacemaking solidly in the biblical vision of the kingdom of God, then place it centrally in the ministry of the Church . . . specify the obstacles in the way of peace, as . . . understood theologically

---

freedoms set forth in declaration can be fully realized."

8   John XXIII, *Peace on Earth (Pacem in Terris)*, papal encyclical (Washington, D.C.: USCC Office for Publishing and Promotion Services, 1963), no. 163.

9   Ibid., nos. 44, 41, 86, 104-106.

10 *The Challenge of Peace*, vii, no. 333. *The Harvest of Justice*, 3.

11 *The Challenge of Peace*, no. 73.

12 Ibid., nos. 23-25.

and in the social and political sciences . . . identify the specific contributions a community of faith can make to the work of peace and relate these to the wider work of peace pursued by other groups and institutions of society.[13]

Although significant theological work on the subject of peacemaking remains, we are not left wanting in the interim. The encyclicals propose insights and orientations that, taken together, form a theological framework for probing the meaning — and the challenge — of peace. This storehouse of resources, both new and old, can assist us in determining what it means to construct authentic peace in the final years of this century and the first years of the next.

I. The Meaning of Peace

To ask oneself the meaning of peace can be an intriguing and surprising exercise. On first thought, the meaning seems obvious. On closer examination, the term, no matter how familiar, has no single, delimited definition, in part because we use the word as both a residual category and as a placeholder.

The word "peace" functions as a residual category when it describes what remains once a distressful event ceases to occur. Dictionaries characteristically treat the word in this manner, defining peace as: a nonwarring condition; an end to strife or dissension; the absence of social disorder; mental freedom from annoyance, distraction, anxiety, or obsession; silence; restraint in speech (as in holding one's peace); or the state after death (as in being "at peace" or "resting in peace").

In defining war, the political theorist Thomas Hobbes gives the classic illustration of peace construed as a residual category. According to Hobbes, war "consists not in battle only or the act of fighting," but also "in the known disposition thereto, during all the time there is no assurance to the contrary." Hobbes concludes his definition with the throwaway comment: "All *other* time is peace."[14] Since there is always some actor with the disposition to fight, since it would be foolhardy indeed to claim assurance to the contrary, Hobbes considers the state of war a permanent condition. The *other* time that is "peace" never occurs. Though Hobbes gives a nod,

---

13 Ibid., no. 25. Underscoring the role of practitioners in shaping the Church's vision of peace, the bishops note that the contribution of those "who have struggled in various ways to make and keep the peace in this often violent age" is essential in the development of this theology (no. 24).

14 Thomas Hobbes, *Leviathan*, C. B. Macpherson, ed. (New York: Penguin, 1981), ch. XIII, 186. Emphasis mine.

in passing, to common parlance, for him peace is the ultimate residual category: a null set.

The word "peace" functions as a placeholder when it stands for a particular value, good, or state of affairs designated as the equivalent of peace. For example, in the aftermath of the Rodney King verdict, marchers protesting racism in American society repeated insistently: "No justice, no peace." This chant captures the insight that conditions of justice are not just *a prerequisite for* peace, but *the substance of* peace.

Scripture supplies some equivalents for peace. Consider the following meanings of the biblical term "shalom": tranquil possession of good things; perfect happiness; well-being; health; cordial understanding made possible by God; harmony with nature, self, others, and God; blessing; rest; glory; riches; salvation; and life! To this list, the Gospels add spiritual well-being through reconciliation effected by Christ, thus underscoring the connection between forgiveness and peace.[15] Notice that these equivalents for peace are not necessarily themselves equivalent. For example, "serenity" and "justice" are not synonyms; however, both words are synonyms for peace.

Given this definitional profusion, discussions of the concept of "peace" in any context, including the theological, easily become diffuse. If peace is only a residual category, or, alternatively, if it is the equivalent of any and all good things, it is difficult to know what it means to create peace or when we succeed in doing so.

II. Peace in Contemporary Catholic Social Thought

One contribution of contemporary Catholic social thought is that it focuses the definition of peace. On balance, recent texts decline to conceive of peace as a residual category; instead, they propose two specific equivalents for peace: justice and authentic development.

A. A Positive Vision of Peace

Even in the context of condemning war in the strongest possible terms, these texts do not refer to peace as a residual category. "Peace is not merely the absence of war."[16] This point deserves emphasis because we

---

15 Xavier Léon-Dufour, *Dictionary of Biblical Theology* (Dublin: Geoffrey Chapman, 1970), 364-367.

automatically associate "the end of war" with "peace." Recall, for example, powerful images in the collective American memory of the explosion of joy in Times Square, August 1945, at the end of World War II. Certainly, the moral obligation to end war commands the highest urgency. However, ending war does not automatically create peace. It may afford a particularly promising opportunity to *construct* peace — one we may choose either to act upon or to squander. The obligation to act upon — not squander — such an opportunity also commands the highest moral urgency. For that matter, the obligation to make peace has urgent priority even when there is no obvious opportunity to do so.

The Challenge of Peace illustrates both a consistent refusal to equate peace with the absence of war and a consistent call to search out possibilities for building peace when there appear to be none on the political horizon. The goal of the pastoral is to set out the overriding obligation to avoid nuclear war. In making that argument, however, the pastoral never concedes to the view that nuclear weapons play an essential role in making and preserving world peace.

In contrast, some international relations theorists argue that the adversarial, bipolar structure of nuclear deterrence is responsible for peace. In other words, the accurate name for the period between 1945-1989 is "The Long Peace," not "The Cold War."[17] This interpretation suggests that there is reason to regret the end of the bipolar order. The wisest U.S. policy, now that the Soviet Union has collapsed, is to maintain bipolar nuclear deterrence. If that proves impossible, then the United States should pursue a policy of "managed" nuclear proliferation.[18]

The Challenge of Peace (not to mention *The Harvest of Justice*) makes a markedly different judgment about the desirability of adversarial bipolarity and its deterrence structure. Published in 1983, *The Challenge of Peace* clearly identifies its context and impetus: a dangerous period within a cold war of indefinite duration. The Cold War may have been "peace of a sort"[19] in comparison to hot war, particularly, nuclear hot war, but it was a real war nonetheless. Waged globally on multiple fronts, this war exacted exorbitant costs and claimed uncounted lives. While the pastoral acknowledges that deterrence may have helped to maintain peace of a sort, it treats deterrence, on balance, as a strategy for waging war, not a structure

---

16 Second Vatican Council, *Pastoral Constitution on the Church in the Modern World (Gaudium et Spes)*, no. 78; nos. 77-81, generally.

17 See, for example, John Gaddis, *The Long Peace: Inquiries into the History of the Cold War* (New York: Oxford University Press, 1987).

18 See, for example, John Mearsheimer, "Why We Will Soon Miss the Cold War," *The Atlantic Monthly*, August 1990. Mearsheimer fears unmanaged nuclear proliferation is more likely than managed proliferation.

19 *The Challenge of Peace*, no. 189.

for keeping peace. It assesses the moral justifiability of deterrence principally in terms of the just-war tradition. Using *ius in bello* criteria to evaluate deterrence implies it is a strategy employed *in war*. The pastoral finds "concrete elements" of nuclear deterrence, as practiced by the United States, morally suspect because the purpose (actual, if not avowed) and probable consequences of these elements do not satisfy the *ius in bello* precepts of noncombatant immunity and proportionality. Although the bishops give deterrence a "strictly conditioned moral acceptance," they reject the idea that deterrence can provide an adequate or long-term basis for peace. Therefore, they hinge this strictly conditioned acceptance on the commitment of the United States government to use the Cold War's "peace of a sort" as "a framework to move toward authentic peace."[20]

Authentic peace, in other words, is different from the absence of hot war or a prolongation of the Cold War status quo. In what we can now acclaim as its most prescient passage, the pastoral (drafts of which circulated during the years when the first Reagan administration was describing the Soviet Union as an evil empire) challenged Americans to believe in the possibility of transforming relations with its archenemy into conditions of authentic peace.

> To believe we are condemned in the future only to what has been the past of U.S.-Soviet relations is to underestimate both our human potential for creative diplomacy and God's action in our midst which could open the way to changes we could barely imagine. We do not intend to foster illusory ideas that the road ahead in superpower relations will be devoid of tension or that peace will be easily achieved. But we do warn against that "hardness of heart" which can close us or others to the changes needed to make the future different from the past.[21]

The pastoral declines to define cold war as "peace" or acquiesce to the view that relations of enmity among nations are inevitable. In contrast, the text emphasizes the positive content of peace and our positive obligation to bring it about. Granted, peace is a gift of God who breaks through existing patterns of history (whether personal or international). It is nevertheless a work of human construction.[22]

Congruent with this approach, *The Harvest of Justice* argues that today's challenge of peace demands aggressive and concerted action to dismantle (not preserve) the bipolar nuclear deterrence structure, prevent nuclear proliferation, and capitalize on the graced opening that the end of the Cold War affords for the construction of an authentic peace. At the end of World War II, leaders compelled by the clarity of catastrophe gathered in San Francisco and Bretton Woods to construct international institutions

---

20   Ibid., nos. 186, 189, specifically; nos. 132, 138, 163-199, generally.
21   Ibid., no. 258.
22   Ibid., no. 68.

intended to ensure collective security, mediate conflict, and contribute to global welfare. Arguing that today's challenge is to take up that task again, *The Harvest of Justice* cautions against two tendencies: (1) continuing to view the international system through outmoded Cold War lenses with faulty depth perception; and (2) retreating into isolation and abdicating the responsibility to build an effective international order.[23] The obligation to develop and act on a correct vision of international needs and possibilities is particularly binding on the United States, given its preponderant power and preeminent position; "a leadership role among nations can only be justified by the . . . willingness to contribute widely and generously to the common good."[24]

B. The Enterprise of Peace

The texts considered in this essay do not settle for a residual notion of peace. Nor do they proliferate positive equivalents for peace until the meaning evaporates, leaving us adrift in vague confusion. The background for discussions of peace in these texts is the gratuity of God's redemptive action in the world, as revealed in Scripture. In the ultimate analysis, peace is grace, that healing gift of God which surpasses understanding.[25] From first to last, it is the gift, the sign, work, and fruit of the Spirit. Against that context, these documents propose two central equivalents for peace: (1) justice and (2) authentic development.

Taken together, these documents argue that justice and authentic development are intrinsically related. To work for social justice means to ensure that all persons have the opportunity to experience authentic human development. This task has interpersonal, national, and international components, all of which are increasingly interdependent. Engagement in this enterprise *is* the call for and life project of every Christian, acting in response to the signs of the times, under the inspiration and power of the Spirit. The *name* for this engagement is solidarity: deliberate action that seeks to transform "structures of sin" into "structures of the kingdom." Solidarity is simultaneously the path to development and to peace. Peace is the outcome of this enterprise.[26]

---

23 *The Harvest of Justice*, 8-18, generally.

24 John Paul II, *On Social Concern (Sollicitudo Rei Socialis)*, papal encyclical (Washington, D.C.: USCC Office for Publishing and Promotion Services, 1987), no. 23.

25 See the reflections in *The Harvest of Justice*, 3.

26 *Pacem in Terris, Populorum Progressio, Sollicitudo Rei Socialis*, and *Centesimus Annus*, generally; *Sollicitudo Rei Socialis*, no. 39, specifically.

III. Peacemaking: A Work of Social Justice and Authentic Development

In undertaking this enterprise, how can we know whether any given social institution accords with the requirements of social justice? In other words, what is the basis for the moral judgment that a particular practice, institution, or society is well ordered, a structure of the kingdom? According to *Pacem in Terris*, the test is the extent to which it upholds human rights.

A. The Centrality of Human Rights

Human rights — moral standards with an explicitly political purpose — are plumb lines for assessing the justice of any fundamental social institution, including the international political economy, the basic social structure which affects the possibilities for human development in all subordinate spheres.

The fulcrum of the human rights approach is the individual human person, the bearer of fundamental and inalienable rights *and* corresponding duties. In *Pacem in Terris*, human rights are inseparable from respective social obligations. The integral link between rights and duties is central to the encyclical's vision of a just and peaceful social order. We can understand why, having seen, to our dismay, the social disintegration and moral disorder that result when the link between rights and duties is severed; when individuals demand their rights against others, but accept no responsibility for themselves and/or no responsibility to defend the rights of others. In *Pacem in Terris*, individuals bear the primary obligation (and authority) to defend and exercise their own rights, to the extent this is possible. From the moral perspective, however, this is not the end of the story. To the right of each person, "there corresponds a duty *in all other persons*: the duty, namely, of acknowledging and respecting the right in question."[27]

The ordinary way persons exercise their joint responsibilities for defending and promoting their own rights, as well as the rights of others, is by developing social practices and structures (whether formal or informal) which have this end in view. Therefore, the ultimate *moral* purpose, thus justification, of any social structure is the defense of human rights against standard threats.[28] A well-ordered society (whether that be a particular

---

27 *Pacem in Terris*, nos. 28-30. Emphasis mine.

family, at one end of the spectrum, or the international political economy, at the other end) is one that carries out its pertinent set of corresponding obligations.

In contrast, a social structure is unjustly ordered when it directly violates human rights or when it fails to devise effective, positive ways to implement the duties to which the basic rights of persons give rise. Egregious injustice results when persons, groups, or countries (usually those with access to relative power, wealth, and opportunity) design social structures in ways that enable them to claim their *own* rights, but neglect or deny the identical rights of others. Such actors "build with one hand and destroy with the other."[29]

In sum, then, *Pacem in Terris* argues that working for social justice means working to institute conditions that protect and promote human rights. It lays out a broad vision of a social, political, and economic order designed to accomplish and responsible for this work. It calls everyone to advance this common good and banish whatever endangers peace.

B. The Most Urgent Task

The liability of a broad vision is that it does not select among competing priorities or identify the most urgent tasks. Among the comprehensive set of human rights and corresponding duties, which ones are fundamental? What is the basis for setting priorities among competing obligations?

Pacem in Terris does present the full complement of human rights. On examination, however, the rights listed illustrate or specify the most basic human right: that is, "the right to life *and* a worthy standard of living." At its core, the right to life comprises the right to bodily integrity and the right to the means and opportunities essential for the proper *development of life*.[30] Specifying this point, a contemporary political philosopher defines the fundamental content of the basic and universal human right to life as: the right to personal and bodily security against violence; the right to the means of subsistence; and the right to free and full participation in the fundamental institutions of society that determine security, subsistence, and participative freedom for oneself and others.[31]

Defending basic human rights is the most urgent priority in the work of social justice and authentic development. Pope Paul VI calls on the world's peacemakers to focus their efforts on this fundamental obligation.

---

28 This notion of "standard threat" is intended to signify a "reasonable" level of social guarantees. Henry Shue, *Basic Rights: Subsistence, Affluence, and U.S. Policy* (Princeton: Princeton University Press, 1980), 17.

29 *Pacem in Terris*, nos. 30-31.

30 Ibid., no. 11. Emphasis mine.

31 Shue, *Basic Rights*.

Far too many persons are crushed by destitution, fratricidal conflicts, and abusive political regimes. Moreover, "the gap as it were is widening between the development of some and the stagnating, even deteriorating, conditions of others." The bitter injustice of entire populations deprived of the necessities of life and subjugated to domination cries out to God. This injustice "must be fought and overcome" through bold initiatives.[32]

The urgent problems Pope Paul VI identifies — fratricidal conflict, destitution, and abusive regimes — correspond directly to the chief threats to the basic human right to life, that is the right to security, subsistence, and participation in the fundamental institutions of society. Countering these threats is the immediate priority and fundamental obligation of the peacemaker.

This obligation has a "positive" as well as a "negative" content. There are actions we *must undertake* (positive obligation) as well as actions we *must not take* (negative obligation) in order to guarantee basic human rights. For example, making safe water available is as essential to guaranteeing the right to life as is preventing the state from using death squads against dissidents. Development is the name for, and the goal of, the positive duties correlative to basic human rights. *Populorum Progressio* concentrates primarily on the obligation to aid the destitute, in response to the global emergency of absolute poverty. However, the encyclical also suggests that ending poverty would contribute to ending fratricidal conflict and political oppression, to the extent that the destitute become able to direct their lives and reorder their societies.[33]

The obligation to alleviate poverty prohibits misuse of resources needed for the task:

> While so many people are going hungry, while so many families are suffering destitution, while so many people spend their lives submerged in the darkness of ignorance . . . every public or private squandering . . . every financially depleting arms race . . . become[s] a scandalous and intolerable crime.[34]

Cutting closer to the marrow, *Populorum Progressio* argues that this obligation also takes precedence over competing claims (ordinarily deemed "legitimate") to the resources needed for the task, including claims by affluent persons *and* nations to their "own" property.[35] "All other rights, whatever they are, including property rights and the right of free trade, must be subordinated" to the basic right of all persons to the means

---

32 *Populorum Progressio*, nos. 21, 26, 29, 30, 32. Paul VI's reference to the widening gap repeats the theme of key United Nations development documents of this time.

33 Ibid., nos. 9, 11.

34 Ibid., no. 53.

35 Ibid., nos. 22-24.

of subsistence.[36] That includes the right of state sovereignty. Affluent nations are obligated to alleviate destitution beyond, as well as within, their borders. The duty of development, in other words, is international, as well as personal and national, in scope. Pope John Paul II reiterates the conviction: the question of social justice has "acquired a worldwide dimension . . . because the demand for justice can only be satisfied on that level."[37]

By focusing on destitution (primarily), fratricidal conflict, and the domination of abusive political regimes, Pope Paul VI defines the essential content of the duty of development. At its core, the obligation of development is the obligation to combat the most serious violations of the basic human rights to security, subsistence, and free participation in the fundamental institutions of society. Because development is synonymous with peace, countering violations against basic human rights is the *sine qua non* in creating conditions of peace.[38]

C. Reading the Signs of the Times

The recent social encyclicals of Pope John Paul II and the American peace pastorals continue this line of moral argument. Moreover, they all demonstrate the importance of reading the signs of the times. The obligation to defend basic human rights is primary and integral to building peace, but knowing how to do so depends on recognizing the particular threats to human rights and the particular possibilities for action that obtain in a given situation. Each of the above texts reads the challenges, obstacles, and possibilities inherent in a specific set of geopolitical and economic circumstances. Reading in nuclear weaponry and U.S.-Soviet antagonism "a threat to human life . . . without precedent," *The Challenge of Peace* focuses on the obligation to transform bipolar nuclear deterrence.[39]

Sollicitudo Rei Socialis reads the consequences of a world divided into blocs that operate to sustain and further promote maldevelopment of every kind. In both the "so-called developed North and the developing South," deliberate political and economic decisions allocate inordinate resources in slavish thrall to "an unacceptably exaggerated concern for security" and to "superdevelopment," thus violating the right of millions to basic security and basic subsistence. In consequence, insecurity and destitution have been increasing within rich and poor countries alike.[40] The most salient indicator of this grievous distortion of resources is the

---

36 Ibid., no. 22.
37 *Sollicitudo Rei Socialis*, no. 10.
38 *Populorum Progressio*, no. 87.
39 *The Challenge of Peace*, i.
40 *Sollicitudo Rei Socialis*, nos. 14, 22, 28, specifically; nos. 16, 17, 42, generally.

dispossession of millions, reflected both in the growing number of refugees and migrants and in the growing worldwide phenomenon of homelessness: "so many men, women, and children who can no longer find a home in a divided and inhospitable world." The "prevailing picture is one destined to lead us more quickly *towards death* rather than . . . *true development* which would lead all towards a 'more human' life."[41]

Faced with these interdependent structures of sin and their disastrous consequences for the weakest persons, the Christian is called to solidarity: deliberate engagement in the work of transforming these structures of sin and ideological idolatry (the all-consuming desire for power and profit) into structures of the kingdom.[42]

> The obligation to commit oneself to the development of peoples is not just an individual duty, and still less an individualistic one. . . .
>
> Collaboration in the development of the whole person and of every human being is in fact a duty of *all towards all*. . . .[43]

Solidarity in the service of authentic development is "the path to peace."[44] The path is long and complex, given human frailty and changing circumstances. Sometimes, those circumstances pose tremendous obstacles; sometimes, they introduce rare opportunity. The task of the peacemaker is to respond to either with action and courage.[45]

Centesimus Annus reads the extraordinary changes in the world that have led to the end of the Cold War and the collapse of ideological frameworks that fueled decades of violent conflict and maldevelopment. Pope John Paul II discerns in this upheaval an opportunity to reform political, economic, social, and military structures of the international system and reconceptualize relationships among them. The encyclical warns against filling the ideological vacuum by absolutizing *any* view of political economy as the *only* route to development.[46] It suggests criteria for assessing whether new political and economic structures contribute to maldevelopment or authentic development. Once again, these markers underline the centrality of basic human rights. With regard to the right of security, is there a commitment to building international structures capable of arbitrating and intervening in conflicts between nations? With regard

---

41   Ibid., no. 24. Emphasis in text. The internal reference is to Pope Paul VI's definition of "true" development.

42   Ibid., no. 37, specifically; ch. V, generally.

43   Ibid., no. 32. Emphasis in text.

44   Ibid., no. 39. Emphasis in text.

45   Ibid., no. 38.

46   John Paul II, *On the Hundredth Anniversary of* Rerum Novarum *(Centesimus Annus)*, papal encyclical (Washington, D.C.: USCC Office for Publishing and Promotion Services, 1991), no. 25, specifically; chs. II, IV, generally.

to the right to subsistence, is there commitment to ending absolute poverty in the developing regions? Is there rejection of the mentality that treats poor people (or nations) as "irksome intruders trying to consume what others have produced?" With regard to the right of participation in the fundamental institutions of society, is there political commitment to instituting authentic democracy that has its solid foundation in respect for human rights? Is there effort to transform *both* state capitalism and state socialism into economic systems characterized by free work, enterprise, and participation, such that the forces of society and state appropriately direct and limit the market? In other words, is the reordering of the political, economic, and social order within and among states based on "a correct understanding of the dignity and rights of the person" and "a coherent vision of the common good"?[47]

Similarly, *The Harvest of Justice* reads the call to peacemaking in a new world in order to name the major tasks that fall particularly on the United States. Today's challenge of peace is: (1) to control and reduce violence and the stockpiles of weaponry and destructive capability, both at home and abroad; (2) to complete the international project (launched by the United Nations after World War II) of ending abject poverty around the globe, in a way that is congruent with preserving and repairing the environment and reducing inequity at home; and (3) to strengthen the United States' commitment to developing effective international institutions and to exercising the leadership and accepting the costs and obligations that preponderant American power and position entail. Because the defense of human rights is an "indispensable condition for a just and peaceful world order," it must be a "consistent and persistent priority for the United States and for a world seeking peace."[48]

IV. The Call to Individual Peacemakers

To review, this essay contends that contemporary Catholic social thought reveals a theological framework that defines peacemaking as a project of social justice and authentic development, at the core of which is the obligation to ensure guarantees for universal and basic human rights. If so, an important question remains: Do these texts give specific guidance to the individual peacemaker?

---

47   Ibid., nos. 27, 51; 28, 32; 34, 46-47.
48   *The Harvest of Justice*, 9 and generally.

In one sense, the answer is "no." In the power of the Spirit, every believer has the authority and the obligation to ponder the signs of the times in the light of the Gospel and figure out the content of his or her particular call to contribute to the creation of conditions of peace. One dimension of the call to be a peacemaker is the obligation to scrutinize one's own life and relationships; talents and resources; skills and opportunities; particular circumstances and the needs those circumstances reveal. "But all this plants within the human being — man and woman — the *seed* and the *requirement* of a special task to be accomplished by each individually. . . . "[49] It is up to each of us to *make the connection* between what we have come to understand and what we know we must, in consequence, do. The task of peacemaking is enormous. No one of us bears the entire burden. But some aspect of the project is some particular person's task and will not be accomplished apart from that individual's contribution. The project of peacemaking — and a needy world — call for all the creativity and commitment we can muster.

In another sense, the answer is "yes." These texts give specific direction on three points. First, in responding to the call to be a peacemaker, it does not suffice to "tend our own gardens." We have to do that, of course, but it does not fulfill the obligation to make peace. The call to peacemaking does not allow us to draw neat boundaries, such that "I acknowledge obligations to these people, but not to those — to this community, but not to that." For example, if provision for education is essential in guaranteeing the basic right to human rights to security, subsistence, and participation, then to that right, "there corresponds a duty in all other persons." We have to be concerned about the education of children in other parts of our city or nation (thus concerned about equitable funding, the elimination of inequality and violence in the schoolroom . . .) and in other parts of the world (thus concerned about foreign aid, diplomatic interaction . . .), and not just about the education of our own children. Otherwise, we build up with one hand and tear down with the other.

Second, the idea that peacemaking is primarily the responsibility of the state, of the "king," has passed.[50] Democracy is a form of government based on respect for the dignity and contribution of each individual. One consequence is that the entire citizenry is chiefly responsible to make peace, not just the elected officials. Ordinary citizens can determine the policies of their country if they put their minds, voices, and votes to it. Ordinary citizens can also let their leaders off the hook by being indifferent to, or uninformed about, policies (about refugees and immigrants, for

---

49 *Sollicitudo Rei Socialis,* no. 30. Emphasis in text.
50 Cf. Aquinas on kingship, Paul E. Sigmund, ed., *St. Thomas Aquinas on Politics and Ethics* (New York: Norton, 1988), 25-29.

example) that contribute to, or hinder, the construction of peace on the national and international level.

Finally, these texts call us to have hope, the indispensable virtue of the peacemaker.[51] We live in a world that defines international relations as "a war of all against all" and an endless struggle for relative power and advantage. The recent history of that world is a dismaying record of worsening violence, weapons of mass destruction, genocide, ethnic cleansing, racial and religious hatred, and war of every kind. One out of five persons in that world is desperately poor. And dictatorial and corrupt regimes continue to subjugate, abuse, and terrorize their populations. In the face of that history, it is extraordinarily difficult, but essential, to sustain hope. If we presume — or conclude — that the forces of violence, poverty, and oppression are bound to carry the day, it will not be possible to persevere in the project of peacemaking, in season and out. Fortunately, nothing is impossible with God. The Resurrection reveals that hope is stronger than history.

---

51 *The Harvest of Justice*, 20-21.

Back to Basics

Moral Reasoning and Foreign Policy "After Containment"

George Weigel

As richly textured and distinctive historical realities, "centuries" do not always follow the arithmetic conventions of our system of dating. The "eighteenth century" took some 126 years to run its course, from the beginning of the great wars between France and England (of which the American Revolution was an episode) until Waterloo. The "nineteenth century" really got under way in 1815 with the defeat of Napoleon; it collapsed 99 years later, with the outbreak of World War I. The guns of August 1914 raised the curtain on the "twentieth century," which ended on August 21, 1991, when the failure of the coup that aimed to restore communism in what was then the Soviet Union marked the conclusion of the great Fifty-Five Years' War against totalitarianism.

And so, the conventional calendar notwithstanding, we are (at the very least) living through the overture to the twenty-first century — which, as Pope John Paul II regularly reminds us, will be the beginning of the third millennium of the Christian era. What is the American task in the world politics of the twenty-first century? What does the Catholic Church in the United States have to say to the country, as it deliberates that grand strategic question?

The country does not need detailed instruction on the fine points of foreign policy from the Church.[1] For to do so would be to reduce the Church and its leadership to the condition of those sundry interest groups which regularly beat down the doors or clog up the fax machines of offices all over Washington. Moreover, according to the teaching of Vatican II, detailed policy prescription is not among the tasks of the episcopal leadership of the Church; the charisms conferred by episcopal ordination are not to be understood as somehow parallel to the competencies acknowledged by election, senatorial confirmation, or executive appointment. Rather, the role of the Church and its bishops, as Pope John Paul II has insisted, is to teach the "truth about man" that is revealed in its fullness by the truth of the Gospel, and to suggest how the moral norms derivative from the "truth about man" can illumine (and discipline) the tasks of the policymaker. Put another way, the task of the National Conference of Catholic Bishops is to help form, through the arts of religious and moral teaching and persuasion, the moral horizon against which the foreign policy of the United States is shaped, and toward which America's action in the world is directed. That is what bishops are supposed to do, as I understand the magisterium of the Church on this point.

Happily, that is also precisely what the country needs right now, at the end of the Cold War and on the cusp of whatever it is that is going to follow the Cold War.

It has become a truism bordering on a cliché to say that we live in a time of transition. While remembering the venerable provenance of such sentiments (as Adam is supposed to have said to Eve on their way out of the Garden of Eden, "We live, my dear, in a time of transition"), I think we can still say, without fear of contradiction or cavil, that ours are especially transitional times.

The great contest that defined world politics since Hitler's reoccupation of the Rhineland — the struggle between totalitarianism and liberal democracy — has been won: and by the party of freedom. As Jeane J. Kirkpatrick put it in early 1992, "For the first time since the spring of 1936, we are not facing mortal danger." Freedom's victory in the great Fifty-Five Years' War has been poorly celebrated in the West; and yet the past decade — and particularly the period between June 1989 (when Poland elected a Solidarity-led government) and August 21, 1991 (when Boris Yeltsin's forces successfully resisted the attempt to turn the clock back to communism in the USSR) — has indeed seen a series of "extraordinary events in which the love and mercy which God the Father has for all his children

---

1 On this point, some reflection on the ways and means by which the USCC exercises the arts of persuasion (also known as "lobbying") on particular pieces of legislation (as suggested by the 1992 USCC "Legislative Priorities" agenda) is surely in order. What does it mean, for example, for the USCC to "support . . . programs of U.S. development assistance," many of which have been shown, empirically, to be failures, and some of which are arguably disconsonant with the teaching of *Centesimus Annus*?

[could] almost be touched" (as the bishops of Europe wrote at the end of their special synod in December 1991).

One reason why the victory of freedom was not fully or properly celebrated was because things got messy, in a hurry, in the early 1990s. For the end of the Cold War did not mean the end of history; it meant the restoration of history to its normal rhythms, patterns, and (lack of) discipline. Thus the immediate post-Cold War period has been marked by several wars, the outbreak of ethnic irredentism and violence, and the accelerating decomposition of nation-states in Africa. (There is also some good news, often ignored, about reasonably successful transitions to democracy and the market in Hungary, Poland, and the Czech Republic; meanwhile, the process of democratic capitalist consolidation continues apace in East Asia and Latin America, sometimes rapidly, sometimes at less than full throttle — but it continues.)

In this "especially transitional" time, calls are frequently heard for a new "master concept" or image that would do for the foreign policy of the twenty-first century what "containment" did for foreign policy in the latter half of the twentieth: provide a template against which individual choices could be measured and cut. But the unsettled circumstances of the present may make any such effort chimerical just now; as Harvard's Joseph S. Nye, Jr., has put it, "The world order after the Cold War is *sui generis*, and we overly constrain our understanding by trying to force it into the procrustean bed of traditional metaphors with their mechanical polarities."[2]

Thus the first order of business today may seem, at first blush, more modest, but may actually be more important for morally sound policy over the long run: to clarify the intellectual building blocks out of which a new "master concept" might later emerge. Catholic understandings of the ethics of international relations can particularly illuminate the moral dimension of this new policy calculus on three key foundational questions.

1. Why Us?

In our present psychological and political situation, the most important thing that the bishops' conference, and indeed the Church as a whole, must teach about peacemaking "ten years after *The Challenge of Peace*" is the moral impossibility of isolationism — in its Old Right, New Left, or libertarian forms. Put another way, the most urgent moral question to be

---

2 Joseph S. Nye, Jr., "What New World Order?", *Foreign Affairs* 71:2 (Spring 1992), 88.

answered in America today, when the topic turns to foreign policy, is — Why engage?

There are many reasons why the new isolationist impulse — whether articulated by aging refugees from the radicalisms of the sixties, nostalgic (and sometimes xenophobic) celebrants of America First, or buttoned-down scholars from the Cato Institute — should be resisted. It is strategic foolishness of a very high order: in a world of proliferating ballistic missile technology where deranged or evil tyrants can acquire weapons of mass destruction and the means to deliver them over thousands of miles, the concept of "Fortress America" is a sorry (and dangerous) fiction.[3] It is politically dangerous: as the debacle in ex-Yugoslavia has shown, absent American leadership, the "new world order" will be characterized by murderous chaos, not by a self-expanding web of collective security. Isolationism is also a recipe for global economic catastrophe and the gross human suffering that would result therefrom: for isolationism, translated into attempts at economic autarky, would almost certainly yield a chain-reaction world trade war whose likely results may be discerned from a brief meditation on the 1930s. The new isolationism, with its call to tend our own republican garden, also misconceives the sources of our domestic woes: SAT scores are not far too low, and teenage pregnancy rates far too high, because there has been an insufficient reallocation of resources from the Pentagon and the State Department to the Department of Health and Human Services and the Department of Education. (When Pat Buchanan and *The Nation* agree on the general outlines of a course of action [or, in this case, inaction], we can be morally certain that the prescription is wrong.)

These strategic, political, and economic points have been made in the early 1990s by competent analysts of both liberal and conservative bent. (Indeed, one of the striking things about the current internationalist/isolationist debate is its reshuffling of the old ideological deck.) But what the Catholic leadership of the United States can do, powerfully and perhaps uniquely, is to explain why isolationism is a *morally* irresponsible option for the United States at this, or indeed any, juncture in history. Put more positively, American Catholics in the 1990s must articulate a persuasive moral rationale for responsible internationalism: what I have called elsewhere an ethic of "idealism without illusions."[4]

---

3 The grim equation of tyrannies + ballistic missiles + weapons of mass destruction also reminds us of the moral imperative of developing adequate measures of strategic defense. On this point, see the recent essay by Robert Jastrow and Max M. Kampelman, "Death in Clusters," *New York Times*, January 13, 1993, A21.

4 See George Weigel, *Idealism Without Illusions: U.S. Foreign Policy in the 1990s*

In making this case, the Church must clarify for our fellow citizens (and, frankly, for not a few Catholics) that the moral duties of nations cannot be understood as simply analogous to the moral responsibilities of individuals. Moreover, the Church must help the country articulate a vision of American moral responsibility in the world that does not smack of unwarranted hubris or national messianism. But these temptations are, in truth, far less pressing at the moment than the temptation to say, "We did our job; we saved the world from Hitler and from Stalin and his epigones; it's time to take care of business at home."

That sentiment is entirely understandable; but it must be firmly challenged, and precisely on grounds of moral realism and moral obligation. Public weariness — or worse, a crabbed, narrow, and selfish view of the American role in the world — must be answered by a realistic, yet more capacious, construal of our duties beyond our borders. If that answer is not given, the result will be greater danger (and suffering) in the world — and, I fear, a crabbed, narrow, and selfish construal of the American possibility at home.

America's international duties are not infinite in number. There are limits to our capacities, as there are limits to our wisdom. But reasonable arguments about limits will be more prudently engaged when they are conducted within the framework of a morally grounded national consensus on the inevitable and unavoidable exercise of American international responsibility in a unipolar world. In the United States today, religious communities remain the most important locus of moral discernment and commitment. And I don't think it hopelessly sectarian to suggest that, among America's many religious communities, Roman Catholicism has the most highly developed tradition of moral reflection on the morality of international public life; moreover, the Church's traditional natural law approach to these questions can serve as an ecumenical and interreligious "grammar" for disciplining the many moral vocabularies in play when Americans consider their responsibilities in the world. That tradition of Catholic moral reflection, plus the lived experience of American Catholics as members of a transnational church, should position Catholicism in the United States to take effective moral leadership in resolving the question, "Why us?" — which really is the first post-Cold War question that has to be answered.

(Grand Rapids: Wm. B. Eerdmans Publishing Co./An Ethics and Public Policy Center Book, 1994).

2. "Interest" and "Purpose"

"Toward what ends?" is the second question on the new agenda. At one abstract level, of course, we know (or should know) the answer: U.S. foreign policy, measured by the norms of Catholic social ethics, should serve the ends of justice, freedom, security (order), the general welfare, and peace — the classic ends of politics in the Western tradition as developed by Christian philosophers and theologians. But the invocation of those grand ends does not get us very far down the path toward coherent and responsible policy.

Perhaps a more fruitful approach would be to think about the classic ends of politics through the prism of the argument that has erupted, since the end of the Cold War, over the definition of the "national interest." Few terms are deployed so frequently, as the debates over Somalia and ex-Yugoslavia attest. But the invocation of the "national interest" is more frequently an incantation, a rhetorical trump card against an opposing position, than a term of analytic and strategic (much less moral) art.

The Church in the United States would do the country a great service were it to help sweep clear from the notion of "national interest" the cobwebs of amoralism that have grown about it since Hans Morgenthau first published *Politics Among Nations*. For whatever Professor Morgenthau's own intentions, the sorry fact is that more than a few of his *soi-disant* disciples have taken the "national interest" to be a category devoid of moral content: indeed, for many policy "realists" today, the "national interest" can be almost mathematically defined in terms of certain key indices of economic and military power. The result has been a schizophrenic foreign policy debate in which it is too often assumed, in the "policy community," that between the worlds of statecraft and morality a great gulf is fixed which no man can cross.[5] This, in turn, has further distanced the government from the citizenry, which remains profoundly uncomfortable with rationales for policy that are grounded solely on the canons of Realpolitik. The confusion is further deepened by the media's

---

5 It should be freely admitted that the realists of the 1930s and 1940s were, in the main, more prescient than their Wilsonian brethren in their assessment of the threats of fascism and communism. And, yes, the policy of "containment" — arguably the most successful U.S. foreign policy in our national history — was largely the construct of realists. But we should not confuse the Niebuhrian realism of the 1930s, 1940s, and early 1950s with the more dessicated "realism" invoked by the Bush administration as justification for its fecklessness in ex-Yugoslavia, or by some of the libertarian critics of the U.S. intervention in Somalia.

tendency to vulgarize the debate, such that it comes down to a contest between "tough-minded realists" and "soft-hearted idealists."

But as John Courtney Murray argued two generations ago, the unsatisfactory quality of the "morality and foreign policy debate" in the U.S. has less to do with differences over concrete applications than it does with the impoverished notions of *morality* that usually inform (and deform) our public life. Put with drastic brevity, the circularity and intractability of the morality-and-foreign-policy debate reflect the continual dominance, as a kind of cultural residue, of certain American Protestant notions of "morality" which sought to apply the norms guiding private life to the exigencies of international public life.[6] It was against this mora*lism* that Morgenthau and other "realist" critics reacted, by trying to "de-moralize" the debate, so to speak. But mora*lism* of this sort ought not be confused with moral *reasoning* as the classic Catholic tradition understands it.

In that tradition (and in other natural law traditions), there is only one human universe or reflection and action: a universe that is at once moral and political. Which means, as the philosopher Charles Frankel used to insist, that Realpolitik (especially in its Bismarckian form) is not an escape from morality; rather, it is a deficient and debased form of morality. The real choice, then, is not between mora*lism* and amorality; the choice is between wiser and dumber forms of moral reasoning.

The classic Catholic insistence that moral decisions are inextricably involved in political choices means, *inter alia*, that the very definition of the "national interest" is itself an exercise in moral reasoning. Charles Frankel once put the matter this way, in terms that Murray would have applauded:

> "The heart of the decision-making process . . . is not finding the best means to serve a national interest already perfectly known and understood. It is the determining of that interest itself: the reassessment of the nation's resources, needs, commitments, traditions, and political and cultural horizons — in short, its calendar of values."

In the Catholic tradition, "interest" (like "power") is not a four-letter word. Moreover, democratic political leaders have a fiduciary moral responsibility to defend the interests of those whom they represent. But that responsibility is best exercised, according to the classic Catholic position, when the notion of "national interest" is married to a concept of American *purpose*. Father Murray put it like this, speaking out of the natural law

---

6 According to Murray, this "older morality" was characterized by voluntarism (i.e., it located the good in the will of God), fundamentalism (in its use of Scripture), subjectivism (in its focus on a moral agent's intentions), and individualism (in that it could not imagine a distinctive discipline of "social ethics" or "political ethics").

tradition which he believed was crucially formative of the political tradition of the West:

> "The tradition of reason requires, with particular stringency today, that national interest, remaining always valid and omnipresent as a motive, be given only a relative and proximate status as an end of national action . . . The national interest, rightly understood, is successfully achieved only at the interior, as it were, of the growing international order to which the pursuit of the national interest can and must contribute."

Is this simply more abstract moral logic-chopping? I think not. Indeed, were we to look for a concrete and successful exemplification of this Catholic claim that the pursuit of the national *interest* can and must contribute (through the mediation of a sense of American *purpose*) to the "growing international order," we need look no farther than President Reagan's epochal 1982 address to the British Parliament in Westminster Hall: which led to the creation of the National Endowment for Democracy — which, in its turn, helped support and sustain the forces that eventually led the nonviolent Revolution of 1989.

3. What "Peace"?

The third foundational building block that American Catholics should help cement into our post-Cold War thinking about foreign policy is the classic Augustinian-Thomistic concept of "peace" as rightly ordered and dynamic political community. Alas, it cannot be said that our own religious community is in a strong position to make this contribution. For as a brief glance through American Catholic newspapers and magazines will readily attest, there remain deep confusions in the Church over the meaning of the "peace" that is to be sought in the politics of nations. But to the confusions (generally found *à gauche*) about peace as the *Shalom* kingdom to be built by human hands have been added confusions off the starboard beam about "peace" as the absence-of-American-participation-in-violent-conflict. Then there are the various New Age (and essentially gnostic) understandings of "peace" as a matter of psychological "healing" (as if foreign policy were a form of therapy and Saddam Hussein a promising candidate for a Twelve-Step program).

And yet the drama of the Revolution of 1989 and the New Russian Revolution of 1991 should have taught both the Church and the country that "peace" between and within nations is, at bottom, a matter of just legal and political structures, capable of mediating the ancient and ongoing argument over "Who rules?" It is these structures which permit the exercise of human freedom, including the fundamental right of religious freedom. It is these structures which create the circumstances in which the kind of "free economy" endorsed by Pope John Paul II in *Centesimus Annus* can develop. It is these structures which permit conflicts over justice to be resolved without the threat or use of mass violence.

In 1983, the bishops were frequently accused of "politicizing" their witness: which was true in the narrow sense that many Catholic political activists seized *The Challenge of Peace* as a weapon in their *bellum contra Reagan*.[7] But I would argue that the real problem was that *The Challenge of Peace depoliticized* the Catholic debate over the pursuit of peace, precisely because it failed to make clear that, in the Catholic understanding of these things, international "peace" is a matter of structures, politics, and law. If the Church in America were to reclaim that largely abandoned aspect of its moral-theological heritage, both the Catholic debate and the wider national debate would be set on a sturdier footing.

Some Obstacles Along the Way

Finally, I should like to mention three intellectual obstacles which, unattended, will impede the Church's capacity to help set a firm moral foundation for the public debate over post-Cold War U.S. foreign policy.

The first of these obstacles is a tendency, in both the NCCB and the Holy See, to take what even a moderate policy realist would have to regard as too optimistic a view of the current capacities of international organizations, and especially of the United Nations. The Catholic instinct in favor of international legal and political structures, whose place in the American debate can be traced back to the World War II allocutions of Pope Pius XII and the pastoral letters of the American hierarchy during the same period, is, to be sure, a specification under modern conditions of the aforementioned classic Catholic concept of peace as *tranquillitas ordinis*: "the tranquillity of order" which is made possible by a rightly ordered political community. Thus, in his 1963 encyclical, *Pacem in Terris*, Pope John XXIII was simply extending this tradition when he wrote of the necessity of an "international public authority" for handling those aspects of the "universal common good" which could not be responsibly managed by nation-states.

But the affirmation of this tradition as a horizon of possibility toward which U.S. foreign policy should aspire, and its embodiment in real-world

---

7 It will be replied that this was not the bishops' intention. That is certainly true of many bishops. But it is also true that the USCC did little to stop, and perhaps more than a little to encourage, this form of "politicization" in the follow-up to the pastoral letter.

international public life, are two distinct matters. And here an argument needs to be engaged. For one might well get the impression, from certain quarters in the Holy See as well as from the National Conference of Catholic Bishops, that the only real obstacle to effective international organizations today is the recalcitrance of nation-states jealous of their individual prerogatives. But this is simply not the case.

The United Nations has enjoyed some significant peacekeeping successes in the early 1990s. But that happy fact does not, alas, substantially alter another, harsher reality: namely, that contemporary international organizations are rife with bureaucracy, with ideological conflict, and, let it be said frankly, with corruption. Nor is it politically feasible to explain to the American people why an international organization, most of whose members are not yet democracies, and whose secretary-general is a career bureaucrat from a thoroughly undemocratic state, should be given significant authority over the design of U.S. foreign policy and significant discretion over the use of U.S. military forces abroad. And, political feasibility aside, some would wonder where the moral justification for such a transfer of authority lay.

The gap between the Church's hopes for a genuine "international public authority" and the realities of international politics today will best be closed, not by premature optimism about the current UN system, but by recognizing that the UN remains a stage on which a script written elsewhere is played out. That recognition in turn provides a motive for effective American and, more broadly, Western leadership in making the UN system work better such that, over time, the UN begins to acquire the kind of legitimacy it now lacks — and which it would be dangerous foolishness to pretend that it now enjoys.

American Catholicism must also internalize more thoroughly the teaching of *Sollicitudo Rei Socialis* and *Centesimus Annus* on the economic and political development of the Third World. In these documents, Pope John Paul II made a decisive break with the curious materialism that had sometimes characterized aspects of modern Catholic social thought on development economics; stressed the importance of entrepreneurial energies (*Sollicitudo*'s "right of economic initiative") in breaking the cycle of poverty; sharply criticized the "corrupt, dictatorial, and authoritarian" governments that were impeding their people's development; and championed "democratic and participatory" polities in which the energies of free people, operating in a free economy, could flourish.[8] Implicit in these teachings is a radical critique of the state-centered development strategies of recent decades.

---

8   John Paul II, *On Social Concern (Sollicitudo Rei Socialis)*, papal encyclical (Washington, D.C.: USCC Office for Publishing and Promotion Services, 1987), nos. 15 and 44.

And yet one reads through much of the American Catholic commentary on Third World issues today with little sense that this critique has been engaged, much less digested. One has even less sense that the Church in America has come to grips with the fact that no positive correlation — none — can be shown between levels of development aid dollars and actual economic development: put bluntly, there is simply no empirical evidence to suggest that more foreign aid buys you (or, rather, the recipient country) more economic development. More positively, the great development success stories to be found among the "little dragons" of East Asia and in Chile have not become part of American Catholicism's normal rhythm of reflection on the transition from poverty to wealth.

The greatest obstacle to Third World development today is not to be found in the developed countries and their supposed niggardliness, but in the "corrupt, authoritarian, and dictatorial" regimes of Africa, Asia, and parts of Latin America. Until the Church clears its collective mind on that central point, and until it welcomes Pope John Paul II's endorsement of the free economy as the engine of economic growth that best reflects the dynamic creativity of the human person, its continuing endorsement of higher levels of foreign assistance, and its preferential option for the poor of the Third World, will ring hollow.

Finally, the Church must overcome its seeming reluctance to reopen a number of just-war questions in the aftermath of the Cold War. Refining the just-war tradition to meet the exigencies of our current situation is an unavoidable and urgent task. Here, particular attention should be paid to those classic *ad bellum* criteria that may have been neglected in our concern to refine the *in bello* criteria of proportionality and discrimination to meet the challenges posed by modern weapons technologies.

Can "resistance to aggression" be the only legitimate *casus belli* in the contemporary world? (And what would constitute "aggression?") Is there room in the just-war tradition for preemptive military action aimed at denying aggressors weapons of mass destruction?[9] Could a threat to the stability of the global economy ever constitute one part of a morally

---

9 In a February 28, 1992, column in *Commonweal*, Father J. Bryan Hehir suggested that "only the resistance-to-aggression rationale should be accepted . . . as a *casus belli*." I regard this as too narrow a construal of the *ad bellum* criterion of "just cause." For Father Hehir's definition would seem to force us to the untenable position that a *casus belli* exists when Burkina Faso invades Mali, but not when recently deceased Kim Il-Sung, Moammar Qaddafi, or Saddam Hussein threatens to do unspeakable damage with weapons of mass destruction. Once again, the "regime factor" has to play a central role in our moral reasoning about the pursuit of peace and its relationship to the proportionate and discriminate — and possibly preemptive — use of armed force.

adequate *casus belli*? Is the United Nations the sole legitimate authority capable of authorizing the use of armed force (preemptively or in response to an aggression already under way)? If so, what is our duty when the UN is clearly in default of its moral responsibilities?

The Catholic Church in the United States cannot settle these questions; but as the chief institutional bearer of the just-war tradition, it has to face up to its responsibility to develop that tradition in the face of the new kinds of threats posed by the post-Cold War world.

This will require, I believe, an abandonment of the "dual tradition" concept promoted by *The Challenge of Peace* and the tenth anniversary statement, *The Harvest of Justice Is Sown in Peace*. The concept is historically dubious, theologically confused, and of limited analytic utility. The just-war tradition is the Church's normative tradition of moral reflection on international politics; it contains within itself a concept of peace; and it certainly contains warrants for the morally justified deployment of nonviolent strategies when circumstances so dictate. But the temptation to elevate the moral status of pacifism in Catholic ethics by appeals to the successful nonviolent resistance mounted by the (nonpacifist) Church in Central and Eastern Europe during the 1980s should be stoutly resisted.

Pacifism is a personal commitment that can, arguably, be reconciled with the demands of Christian conscience. But the pacifist conscience, *per se*, can provide no serious counsel to the statesman. And to suggest that it does distracts our attention from the crucial business at hand, which is to refine the just-war tradition's criteria in light of the signs of the times.

A Community of Prayer and Discernment

With the end of the Cold War, humankind seemed poised to take what Pope John Paul II proposed at Hiroshima in 1981: "a major step forward in civilization and wisdom." The moral realism of the Catholic tradition, rooted in the Church's incarnational humanism, is a powerful instrument for discerning the "oughts" that are deeply embedded in the political decisions that drive us further along the path toward "civilization and wisdom" — or that push us back toward the barbarism of a Hobbesian world in which all are at war with all. The responsibilities of the National Conference of Catholic Bishops are not the same as the responsibilities of the United States government, and the United States Catholic Conference is not a parallel Department of State. But the NCCB and USCC are (or should be) the bearers of a rich tradition of moral wisdom that is especially pertinent to the kind of new strategic reflection required of our public officials today. Ours is a time of back-to-first-principles; and the Catholic heritage of moral reflection on international politics is very much a "first principles" tradition.

But the Church will be remiss in its public duties if it is not, first and foremost, a community of prayer for peace. The extraordinary witness of the resistance Church in Central and Eastern Europe has been a powerful reminder of the potency of prayer: within the Church and on the world of affairs. Indeed, in the underground prayer of the resistance Church during the long, dark night of communist persecution, we can see a contemporary illustration of the truth first enunciated about prayer in the medieval mystical text, *The Cloud of Unknowing*: "The whole of mankind is wonderfully helped by what you are doing, in ways you do not understand."

The moral wisdom of our tradition is a precious resource. It deserves to be brought to bear on the debate about America's role in a post-Cold War world. But that intellectual witness, if you will, has to emerge out of a distinctively ecclesial context if it is to be true to itself. The more Roman Catholics in America are a people of prayer, the more we will be a Church meeting the many challenges of peace.

II.

Human Rights, Self-Determination, and Sustainable Development

Towards an Effective Human Rights Agenda

James K. Bishop

As the second millennium of the Christian era concludes, the world is remarkably receptive to the message of the carpenter from Galilee. Historians of the human rights movement trace the articulation of its precepts back to the philosophers of the Enlightenment. But what scholarly treatise expressing these principles was not influenced by Jesus' simple admonition to love one's neighbor as oneself?

Remarkable Progress

Televised images of man's persistent barbaric behavior and the eventual testimony of those who are violated beyond the sight and hearing of any journalist so shock the emotions that it is possible to overlook the breadth and depth of the global commitment to human rights. The media's understandable spotlight on the frustrations of humanitarian intervention in Somalia may lead one to forget that the international community put its solidarity with the suffering Somali people ahead of traditional deference to sovereignty when the Security Council sent armed forces to open relief pipelines blocked by the country's warlords and thugs. The creation by the Security Council of a tribunal mandated to investigate and try those accused of war crimes in the former Yugoslavia is another reflection of the strength and range of the belief that all mankind shares responsibility for the protection of those who are not shielded from abuse by their own authorities. The creation in December 1993 of the post of UN High Commissioner for Human Rights is but the latest indicator of the positive momentum the human rights movement has developed. Well-founded skepticism about the fidelity of public figures in many countries to the causes they espouse can obscure the often genuine commitment which many world leaders are showing to curbing human rights abuses.

At the World Conference on Human Rights held in June 1993 in Vienna, delegates of those governments sincerely committed to continuing human rights advances isolated and overwhelmed representatives of those states trying to use the meeting to checkmate further progress. The conference reaffirmed the worldwide applicability of the principles expressed in the Universal Declaration of Human Rights adopted 45 years earlier. The conference then broke new ground, calling *inter alia* for greater respect for the rights of women and lending its support to calls for the UN General Assembly to consider creation of the post of High Commissioner for Human Rights.

In the United States, at the urging of the Bush administration, the Senate gave its advice and consent to ratification of the International Covenant on Civil and Political Rights in 1992. Secretary of State Christopher told his World Conference audience in Vienna that the Clinton administration would request the consent of the Senate to ratification of the International Covenant on the Elimination of All Forms of Racial Discrimination (now ratified) and then turn its attention to three other signed but unratified human rights accords. In a related development, the new American administration in the weeks before the conference reversed the stance of its Republican predecessors on economic, social, and cultural rights. The Reagan and Bush administrations had insisted on characterizing them as objectives rather than rights, denying them the status clearly conferred by the Universal Declaration, as well as by Pope John XXIII in his encyclical *Pacem in Terris*. There was a further breakthrough when the Clinton administration reversed the U.S. position on the right to development, again moving the United States back into the mainstream of international opinion by acknowledging at least implicitly that the solidarity of mankind obliges those who are well endowed to share their resources with those with insufficient resources to live a life consistent with maintenance of human dignity.

The flood tide of democratic fervor washing over so much of the world carries with it the promise of much greater respect for human rights than accorded heretofore. Across the 11 time zones of the Russian Federation, the inhabitants struggle to secure for themselves the liberties denied them throughout centuries of despotic rule. On African savannas, deep in the continent's rain forests, and on the potholed streets of its decaying cities, those who have been exploited by indigenous autocrats or by the rear guard of colonialism are savoring political empowerment and the rule of law. Fragile peace accords in the proto-democracies of Central America offer to many inhabitants the possibility that their hopes for justice will be realized. Prosperity in several of the nations on the Pacific's Asiatic Rim is being accompanied by liberalization of political structures and processes. Genuine peace in the Middle East would undercut the political foundations of some of the region's despots and calm the passions which have provoked violations of the rights of Palestinians and Israelis alike.

Saddened and even horrified as one may be by the persistence of man's abuse of his fellow man, there is some solace in reflection on the drive the international human rights movement has developed in recent years. From the Treaty of Westphalia in 1648 until the current century, governments were left free by other states to abuse their citizens if rulers wished. The first civil restraint on international behavior did not become effective until a ban on the slave trade began to be enforced by the British Navy early in the last century. Only in the interwar period of this century did it prove possible to establish some internationally recognized standards intended to protect workers from abuse.

Adoption of the Universal Declaration of Human Rights did nothing to shut down the Gulag or to end legalized racism in the United States. But after the American civil rights movement achieved the latter objective, Americans could call for an end to oppression abroad without being silenced by the rejoinder that a country which refused to recognize the fundamental rights of its own minorities could not castigate other nations for abusing the rights of some of their citizens. By the mid-seventies, the legislation which prohibits U.S. assistance to governments deemed to systematically violate their citizens' basic human rights was on the books. And as we remember a few years later, President Carter had made human rights a cornerstone of American foreign policy.

Although the Reagan and Bush administrations were criticized for pulling the U.S. government back from the vanguard of the human rights movement, historians may see these 12 years as the period during which human rights considerations became internalized in the conduct of American foreign policy. As it had been during the Carter administration, the East-West struggle continued to be viewed as justifying continued collaboration with governments which engaged in substantial human rights abuses. But even client states and close allies were held to account in the State Department's increasingly candid human rights reports. American ambassadors from Chile to Israel confronted cabinet ministers and heads of state over the depredations of their soldiers and policemen. American assistance was reduced or terminated when local governments ignored diplomatic demarches and public criticism. Human rights became a central issue in our relationship with the USSR as they are in our relations with China today.

Additional good news for the human rights movement has been more creative use of foreign aid to protect human rights. Instead of employing it solely as a negative sanction, suspending, reducing, or cutting off assistance when there are serious violations, aid is being increased to nations which take bold steps to improve human rights, e.g., to Zambia after free elections toppled the party and the ruler which had dominated political life since independence decades earlier. Moreover, assistance programs designed to protect human rights by strengthening the rule of law are being implemented in several of the countries of the former Soviet Union as well as in other parts of the world. At the grass roots level, local human rights organizations are receiving the funds and technical assistance needed to rent office space, conduct training sessions, monitor elections, and so on.

Within the nongovernment human rights community, there has been a similar evolution. Instead of just investigating human rights abuses, publicizing them, and calling for sanctions, some of the major organizations have started to use their resources to train foreign human rights monitors. Together with like-minded governments, they have called for more human rights training by the UN Human Rights Commission as well as by peacekeeping missions.

Even U.S. military assistance programs are being used to support human rights. Training programs are being conducted both in the United States and abroad for foreign military personnel in which they are instructed in their responsibilities under international human rights law and the Geneva Conventions. Special programs have been designed to strengthen judge advocate generals and their staffs so that they can investigate and prosecute human rights offenders within military establishments. On human rights grounds, the Bush administration placed a moratorium on the export of land mines and the current administration favors an eventual international ban.

The end of the Cold War has made the practice of human rights diplomacy more satisfying. In international fora, the Cubans and other Soviet surrogates first were abandoned by their Eastern European allies and then undercut by the demise of communism and the breakup of the Soviet empire. The nonaligned movement fractured as genuine democrats took office in Latin America and Africa. With apartheid joining communism in the septic tank of history, it became even more difficult to distract attention from the human rights abuses of the nonaligned themselves. Human rights coalition building took on new parameters as regional solidarity was sundered.

The United Nations' new secretary-general was quick to appreciate the possibilities for improving human rights offered by the international realignment. As the violence of armed conflict is the force most destructive of human rights, Boutros Boutros-Ghali, in his July 1992 report to the Security Council entitled *An Agenda for Peace*, proposed bold but practical measures to achieve the objectives of the United Nations Charter, including "justice and human rights." In his vision, the UN could meet this objective by engaging in more preventive diplomacy and by going beyond the organization's traditional peacekeeping role to try to make peace when belligerents would not accept the ceasefire required for the stationing of blue berets. Declaring that "the time of absolute and exclusive sovereignty, however, has passed," Boutros-Ghali called *inter alia* for UN military intervention under chapter 7 of the Charter. He recommended the designation of "peace-enforcement units" which could be authorized by the Security Council to deploy in situations so violent they went beyond the mandates of peacekeeping forces and the expectations of peacekeeping force contributors.

President Bush's endorsement of many elements of the "Agenda for Peace" and his concurrent offer to allow military forces designated by other nations for UN service to train at an American base caught many off guard. Unfortunately, both Boutros-Ghali's noble initiative and American willingness to participate in such interventions have become victims of the incompetence with which the first such intervention was conducted.

Somali Misstep

As originally conceived by those American diplomats who first urged that the United States mobilize support for a UN military intervention in Somalia, the UN troops were to establish "zones of tranquility" in central and southern Somalia to permit relief workers to reach the hundreds of thousands of additional Somalis otherwise expected to die of famine and its consequences. Rather than confronting blue berets in Mogadishu's crowded narrow streets, the warlords who had ravaged the capital would find themselves abandoned as their supporters left Mogadishu to trade their weapons for food at distribution points. Helicopter gunships and armor would protect the distribution centers from the armed pickups of the warlords.

The decision to send UN forces into Mogadishu assigned greater importance to logistics than to politics and reflected culpable ignorance of Somali character. It is particularly hard to understand why the American commanders who led UN-authorized forces into Mogadishu established their headquarters within spitball range of the country's most belligerent warlord. Although easier to understand, it is equally regrettable that the Bush administration, having had the compassion to dispatch American forces to undertake a peacemaking mission otherwise beyond the capacity of the United Nations, tried to mislead the public about the difficulty of the mission on which American troops had been sent. The claim that these forces would be withdrawn prior to the change in administrations the following month was transparently false. Moreover, by putting first priority on the early departure of U.S. troops, both the Bush and Clinton administrations distracted the attention of the United Nations from the need to jump-start the process of political reconstruction. Then a combative retired admiral was allowed to browbeat Washington into supporting the militarization and Americanization of United Nations operations in Mogadishu.

The massacre of the American patrol sent into hostile territory without the armor needed to defend itself has provoked a perverse reaction. Those actually responsible for this fatal miscalculation escape sanction while the United Nations is scapegoated for an operation conducted without its cognizance. The UN intervention now appears foredoomed by the American decision to withdraw the U.S. forces whose presence encouraged other nations to contribute troops to the operation. Prospects for further UN humanitarian interventions are set back by the cries of American politicians objecting illogically to U.S. troops being placed "again" under United Nations command. Hoodlums and despots elsewhere are emboldened to threaten U.S. forces by the vacillation of American politicians responding to the mood swings of talk show hosts.

One hopes that with respect to humanitarian interventions to protect human rights, the Somali experience will prove to be a case of one large step backwards after several steps forward, and that the disaster likely to take place with the withdrawal of American troops will refocus attention on the need to take the preparatory and follow-up steps recommended by Boutros-Ghali.

Other United Nations initiatives related to human rights have fared better. The creation of the Department of Humanitarian Assistance headed by an under secretary reporting directly to the secretary-general was prompted by the slow and otherwise inadequate response of UN agencies to the loss of life and suffering caused by disasters in northern Iraq, Somalia, Liberia, and elsewhere. Although UN agencies have resisted the effort to give the new under secretary authority to coordinate their responses to such crises, the department exists and it has begun to provide some additional protection of the rights to life, food, shelter, and medical care of those caught up in conflict or displaced by it.

The United Nations Truth Commission, established by the El Salvador peace settlement brokered by Boutros-Ghali's predecessor, significantly advanced the cause of human rights when it identified those it believed responsible for the human rights violations it investigated. During the Cambodian peacekeeping operation, a very small human rights staff impressed observers with how much a few dedicated UN officials could achieve in curbing abuses and supporting local human rights activists.

One can take satisfaction in the fact that major regional organizations also are becoming active in defending human rights. The Organization for African Unity has begun to dispatch peacekeepers, human rights monitors, and election observers to trouble spots throughout the continent. The Organization of American States took another step away from its traditional reluctance to become involved in the internal affairs of member states when it rejected the military takeover in Haiti and later joined the United Nations in sending human rights monitors to that country. The Conference on Security and Cooperation in Europe is in the vanguard of efforts to protect the human rights of minorities and has appointed a senior European statesman to be its High Commissioner for Minorities. It also dispatches courageous human rights observers to conflicted areas.

Activists at Odds

While respect for human rights is on the upswing, human rights practitioners sometimes show too little respect for each other. The report of the panel commissioned by Secretary of State Christopher to examine the conduct of Foreign Service and other State Department personnel in dealing with human rights violations in El Salvador called attention to how poorly served the human rights cause is when U.S. government officials and private sector activists come to regard each other as antagonists. Mutual suspicion precludes collaboration. Energies better directed at helping the victims of injustice are squandered on vituperation. While there are ideological zealots in both the government and private groups who have other agendas which sometimes override human rights concerns, most of the public servants and nongovernmental organization representatives defending human rights act on the basis of very similar commitments. But in the private sector, some advocates interpret the refusal of public officials to mechanistically apply "a single standard" as sympathy for the human rights offender. Government officials in turn sometimes accuse private human rights advocates of employing a double standard in which abuses committed by governments are condemned more strongly than abuses by their opponents.

Cars are built by mechanistic application of uniform standards, but greater subtlety obviously is required to influence human behavior. The complexity of human interaction creates ambiguous situations that challenge the ethicist. It may be more productive to accept the fact that partial relief from abuse is all that can be achieved in particular circumstances, rather than preclude partial relief by fruitless insistence on an absolute end to abuse. Sometimes avoidance of a greater evil may even require continued association with those guilty of serious human rights abuses.

Examples of the circumstances which give rise to such tensions include the current situation in Turkey. The government's abuse of its Kurdish minority and regime opponents is well documented. But the cutoff of U.S. military and civil assistance urged by some human rights groups would prompt an estrangement in U.S.-Turkish relations, which most likely would lead to Turkish refusal to permit U.S. and other Western warplanes to continue to overfly northern Iraq from Turkish bases. Expulsion of these aircraft from Turkey almost certainly would prompt Saddam Hussein to attack the Kurds in the north of his country. The end result would in no way improve the human rights situation in Turkey, while human rights would be massively violated by an Iraqi government which in the past has not hesitated to employ even poison gas against its own citizens.

The issue of amnesty provides another example of conflict among human rights activists. Some advocates both in and out of government insist that there can be no amnesty for serious human rights violators, all of whom should be brought to justice. Some diplomats charged with negotiating an end to conflicts object that rejecting amnesty can prolong conflict and associated human rights abuses, particularly in situations where the leaders whose agreement is necessary for negotiated solutions are themselves charged with major human rights violations. Is either of these positions unquestionably more consistent with moral principles and human solidarity? Should outsiders tell those who will suffer most directly from prolonged conflict that they should not put down their arms under conditions they find acceptable?

Haiti provides many examples of the dilemmas which confront human rights practitioners. One of the most serious is the predictable but undesired consequences of economic sanctions. The difficulties relief agencies have experienced in distributing food to the hundreds of thousands of Haitians who depend on such assistance for survival was foreseen. Was it rational to expect that the Haitian military would allow relief agencies to continue to receive food while their gas tanks were empty or could be filled only by paying premium prices for smuggled gasoline? Dying babies rarely prompt military despots to accept early retirement.

Certainly there are many situations in which human rights can be defended by the use of economic sanctions. And sanctions unlikely to be effective in changing the behavior of one government nevertheless may be justified because demonstrating willingness to use them may deter another government from abusive behavior. The Thai military's withdrawal from politics two years ago following American suspension of high-level military contacts, lethal weapons deliveries, and joint exercises after troops killed civilian demonstrators was an effective use of economic and diplomatic sanctions. In 1992, the usurpation of legislative and judicial authority by Guatemala's President Serrano was aborted and Serrano was forced into exile largely by withdrawing the preferential tariffs given some Guatemalan exports in the U.S. market. President Fujimori of Peru decided to return to constitutional rule after the U.S. and some other IMF members blocked his government's access to that institution's resources.

There is no likelihood that the religious zealots who dominate Sudan's government and persecute its non-Muslim peoples will stop murdering and torturing their compatriots because the U.S. has cut off military and development assistance. But the governments of Kenya and Malawi freed political prisoners, permitted internationally monitored balloting, and undertook other reforms after the U.S. cut off aid to Sudan and Mauritania on human rights grounds and reduced aid to Kenya and Malawi for the same reason. In Burundi, military officers who seized power and murdered the democratically elected president were disavowed by other elements of the military after Western envoys condemned the takeover and indicated that the would-be usurpers would receive no assistance from their governments.

Rebuffing the Counteroffensive

While the sickening human rights violations in Bosnia, Somalia, Haiti, and elsewhere have few apologists, authoritarian regimes which see their legitimacy threatened by scrutiny of their abusive behavior still make some headway questioning the universality of human rights standards. Claims that poverty, cultural preferences, or the threat of religious fundamentalism justify practices clearly in conflict with the Universal Declaration elicit unwarranted credence among those who focus on the kernel of truth in the rationales confected rather than analyze them rigorously.

Human rights abusers who argue that their impoverished regimes cannot be expected to meet the same standards as governments of wealthy nations sometimes need to be reminded that abuses of rights related to the physical integrity of the person, which are the most severe abuses, generally cost a government little to correct. By successfully prosecuting and appropriately punishing a few senior offenders, any government can begin to convince its officials that extrajudicial killings, torture, and extrajudicial confinement are unacceptable. Similarly, protection of the fundamental freedoms of speech, religion, press, association, and representation cost a government relatively little in financial terms. While many Third World governments cannot provide even cabinet ministers with all of the comforts available to inmates of Nordic prisons, some of the world's poorest regimes, e.g., that of post-Menguistu Ethiopia, have shown that even an impoverished state can meet the basic needs of prisoners for food, sanitation, shelter, and health care.

There also are good responses to be made to the Muslim and east Asian states which claim exemption from the Universal Declaration on the grounds that the civil and political rights that document proclaims enshrine "Western" values inconsistent with their cultural and religious norms. A first obvious fallacy in this argument is the assumption that any culture's norms are static. Slavery once was tolerated by most cultures and now is formally condemned by all governments. Infanticide, cannibalism, and female circumcision are practices still viewed positively in some cultures but nevertheless opposed by the governments rooted in those cultures. Another fallacious proposition is that cultures are autonomous and their individuality must be protected from foreign contamination. Mohammed was not a Malaysian nor was Marx Chinese but the teachings of each have shaped the cultures of those who would reject human rights on the grounds that they are Western and therefore alien to their value systems.

Opponents of the universality of human rights sometimes also misrepresent their own norms. The precepts of most ethical systems advocate respect for most of the rights specified in the Universal Declaration. The teachings of Confucius, sometimes cited by east Asians as justification for maintenance of despotic states, proclaim the right of the governed to unseat an unjust ruler. Other human rights opponents fail to acknowledge that within their own cultures major concessions already have been made successfully to twentieth-century concepts. Thus, while women may be second-class citizens in many of the nations of the Islamic world, they also serve as the heads of government of Turkey and Pakistan.

Some defenders of autocratic regimes in the Middle East claim that a government need not be democratic to be genuinely representative as rulers keep in touch with their subjects through appointed councils. These apologists merit no more credence than those who claimed 30 years ago that one-party government was more appropriate than multi-party government to African culture and that one-party government would honor democratic values. Ignored by supporters of both propositions, the infallible prediction of Lord Acton is and was on the adverse consequences of concentrated political power.

In several of the secular states of the Islamic world and elsewhere the specter of fundamentalism is employed to justify severe restriction of basic freedoms, to excuse torture of suspects and prisoners, and, in the case of Algeria, to abort the democratic process. While some religious extremists, undoubtedly, are opportunistic in their espousal of basic political freedoms, their followers' commitment to religious extremism also can be superficial. Participation in representative government can contain religious fanaticism, as is the case in India, Israel, and Jordan. Repression may legitimize it, as appears to be happening in Algeria and may be taking place in Tunisia and Egypt. Weak democracies could be hijacked by those who would abuse the rights of others to perpetuate their rule. But representative government's fate is sealed, not merely at risk, when its self-proclaimed defenders extinguish or hamstring it in the name of its protection.

There are several responses to those governments which try to excuse their violations of their citizens' rights as necessary to permit economic development. Here the obvious kernel of truth is that a disciplined population is more likely to accept the sacrifices which encourage economic growth than is the population of a state which can vote out of office public officials seen to be asking too much of the taxpayers. The history of the Soviet Union demonstrates three of the grave dangers in subordinating human rights to development. The first is that the price of this strategy measured in human lives sacrificed and ruined can clearly be excessive by any standard. The second is that development decisions made without broad input can be wasteful economically and disastrous ecologically. The third is that the controls of a police state fatally inhibit the creativity, risk taking, and factor of production mobility needed for success in today's global economy. The altered dynamics of international political life, particularly the widespread preoccupation with human rights in both the developed and developing worlds, make anachronistic the belief that Third World leaders should be allowed to restrict civil and political rights until economic growth takes off and improved living standards make politics less disruptive.

Conclusion

As the international community considers how to redesign the global political framework to better prevent and resolve armed conflict, the admonition "there can be no peace without justice" is more applicable than it ever was during the Cold War. The human rights community has the opportunity to move toward protection of the full range of rights specified in the Universal Declaration. However, given the persistence of horrific human rights abuses, it should continue to focus its greatest efforts on defending the physical integrity of the person in those scores of countries where extrajudicial killings and torture continue to occur. The sad history of UN intervention in Somalia should prompt better preparation of future humanitarian interventions, not permanent retreat from the peacemaking role urged by Secretary-General Boutros-Ghali.

For human rights advocates in the United States, both in and out of government, it is time to leave behind the recriminations of the Reagan--Bush era and work together. Human rights will be more effectively protected working energetically on incremental improvements than by uncompromising rhetorical insistence on immediate and perfect compliance with international norms. There are some human rights issues on which good faith advocates honestly can disagree. But claims that underdevelopment or cultural peculiarities exempt a society or nation from international human rights standards deserve a stiff rebuff.

In a world fractured by so many ethnic and religious cleavages, the solidarity manifest in the worldwide human rights movement provides special encouragement to Christians and others who believe that every man should be his brother's keeper.

Religious Nationalism and Human Rights

David Little

Religious nationalism is a fact of contemporary international life. Whether the issue is building, restructuring, or maintaining a nation the process is, in many parts of the world, entangled with religion. Frequently, the effects are violent and constitute a threat to peace, as the bishops' statement, *The Harvest of Justice Is Sown in Peace*, declares.[1]

Editors' Note: The opinions expressed here are the author's own and do not necessarily express the views of the United States Institute of Peace.

---

1 "One of the most disturbing threats to peace in the post-Cold War world has been the spread of conflicts rooted in national, ethnic, racial, and religious differences. While the end of the Cold War may bring new hope for ending some of these conflicts, others continue with their bloody logic largely unaffected by recent events, and still others, frozen by the Cold War, have erupted with a new and deadly fury, fueled by the dangerous virus of extreme nationalism." National Conference of Catholic Bishops, *The Harvest of Justice Is Sown in Peace* (Washington, D.C.: USCC Office for Publishing and Promotion Services, 1994), 11.

Examples from recent experience abound: Iran, Israel, Pakistan, Sudan, Sri Lanka, India, Northern Ireland, Tibet, Azerbaijan, and Armenia, the warring states of the former Yugoslavia, etc. Nor, for that matter, are the "developed" countries altogether exempt from the impact of religious nationalism. The simmering ethnic and religious tensions in Western Europe just now are an illustration. So is the influence of the Moral Majority and related movements on American public life during the 1980s, and the continuing presence of the "religious right" in American politics.

The notions of "nation" and "nationalism" as we use them today are relatively recent, as is the passion for achieving "national self-determination." Up through the Middle Ages, it was not customary in Europe or elsewhere to draw sharp political boundaries between different "peoples," each with their peculiar language and culture. It was in the "modern world" that one people took to identifying itself over against others by establishing its own government inside a clearly defined territory. So arose the modern obsession with the "nation-state": a people or nation achieves self-fulfillment by governing itself within a given area.

The way that nineteenth-century European imperialism and colonialism disseminated these ideas across the globe is a familiar story. Contemporary instances of "the dangerous virus of extreme nationalism," as the bishops put it, are often a reaction, directly or indirectly, to expansionist adventures and arrangements that were themselves inspired by nationalistic competition mostly among Western powers. The present map of Africa, the Middle East, and South Asia bears eloquent testimony to that influence.

But if the rise of modern nationalism is a fairly straightforward matter, the connection between religion and nationalism needs a comment or two, for it has become, in fact, a controversial question. For their part, the bishops claim that religious conflicts, including those associated with religious nationalism, are not usually caused by religion at all, but by other factors, such as political or economic discrimination and injustice. They also assert that rather than generating enmity, "authentic religious belief" is typically "a powerful moral force for nonviolent human liberation," as exemplified by recent occurrences in Eastern Europe, South Africa, and the Philippines.[2]

---

2 Their full statement is as follows: "In most so-called religious conflicts, political, economic, and ideological factors, rather than religious antagonisms, are the predominant causes of tension and violence. Instances of religion['s] being the principal cause of conflict are extremely rare.

"From Central America and Eastern Europe to South Africa and the Philippines, authentic religious belief, rather than being a cause of conflict, has been a powerful moral force for nonviolent human liberation ... Religious

According to one recent study, there is empirical evidence that — in the last decade anyway — religion is "seldom the root cause" of communal conflict.[3] On the other hand, the same study reports that cultural (including religious) differences do have a moderate influence, at least, on the antagonism that often develops between majorities and minorities in plural societies, especially over the distribution of economic advantages. This is because custom, language, religion, and so on give to the majority a rationale or warrant "for denying access to people who are 'different,'" and because cultural differences "make it difficult for minorities to operate effectively in institutions established by dominant groups."[4] These results, among others, suggest that religion is frequently not incidental as a contributing factor to communal conflict,[5] including conflict related to religious nationalism.

The proposition contained in the bishops' statement that "authentic religious belief" is typically a cause not of conflict but of nonviolence and peace begs some questions. It appears to assume that only such religious belief as leads to nonviolence and peace is indisputably authentic. But then the connection is not causal but definitional, and the definition, of course, will require some special justification (which is not supplied in the statement). Certainly, it will be necessary to explain exactly what is meant by authentic belief, as well as why, in various traditions, belief that is authentic might not, under some conditions, inspire violence. Until these questions are disposed of, it is reasonable to retain an open mind concern-

---

nationalism, and religious conflict, while potentially serious problems, are best confronted by an increase, not a disparagement, of authentic religious behavior." *The Harvest of Justice Is Sown in Peace*, 11.

3 See Ted Robert Gurr, et al., *Minorities at Risk: A Global View of Ethnopolitical Conflicts* (Washington, D.C.: United States Institute of Peace, 1993), 317. "Only eight of the forty-nine militant sects in the study are defined solely or mainly by their religious beliefs." Cf. 116.

4 Ibid., 57-58. The data show "moderate correlations" between cultural differentials and economic differentials, and to a slightly lesser degree, economic discrimination (see part 2 of table 2.5, 54-55). Gurr's comments in other parts of the book illustrate the statistical conclusions. In Asia, "[I]ndigenous origins and religious beliefs account for the high cultural differentials that typify [Asia]. These cultural differentials in turn tend to reenforce economic differentials . . . " (65). Elsewhere in the book, Gurr and his associates speak somewhat more generally about the influence of religion on conflict that has a strong nationalistic character. In Sub-Saharan Africa, and especially in Sudan, the "intensity of the conflicts has been exacerbated by substantial cultural differentials, especially the Arab Muslim-versus-Christian (and animist) cleavage that divides contenders . . . " (65). "Religion is a major issue of ethnic differentiation and divisiveness in [Eastern Europe] . . . " (182).

5 Ibid., 317.

ing the relation between religion (whether authentic or inauthentic) and conflict.

There are two important truisms that help to identify, in general, the connection between nationalism and religion. First, as Woodrow Wilson, "the father of self-determination," stressed over and again, there is a strong natural affinity between religious commitment and patriotism, or devotion to the national cause. The nation becomes the symbol of a "sacred" cultural and linguistic heritage. It involves questions of ultimate meaning and legitimacy that are expressed in solemn public ceremonies and rituals, and it is to many citizens the sort of thing that gives final purpose and direction to life. The nation is something to die for. It inspires self-denial on behalf of a greater good: "Ask not what your country can do for you. Ask only what you can do for your country," as President Kennedy memorably put it in his inaugural address.

In other words, the virtues of nationalistic devotion have a religious flavor to them. It is no doubt for that reason that the much-discussed idea of "civil religion" seems so compelling. If contemporary nation-states are conceived of in religious or quasi-religious terms, it is hardly surprising that national cults would proliferate and flourish to the degree they have.

The second obvious link between nationalism and religion has to do with the impulse of the modern nation to monopolize successfully "the legitimate use of physical force within a given territory," in Max Weber's famous formulation. As mentioned, the whole point of "national self-determination" is to achieve statehood by means of consolidating political and legal control. That kind of control involves having the *legitimacy* to exercise force, and to organize and maintain the state.

This is where religion comes in; it frequently supplies such justification. In Judaism, Islam, and Christianity, "Yahweh," "Allah," and "God" are all described, among other things, as supreme political and legal rulers. As "mighty warriors," "just kings," or "righteous judges," they are believed to possess rightful authority to employ force and regulate public affairs, as well as to delegate that right to earthly authorities.

Even in the New Testament, with its attention to nonviolence and martyrdom, there is St. Paul's explicit approval of the use of the sword by authorized governments. Similarly, while Buddhism exhibits a strong preference for nonviolence and monastic withdrawal, it simultaneously emphasizes the role of the "universal king" as a righteous ruler and the embodiment of justice. Toward establishing dominance, Buddhist kings may use force, at least provisionally. In short, religion is typically concerned to set ultimate standards for the use of force and the conduct of political and legal affairs. That is a subject of deep sacred significance, and it lies close to the heart of religious belief and practice.

It is, therefore, not hard to understand why religion would come to play the important role it frequently does in the process of building and preserving a nation-state. Religion and nationalism share a common concern over political legitimacy.

Of course, to indicate the way religion and nationalism sometimes go together is *not* to suggest that it must necessarily be so. Traditions like Judaism, Christianity, Islam, and Buddhism are complicated affairs, with all sorts of different themes and counterthemes. Some of those themes — for example, the emphasis on universal benevolence, tolerance, and peaceful persuasion rather than coercion — cut against the violent parochialism and ethnocentrism so often associated with nationalism.

Still, the reasons for a recurring affinity between religion and nationalism cannot be ignored, particularly at present, when there is so much available evidence all around.

The Current Shape of Religious Nationalism: Three Examples

We may look, briefly, at three examples of religious nationalism: Ukraine, the Sudan, and Sri Lanka, selected because of their religious, political, and geographical diversity.[6]

Ukraine

One of the most obvious lessons of the history of Ukraine is the interconnection of beliefs about religion and national identity. For one thing, the very names of the disputing groups are significant. There are the *Russian* Orthodox (or so they were known until the advent of an independent Ukraine); the *Ukrainian* Independent Orthodox (independent of the Russians, that is); and the *Ukrainian* Catholics. The religious identity of each of the groups is at the same time national and political, and much of the current controversy over church property and jurisdiction runs to disagreements over which church is most loyal to the authentic national tradition.

---

6 These three examples are selected from a series of seven case studies of religious nationalism currently being conducted by a United States Institute of Peace working group on religion, nationalism, and intolerance. For fuller accounts of Ukraine and Sri Lanka, see David Little, *Ukraine: The Legacy of Intolerance* (Washington, DC: U.S. Institute of Peace, 1991), and David Little, *Sri Lanka: The Invention of Enmity* (Washington, DC: U.S. Institute of Peace, 1994). A report on the Sudan (tentatively entitled, "Sudan: Plural Society in Distress") will be published in 1995.

The Russian Orthodox have contended that as Ukraine is really part of greater Russia, so churches with Orthodox roots, like the Independent Orthodox and the Ukrainian Catholics, have no separate legitimacy. They ought to be members of the Russian Orthodox Church. By contrast, the Independent Orthodox followers consider themselves to be the bona fide representatives of Ukrainianism over and against Russian political and religious imperialism. Furthermore, some members regard their country-men, the Ukrainian Catholics, to be grossly disloyal for having turned their backs on Orthodoxy and sworn allegiance to a "foreign Western power," namely, the pope in Rome.

The Sudan

A militant Islamic group, known as the National Islamic Front, seized the government by means of a military coup in June 1989, and is now attempting to impose a highly authoritarian Islamic regime upon all of the Sudan. The country is divided between an Arab, Islamic north and a black African Christian and animist south, and the civil war between the north and the south is very much a contest over conflicting religious and ethnic identities.

The government has already begun to suppress and persecute unsympathetic Muslims, as well as Christians and other non-Muslims throughout the country. It is purging the universities and business firms of dissenters, and using force and other coercive means to require compliance with Islamic law.

Sri Lanka

In Sri Lanka, an extremist element gained control of the government in the 1950s. They declared the Buddhist majority to be "the chosen people," fully authorized by their religious tradition to favor their own language and culture, and therefore fully justified in discriminating against the minority Tamil population in education, public employment, and so on. As might be expected, the Tamil minority has in response developed its own version of the "chosen people" syndrome, and the conflict between these two religious and cultural visions has led to a bloody and ongoing civil war.

It seems clear that the conflict is, at bottom, a product of the government's having taken sides, and having favored, at certain crucial points in recent Sri Lankan history, the majority cause over and against the minorities. Rather than enforcing the neutrality of the agencies of law and order, civil service, police, and welfare agencies, the government has recurringly understood itself as called upon to embody and promote Sinhala nationalism, "with its potent mix," in the words of one author, "of race, religion, and language."[7]

In these and other examples, religion undoubtedly gets used or manipulated for political gain. Nevertheless, it is important that religion (and not something else) gets used, because the combination between religion and nationalism is particularly volatile and highly divisive. When national identity and religious identity are combined, as they have been in Ukraine, the Sudan, and Sri Lanka, the stage is set for civil strife among different religious and ethnic groups within the same society. So long as one religion constitutes the badge of true citizenship, citizens who do not share that religion will be disadvantaged.

A Human Rights Approach to Religious Nationalism

It is unlikely, to say the least, that there are any handy solutions to the bloody conflicts, or to the promise of such conflicts, that are generated by religious nationalism.

Nevertheless, the bishops appear to have it right when they declare: "Nationalist conflicts often arise out of injustice and, in turn, can create new forms of injustice. Militant nationalism is less likely to flourish where there is a commitment to fundamental human rights — civil, political, economic, social, and cultural. Full respect for freedom of religion and minority rights is especially crucial. . . . Self-determination and human rights must be firmly linked to a commitment to tolerance and solidarity."[8] The human rights approach to ameliorating conflict associated with militant nationalism has a special appeal. It has stood the test of extensive international and intercultural reflection and discussion, and, as a result, is a way of thinking that has already been introduced into the consciousness of peoples around the world.

Of special importance are the ideas underlying the provisions that are enshrined in the international human rights documents concerning freedom of religion and conscience, most particularly in the Universal Declaration of Human Rights, the International Covenant on Civil and Political Rights, and the United Nations Declaration on the Elimination of Intoler-

---

7 Stanley Tambiah, *Sri Lanka: Ethnic Fratricide and the Dismantling of Democracy* (Cambridge: Harvard University Press, 1986), 76.

8 *The Harvest of Justice Is Sown in Peace*, 12.

ance and Discrimination Based on Religion or Belief (adopted by the UN General Assembly in November 1981).

The central issue is identified in part of Article 2 of the Declaration against Intolerance:

> (1) "No one shall be subject to discrimination by any State . . . on grounds of religion or other beliefs. . . . (2) [T]he expression 'intolerance and discrimination based on religion and belief' means any distinction, exclusion, restriction, or preference based on religion or belief and having as its purpose or as its effect nullification or impairment of the recognition, enjoyment, or exercise of human rights and fundamental freedoms on an equal basis."

The assumption here is radical: It introduces considerable distance between religion and the state, if it does not dissociate them altogether. Accordingly, *the grounds on the basis of which a government legitimates its monopoly of force are sharply distinguished from religious belief of any kind*. That means, as Article 2 makes clear, that participation in public or political life may not be subject to any religious test whatsoever. If it can be demonstrated that religious affiliation or outlook creates civil advantages or disadvantages, such outcomes must be considered to be violations of "internationally recognized human rights." Furthermore, physical force, or the other enforcement mechanisms of the state, may not be used so as to accord special advantages to one religious group over another.

The human rights documents undercut many of the assumptions of religious nationalism. They do that by positing an explicitly nonreligious basis for political authority and the exercise of force. Because, as the Preamble to the Declaration against Intolerance puts it, "disregard and infringement of . . . the right to freedom of . . . conscience [and] religion . . . have brought . . . wars and great suffering to [human]kind . . . ," the proper solution is, simply, *to desanctify the civil order*. It is to differentiate as much as possible between religious authority and civil authority, between religious communal identity and political communal identity.

The idea is that such a system would create a new common, inclusive basis for peace and mutual respect among competing communities. Under such a conception, each party would, of course, lose the hope of ultimate political control over the other. But surrendering such a hope would in itself be the foundation for peace. Each party would thereby gain an opportunity for fair and equal participation in a religiously unbiased political system.

The idea that lies behind these provisions, as it emerged painfully from Western experience, is that there is a fundamental distinction between the "inner forum" and the "outer forum," between the "conscience," or the center of deep personal commitment and conviction, on the one hand, and the civil government on the other.

The law of the spirit is not the same as the law of the sword. That means that if one comes to authentic religious or other basic beliefs, those beliefs may be won only by continuing inner struggle. That struggle must finally be resolved by personal judgment, arrived at in consultation with whatever people one may choose of one's own volition to associate with. Deep, inward, conscientious beliefs cannot be produced by external compulsion, certainly not by civil coercion. Compelled belief is no belief at all.

On the other hand, it is perfectly intelligible to speak of being deterred or restrained from doing overt harm or violence to others by means of "outward" or physical force. Controlling acts of that kind is, as the human rights documents suggest, where the state comes in. The state is in business to protect, rather than impede, the free exercise of conscience by effectively guaranteeing equal rights and privileges to all, regardless of "race, colour, sex, language, *religion*, political or other opinion, national or social origin, property or other status," in the words of Article 2 of the Universal Declaration. By definition, there may be no preferential treatment for one form of religious identity over another, just as there may not be discrimination on grounds of race, ethnicity, sex, property, and so on.

The notion here is revolutionary. *It entails that political or governmental authority properly rests upon what human beings hold in common, not upon what distinguishes them or makes them different.* Not all human beings hold the same religious beliefs, just as they do not possess the same amount of property. They are not all born in the same ethnic tradition, nor do they have the same race or sex. In contrast, they all *do* commonly experience the pain and distress of enforced confinement, of severe physical suffering, of being deprived of property, sustenance, limb, or life.

Accordingly, the state ought to operate in the name of protecting people from violations of those common human aversions. It ought to protect all people equally against being arbitrarily imprisoned, killed, injured, robbed, victimized. Insofar as the state provides equal protection of that sort, it frees its citizens to relish their differences so long, of course, as those differences are expressed in a way that respects that which human beings hold in common.

Is the Human Rights Approach Antireligious?

It will be objected, no doubt, that this proposed human rights solution to the problem of religious conflict is "pure secularism," that it is a way of denaturing and trivializing religion by privatizing it and divorcing it from civil influence.

Three responses can be made to such an objection. First, parts of different religious traditions perceive and sometimes emphasize the distinction between spirit and sword. Obviously, there are different interpretations among Judaism, Christianity, Islam,[9] and Buddhism regarding just where the line should be drawn, as there are varying interpretations within each of these traditions over that question.

Still, if there are foundations within the different traditions for distinguishing spirit and sword, then it would be incorrect to say that advocating the separation of the spiritual and civil spheres along the lines of the human rights approach is totally antireligious. It is true, religious believers will have to decide to favor certain parts of their traditions and reject others if they are to embrace the human rights approach. But that is hardly abandoning religion altogether as a basis for peace.

Second, though it is open to discussion, there is reason to believe that the human rights approach represents a dramatic challenge to the various religious traditions. It asks believers not to deny their heritage, but to reexamine it critically in light of the following question: Does not a careful reading of each tradition reveal what countless historical and contemporary examples reveal — that the religious impulse to peace is actually thwarted, not fulfilled, when one religious group dominates others by civil means, when civil benefits and burdens are distributed unequally "on the basis of religion or belief"?

Third, since free speech and assembly are protected by the human rights instruments, religious people are not excluded from entering into civil discourse and lobbying for whatever opinions they may hold, so long as they respect the equivalent rights of others. Moreover, insofar as a civil system that institutionalizes human rights protects the freedom and integrity of conscience and the equality of civil opportunity for all citizens, including all religious citizens, it would be a mistake to describe that system as totally antireligious.

---

9 See David Little, John Kelsay, and Abdulaziz Sachedina, *Human Rights and the Conflict of Cultures: Western and Islamic Perspectives on Religious Liberty* (Columbia, S.C.: University of South Carolina Press, 1988), for a discussion of the complexity of the Islamic tradition regarding freedom of conscience.

Conclusion

It is true that the human rights approach favors a "secular" or "neutral" reference point for organizing and legitimating the modern nation-state. That approach rests on the belief that differentiating as much as possible between religion and the state — between the law of the spirit and the law of the sword — is an important step toward civil peace.

In some respects, of course, such a reference point is at best an ideal. In the real world, only approximations are possible. Still, the unmistakable assumption of the human rights approach is that trying to approximate the ideal is a meaningful exercise and well worth the effort.

The three cases of religious nationalism briefly described here provide support for that assumption. The spectacle of the governments of Ukraine, the Sudan, or Sri Lanka abandoning or being encouraged to abandon all semblance of neutrality, of openly siding with one religious and ethnic group over and against others, is surely cause for the greatest apprehension. There is good reason to assume that the lesson applies elsewhere as well.

Identity, Sovereignty, and Self-Determination

Jean Bethke Elshtain

Nationalism is the great political passion of our time. That this is so is surprising and, for many, disturbing. Political scientists and analysts over the years predicted confidently that nationalism would cease to be a powerful force as the world moved toward ever-expanding rationalism, enlightenment, and universalism. (Religion, of course, was slated for disappearance, too, as yet another atavistic force.) Perhaps this helps to account for the shock waves ricocheting through the academic world post-1989. For the Christian, however, much of what is happening seems perhaps all too predictable in a fallen world in which human beings are always tempted by power and some among us are quite overtaken by hatred and a lust to dominate. I want to explore, briefly, the interwoven themes of self-identity, self-determination, and nationalism in the penulti-mate realm in which each takes shape: the world of states, would-be states, political rule, and civic life.

There are some things we ought by now to have learned. One is that the imperial suppression of particular national identities is temporary and, moreover, that these identities, once permitted expression, are likely to take shape in militant, even ferocious, forms. As Sir Isaiah Berlin points out, "People tire of being spat upon, ordered about by a superior nation, a superior class, or a superior anyone. Sooner or later, they ask the nationalist questions: 'Why do we have to obey them?' 'What right have they?' 'What about us?' 'What can't we . . . ?'"[1] In her excellent book on nationalism, Liah Greenfield argues: "National identity is, fundamentally, a matter of dignity. It gives people reasons to be proud." Peoples historically — including our own foremothers and forefathers — fought "over respect due to them, rather than anything else."[2] Vaclav Havel speaks of the "desire to renew and emphasize one's identity" as a force that lies behind "the emergence of many new countries. Nations that never had states of their own feel an understandable need to experience independence."[3] Between 1945 and 1978 alone, 66 new states were born out of the wreckage of old colonial empires. Each colonial struggle gave birth to new nationalisms.

The nation-state model may have emerged historically as a Western invention, but with the Treaty of Westphalia in 1648 this form has been embraced worldwide. Aggrieved peoples want, not an end to the nation-state or to sovereignty or national autonomy, but an end to Western colonial or Soviet or other "external" dominance of their particular histories, languages, cultures, and wounded sense of identity. Catholic social thought has long recognized the validity and importance of self-determination, tying this concept to the need to work to achieve a common good and to a vision of human dignity tied "unquestionably," according to Pope John XXIII in *Pacem in Terris*, to the "right to take an active part in government. . . ."[4] In that great document, the pope reminds us that no human being is "by nature superior to his fellows, since all men are equally noble in natural dignity. And consequently there are no differences at all between political communities from the point of view of natural dignity."[5] Yet is this not what nationalism always violates by insisting that some states, or peoples, are in fact not only different from others, given their history and culture, but superior, too? Is not equal dignity of all peoples necessarily violated by nationalism?

George Orwell, for one, thought so. Orwell, in his essay "Notes on Nationalism," traces the drastic simplifications and overwrought evocation of competitive prestige in which the nationalist, one who uses all "his mental energy either in boosting or in denigrating," indulges. Orwell calls

---

1 Isaiah Berlin, "Two Concepts of Nationalism," *New York Review of Books* (November 21, 1991, 19-23), 20.

2 Liah Greenfield, *Nationalism: Five Roads to Modernity* (Cambridge, Mass.: Harvard University Press, 1992), 487-488.

3 Vaclav Havel, "The Post-Communist Nightmare," *New York Review of Books* (May 27, 1993, 8-10), 8.

4 Pope John XXIII, "Pacem in Terris," in *The Encyclicals and Other Messages of John XXIII* (Washington, D.C.: TPS Press, n.c.), 347.

5 Ibid., 350.

nationalist thought obsessive and indifferent to reality — persisting on a plane far removed from the concrete truths of everyday social life. The nationalist (by contrast to the civic patriot, of whom I will say more below) classifies people like insects and assumes that "whole blocks of millions or tens of millions of people can be confidently labeled 'good' or 'bad'" and, as well, he insists that no other duty must be allowed to override or even challenge that to the nation-state. The nationalist evokes power as force — we need more of it, we can never have enough of it, somebody else is creeping up on us and may soon have more than we do — and he sinks his own individuality into an overarching identification with the collective.[6]

But Orwell also endorsed a robust version of patriotic or civic identity, as do I, a form of identification always wary and cautious of nationalistic excess because the temptations of national identity push in a triumphalist direction. How do we sort this out with *Pacem in Terris* and the U.S. bishops' *The Harvest of Justice Is Sown in Peace* in mind? The bishops, too, endorse self-determination and claim that it "should neither be dismissed as always harmful or unworkable nor embraced as an absolute right or a panacea in the face of injustice. . . . While full political independence may be morally right and politically appropriate in some cases, it is essential that any new state meet the fundamental purpose of sovereignty: the commitment and capacity to create a just and stable political order and to contribute to the international common good."[7] I take the bishops, in line with their own previous document, *The Challenge of Peace*, and the long tradition of papal proclamations in this matter, to be lifting up a *via media*, a moderate but firm course charted between the Scylla of sovereign absolutism or an absolutizing of particular national identities, on the one hand, and the Charybdis of an arrogant universalism or imperialism running roughshod over self-determination and diversity, on the other. Let us examine this possibility further.

Identity with a nation goes deep. In his work on *The Political Life of Children*, Robert Coles found attachment to a homeland, or an imagined homeland, in the symbolism and imagery deployed by children. "Nationalism works its way into just about every corner of the mind's life," Coles writes. Children have ready access to a nation's "name, its flag, its music, its currency, its slogans, its history, its political life," and this personalized

---

6 George Orwell, "Notes on Nationalism," *The Collected Essays, Journalism, and Letters of George Orwell*, Sonia Orwell and Ian Angus, eds., vol. 3 (New York: Harvest, HBJ, 1968, 361-379), 362-363.

7 National Conference of Catholic Bishops, *The Harvest of Justice Is Sown in Peace: A Reflection of the National Conference of Bishops on the Tenth Anniversary of* The Challenge of Peace (Washington, D.C.: USCC Office for Publishing and Promotion Services, 1994), 11-12.

yet political identity shapes their outlooks and actions. Entrenched notions of a homeland are double-edged, at once inward looking, a place where one "gets one's bearings," and outward projecting, distinguishing, and perhaps protecting "us" from "them," from foreigners who, all too easily, may become enemies. Both aspects of homeland and nationalist imagery turn up "in the developing conscience of young people" everywhere.[8] John Keane, a British theorist of civil society, that realm of associations and solidaristic possibilities greater than the individual but 'beneath' the state, writes: " . . . the birth of democracy required among its citizens a shared sense of nationhood, that is, a collective identity of people who share a language or a dialect of a common language, inhabit or are closely familiar with a defined territory, experience its ecosystem with some affection, and share a variety of customs, including a measure of memories of the historical past, which is consequently experienced in the present tense as pride in the nation's achievements and, where necessary, an obligation to feel ashamed of the nation's failings."[9] All of this sounds quite unexceptionable. But we all know the troubles that national identity trails in its wake and why there is so much cause for concern.

If we want to focus our attention on the downside, all we need do is turn on the evening news and get the latest body count from Sarajevo, a city that before the past two years was primarily codified as the place in that little-known region, the Balkans, where the Archduke Franz Ferdinand was assassinated in 1914, triggering the events that led to the bloodletting of what used to be called "the Great War." How, in a way, dismally appropriate that the most destructive features of the new nationalism should be manifest here. We know what these are: a ruthless granulation of political entities in the name of a principle of the unimpeachable singularity of national, linguistic, cultural, even racial identities coupled with the dangers of "mixing" any group with any other. Let me suggest that we not rush to judge the Balkans, to dismiss this region and its people as primitives and fanatics, but to permit these terrible events to instruct us on the *always* present dangers in nationalism and national self-identity. We can and must be instructed without abandoning altogether the inherent integrity implicit in the *ideal* of self-determination, an ideal tied to self-respect and to the possibility that men and women, acting together, may know a good in common they cannot know alone.

What we see unfolding in the Balkans is a very old phenomenon, one from which our own society is by no means exempt. In harsher forms of multiculturalism, for example, do we not see an assertion of the absolut-

8   Robert Coles, *The Political Life of Children* (Boston: Atlantic Monthly Press, 1986), 60, 61, 63.
9   John Keane, "Democracy's Poisonous Fruit," *Times Literary Supplement*, August 21, 1992, 10-12), 10.

ism of particular identity? Going beyond rightful claims to self-respect and civic equality, multicultural absolutists insist that identities must not be mixed, that, quite literally, whites and blacks, or men and women, or homosexuals and heterosexuals, inhabit incommensurable epistemological universes. This is a view neither the civic liberal nor the Christian can accept. For the civic pluralist and the Christian alike embrace universalist aspirations and possibilities, affirming the idea that we can and must reach out in gestures of solidarity, friendship, and citizenship to those different from ourselves. As G. M. Tamas puts it, the "ethnocultural" version of identity and nationalism is that "others ought to be elsewhere; there is no universalistic, overriding, transcontextual principle 'legitimizing' mixture, assimilation or diversity within the same politico-symbolic 'space.'"[10] Those who break bodies politic "into warring ethnocultural enclaves" disdain nineteenth-century liberal and civic republican ideas of citizenship, for these accepted the possibility of, and, in some instances, the necessity for, a form of national identity not reducible to ethnicity or culture as that which is simply given. The 'new' ethnocultural nationalism, "particularly in the extreme shape it had taken in Eastern Europe, cannot and does not want to answer political questions. It is mostly a repetitive reaffirmation of identity." The only precept proffered by the ethnoculturalist is "Be what you are," as an essentialist prescription.[11] This is, then, by contrast to an alternative *civic* ideal, one chastened by recognition that "others are before and among me," that I am not hunkered down, alone, with others exactly like myself.

The post-World War II popes, the U.S. bishops, and civic patriots (in contrast to very uncivil nationalists) all recognize this latter reality. The Christian, in fact, is *obliged* in this matter. Christianity is not primarily a civic religion. It arose in opposition to the Empire and has struggled mightily (perhaps, at times, not as mightily as it ought) against tight assimilation of *regnum* to *sacerdotium*. We — we human begins in the *saeculum* — are always in "the Empire," in a political formation of some sort or another. But the claims of a body politic, including the vast pretensions embodied in the classical notion of *sovereignty*, must always be checked and balanced against other claims. Identity with, and obligation to, a nation-state is never absolute. We rightly fear forms of nationalism that feed on hatred of other ways of life. But much of the new nationalism, the remarkable outbursts of civic energy from suppressed peoples, speaks in and through a rhetoric that taps universal claims and concerns.

---

10 G. M. Tamas, "Old Enemies and New: A Philosophic Postscript to Nationalism," *Studies in East European Thought* (Netherlands: Kluwer Academic Publishers, 1993, 107-126), 120.

11 Ibid., 121.

The independence movements in the Baltic states, Solidarity, Civic Forum, and others protested their control by the Soviet empire, first, because it violated principles of self-determination imbedded in international law and shared understandings and, second, because it trampled on basic human rights, including the right to participate in, and help to choose, a way of life. Such appeals are at once universal *and* particular, tapping old identities but energizing new political recognitions. Hopefully, peoples who proclaim their devotion to human rights as a universal principle can be held accountable in ways rapacious, nationalistic destroyers, who scoff at such niceties, cannot. (Though one must, of course, *attempt* to hold them accountable.) This "middle way" — once again as an alternative to warring racial and ethnic groupings or the homogenized stability of efficiently managed imperialism — seems to me the only possible course that respects claims to self-determination yet holds forth the prospect of a painfully attained and perhaps, for that reason, even more deeply cherished civic order based on universal principles of recognition.

Perhaps a concrete example of this delicate balancing act is necessary. I rely here on press reports of Pope John Paul II's visit to the Baltic States in September 1993. The situation in Lithuania was particularly delicate for the pope because "Polish nationalists for their part have tried to exploit the alleged mistreatment of the three hundred thousand-strong Polish minority in Lithuania." Thus, "the pope had to be very careful not to offend Lithuanian sensibilities," he being not only the pope but a Pole associated with Polish aspirations to self-determination. It is worth reminding the reader that much of today's Lithuania was once part of Poland. The Lithuanian capital, Vilnius, is Poland's "Wilno," dear to the hearts of Poles everywhere, in part because it is the home of Adam Mickiewicz, the greatest Polish poet. But Pope John Paul, while acknowledging the love Poles have for that particular place, used the Lithuanian name "Vilnius" and not the Polish "Wilno" throughout his pastoral visit, including the one time he spoke Polish — when he delivered Mass in the main Polish-language church in Vilnius. For the rest of his visit, "the pope spoke . . . Lithuanian which he had learnt for the occasion" and "this made a tremendously positive impression on the Lithuanians." The Poles "were not so pleased, but coming from the pope they had to accept it. The pope exhorted the Poles to identify fully with Lithuania, and not to dwell on the past — by which he meant not to endlessly recall the time when Vilnius was part of Poland. . . ."[12] This wonderful account shows the ways in which ethical space can be created or expanded for a form of civic identification *sans* irredentist or chauvinistic aspirations. One might say that "eternal vigilance is the price of civic moderation."

---

12 I here rely on Anatol Lieven's account, "The Pope's Balancing Act," in *The Tablet* (September 18, 1993), 1208-1209.

This brings me to a few final words about the claims of sovereignty and self-determination. Post-Nuremberg, such claims cannot trump all other claims in any instance of conflict. The issue of crimes against humanity and human rights has been a shaping force in the world arena and will continue to be such. Human rights may be a weak reed against a deadly force but it is often the only weapon beleaguered peoples have and it offers a lever others can use to enforce the notion that geopolitical and cultural definitions of nationhood must, at this time in history, be open to chastening by universal principles. Of course, the Church has always advocated such chastening. But as we enter the twenty-first century, a bevy of international associations promulgates and nurtures this conviction as well.

The plurality of cultures is irreducible. A world of many nations, each with its own particular marks of self-identity, reminds us that we are not alone and that we cannot and ought not make the world "one" by cruelly obliterating diverse ways of life. Indeed, one of the most insidious aspects of communist "universalism" was precisely its need to crush difference, "to make everything the same," in the words of Havel. Havel goes on: "The greatest enemy of communism was always individuality, variety, difference — in a word, freedom. From Berlin to Vladivostok, the streets and buildings were decorated with the same red stars. Everywhere the same kind of celebratory parades were staged. Analogical state administrations were set up, along with the whole system of central direction for social and economic life. This vast shroud of uniformity, stifling all national, intellectual, spiritual, social, cultural, and religious variety, covered over any differences and created the monstrous illusion that we were all the same."[13] No, we are not the "same." But we do *share* a capacity for identification with the idea of a plural political body; we all require self-dignity; we all yearn for a decent life for our children.

This latter universalism is as different from the false universalism Havel scores as the night is to the day. In the words of Pope John Paul II, "a falsely united multinational society [the Soviet empire] must not be succeeded by one falsely diversified." (Here the pope refers to the "racist pretensions and evil forms of nationalism . . . ")[14] A universalism that sustains respect for difference is a universalism aware of our human need for concrete reference groups in order to attain and to sustain individuality and identity. As a version of national identity, the form of membership I wish here to commend softens but does not negate altogether the idea of sovereignty. The alternative to strong theories of sovereignty that place duty and loyalty

---

13 Havel, "Post-Communist Nightmare," 8.
14 "Pope sees false nationalism tearing at Europe," *The Tablet* (December 4, 1993), 1599.

to the nation-state above all other duties and loyalties is "sovereignty . . . in the service of the people," in the words of the U.S. bishops.[15]

Vaclav Havel writes of politics — a politics of civic self-determination — as a form of "practical morality . . . humanly measured care for our fellow human beings." Scoring the "arrogant anthropocentrism of modern man," an arrogance that has its political culmination in triumphalist accounts of sovereignty and nationalism, Havel opts for limited ideals of identity and responsibility — ideals that cannot be cut to the measure of a man's hubris.[16] Politics, on this account, has to do with having a home, with being at home, with tending to one's particular home and its place in the wider world in which one gets one's bearings. Pope John Paul has also elaborated an alternative to statist versions of sovereignty. In one early formulation, he argued that: "The state is firmly sovereign when it governs society and also serves the common good of society and allows the nation to realize its own subjectivity, its own identity."[17] Insofar as I grasp the version of sovereignty here advanced, sovereignty is located neither "in" the state per se, nor in an unmediated construction of the "sovereign will" of the people but, rather, in the multiple associations of civil society in dialogue with one another as "subjects." This dialogue creates, or concatenates into, a political body whose legitimate purpose is to see that rules for civil contestation are followed and that the various loci of human social existence, necessary to human dignity and freedom, are protected and served. The coexistence of overlapping, porous entities is assumed. This is a dialogical, by contrast to a monological, political ideal.

With Isaiah Berlin, I "do not wish to abandon the idea of a world which is a reasonably peaceful coat of many colors, each portion of which develops its own distinct cultural identity and is tolerant of others."[18] Indeed, this ideal offers the strongest alternative to the cruelty and torment of a rapacious and narrow nationalism, on the one hand, or a watery universalism or impositional empire that either cannot inspire or cruelly commands people's loyalties, on the other. We live in a dangerous time, shaped by powerful forces most of us had no direct hand in shaping. But we are not helpless before such forces: that is the humble but powerful message of *The Harvest of Justice Is Sown in Peace.*

---

15 *The Harvest of Justice Is Sown in Peace,* 3.

16 These insights and words are found throughout Havel's works. The reader might want to consult both early and late essays, say, *Vaclav Havel, or Living in Truth,* ed. Jan Vladislav (London: Faber and Faber, 1987) and Vaclav Havel, *Disturbing the Peace* (New York: Alfred A. Knopf, 1990).

17 Cited in Timothy Garton Ash, *The Uses of Adversity: Essays on the Fate of Central Europe* (New York: Random House, 1989), 43. From a homily at Jasna Gora in 1983.

18 Berlin, "Two Concepts of Nationalism," 21.

Peace and the Moral Imperative of Democracy[1]

Bruce Russett

For nearly half a century, the United States and its allies carried out a policy of containment, to prevent the spread of communist ideology and Soviet power. That policy ultimately succeeded, spectacularly. Now it must be replaced by another policy, one designed to consolidate the new acceptability of free institutions around the world. The post-Cold War era presents more than just the passing of a particular adversarial relationship; it offers a chance for fundamentally changed relations among nations.

Supporting democratization should be a moral imperative for two reasons. First, democracy is a desirable form of government on its own merit. It both reflects and promotes human dignity. Undemocratic institutions — even benevolently ruled ones — lose touch with the needs of their peoples, and shut themselves off from information that might prevent egregious missteps. Democracy is not perfect, and should not be forced upon peoples who do not wish it. But for many countries, it is better than the alternatives they have tried and from which they have suffered. Recall

---

1 This chapter summarizes research reported in detail in Bruce Russett, *Grasping the Democratic Peace: Principles for a Post-Cold War World* (Princeton, N.J.: Princeton University Press, 1993).

E. M. Forster's "two cheers for democracy" on these grounds. Reflecting modern Catholic teaching, in *The Challenge of Peace* (especially paragraphs 251-53), the U.S. bishops called for support of democracy and human rights. In *The Harvest of Justice Is Sown in Peace*, they repeatedly affirm that commitment, most notably in the Introduction (also see II.B) which lists "support for human rights and democracy" among "essential works of peace."

Second, we now have solid evidence that democracies do not make war on each other. While this particular connection and the causal reasoning are not explicitly made by the bishops, both deserve thorough attention. Foreign policy for the post-Cold War world can be built on a policy of enlarging the zone of democratic peace.

Democracies Rarely Fight Each Other

The vision of a peace among democratically governed states has long been invoked as part of a larger structure of institutions and practices to promote peace among nation-states. In 1795, Immanuel Kant spoke of perpetual peace based partially upon states sharing "republican constitutions." His meaning was compatible with basic contemporary understandings of democracy. Of the elements of such a constitution, he identified freedom, with legal equality of subjects, representative government, and separation of powers. The other key elements of his perpetual peace were "cosmopolitan law" embodying ties of international commerce and free trade, and a "pacific union" established by treaty in international law among republics.

Woodrow Wilson expressed the same vision for the twentieth century. His Fourteen Points sound as though Kant were guiding Wilson's writing hand. They included Kant's cosmopolitan law and pacific union. Point three demanded "removal, so far as possible, of all economic barriers and the establishment of an equality of trade conditions among all the nations consenting to the peace and associating themselves for its maintenance." The fourteenth point was, "A general association of nations must be formed under specific covenants for the purpose of affording mutual guarantees of political dependence and territorial integrity to great and small states alike." He did not explicitly invoke the need for universal democracy, since not all of America's war allies were democratic. But his meaning was clear if one considers the domestic political conditions necessary for his first point: "Open covenants of peace, openly arrived at, after which there shall be no private international understandings of any kind but diplomacy shall proceed always frankly and in the public view." His 1917 war message to Congress asserted that "a steadfast concert of peace can never be maintained except by a partnership of democratic nations." This vision once sounded utopian, but now, at the end of the twentieth century, it is newly plausible.

In the contemporary era, "democracy" denotes a country in which nearly everyone can vote, elections are freely contested, and the chief executive is chosen by popular vote or by an elected parliament. Democracies are not necessarily peaceful in general — we all know the history of democracies in colonialism, covert intervention, and other excesses of power. Certainly democracies are as violence-prone in their relations with authoritarian states as authoritarian states are toward each other. But the relations between stable democracies are qualitatively different.

Democracies are unlikely to engage in militarized disputes *with each other* or to let any such disputes escalate into war. In fact, they rarely even skirmish. Since 1946, pairs of democratic states have been only one-eighth as likely as other kinds of states to threaten to use force against each other, and only one-tenth as likely actually to do so. Established democracies fought *no wars* against one another during the entire twentieth century. (Although Finland, for example, took the Axis side against the Soviet Union in World War II, it engaged in no combat with the democracies.)

The more democratic each state is, the more peaceful its relations are likely to be. Democracies are more likely to reciprocate each other's behavior, to accept third-party mediation or good offices in settling disputes, and to settle disputes peacefully. Democracies' relatively peaceful relations toward each other are not spuriously caused by some other influence such as sharing high levels of wealth, or rapid growth, or ties of alliance. The phenomenon of peace between democracies is not limited just to the rich industrialized states of the global North. It was not maintained simply by pressure from a common adversary in the Cold War, and it has outlasted that threat.

The phenomenon of democratic peace can be explained by the pervasiveness of normative restraints on conflict between democracies. That explanation extends to the international arena the cultural norms of live-and-let-live and peaceful conflict resolution that operate within democracies. The phenomenon of democratic peace can also be explained by the role of institutional restraints on democracies' decisions to go to war. Those restraints ensure that any state in a conflict of interest with another democracy can expect ample time for conflict-resolution processes to be effective, and that the risk of incurring surprise attack is virtually nil.

Evidence supports both explanations. They are not fully separable in theory or in practice. Both make a contribution, and the two kinds of influences reinforce each other to produce the phenomenon of democratic peace. Some evidence suggests that the normative explanation is the more powerful. Democratic norms, as measured by the absence of violence in domestic politics and the duration of stable democratic regimes, are somewhat more strongly associated with peace between democracies than are measures of specific institutional constraints. The spread of democratic norms and practices in the world, if consolidated, should reduce the frequency of violent conflict and war. Where normative restraints are weak, democratic institutions may provide the necessary additional restraints on the use of violence against other democratic states.

In the world of ancient Greece, institutions to limit the resort to force by democracies were almost entirely lacking, and the norms that democracies should not fight each other were nascent and weak. Some democracies — notably Athens and Syracuse — did fight each other. But when they did, perception of political instability in the adversary state, and misperception of its democratic nature, played an important role in instigating the war. Nonindustrial societies studied by anthropologists also show restraints on warfare among democratically organized polities that typically lack the institutional constraints of a modern state. Despite that absence, democratically organized units fight each other significantly less often than do nondemocratic units. And here too political stability again proves an important restraint on the resort to violence by democratically organized units. Finding the relationship between democracy and peace in preindustrial societies shows that the phenomenon of democratic peace is not limited to contemporary Western democracies.

During the Cold War, Soviet-American hostility was overdetermined. The very different political systems of the two superpowers, with their built-in ideological conflict, ensured a deadly political and military rivalry. So too did the systemic stresses of two great powers, each leading a big alliance in a bipolar confrontation, which ensured that each would resist any enhancement of the other's strength as a threat to its own security. But the end of the Cold War destroyed both those sources of hostility. The ideological conflict dissolved with the end of communism, and the bipolar confrontation collapsed with the Soviet alliance system and the Soviet Union itself. Given the revolutionary changes both in the global system and in the states which comprise it, the old bases for evaluating the character of international relations have also collapsed.

The end of ideological hostility matters doubly because it represents a surrender to the force of Western values of economic and especially political freedom. To the degree that countries once ruled by autocratic systems become democratic, the absence of war among democracies comes to bear on any discussion of the future of international relations. The statement that in the modern international system democracies have almost never fought each other represents a complex phenomenon: (a) democracies rarely fight each other (an empirical statement) because (b) they have other means of resolving conflicts between them and therefore do not need to fight each other (a prudential cost-benefit statement), and (c) they perceive that democracies should not fight each other (a normative statement about principles of right behavior), which reinforces the empirical statement. By this reasoning, the more democracies there are in the world, the fewer potential adversaries we and other democracies will have and the wider the zone of peace.

This means that the *possibility* of a widespread zone of democratic peace in the contemporary world exists. To turn that possibility into a policy to promote democratic peace, several fundamental problems must be addressed: the problem of consolidating democratic stability, the interaction of democracy with nationalism, and the prospects for changing basic patterns of international behavior.

Strengthening Democracy and Its Norms

The need to act to strengthen democracy in successor states of the former Soviet Union is, in terms of the above principles, apparent. But expectations that the United States (and perhaps its allies) will effectively do so may be unfounded. It is an old American foreign policy error to exaggerate the effect the United States can have on others. It is an even greater mistake in an era when the United States lacks the economic resources it could muster in earlier decades. More to the point, the United States has lacked the will to employ the resources it does have. Its contribution to economic recovery in the former Soviet Union has amounted to only a miserly fraction of Germany's, even excluding Bonn's expenses in the territories of former East Germany. There is no massive American Marshall Plan to consolidate democracy, and external assistance will be limited under the best of circumstances. But amid all the helpful internal conditions for aspiring democracies, external influences can make a contribution — often modest, sometimes critical.

The literature on the "prerequisites" of democracy is vast and often deeply flawed — ethnocentric and too enamored with economic preconditions. Yet some things have been learned, and stated with some modesty, in recent analyses. Among several good efforts, the most prominent may be Samuel Huntington's.[2] Since he reviews and synthesizes much of

---

2 Samuel P. Huntington, *The Third Wave: Democratization in the Late Twentieth Century* (Norman: University of Oklahoma Press, 1991).

the earlier literature, a summary of his conclusions will suffice. First, he identifies five changes in the world that played significant parts in *producing* the latest wave of recent transitions to democracy: (1) deepening legitimacy problems of authoritarian governments unable to cope with military defeat and economic failure, (2) economic growth that raised living standards, educational levels, and urbanization — raising expectations and the ability to express them, (3) changes in religious institutions that made them less defenders of the status quo than opponents of governmental authoritarianism (for example, by the Catholic Church in the Philippines, Eastern Europe, and parts of Latin America), (4) changes in the policies of other states and international organizations, to promote human rights and democracy, (5) "snowballing" or demonstration effects, enhanced by international communication, as transitions to democracy in some states served as models for their neighbors.

Huntington also lists conditions that favor the *consolidation* of new democracies: (1) experience of a previous effort at democratization, even if it failed, (2) a high level of economic development, (3) a favorable international political environment, with outside assistance, (4) early timing of the transition to democracy, relative to a worldwide "wave," indicating that the drive to democracy derived primarily from indigenous rather than external influences, (5) experience of a relatively peaceful rather than violent transition, and (6) moderation in the number and severity of the problems confronted.

Such lists do not lead to simple diagnosis or prescription, with "necessary" or "sufficient" conditions, but they do offer a helpful focus for discussion. Most importantly, they single out both internal and external influences on the process of democratization. Internal influences are certainly prominent, especially in the consolidation list. It is hard to imagine a successful stabilization of democracy without many or most of them. But the list of international conditions is impressive also. Favorable international conditions may not be essential (either alone or in combination) in every case, but they can make a difference, and sometimes a crucial one when the internal influences are mixed. The United States and its allies have made a difference — for the defeated Axis powers after World War II, and sometimes since.

Currently, with economic conditions so grim in much of the Third World, Eastern Europe, and the former Soviet Union, and the consequent dangers to the legitimacy of new democratic governments, external assistance — technical and financial — is especially important. Rather small amounts — but more than have been forthcoming to date — could make a difference. As a stick, aid can surely be denied to governments that regularly violate human rights, for example, of ethnic minorities. Clear antidemocratic acts, such as a military coup or an aborted election, can be punished by suspending aid. As to the carrot of extending aid on a conditional basis, broader goals of developing democratic institutions require creation of a civil society, and are less easily made conditional. Recipients may see multilateral aid, with conditions of democratic reform attached, as a less blatant invasion of their sovereignty than aid from a single country. Without exaggerating the prospects for success, it would be a terrible loss if the United States and other rich democracies did not make serious efforts. It would be a loss, to themselves as well as to the peoples of the struggling democracies.

A special complication, one hardly unique to the current era but felt acutely now, is nationalism in the quilt of ethnicities left behind from the former Soviet empire. With its combination of inclusion and exclusion, nationalism readily conflicts with the quasi-universalistic ethos of "democracies don't fight each other." Hatreds, long suppressed, emerge to bedevil any effort to build stable, legitimate government. They bring border conflicts to liberate or incorporate "oppressed" minorities, and civil wars. Civil wars often are contests between ethnic groups for exclusive control of the central coercive institutions of the state. The conflict then becomes one over the right of some minority ethnic groups to secede from the control of those institutions, and in doing so frequently take with them other ethnic groups who may in turn consider themselves oppressed by their new government. Neither the institutions nor the experience of "live and let live" may exist.

An irony is that the initial creation of democratic institutions can contribute to the explosion of ethnic conflicts, by providing the means of free expression, including expression of hatred and feelings of oppression. That does not mean, however, that the solution lies in less democracy. Rather, it likely lies in devising institutions, and nurturing norms and practices, of democratic government with respect for minority rights. (See *The Harvest of Justice*, section II.D.1,2.) It may also require allowing the secession of groups who are not satisfied that their rights and interests can be sufficiently respected under a single government. A consolation may be that nationalism in a democratic era probably dooms any substantial effort of imperialism to incorporate into a larger political unit different ethnic groups against their will. The will of acquired peoples to separation can be repressed only at great cost and risk. The creation of institutions, norms, and practices to protect minorities has never been easy. But it presents the fundamental challenge of world political development in this era.

Recall the requirement, for a democratic peace, of stability of democracy and perceptions of stability. For the near future, at least, that condition is likely to be in short supply in much of the world. If one's neighbor has vast unsolved economic problems, is it politically stable? Has it experienced democracy long enough, with some success in managing its problems, to be stable? If it is "democratic" for some, even a majority, of its citizens, but forcibly represses its minorities, is it "stable?" Many of the new states of the old Soviet Union fail these and other tests. Some have not yet had a real democratic transition.

Georgia, for example, did elect, by reasonably democratic procedures, Zviad Gamsakhurdia as president when it was still a republic in the Soviet Union. But on independence, he seized dictatorial powers. In January 1992, he was finally overthrown in bitter fighting and replaced (but not by election) by Eduard Shevardnadze, who fought off a subsequent coup attempt. Elections to confirm Shevardnadze's status as democratic leader were not held until October 1992. Gamsakhurdia reemerged to lead an insurgency. Meanwhile, severe ethnic violence continued in the secessionist region of Abkhazia. Georgia in 1993 may have been an aspiring democracy or a nascent democracy, but it was not yet a stable democracy nor, by any reasonable international standard, even just a "democracy." Until its democracy is established, it should surprise no one if Georgia or states like it get into war with their neighbors. Nor would such a war invalidate a "democracies don't go to war with each other" generalization.

Peace Will Not Be Built by War

Understanding that democracies rarely fight each other, and why, has great consequence for policy in the contemporary world, as well as for theoretical debates. It should affect the kinds of military preparations believed to be necessary, and the costs one would be willing to pay to make them. It should encourage peaceful efforts to assist the emergence and consolidation of democracy. But a misunderstanding of it could encourage war-making against authoritarian regimes, and efforts to overturn them — with all the costly implications of preventive or hegemonic military activity such a policy might imply.

Recollection of the post-1945 success with defeated adversaries can be both instructive and misleading. It is instructive in showing that democracy could supplant a thoroughly discredited totalitarian regime, at a time when authoritarianism in general was not held in high esteem globally. It can be misleading if one forgets how expensive it was (Marshall Plan aid, and important economic concessions to Japan), and especially if one misinterprets the political conditions of military defeat. The allies of the anti-Axis coalition utterly defeated the old regimes. To solidify democratic government, the allies conducted vast (if incomplete) efforts to remove the former elites from positions of authority. But they had something to build on, in the form of individuals and institutions from previous experiences with democracy. The model of "fight them, beat them, and then make them democratic" is irrevocably flawed as a basis for contemporary action. It probably would not work, anyway, and no one is prepared to make the kind of effort that would be required. Not all authoritarian states are inherently aggressive. Indeed, at any particular time, the majority is not. A militarized crusade for democracy is not in order.

External military intervention, even against the most odious dictators, is a dangerous way to try to produce a "democratic world order." Sometimes, with a cautious cost-benefit analysis and with the certainty of substantial and legitimate internal support, it might be worthwhile — that is, under conditions when rapid military success is likely *and* the will of the people at issue is clear. Even so, any time an outside power supplants any existing government, the problem of legitimacy is paramount. The very democratic norms to be instilled may be compromised.

At the least, intervention should not be unilateral. It must be approved, publicly and willingly, by some substantial international body like the United Nations or the Organization of American States. Under most circumstances, even such international bodies are better used as vehicles to promote democratic processes at times when the relevant domestic parties are ready. Peacekeeping operations to help provide the conditions for free elections, monitor those elections, and advise on the building of democratic institutions are usually far more promising than is military intervention.

With the end of the Cold War, the UN has experienced highly publicized troubles in Somalia and the former Yugoslavia as it tries to cope with a range of challenges not previously part of its mandate. Nevertheless, its successes, though receiving less attention, outnumber the failures. It has emerged as a major facilitator of peaceful transitions and democratic elections in such places as Cambodia, El Salvador, and Namibia. Its Electoral Affairs Unit has provided election assistance to 36 states. As expressed in Secretary-General Boutros-Ghali's *Agenda for Peace*, the UN has a new mission of "peace-building," attending to democratization, development, and the protection of human rights. It is newly strengthened, but it is also newly and enormously burdened. In *The Challenge of Peace* (paragraph 268), the U.S. bishops called for support of the United Nations. It deserves that support even more so now. The bishops explicitly give it, endorsing (Section III.A; also see II.A) "the capacity of the United Nations and other multilateral institutions to promote human development, democracy, human rights, and peace."

Can a Wider Democratic Peace Be Built?

New democracies should be supported financially, politically, and morally. Successful transitions to democracy in some countries can supply a model for others. Simply understanding the sources of democratic peace can have the effect of a self-fulfilling prophecy. Scholars sometimes create reality as well as analyze it. In a world where democracy has become widespread, understanding the fact of the "democratic peace" proposition will help to make it true.

So too will wider acceptance of the norm. Political discourse is, for instrumental as well as moral reasons, largely normative. Insofar as norms guide behavior, repeating those norms helps to make them effective. Repeating the norms as descriptive principles can help to make them true. Repeating the proposition that democracies should not fight each other helps reinforce the probability that democracies will not fight each other. Norms may be violated and break down. Nevertheless, norms do constrain behavior, both by affecting what one wants to do and what one may be able to persuade others to do or not to do.

In turn, a stable and less menacing international system can permit the emergence and consolidation of democratic governments. Dire warnings of a world of "garrison states" may have been extreme, and some of the charges about a "military-industrial complex" a quarter of a century ago were shrill and exaggerated. Nevertheless, international threats — real or only perceived — do strengthen the forces of secrecy and authoritarianism in the domestic politics of states involved in "protracted conflict." Relaxation of international threats to peace and security reduces the need, and the excuse, for repressing democratic dissent. Democracy and the expectation of international peace can feed on each other to ease both the real and the perceived dangers of a still-anarchic international system.

An evolutionary process may even be at work. Because of the visible nature and public costs of breaking commitments, democratic leaders may be better able to persuade leaders of other states that they will keep the agreements they enter into. Democracies more often win their wars than do authoritarian states. They seem to be more effective in marshaling their resources, and with free speech and debate they are more accurate and efficient information processors. Authoritarian governments that lose wars are often overthrown subsequently, and may be replaced by democratic regimes.

Perhaps major features of the international system can be socially constructed from the bottom up; that is, norms and rules of behavior internationally can become extensions of the norms and rules of domestic political behavior. The modern international system is commonly traced to the Treaty of Westphalia and the principles of sovereignty and noninterference in internal affairs affirmed by it. In so doing, it affirmed the anarchy of the system, without a superior authority to ensure order. It also was a treaty among princes who ruled as autocrats. Our understanding of the modern anarchic state system risks conflating the effects of anarchy with those stemming from the political organization of its component units. When most states are ruled autocratically — as in 1648 and throughout virtually all of history since — then playing by the rules of autocracy may be the only way for any state, democracy or not, to survive in Hobbesian anarchy.

The anarchic security dilemma of threat, counterthreat is what drove the pessimism of "realists" like Hans Morgenthau and Rheinhold Niebuhr. Alexis de Tocqueville's doubts about democracies' ability to pursue stable and enlightened foreign policies are well known. But Tocqueville was writing in 1835, mindful of an international system in which the vast majority of states were still autocracies. A democracy which tried to operate by democratic norms was at a great disadvantage, and might well shift policy unstably in trying to adjust to the risks.

The emergence of new democracies with the end of the Cold War presents an opening for change in the international system more fundamental even than at the end of other big wars — World Wars I and II and the Napoleonic Wars. For the first time ever, in 1992 a virtual majority of states (91 of 183) approximated reasonable standards employed for democracy. Another 35 were in some form of transition to democracy.[3] Democracy in many of these states may not prove stable. This global democratic wave may crest and fall back, as earlier ones have done. But states probably can become democratic faster than they can become rich. If the chance for wide democratization can be grasped and consolidated, world politics might now be transformed.

A system composed substantially of democratic states might reflect very different behavior than did the previous one composed predominantly of autocracies. We "won" the Cold War, at immense cost. If we should now let slip this marvelous short-term window of opportunity to solidify basic change in the international order at much lower cost, our children will wonder. Some autocratically governed states will surely remain in the system. But if enough states become stably democratic in the 1990s, then in the majority of interactions there will be a chance to reconstruct the norms and rules of the international order to reflect those of democracies. A system created by autocracies centuries ago might now be re-created by a critical mass of democratic states.

---

3 R. Bruce McColm, et al., *Freedom in the World: Political Rights and Civil Liberties 1991-1992* (New York: Freedom House, 1993), 47.

"They will not hurt or destroy on all my holy mountain!"

—Isaiah 11:9

Dianne Bergant, CSA

The National Council of Catholic Bishops begins its recent pastoral letter on war and peace, entitled *The Harvest of Justice Is Sown in Peace*, with a discussion of "an often neglected aspect of *The Challenge of Peace*," namely, "the spirituality and ethics of peacemaking." The bishops insist that "true peacemaking can be a matter of policy only if it is first a matter of the heart."[1] The following reflections have been inspired by the conviction that the "matter of the heart" that must underlie policy is indeed nothing less than authentic metánoia, a radical change of mind, or conversion of heart.

The following article will address an aspect of this *metánoia* that is frequently overlooked, that is, the need to devise a worldview based on principles of overall symbiotic balance in nature rather than on principles

---

1 National Council of Catholic Bishops, *The Harvest of Justice Is Sown in Peace* (Washington, D.C.: USCC Office for Publishing and Promotion Services, 1994), 3.

of human domination over nature. The ecological challenges of our day are evidence of the need of a worldview based on principles of interrelatedness, and of an ethics that goes beyond regarding the rest of creation merely as possessing instrumental value contingent on human dominion. Such an ecologically sensitive worldview will require the reinterpretation of one aspect of the "just-war" tradition, namely, the principle of proportionality. Selected biblical passages will be examined in order to show that the biblical tradition presumes such interrelatedness, and that contemporary rereading of the tradition calls for an ecologically sensitive understanding of proportionality. The title of the article is taken from a messianic poem which describes idyllic conditions when the disorders in nature will be restored to their pristine harmony. With their pastoral reflection, the bishops are calling us to just such a vision of peace.

Proportionality: Criterion for a "Just War"

An authentic spirituality of peacemaking must deal honestly and realistically with the reality of human aggression in a disordered world. We shirk our responsibility if we espouse a naivete that ignores the greed and exploitation of which the human heart is capable, or leave to others the task of redressing the evils of society. Peace is rooted in justice, and justice must be cultivated, maintained, and defended. The cultivation and maintenance of justice and peace require social and economic structures and policies that support and enhance the human dignity of all. The defense of justice and peace frequently requires force. The question then is not: Shall we defend? But rather: How shall we defend?

One of the theories that the Christian tradition has formulated to address conflict is its "just-war" teaching. This teaching is, in fact, an attempt to limit the armed confrontation that appears to be inevitable. It "begins with a strong presumption against the use of force and then establishes the conditions when this presumption may be overridden for the sake of preserving the kind of peace which protects human dignity and human rights."[2] Believing that the "just-war" tradition is "often misunderstood or selectively applied," the bishops summarize the major components of this traditional Catholic teaching. They list criteria both for the justification for the use of force (*jus ad bellum*) and for restraint in the midst of war (*jus in bello*). The first set of criteria includes: just cause,

---

2 Ibid., 5.

comparative justice, legitimate authority, right intention, probability of success, proportionality, and last resort. The second set includes: noncombatant immunity, proportionality, and right intention. Both lists contain the principle of proportionality. The concern regarding *jus ad bellum* is that "the overall destruction expected from the use of force must be outweighed by the good to be achieved."[3] Regarding *jus in bello*, the concern is "to avoid disproportionate collateral damage to civilian life and property."[4]

From its inception at the time of Augustine through its development to the present time, this "just-war" teaching has sought to balance the serious moral problem of warfare with the equally serious moral right and responsibility of a nation to defend its citizenry. However, the destructive capacity of contemporary weaponry has caused recent religious leaders to question the legitimacy of modern warfare.[5]

The attention in these statements usually centers on the question of just means, specifically the inevitable involvement of noncombatants and the disproportionate destruction of human life and property, realities that have become unavoidable consequences of modern arms. However, to date, the threat to delicate ecosystems posed by the force of weaponry, whether nuclear or conventional, has not been a major consideration when the principle of proportionality is addressed. Nonetheless, as people of the world are becoming more and more sensitive to ecological values, they recognize that, besides threatening human survival and property, the production and accumulation, let alone the activation, of exorbitant explosive munitions, chemical biocides, and incendiaries are threatening various fragile ecosystems with irreversible consequences.[6] Ecological sensitivity has inaugurated a new era in our understanding of moral responsibility.[7]

---

3 Ibid., 6.

4 Ibid., 6.

5 Pius XII, "Christmas Message" (1948); John XXIII, *Pacem in Terris* (1963), no. 137; Paul VI, "Address to the General Assembly of the United Nations" (1965), no. 2; *Pastoral Constitution on the Church in the Modern World* (1965), no. 80; John Paul II, "Homily at Bagington Airport," Coventry (1982), no. 2; National Conference of Catholic Bishops, *The Challenge of Peace: God's Promise and Our Response* (Washington, D.C.: USCC Office for Publishing and Promotion Services, 1983), no. 219.

6 A. A. Pirazizy, "Environment of War and Cataclysmic Alteration of Biogeochemical Cycle: Deliberate Extermination of Posterity," in K. S. Ramachandran, ed., *Gulf War and Environmental Problems* (New Delhi: Ashish Publishing House, 1991), 2.

7 See, e.g., Ian G. Barbour, ed., *Western Man and Environmental Ethics: Attitudes Toward Nature and Technology* (Reading, Mass.: Addison-Wesley, 1972); Hans Jonas, *The Imperative of Responsibility: In Search of an Ethics for the*

It is a scientific truism that the slightest alteration in the chemical composition of the atmosphere activates climatic modifications. If the slowly accumulated effects of industrialization have already resulted in acid rain as well as measurable global warming and CO_2 doubling which affects vegetational water use, the consequences of accelerated combustion emission can only dramatically escalate the destruction. Furthermore, unlike the battle itself, environmental effects are not confined to the political boundaries of conflict. The contamination of the air and water spreads across the globe. According to the Pentagon, in the course of two weeks during the Gulf War, more explosives were dropped than in the entire Second World War.[8] The ecological aftermath of this destruction in both the desert itself, its surrounding environs, and the atmosphere has not even as yet been estimated.

The recent Gulf War has introduced a phenomenon referred to as the "Dark House Effect." Just as the "Green House Effect" has changed the composition of the global atmosphere, so the "Dark House Effect" caused by the oil slick has left its mark in the ocean. The thick oil has prevented the sea from swelling, thus altering the distribution of nutrients to marine organisms. It has also limited the penetration of light necessary for photosynthesis to take place. Both of these processes are essential procedures in the progress of the food chain. A wide variety of marine plants and animals has been exposed to the toxins in the oil itself, as well as in the oil-neutralizing chemicals used to break up the slick. This contamination, which is likely to remain for at least a decade, has "the potential to kill about two million birds and annihilate the fragile marine ecosystem."[9] The extent to which the delicate ecological balance, already modified, can continue to support certain forms of life is unknown.[10]

Facts such as these certainly call for a reevaluation and a more comprehensive reinterpretation of the principle of proportionality. War and the preparations for war can no longer be viewed from an exclusively anthropocentric point of view. Their ecological costs must also be calculated.[11] We must consider whether or not the massive amounts of re-

---

Technological Age (Chicago: University of Chicago Press, 1984); James A. Nash, *Loving Nature: Ecological Integrity and Christian Responsibility* (Nashville, Tenn.: Abingdon, 1991); Carol S. Robb and Carl J. Casebolt, eds., *Covenant for a New Creation: Ethics, Religion and Public Policy* (Maryknoll, N.Y.: Orbis, 1991).

8 M. K. Patel and T. N. Tiwari, "Oil Pollution in the Persian Gulf and Its Ecological Impact," in K. S. Ramachandran, ed., *Gulf War and Environmental Problems*, 90.

9 A. A. Pirazizy, "Environment of War and Cataclysmic Alteration of Biogeochemical Cycle: Deliberate Extermination of Posterity," in K. S. Ramachandran, ed., *Gulf War and Environmental Problems*, 10.

10 Jonathan Schell, *The Fate of the Earth* (New York: Alfred A. Knopf, 1982), 91-93.

sources and energy consumed, and the enormous quantities of non-disposable toxic and radioactive wastes produced in the testing and use of weaponry justify the depletion of natural wealth and the destruction of ecosystems. The social consequences of war also place extraordinary burdens on ecosystems of the land to which refugees flee. These areas are expected to produce food, clothing and shelter for, and dispose of the waste of, more people than they normally hold. Experience has shown that while war may destroy one region, it usually depletes others as well. It is clear that the ecological balance of the earth is placed in serious jeopardy whenever armed conflict breaks out anywhere in the contemporary world.

The Integrity of Creation

These reflections in no way challenge the significance of the principle of proportionality. On the contrary, they depend upon it. Indeed, they seek to broaden the scope of its importance. No longer can we confine its applicability exclusively to war's effect on human life, culture, or property. The principle of proportionality must now be considered within the context of the integrity of creation, a concept that has been defined in the following way: "The value of all creatures in and for themselves, for one another, and for God, and their interconnectedness in a diverse whole that has unique value for God, together constitute the integrity of creation."[12] This interconnectedness has led us to see that the question forced upon us by the reality of war is not simply a matter of the value of human life. Rather, it is a matter of all life as we know it, for to disrupt our own environment is to threaten the entire ecosystem of which we are a part.

The integrity of creation is not one issue among many. It is fundamental to all issues. Science and technology have sometimes led us to believe that we can step outside of our environment to examine it and control it. It is important to remember that we do not merely live within our environment as we live within a building. We may be a unique dimension of the natural world, but we are not separate from it. We are part of it, and it is part of us. The world flows through us as breath and blood and food. We are not disinterested bystanders but participants in the wondrous workings of nature. We did not weave the web of life; we are strands within it. We may be able to discover and direct the laws of nature, but we are still

---

11 Cf. James A. Nash, *Loving Nature*, 219 ff.
12 C. Birch, W. Eakin, and J. B. McDaniel, eds., *Liberating Life* (Maryknoll, N.Y.: Orbis Books, 1990), 277.

subject to them. We may be able to control these laws, but we cannot significantly alter them. What we can do (and are doing) is alter the makeup of our own environment, i.e., those conditions, circumstances, and influences surrounding and affecting our physical health and life and the physical health and life of all other creatures that make up our ecosystem. The findings of modern physics and of molecular biology provide us with powerful illustrations of our connectedness with the rest of creation.[13]

Human beings, especially in the West, have been reluctant to consider themselves as part of nature. Often we have preferred an idealistic dualism that separates humanity from the rest of the natural world. Nonetheless, humankind is embedded in nature, in the very creative matrix that has given life and continues to give life to new forms of genetic codes and, therefore, to new species and their individual members through what is called "natural selection." Nature is also embedded in human beings. "We are truly children of the universe, made of the same stuff as are the mountains and the rain, the sand and the stars. We are governed by the laws of life and growth and death as are the birds and the fish and the grass of the field. We thrive in the warmth and through the agency of the sun as does every other living thing. We come from the earth as from a mother, and we are nourished from this same source of life."[14]

The prevailing Western paradigm has typically viewed human beings as subjects standing outside of and dominant over nature as objectified. However, modern science demonstrates what traditional people have long believed: humankind is organically interconnected with nature's processes. It refocuses our perspective, enabling us to realize that the theme of liberation can be applied to questions dealing not only with the human family, but also with all life forms and, indeed, with the earth itself. As Western people begin to acknowledge this concept, they realize that it compels us to link concerns of social justice with concerns of ecological sustainability. These are not alternative human concerns and they should not be pitted against each other. In fact, there can be no justice without sustainability and no sustainability without justice.

In this vein, our kinship with the rest of the natural world challenges us to explore the implications of the principle of proportionality relative to the viability of contemporary armed conflict, broadening the context of

---

13 L. Prigogine and I. Stengers, *Order Out of Chaos: Man's New Dialogue with Nature* (New York: Bantam Books, 1984); Arthur Peacocke, *God and the New Biology* (London: J. M. Dent, 1986); Stephen W. Hawking, *A Brief History of Time* (New York: Doubleday, 1988).

14 Dianne Bergant, *The World Is a Prayerful Place* (Collegeville, Minn.: Liturgical Press, 1992, reprint edition), 28.

consideration from one that is merely anthropocentric to one that is more biocentric or geocentric.

Anthropocentrism and Biblical Interpretation

Traditionally the worldview of Christian believers has been shaped by a form of anthropocentrism. Critics of this point of view, prominent among them Lynn White,[15] blame the Christian perspective, or an exaggeration of it, for much of the turmoil in contemporary society as well as for the current and pressing global environmental crises. On the other hand, its supporters assert that an anthropocentric bias can be validated by the biblical tradition, specifically the Genesis 1 creation narrative where the first man and woman are given the commission to subdue the earth and have dominion over the rest of creation. According to this view, humankind was not only the culmination of creation but also its goal. It is easy to understand how human beings imbued with such a worldview and biblical understanding might be prompted to exploit the natural world in order to accomplish their own goals.

Insights from contemporary interpretive theory along with current readings of several biblical texts raise a number of questions that challenge the soundness of such an anthropocentric viewpoint and, consequently, any argument based on it. In the first place, contemporary interpretive theory has helped us to realize that we ourselves do not come to the text with value-free objectivity but rather with a certain assumptive worldview. Following on this insight, we must ask: Is it possible that an anthropocentric type of worldview has been imposed by the biblical reader rather than implied by the biblical author? It may well be that the literary structure of Genesis 1, fashioned to make a point totally unrelated to ecological issues, lent itself to a Platonic hierarchical interpretation, an interpretation that has been passed down to us.

Historical-critical analysis has provided us with insights not only into the meaning of the text but also into the function that the particular tradition may have performed within an ancient community quite different from our own. It further serves to differentiate, when appropriate, between the focus of a particular passage (e.g., theocentric, ethnocentric, cosmocentric) and the underlying or more fundamental worldview of the socie-

---

15 Lynn White, "The Religious Roots of Our Ecological Crisis," *Science*, vol. 155 (1967), 1203-1207.

ties that produced the text and transmitted it through the ages. Thus we can ask: Could it be that a text's apparent anthropocentric emphasis simply marks the limitations of historical culture and really serves a theological or social rather than some ontological end? For example, might the striking hostility toward natural forces, as described in some biblical texts, actually be a monotheistic polemic against nature deities that might have been thought to rival the sovereignty of YHWH, rather than against the forces of nature as we have come to know them? Likewise, is it possible that what appears to be an anthropocentric bias might instead be an ethnocentric argument or a defense of some prominent social stratification? (The present study will demonstrate that, indeed, this is often the case.)

To question Israel's presumed anthropocentrism is not to deny the obvious fact that the ancients viewed humankind as privileged among the other creatures. At issue is not humankind's prominent place in creation, but the meaning of the charges given to it in the accounts. There we read that human beings were told to "subdue, have dominion over" (Gn 1:28), "serve and guard" (Gn 2:15) the world and the living things within it. Such a directive certainly places them in a position of privilege and control. This view of humankind is in sharp contrast to Mesopotamian myths which portray human beings as created to bear the yoke of the gods, ministering to them, and relieving them of the burden of daily work.[16] In Israel's myths, human beings are detached from the life of the gods in the realm of the divine, and are occupied with human concerns, exercising authority and control in the world of men and women. Despite this obvious privilege, such an anthropocentric inclination does not mean that humankind should be regarded as the pinnacle for which everything else was made, in terms of which everything else is measured, and toward which everything else progresses to fulfillment.

The Integrity of Creation in the Priestly Tradition

Most interpreters contend that the Bible displays a fundamentally theocentric (God-centered) perspective within which the principal value of creation lies less in its usefulness to humans (instrumental value) than in the fact of its existence from God (intrinsic value). No one would deny

---

16 S. G. F. Brandon, *Creation Legends of the Ancient Near East* (London: Hodder and Stoughton, 1963), 115.

that creaturely limitations make it impossible for us to measure reality from anything but a human point of view. However, it is quite another matter to maintain that humankind is itself the actual measure of everything. The intrinsic value of all creatures is presumed in biblical passages such as the creation narratives (Gn 1-3), the account of the Noachic covenant (Gn 9), the YHWH Speeches (Job 38-41), and various other poetic sections (e.g., Ps 104, Eccl 3:1-9, etc.). There we see that the world has not been created merely for human use. The Bible is very clear on this point. The man and the woman may have been told "to subdue and have dominion" (Gn 1:26, 28), "to serve it and to guard it" (Gn 2:15), but the primary relationship they have with the rest of creation is less mechanistic than it is organic. New readings of biblical material demonstrate this.

The first chapters of the Book of Genesis contain two separate and very distinct accounts of creation. Although they originate from different times in Israel's history and convey distinct theological perspectives, they both embrace an anthropological perspective that is organic and an understanding of human privilege that bespeaks ecological responsibility rather than rapacious domination. In the first account (Gn 1:1-2:4a), the structure of the section describing the creation and blessing of living beings (Gn 1:24-28) suggests that the verses reporting human creation (vv. 26-27) were originally an independent motif,[17] which disrupts one of the literary patterns of the unit. In the description of the creation of water animals and birds of the air, three divine actions are mentioned: "God said ... God created ... and God blessed" (vv. 20-22). The blessing, "Be fertile and multiply and fill the water ... and ... the earth," is a blessing upon the animals to populate their respective habitats. Part of this pattern is repeated in the description of the creation of the land animals: "God said .. . God made" (vv. 24-25). There is no mention of a blessing. The report of the creation of humankind (vv. 26-27) follows the initial pattern. As the text stands, the blessing that may have originally belonged to the land animals: "God blessed them ... Be fertile and multiply and fill the earth," has been expanded to include a directive that is addressed to the human beings: "subdue it; and have dominion" (v. 28). The added directive does indeed point to human privilege, but the incorporation of human creation at this point in the account links humankind with the other land animals.

A second pattern confirms this link. Eight distinct acts of creation (light, firmament, earth, vegetation, heavenly lights, birds and fish, land animals, and humankind) are accomplished in six days, one each day with the exception of the third and the sixth days when two creative works are accomplished. The acts of the last three days correspond to the acts of the first three days:

---

17 Clauss Westermann, *Genesis 1-11: A Commentary* (Minneapolis, Minn.: Augsburg Publishing House, 1984), 22 ff.

day 1: light	day 4: heavenly lights
day 2: firmament separating the waters	day 5: birds that fly across the firmament, fish that swim in the waters
day 3: earth & vegetation	day 6: land animals & humankind

This pattern shows that just as the firmament controls the habitats of both the birds and the fish, so is the earth the habitat of both land animals and humankind. The order described within this passage and the literary symmetry of the verses themselves also prepare the reader for the report of the establishment of the day of rest (2:2f), the real culmination of creation. An understandable anthropocentric interest in the creation of humankind has too frequently resulted in a misreading of the importance of this rest. It must be noted that this is not yet the Sabbath. It is not the rest of humankind; it is the rest of God.

Commonality notwithstanding, there are other literary features that make the creation of humankind distinctive. The verb forms are different. The cohortative, "Let us make" (v. 26), which expresses self-deliberation or consultation is used rather than the jussive, "Let the water teem . . . Let the earth bring forth" (vv. 20; 24), which expresses direction. Also, humans are made "in our image, after our likeness" (v. 26) rather than "according to (their) kind" (vv. 21; 24f). Such a break in poetic structure and such peculiarity in literary style were ways of calling attention to something in the narrative, in this case, the distinctiveness of humankind.

Although they are closely associated with the land animals with which they share the same habitat, an affinity not to be ignored, only the human couple is made in the image/likeness of God. This motif carries clear royal connotations. Royalty were often considered human images of the deity. There are Mesopotamian myths that tell of a god forming a mental image and then creating another god according to that image.[18] Israel reinterpreted this theme by characterizing its monarch as a human creature rather than a deity, but still as an image of the god. In this narrative, the human couple alone is given the directive to "subdue" and "have dominion" (v. 28), unquestionably a royal prerogative. Being made in the image of God, Israel's king was referred to as the 'son of the god' (cf. 2 Sm 7:14; Ps 2:7), ruling in the land and over the land in the place of the god.[19]

It is important to remember that the image was not the deity, but was a representation of the sovereignty of the deity, designating the locale and extent of its rule. Accordingly, it would seem that this kind of royal authority was provisional and contingent on the good will of the god.[20] This account

---

18 Samuel Noah Kramer, *History Begins at Sumer* (Garden City, N.Y.: Doubleday [Anchor Books], 1959), 109.

19 Aage Bentzen, *King and Messiah* (London: Lutterworth Press, 1955), 43.

of the creation of humankind suggests that Israel's royal tradition resembles that of the Mesopotamians, who regarded royal rule as a necessary remedy for social turmoil, rather than that of the Egyptians, who viewed royalty as an inherent component of the structure of the world. In other words, in Israel's tradition, human privilege is more a social convention than it is a cosmic determination.

This brief analysis shows that the Israelite worldview underlying the Priestly account of creation was clearly theocentric, not anthropocentric. Any reading of the narrative that would suggest autonomous human sovereignty or absolute dominion overlooks the implications of Israel's royal theology. The monarchy, represented here by primeval humankind, was entrusted with God's world to manage its riches and to foster the forces of life within it, not to ravage it in order to accomplish mere human goals. This short explanation of the Priestly creation account emphasizes its teaching on both humankind's affinity with and distinctness from the rest of creation. It demonstrates that the anthropocentric focus is really an argument in defense of the privilege and responsibility of the social institution of the monarchy, not merely the superiority among creatures of the human couple. Thus, this account should no longer be used to justify environmental indifference, much less exploitation.

Scholars have long recognized the thematic unity of Genesis 1-11. However, only recently have some pointed out a deliberate literary structure behind the arrangement of the various stories in the collection.[21] This structure reveals a parallel between the creation account and the story of the flood, and it strengthens the already accepted contentions that the two narratives not only come from the same theological source but should be understood in relation to each other.

In the traditions of many early civilizations, the creation narrative was actually an account of a primeval flood and the individual saved from this destructive deluge was the first created human being. Therefore, both creation and flood were viewed as primeval happenings, not as historical events. Scholars currently agree that the Priestly narrative of the flood and the eventual recession of the waters (Gn 7-9) is another creation story highlighting much of the same theology found in Genesis 1 and containing some of the same vocabulary. The abyss (t^ehôm), that was in place before God separated the waters (1:2), is what burst open causing the flood (7:11) and was closed when God decreed the flood's end (8:2). Both narratives mention a wind (*rûah*) that swept over the cosmic abyss (1:1; 8:1) and a blessing of fertility (1:22; 8:17). In both passages, the blessing includes a

---

20 Cf. Douglas John Hall, *The Steward: A Biblical Symbol Come of Age* (Grand Rapids, Mich.: Eerdmans, 1990).

21 Gary A. Rendsburg, *The Redaction of Genesis* (Winona Lake, Ind.: Eisenbrauns, 1986), 8, no. 2.

directive to rule over the animals (1:28; 9:1-2). In addition to these literary correspondences, both passages allude to the organic relationship that exists between humankind and the rest of creation. In the flood narrative, this is evident in the account of the covenant.

Much has been written about the covenant that God made with Noah (9:8-17).[22] Actually, this was not merely a pact made with human beings and through them with the rest of creation. It was made directly between God and the earth (vv. 13,16), between God and all living beings (vv. 9-10,12,15,17). It was, in fact, a promise that chaotic waters would never again return to destroy creation. The bow in the sky was an eternal sign of that promise. Within a creation/flood tradition, the battle was not between human beings and chaotic forces within nature; it was between YHWH, the Creator-God, and the forces of primeval chaos. The bow was probably more than a colorful arc in the sky. Most likely, it represented the weapon of the divine warrior, who was victorious over mythological forces. This interpretation is supported by several Mesopotamian artifacts depicting the arrows in the creator-god's quiver as lightning bolts. Hanging the bow in the sky was then a sign that the primeval war was over, the victory had been won, and all of creation could rest secure. Like the divine rest after creation (Gn 2:2-3), hanging up the bow heralded the establishment of *shlôm*.

The significance of the theology contained in this account cannot be overestimated. It is a clear example of the tradition's recognition of the intrinsic value of all creation and the interconnection between humankind and the rest of nature. The covenant with its promise of *shlôm* was made with all of creation, not merely with humankind in the person of Noah. Humankind may enjoy a position of privilege, but this privilege is exercised as an integral part of an interrelated and interdependent organic universe.

Literary studies have shown a correlation between the account of the creation and appointment of the world (Gn 1:1-2:4a) and the construction and appointment of the wilderness sanctuary (Ex 39:42-40:33).[23] This point is further borne out by the fact that both the creation narrative and the list of stipulations regarding the sanctuary end with reference to rest on the seventh day, the sign of completion (Gn 2:2-3; Ex 31:12-17). Characteristically, rest signifies the conclusion of creation. It implies that the order established by the deity is permanent and will not be disturbed by another creative act. By giving liturgical meaning to this rest, the Priestly writer accomplished two different but related goals: a day of rest was taken

---

22 Charles S. McCoy, "Creations and Covenant: A Comprehensive Vision for Environmental Ethics" in *Covenant for a New Creation: Ethics, Religion and Public Policy*, 212-225.

23 Cf. Joseph Blenkinsopp, "The Structure of P," *Catholic Biblical Quarterly*, vol. 38 (1976), 275-292.

out of the primeval realm; and the Sabbath was invested with cosmic significance.

Similarities between creation and the sanctuary do not end here. The wilderness sanctuary shares many characteristics with the ark of Noah; both were constructed according to divine specifications. Furthermore, after the flood, the restored earth emerged on the first day of the liturgical year, the same day on which the sanctuary was established and consecrated (Gn 8:13; Ex 40:2).

The parallels between the accounts of creation and the flood on the one hand and the construction of the sanctuary on the other suggest that the Priestly version of the primeval happenings (creation and flood) both point to and are subordinate to the historical building of the sanctuary. If this is true, then it was the construction of the sanctuary and not the creation of humankind which was the real climax of creation.[24] Such a conclusion appears quite reasonable when one remembers that the Priestly writers probably had witnessed the demise of the monarchy, and consequently promoted the importance of cultic observance as a real source of the regeneration of the exiled community. Thus, in this tradition, humankind is not the pinnacle for which everything else was made, in terms of which everything else is measured, and toward which everything else progresses to fulfillment. What appears to be anthropocentrism (human privilege accorded the first couple) is really sociopolitical hierarchy (royal primacy). Furthermore, even this apparent social preeminence is subordinate to the importance of the sanctuary. Thus the real significance of the narrative is ethnocentric liturgical compliance.

The Integrity of Creation in the Yahwist Tradition

In Genesis 2, the account of human creation is told in a manner quite different from that found in Genesis 1. Here the order of the cosmos is not described, the luminaries have not been set in the heavens, and the human creation is brought into a world depicted as a wilderness. This author proposes a terrestrial focus rather than the celestial one of the Priestly writer. In this account, the importance of the ground cannot be overstated. All of this suggests that the author did not intend that this account be viewed as an explanation of the origin of the world.

---

24 Ibid., 286.

The desolation of the land is due to the lack of rain and the absence of a human being to till (serve) the ground. Without moisture and human toil, the earth cannot bring forth vegetation (2:5). The rain, so necessary for life, is supplied by God alone. It seems, however, that the earth is incomplete without someone to work the land and, thereby, enable the herbs of the field to sprout forth. The word that expresses this working is *bad*, which also means 'to serve' and which implies a certain like of relationship. The tiller of the ground either is the servant of the ground itself, or is a servant of another, working the ground for that other. The admonitions within the text are evidence that the human creature is serving God by serving the ground. It is also clear that the fertility of the ground is dependent on human and divine collaboration.

Verse 7 is often called the *locus classicus* of ancient Israelite anthropology. After the LORD God caused the mist or spring to come up from the earth and give drink to the ground, the LORD God took some dust from that ground and formed a human creature, as a potter would form a piece of art (cf. Is 29:16; 41:25; 43:1,7; 45:9,18; Jer 18:4,6). The relationship between the human creature of the ground and the ground itself is clear from the creative act (being formed), from the material that was used (dust from the ground), and from the play on words between *dm* (man or humankind) and *admâ* (ground). The human creature taken from the ground will in turn work the ground that has been watered by God. Only then will the herbs of the field be able to sprout forth. Later in the narrative we read that the trees (v. 9) and the beasts of the field (v. 19) are brought forth from this same ground. As was the case in the first creation tradition, here too the human beings have both a direct affinity with the rest of creation and a duty toward it. In the Priestly account, humankind was charged with the administration of the earth. Here it is responsible for its fruitfulness.

Though made of the ground, this human creature is not yet a living being. Only by means of a second creative act is this accomplished. It is when God breathes the breath of life into its nostrils that the creature comes alive. This does not mean that the other creatures lack the breath of life (cf. Eccl 3:19-20). One must remember that these accounts are narrative signs of theological and/or cultural realities and are not to be understood literally. The author has set out to show both the affinity that exists between human beings and other land animals, and the unique character of the former in respect to the latter. The creation of the first human being took two deliberate divine acts; this was a way of showing the special character of this creature.

In the Yahwist account, no life existed before the human creature, and the creature did not live before receiving the breath of life from God. It is clear that God is the source of life, but life comes to the earth through human agency. This theological anthropology could be a polemic against those who might have been tempted to regard a human ruler as an actual divine benefactor. It would serve as a reminder of the humble origins of the monarchy. At the same time, it would underscore the indispensability of human instrumentality in some of the life processes of the earth.

The Integrity of Creation and Proportionality

Reading the creation accounts through an ecologically sensitive lens underscores the need of a new paradigm for understanding reality,[25] a paradigm built on the principles of interrelatedness and interdependence,[26] a paradigm that is both scientifically sound and biblically grounded.[27] This sensitivity does not presume adherence to some form of 'deep ecology' or biotic egalitarianism. Relevant species differences do justify unequal treatment.[28] However, an anthropocentric disregard for the integrity of creation, whether unintentional or deliberate, can no longer be tolerated.

For too long we may have viewed ecologists as single-issue advocates and have dismissed their concerns as those of specialists or extremists. If we have done this, it has been to our detriment, for living in harmony with the natural world is fundamental to living in harmony with each other. We already fight wars over land and/or control of natural resources. If we concentrate on social harmony with little or no regard for ecoharmony, we may soon exhaust the planet's ability to support us. We have no more right to exploit and selfishly manipulate the natural world than we have the right to exploit and manipulate other people. Furthermore, both will retaliate.

Realizing that armed conflict may be the only option open to those intent on defending justice and peace, the principle of proportionality must

---

25 Thomas S. Kuhn, *The Structure of Scientific Revolutions*, 2d ed. (Chicago: University Press, 1970); H. Kung and D. Tracy, eds., *Paradigm Change in Theology* (New York: Crossroad, 1989).

26 Carolyn Merchant, *The Death of Nature* (New York: Harper Collins, 1980); Paul H. Santmire, *The Travail of Nature: The Ambiguous Ecological Promise of Christian Theology* (Minneapolis, Minn.: Fortress, 1985); C. Birch, W. Eakin, and J. B. McDaniel, eds., *Liberating Life* (Maryknoll: Orbis Books, 1990).

27 Ian Bradley, *God Is Green: Ecology for Christians* (New York: Doubleday, 1990); Denis Edwards, *Made From Stardust: Exploring the Place of Human Beings Within Creation* (Victoria, Australia: Collins Dove, 1992).

28 James A. Nash, *Loving Nature*, 173-191.

include some of the following considerations: "First, human technologies should function in an *integral relation with earth technologies* . . . ; second, we must be clear concerning *the order of magnitude* of the changes [that will result] . . . ; third, sustainable progress must be progress for *the entire earth community* . . . ; fourth, our technologies...*need to take care of their waste products* . . . ; fifth, there is need for a *functional cosmology*, a cosmology that will provide the mystique needed for this integral earth-human presence.[29]

If committed Christians disagree over the validity of the use of armed force in defending justice and peace, they will also most likely entertain various views regarding the issue of biotic rights and ecological justice. Still, the consequences of accelerated ecological devastation caused by munitions cannot be ignored. They bid us broaden our understanding of moral norms and redefine the perimeters of our worldview. "At its heart, today's call to peacemaking is a call to conversion, to change our hearts, to reject violence, to love our enemies,"[30] and to cherish our earth.

---

29 Thomas Berry, *The Dream of the Earth* (San Francisco: Sierra Club Books, 1988), 65-67.
30 *The Harvest of Justice Is Sown in Peace*, 20.

Humane Development

The Political Economy of Peace

Charles K. Wilber

Introduction

With the demise of communism in Eastern Europe and the Soviet Union, the major threats to peace are economic conflicts — over internal development strategies and the rules of international trade and finance.

The direct human cost of over one hundred cases of international and civil wars in the underdeveloped countries since World War II has been a terrible addition to the daily burdens of poverty and deprivation. By 1980, more than ten million people had been killed in these conflicts, while many millions more had been maimed or injured.[1]

More than a quarter of a century ago, Pope Paul VI told us: "Development is the new name for peace."[2] More recently Pope John Paul II warned that:

---

1 *The Challenge to the South*. The Report of the South Commission (New York: Oxford University Press, 1990), 53.
2 Paul VI, *Populorum Progressio*, Part IV.

It must not be forgotten that at the root of war there are usually real and serious grievances: injustices suffered, legitimate aspirations frustrated, poverty, and the exploitation of multitudes of desperate people who see no real possibility of improving their lot by peaceful means.[3]

With the end of the Cold War and the discrediting of socialist approaches to development, it is to capitalist development strategies that the former communist countries and underdeveloped nations alike now turn. But contrary to some commentators, there is more than one capitalist road. The simple "shock" therapy of complete free markets that has been recommended for Poland, Russia, and the other former communist countries is not the only possible strategy. In fact, this strategy has almost never been followed in the past, either by developing or developed countries. The history of economic development demonstrates that free markets have always been subjected to intervention and regulation in an attempt to control their destructive tendencies while harnessing their creative forces for a more humane development.

Economic Development in the Postwar Period

Development economics was born after World War II with the acceptance of the inevitability of political, social, and economic change. The problem of the poor countries of Eastern Europe was the genesis of much of the initial work, and then the success in rebuilding Europe and Japan emboldened development economists to extend their work to the rest of the world. Development thought incorporated an optimism that change could be for the better and that conscious reflection on and control over change, often through national governments and international organizations, could harness change and bring about development.

Thus the 1950s and 1960s were marked by an optimism that world poverty could be conquered by economic growth. Since economists assumed that the question of the nature of a good society was already answered, the issue became one of solving certain practical problems. The good society was simply assumed to be an idealized version of the United States economy, that is, a consumer society. The key to a consumer society was growth of per capita income. Thus the vast bulk of the

---

3 John Paul II, *On the Hundredth Anniversary of* Rerum Novarum *(Centesimus Annus)*, papal encyclical (Washington, D.C.: USCC Office for Publishing and Promotion Services, 1991), no. 52.

development literature focused on growth rates as the *deus ex machina* to solve all problems.

The 1970s saw that hope dashed by growing unemployment and inequality and the intractability of absolute poverty in the Third World. However, the 1970s also witnessed the birth of a new optimism to replace the old. The pursuit of "growth with equity" or a strategy of targeting "basic human needs" would succeed where economic growth failed.

The 1980s ushered in a period of greater caution. It became widely recognized that world poverty would not be eliminated with simple economic panaceas. Resource shortages (particularly of energy), environmental destruction, rising protectionism in the industrial world, militarism in the Third World, the international arms race, and the structure of the world economy all made the design of development strategies a complex problem in political economy rather than a simple technical economic issue.

Economists became more aware of the problems created by fast economic growth and slow social change, as well as the difficulty of defining development correctly.[4] Development economics had to learn that "all good things do not go together," that rapid growth and economic development may be accompanied by severe social and political problems such as the loss of deeply felt cultural values, the breakup of community, and the emergence of authoritarian governments.

The 1980s' loss of momentum, of hope in development, and of the courage to proceed stimulated free market economists to attack development economics, attributing slackening development to the interference of government in the normal functioning of the economy, in particular, to distortion of the resource allocation role of prices.

This free market stance gained wide acceptance among economists who worked on Third World countries. In part, this was a reflection of the World Bank's growing role in research on economic development. Unfortunately, the postwar decade of poorest development performance, the 1980s, was the decade the Bank's program was implemented most widely. This was a lost decade for much of the Third World in terms of economic development. For example, GDP per capita actually fell between 1980 and 1988 at an annual average rate of 3.7 percent in Africa, 1.0 percent in Latin America, and 3.4 percent in West Asia. In Southeast and East Asia, it increased by 2.9 percent per year.

Despite the slowdown of the 1980s, much has been accomplished since 1945. There has been rapid growth of GNP throughout the world, infant mortality has decreased dramatically, and life expectancy has in-

---

4 A. K. Sen, "Development: Which Way Now?" *Economic Journal*, 93 (December 1983), 745-62.

creased rapidly; access to education has been extended far beyond what would have been imaginable in 1945.

It is now the last decade of the twentieth century, a time when the old verities are collapsing. The Cold War has ended; the Eastern European countries are moving from centrally-planned economies of the Second World to market-oriented underdeveloped countries of the Third World. Regional and ethnic conflicts are moving to center stage in the international political arena with the most notable examples being the Gulf War in 1991 and the internal conflicts in the old Yugoslavia, in Somalia, and in the republics of the former Soviet Union. The prospects for development may fade even further in Africa, Asia, and Latin America if the industrial countries' development assistance becomes focused on aiding the Eastern European countries.

If one version or another of capitalist development is going to be the means of attaining a better life for most of the peoples of the world, an understanding of capitalist development is essential.

The Nature of Capitalist Development

To understand economic development requires us to realize that an economic system is a human creation. As a human creation, it solves certain problems while causing other ones.

Two facts stand out from an examination of the history of capitalist development. It is undisputed that it has been successful in producing unprecedented amounts of goods and services. It is equally clear that capitalist growth has proceeded unevenly between countries and within regions, creating great disparities of wealth and income, and that it has always proceeded cyclically, through euphoric booms and painful busts in every country and region. This process has extended to individual industries and even households.

One of the great economists of the twentieth century, Joseph Schumpeter captures the positive side of this dynamic process in his concept of "Creative Destruction":

> The fundamental impulse that sets and keeps the capitalist engine in motion comes from the new consumers' goods, the new methods of production or transportation, the new markets, the new forms of industrial organization that capitalist enterprise creates. . . . [These developments] incessantly revolutionize the economic structure *from within*, incessantly destroying the old one, incessantly creating a new one. This process of Creative Destruction is the essential fact about capitalism.[5]

Such a vision is scant solace to workers thrown out of their jobs, farmers facing a collapse of demand for their produce, or towns and villages which progress leaves behind. It is important to understand that the strengths of capitalist development are also its weaknesses.

There are two possible responses to this reality. The first proclaims that there is no alternative to allowing the "natural" laws of the economy to work themselves out. Attempts to reform capitalism will only cause greater harm. The second argues that, in fact, capitalism can be, needs to be, and has been reformed without destroying the creative dynamics of the system.

People always have attempted to subordinate economic forces to their values as embodied in social, religious, and political institutions. During the past 60 years, people have turned ever more to government as the social institution with the task of softening the destructive side of economic forces. The great economic debate in the U.S., and now in much of the developing world, is: Can the destructive side of the capitalist development process be mitigated while doing minimal damage to the creative side?

Since economies are human creations, they can be improved through human action. Many steps to affect the economy can be taken by individuals, and the fulfillment of human needs must be an essential goal of every economy. However, government as a social institution must play an important role. Clearly, not all government actions are effective, but a positive role for government is indeed possible and is the result of a well-functioning democracy. Government can be the instrument wielded by men and women to attenuate the effects of the destructive side of economic development.

However, individual self-interest and government actions alone are inadequate to meet the challenges of a humane development. Single-minded pursuit of self-interest as adulated in free market theory is often detrimental to others and in numerous instances prevents greater gains from occurring. Cooperative behavior elicited through institutions such as credit unions, churches, and neighborhood associations can be fulfilling to the individuals involved, can encourage such behavior on the part of others, and can help in confronting the challenges of developing and running a modern economy.

A successfully developing economy will combine all three types of action. And it will do so to ensure that the economy serves the goals set by the people of that society.

---

5 Joseph A. Schumpeter, *Capitalism, Socialism, and Democracy*, 3d ed. (New York: Harper & Brothers, 1950), 83.

Goals and the Economy

Humane development is a question of *being more* rather than *having more*, of knowing how to live rather than just knowing how to make a living.[6] If this is the case, then it must be realized that there is no single criterion — such as per capita GNP growth — to measure humane development. Rather, success can only be assessed in reference to the needs of the human beings who constitute the economy.

What can be said about indicators of successful performance in fulfilling human needs in a developing economy? Dealing with this problem requires looking at broader psychological studies and at information which is gathered across different societies. Following the work of Denis Goulet,[7] which draws upon cross-cultural studies that attempt to identify basic human needs, three goals can be specified for a humane development strategy.

The first is what Goulet calls "life-sustenance," which corresponds generally to physiological needs or what we call basic material goods. Every society strives to provide its citizens with the basic goods that are necessary for life — adequate food, water, housing, clothing, education, and health care — and an economy is successful if it can provide them.

It is useful to further specify basic material goods. One manner is to differentiate among three types of goods. The first are necessities such as food and water. Within some limits, needs in this realm are clear. The second type of goods are "enhancement goods," which make life more vital, more interesting, more worth living. Examples might be music, various forms of entertainment, some household goods, and so on. The third level of goods involves what are commonly known as luxury goods. Driving a Mercedes instead of a Chevrolet, eating Chataeubriand in a French restaurant instead of cooking a hamburger at home, and wearing a silk shirt instead of cotton are all instances of consuming luxury goods.

All agree that basic needs must be met. Most believe that enhancement goods are worthy of pursuit. There is less accord on luxury goods. The traditional free market development strategy claims that individual wants are unlimited and that luxury goods satisfy wants the same as basic goods. However, reliance on individual consumption demand, in the face of the large income inequalities characteristic of poor countries, means that automobiles will be produced instead of bikes and buses, individual washing machines and dryers for a few instead of laundromats for many, Coca Cola instead of milk.

---

6 See *Populorum Progressio*, Part I.
7 Denis Goulet, *The Cruel Choice: A New Concept in the Theory of Development* (New York: Atheneum, 1971), 241-45.

A second component of societal goals found in most societies is esteem and fellowship. The developing economy should provide a sense of worth, of dignity to its citizens. One's goods can be a measure of societal esteem, but surely there are other important elements. The institutions in which citizens work should support them physically and give them a sense of belonging and of contributing to an important undertaking. Society should have clubs, churches, or other entities which support the individual. If the family is the basic social and economic unit, as is the case most everywhere, the economy should provide support and encourage in families a sense of self-esteem that can help sustain them. Another term for this is fellowship; the economy should promote correct relations among its participants, and to the extent it can, should keep life from being "nasty and brutish," while providing basic material goods to lengthen it.

Even if material economic well-being were at the heart of social success, surely fellowship would be the lifeblood that sustains the community, the cohesion that makes one individual feel a closeness and a unity of purpose with others in that society, whether known personally or not. Consequently, another goal of economic development, in addition to providing for the material needs of its members, must be to encourage the growth of widely shared esteem that yields a life-giving and life-sustaining fellowship.

This implies an element of equity among citizens. No modern society could provide esteem or fellowship which gave minimal income to most of the population, but fabulous wealth to a few families. Equity, of course, does not necessarily mean equality, but it does mean that there be some consensus regarding the justness of the distribution of wealth and income.

The third goal of economic development is freedom. However, freedom is a difficult goal to specify clearly. It obviously does not mean that all individuals may do whatever they wish, for that would be anarchy and the death of society. At its weakest, an increase in freedom means that the range of options open to the individual or the group has increased, that there are more choices available. This has its physical side in choice of goods, but it can also operate in other spheres such as the political or religious.

There are three component parts to the goal of freedom. The first, and the one which is usually at the center of much economic theorizing, is the provision of consumer sovereignty. Individuals should be able to choose the goods that they wish to consume. But, as noted above, if there is great inequality in the distribution of income this can lead to production of many luxury goods while the basic needs of many go unmet.

The second part is worker sovereignty. People must have a choice of jobs, jobs they find meaningful and that enhance their human capacities. There must be mechanisms for finding people's preferences on work and creating the types of jobs required. A variety of mechanisms could satisfy this need: labor mobility among jobs of widely different character, some degree of control by workers over their job situations, or provision of capital resources to laborers to allow them to establish their own undertakings. Whatever the mechanisms, this characteristic is important because work plays an important part in human development.[8]

Third, a society must provide citizen sovereignty, a mechanism to aggregate people's preferences for community. What kind of community do people want? What kind of environment do they want? The concept of citizen sovereignty implies that a way to express preferences and to control communities is provided to the citizen. A number of mechanisms may be found which satisfy this requirement, in addition to normal democratic voting procedures. One way of enhancing citizen sovereignty could be through strengthening local groups for citizen participation in decision making, e.g., parent-teacher organizations, zoning boards, and citizen review boards of economic planning offices and other public agencies. Or perhaps local residents might participate in the operation of local industries in their areas, by electing representatives to firms' boards of directors to minimize the negative aspects of industrial production such as noise and pollution.

The three goals for a humane development strategy — life sustenance, esteem and fellowship, and freedom — seem to characterize all societies and can serve as criteria to examine the nature of humane development. The existence and acceptance of these or some other goals are central to an examination of various approaches to economic development — unless one is content to accept whatever result a free market strategy gives.

Attaining these goals, while dealing with the latent conflicts in the process of economic development, will be possible only if people are willing to cooperate in the difficult adjustments necessary to transform the economy. That requires policies to be developed and implemented at the lowest feasible levels, an embodiment of the principle of subsidiarity.[9]

In the process of development, national institutions can become too large, too uncontrollable, too unresponsive. Modernizing capitalist economies are characterized by largeness of firms and government institutions — what Peter Berger calls megainstitutions.[10] Socialist economies share

---

8 See John Paul II, *Laborum Exercens*, encyclical letter (Washington, D.C.: United States Catholic Conference, 1981).

9 Pius XI, *On Reconstructing the Social Order (Quadragesimo Anno)*, papal encyclical (Washington, D.C.: National Catholic Welfare Conference, 1931), no. 79. Also see *Centesimus Annus*, no. 48.

10 Peter Berger, "In Praise of Particularity: The Concept of Mediating Structures," *Review of Politics* (July 1976).

this same characteristic. Their economic institutions are even larger and more bureaucratized than the ones in capitalist economies.

Development tends to create a fundamental division of social, political, and economic life. Put most simply, the dichotomy is between the megainstitutions and the private life of the individual. People could cope with these megainstitutions if the process did not so deinstitutionalize their private life. People have always found their identity through, and, in turn, impressed their values on, the megainstitutions through what Berger calls "mediating structures." This is where freedom is nurtured and protected, where the counter to bureaucracy lies, where moral values can play a role in resource allocation. However, this interlocking network of mediating institutions — family, church, voluntary association, neighborhood, and subculture — becomes severely weakened during the development process by growth of megainstitutions that take over many of their traditional functions.

Some point to corporations and the market as the dominant factor in the erosion of these instruments of subsidiarity, and look to government for protection and countervailing power. Others point the accusing finger at government itself, exonerating the private sector, and look to individual effort for the source of rejuvenated mediating institutions.

Both approaches are partial and will be unsuccessful. Credit unions, employee stock ownership plans, and neighborhood associations have all been grass-roots responses to the dichotomization of modern life. Thus, economic policy must provide encouragement for the growth of mediating institutions, not-for-profit organizations, private voluntary organizations (PVOs), and nongovernmental organizations (NGOs).

Only if economic behavior is constrained by moral concerns that transcend self-interest, and that call into question that self-fulfilling "myth of self-interest,"[11] can humane development policies be formulated. The next section briefly sketches some aspects of a humane development strategy.

Humane Development Policies

Humane development requires both national policies on the part of developing countries and new international policies by the leading developed countries.

---

11   See Michael J. Himes and Kenneth R. Himes, "The Myth of Self-Interest," *Commonweal* (September 23, 1988), 493-98.

National Policies. In the Third World there is emerging a clearer understanding of both the successes and limitations of past development strategies. There is also a profound disillusionment with the free market policies pressed upon them by the World Bank, the IMF, and the United States.

The countries of the Third World cannot count upon a favorable international environment during the remainder of the 1990s — large amounts of foreign aid, reduced protectionism by the industrial countries, or rapid expansion of world economic growth. Thus, they must rely more on their own efforts and create new strategies of humane development. Such new strategies must be country specific but will need to be guided by similar basic principles if humane development goals are to be achieved.[12] Thus the focus of development must be on food security, health, education, and employment, all of which are essential for enhancing human capabilities.

Development experience since World War II has demonstrated that meeting the basic needs of the people requires a rapidly growing economy, including the rapid expansion of industry and the use of modern technology. However, economic growth by itself does not ensure humane development. The process of growth, including the choice of types of industry and technology, has to be focused on providing employment to raise the income and productivity of the poor and to promote a sustainable use of scarce natural resources and the environment.

The South Commission has insisted on the importance of equitable development:

> Concern for social justice has to be an integral part of genuine development. A fairer distribution of income and productive assets like land is essential as a means of speeding up development and making it sustainable. The development of human resources should similarly be an important concern, as it can simultaneously bring equity and efficiency into the economy. In their measures to enrich the capabilities of their people, the countries of the South should seek to achieve . . . universal primary health care, literacy, and elementary education; a substantial increase in secondary and higher education, and in vocational and technical training; and a slowing down of population growth.[13]

They also point out that humane development needs to be consistent with the evolving culture of the people. While development forces changes in cultural norms, values, and beliefs, it needs to be oriented so that it is not antithetical to the culture of a people but contributes to its internal evolution.

---

12 The following is drawn from *The Challenge to the South*, 79-141.
13 Ibid., 80.

A development strategy based on attaining the lifestyles and consumption patterns of the advanced countries would be clearly inconsistent with humane development. Such a strategy would lead to increased inequalities because high consumption levels could be achieved for only a few and it would lead to a high level of imports and energy use.

A broad-based agricultural program with sustained improvement in the productivity and income of the rural poor is central to achieving food security. A strategy focused on modernizing small and middle-sized farms to achieve food security is the best way for agriculture to contribute to humane development.

A key to carrying out a humane development strategy is increased democratization of political structures and modernization of the state apparatus. Not only should democratic institutions be created and strengthened, but nongovernmental and voluntary organizations should be encouraged to assume responsibility for some of the medical, educational, and social aspects of development. Their ability to mobilize human and financial resources at the grass-roots level should not be overlooked.

Clearly, humane development begins at home. Poor countries must carry the major burden of organizing the development effort. However, advanced countries can ease the burden with appropriate foreign aid and technical assistance, and, most importantly, by reforming the international economic system and their own trade policies.

International Policies. To develop solutions for the international problems facing underdeveloped countries, it must be understood how the world economy differs from a country's domestic economy. In every domestic economy, there is a sovereign power — the central government — that establishes the framework and rules for carrying on economic exchange. In the U.S., for example, the Constitution empowers the federal government to regulate interstate commerce. No state can impose import tariffs on goods produced in other states. The federal government sets minimum wages, environmental regulations, payroll taxes, safety requirements, and so on, that are binding on all of the states.

This is not the case in the world economy. There is no central government to set the rules. Prior to World War I, the hegemonic power of Great Britain set the rules of the international economy. During the interwar years, Great Britain was too weak to do so and the result was chaos in the international economy. After World War II, the Bretton Woods Agreement and the hegemonic power of the United States controlled the world economy. As the Bretton Woods system was abandoned and the power of the U.S. waned, coordination in the international economy was left to unregulated markets. Economic summits have been tried to reestablish international coordination, but it is difficult to reconcile the differing economic interests of the countries involved.

New international agreements are needed if restructuring of the international economy is to be successful and achieved with minimum conflict. The Bretton Woods system deliberately interfered with the workings of international markets. Exchange rates were fixed, resources were to be provided to countries whose investment needs were greater, and countries that ran into international payments difficulties could obtain temporary adjustment loans.

The Bretton Woods system performed relatively well for almost 30 years. The move to organize the world economy on market principles has been far less successful. World economic growth has slowed down, and in many areas of the Third World actually has become negative during the 1980s. Trade imbalances have become extreme. Instability of exchange rates has become endemic in many areas, particularly in Latin America where currency depreciations of two to three hundred percent in a matter of months is not at all uncommon. And the international debt owed by many developing countries can only have a severe constricting effect in years to come.

More stability is needed in the international economy. First of all, the debts of Third World countries need to be dealt with on a basis that will allow them to resume growth. This may require some form of debt forgiveness. The Europeans and especially the Japanese are leading in this area. Next, an attempt must be made to move back to more stable exchange rates by reaching international agreements on ranges of rates and mechanisms to support them. The industrial countries have done this with some success for the dollar, but it should be extended to the currencies of developing countries. The only way this will work is if countries begin to deal with international capital flows, making them less fluid by regulating them and beginning to tax them. The goal of free capital flows is to move capital to where it can contribute most to production. In fact, however, capital moves as much for speculative and financial reasons that often have little to do with productivity.

The interdependent nature of international markets and of the various national economies means that individual policies regarding exchange rates, trade, capital flows, and debt issues will be more effective if set within supranational programs that encourage and coordinate them. Just as it has been necessary for all countries, developed and underdeveloped alike, to introduce various measures to control the workings of their domestic economies for the common good, it is time to extend those measures to the international economy. Countries cannot continue to practice one kind of economics up to their frontiers and another kind beyond them.

The North American Free Trade Agreement (NAFTA) may be the first step toward creating a trading bloc encompassing the whole Western Hemisphere to counter the potential trading blocs centering on the European Economic Community (EEC) and on Japan and the Pacific Rim. If so, these three trading blocs may be able to bring stability to the international economy by negotiating new rules and regulations. That is, each free trade bloc can be given some of the powers necessary to control the destructive processes of capitalist development. Also, having a few blocs negotiating with each other may be easier than under the present system where the most reluctant country sets the pace.

Within such trading blocs, developing countries could have freer access to the domestic markets of the developed countries and, at least potentially, could attract more investment funds for their development needs. Of course, this will not just happen but must be planned as part of the trade agreement. Also, the growth of these trading blocs poses the danger of heightened conflict among them. The point is not that trading blocs *should be* adopted as the solution to international stability; rather that they *are* being put together.

Easier access to the markets of developed countries, more financial assistance and private investment from the developed countries, and increased stability in the international economy — these are the things with which developing countries need help.

Conclusion

Humane development in the Third World and in the former communist countries of Eastern Europe is essential to peace in the world. As the Vatican's Justice and Peace Commission said at the UN Conference on Trade and Development (UNCTAD) VI: " . . . the gulf that separates the standard of living [between rich and poor countries] . . . is still intolerably wide, and is an acute cause of the odium and violence that have characterized the last two decades of human existence. Unless such basic injustices are eliminated or at least alleviated in the short term, world peace becomes an unattainable mirage."[14]

In turn, a strategy that softens the destructive aspects of free market capitalism is essential for humane development. This will require the best efforts of the poor countries themselves *and* the cooperation of the advanced countries to aid them in that project. This is a serious challenge to the peoples of the advanced countries, for as Pope John Paul II has said: " . . . the poor — be they individuals or nations — need to be provided with

---

14 Pontifical Commission of Justice and Peace, *International Economics: Interdependence and Dialogue*, Contributions of the Holy See on the Occasion of UNCTAD VI (Vatican City, 1984), 11.

realistic opportunities. Creating such conditions calls for a concerted worldwide effort to promote development, an effort which also involves sacrificing the positions of income and of power enjoyed by the more developed economies." He goes on to add: "This may mean making important changes in established lifestyles, in order to limit the waste of environmental and human resources, thus enabling every individual and all the peoples of the earth to have a sufficient share of those resources."[15]

This is a challenge that the United States and the other advanced industrial countries must meet if the world is to live in peace and harmony in the twenty-first century.

---

15 *Centesimus Annus*, no. 52.

III.

Global Institutions

Strengthening Global Institutions

Alvaro de Soto

The euphoria at the fall of the Berlin Wall in 1989 was felt perhaps more than anywhere else at the United Nations. It gave rise to hope that, for the first time since the UN Charter was signed in 1945, magnificent feats might be accomplished through international cooperation, and the collective security system as embodied in the Charter would flourish and belatedly fulfill its promise. Signs began to appear that this hope might be realized, as efforts picked up by, in, or through the United Nations to end the war between Iran and Iraq and settle long-festering conflicts fueled by the Cold War in Angola, Cambodia, El Salvador, Mozambique, and Nicaragua. The enthusiasm reached a high pitch when a coalition of states, with the Security Council's authorization, removed Iraq's invading army from Kuwait in an astonishing show of will coupled with the force to impose it.

After the fall of the Berlin Wall and the crumbling of the Soviet Union, the 15-member Security Council gathered for the first time at the Summit, in January 1992, in order to bury the Cold War and to initiate a reflection about the United Nations at a moment of promise. There was talk about the end of history, with the triumph of liberal democracy. The Summit coincided with the end of Javier Pérez de Cuéllar's decade in office as the fifth UN secretary-general and the inauguration of Boutros Boutros-Ghali as the sixth. Expectations were high when the gathered leaders asked Boutros-Ghali to provide his analysis and recommendations on how to strengthen the role of the United Nations, mainly in the fields of preventive diplomacy, peacemaking, and peacekeeping.

The secretary-general presented his report, *An Agenda for Peace*, to the members of the United Nations in June 1992. In it, he presented his vision of what the aims of the United Nations must be:

- To seek to identify, at the earliest possible stage, situations that could produce conflict, and to try through diplomacy to remove the sources of danger before violence results;

- Where conflict erupts, to engage in peacemaking aimed at resolving the issues that have led to conflict;

- Through peacekeeping, to work to preserve peace, however fragile, where fighting has been halted and to assist in implementing agreements achieved by the peacemakers;

- To stand ready to assist in peace-building in its differing contexts: rebuilding the institutions and infrastructures of nations torn by civil war and strife; and building bonds of peaceful mutual benefit among nations formerly at war;

- And, in the largest sense, to address the deepest causes of conflict: economic despair, social injustice, and political oppression. It is possible to discern an increasingly common moral perception that spans the world's nations and peoples, and which is finding expression in international laws, many owing their genesis to the work of this organization.

The secretary-general's recommendations for action drew upon ideas and proposals received from governments, regional agencies, nongovernmental organizations, and institutions and individuals from many countries. The manifest desire of the membership to work together, he said, was a new source of strength in our common endeavor. Success was far from certain, however: "While my report deals with ways to improve the organization's capacity to pursue and preserve peace, it is crucial for member states to bear in mind that the search for improved mechanisms and techniques will be of little significance unless this new spirit of commonality is propelled by *the will to take the hard decisions demanded by this time of opportunity*."

An Agenda for Peace was widely reported on and discussed at the time of its publication and in the months thereafter. It rapidly became the centerpiece of debate on the use of the UN's instrumentalities in the work of peace. The thrust was, as the Security Council requested, to strengthen the capability of the United Nations to discharge its responsibilities in preventive diplomacy, peacemaking — which at the United Nations is a synonym for diplomacy rather than imposition of peace by force — and peacekeeping, to which he added postconflict peace-building, which is the set of actions necessary to prevent recurrence of conflict once fighting has stopped.

The recommendations include a strengthening of the United Nations' capability to learn of impending crises, measures to speed up deployment of military personnel, prompt and full payment of dues by members to shore up the UN's precarious financial situation, identification and ear-marking of troops, logistics, and other facilities to be on call when needed, preventive deployment of military personnel, and tightened coordination of the agencies and programs of the UN system to help in building the peace.

Soon after *An Agenda for Peace*, however, the difficulties associated with applying tried methods to the new challenges which surfaced at the end of the Cold War became apparent. A set of problems which for decades had lain muffled by an authoritarian mantle, including ethnic and religious tensions, fermented once again and led to explosions in the former Yugoslavia and in parts of the former Soviet Union. With the waning of interest of distant powers which had competed during the Cold War, state institutions came under severe strain in Liberia and Somalia and threatened to do so in other African nations, most recently in Rwanda. Virtual implosions occurred, accompanied by massive flows of persons, famine, and huge loss of life. The proliferation of modern weaponry and its increasing deadliness provided fuel for these conflagrations.

Setbacks arose in peace processes under way in Angola, postwar Nicaragua, and even El Salvador. Progress to settle the dispute over the Western Sahara, already slow, seemed to grind to a halt. In a matter of months following the Security Council Summit, the background scenery seemed to cloud over, changing from uniform hope and justified expectation to crisis and danger.

The Growing Challenge

Besides the peace/war problems, issues which have always been around have grown out of proportion. Some of these issues are not formally on the agenda of the UN Security Council since they are not seen as direct threats to international peace and security, which are the council's province.

Populations have increased greatly. The environment is under severe strain. Humanitarian disasters strike the poorer regions of the globe, with a devastating toll in hunger, disease, and death. While some countries of the Third World are finding prosperity, large areas in Africa and even booming Asia are still suffering poverty. Latin America's recovery is deceptive, for it camouflages a huge gap between the rich élites and the poor majorities as well as the fact that close to half of the population remains below the poverty line. Waves of beleaguered people beat at the doors of the industrialized West, which itself is no longer free from problems long thought buried, or from those that grow out of urban decay.

With instant communications and rapid travel, frontiers are not the barriers they used to be. Thus, while these problems may not be on the agenda of the Security Council, they unmistakably represent an unstable, peace-threatening panorama.

Some of these problems are dealt with as part of the vast array of the UN's activities in the fields of law, development, human rights and humanitarian assistance, and the environment, many of which have been the bread and butter of its daily endeavors even through the lean years. There is a pressing need for global problems such as these to be intelligently and efficiently addressed, and the distinction between global, regional, national, and even local problems is increasingly blurred. Progress in these areas can help provide the underpinnings of peace.

Despite the foreboding symptoms, there is a surprising degree of uncertainty, even bafflement, regarding how and whether to enhance international cooperation by using global institutions. Unfortunately, the problems will not go away if ignored or if not properly addressed. Rather, they will make their pressure ever more greatly felt, and build up a compounded debt for our children — if they do not before then lead to direct threats to peace and security requiring military action in defense of international security. While the stark, direct peace/war issues on the Security Council's agenda are the immediate concern, these fundamental questions cannot fail to be part of the reflections of the National Conference of Catholic Bishops as it marks the tenth anniversary of the pastoral letter *The Challenge of Peace*.

To mark this anniversary with such a reflection is a most welcome initiative. It comes at a time when, here and there, a wry, bittersweet nostalgia for the predictability of the Cold War has begun to well up. Some ask whether the 1992 proclamation by the Security Council Summit of a new era, perhaps even a new world order, was premature. Is the United Nations capable of traversing the minefield before it? Do the members of the United Nations want it to do so? Are they prepared to provide it with the necessary means? These are the kinds of questions we face as the Bishops' Conference issues *A Harvest of Justice Is Sown in Peace*, a most timely contribution as the United Nations prepares for its 50th anniversary.

A mere two years after the Security Council Summit, buffeted by concrete challenges that have put it to the test, the United Nations has moved to a crisis of credibility, all the more serious given the zenith of expectations to which it had risen. In light of the pressure for attention and the competition for action, at a time of dwindling resources and a rebirth of isolationism, the United Nations sometimes finds itself in the invidious position of having to choose which challenges it will undertake. There is a strong, perhaps not entirely mistaken, perception that decisions on where to act are being taken because of public pressures, principally in the West, generated by vivid, on-the-spot television images. Whether or not this is true, there are fundamental ethical questions which must be addressed and in which the Church has an important say.

Despite the growing complexity and danger, little reflection seems to be occurring on how to grapple with the challenge. The responsibilities facing the international community, and hence the United Nations and regional organizations, have grown exponentially, with the proliferation of situations pressing, if not actually competing, for the international community's attention. The United Nations and some of the regional organizations are being forced to innovate and experiment, sometimes with little time to ponder carefully the consequences of some of their decisions. They have entered this hazardous new period without having previously taken "the hard decisions demanded by this time of opportunity," as the secretary-general urged in *An Agenda for Peace*.

The Security Council does not seem inclined, indeed may not be suited, to formulate overall policy in the abstract; policy is made case by case. Much huffing and puffing went into bringing down the Berlin Wall, but no thought went into planning the aftermath. Some say that the United Nations is much like a vehicle undergoing repairs while hurtling over rugged terrain at 100 miles per hour. The beleaguered secretary-general is the mechanic, and there does not seem to be anyone handing him the tools and the spare parts to get the job done. Even his bills are not being paid, except by a hardy few.

At the United Nations these days, it is very much life on the edge. It is difficult to open a newspaper without reading six or seven stories which in one way or another concern the United Nations. Some of them, such as Angola and Liberia, are tragic. Others, such as Western Sahara, seem to be at a standstill. South Africa seems to be emerging with great hope from the long night of Apartheid. In Cyprus — one of the oldest peacekeeping operations, a dubious accomplishment — the peacekeeping has been successful, but the peacemaking has not kept pace. Cambodia defied most predictions and successfully held elections that led to the constitution of a coalition government, though the Khmer Rouge have yet to disarm and join the emerging body politic.

In the last two years, the United Nations has taken on a growing number of peacekeeping operations in situations of internal conflict, with all the uncertainties this entails and for which, some argue, it was not designed. Nine out of 18 of the current peacekeeping operations are in internal settings. The Security Council has launched a UN-commanded operation in Somalia under Chapter VII of the Charter, which allows use of force. The mixed blessing of modern communications brought to TV viewers in 1993 confusing images of disarray and horror in Bosnia, Haiti, and Somalia, which seemed to bleed into each other to produce a sensation that the international community was lurching to and fro without a clear idea of where it was heading. In Bosnia, the United Nations, the European Union, and even NATO have until recently been accused of lacking the political will and firmness to stop the conflict. In Haiti, the United Nations and the Organization of American States (OAS) have been criticized as ineffectual. In Somalia, the United Nations has been criticized for overextension and unnecessary use of force. Leaving aside the unfairness of these attacks, the capacity of the existing institutions of the international community to deal with these crises is increasingly being called into question.

Three Operations under the Glare of the Media

Bosnia, Haiti, and Somalia are three cases in which the United Nations has most notoriously been drawn into experimentation and innovation without anything resembling a clear script. While risk and danger go hand in hand with experimentation and innovation, and the United Nations is coming out of these episodes wiser, it has not emerged unscathed.

The UN's involvement in the former Yugoslavia came about without the world organization seeking it. European mechanisms were set up to deal with them but were unable to cope by themselves. The original division of labor between Lord Carrington's European community-sponsored conference, which sought to stop the fighting and solve the underlying issues through negotiation, and the United Nations, which was asked to set up a peacekeeping operation, beginning with Croatia, was not comfortable. By mid-1992, the United Nations found itself being asked to carry out tasks without participating in their design. This problem was to a large extent overcome at the London conference in July 1992 when the United Nations became engaged in leading the negotiation together with the European community.

By that time, however, a new and far more dangerous situation had emerged with the breakup of the Yugoslav state, the recognition of Croatia and its admission to the United Nations (without previously solving the issue of the Serb population in that country), and the breakout of fighting in Bosnia and Herzegovina. The United Nations had originally entered Yugoslavia in a traditional peacekeeping mode, placing lightly armed personnel between combatants who had ceased firing and supervising the withdrawal of soldiers from UN "Protected Areas." This assumed that the belligerent parties would refrain from fighting, withdraw, and cooperate with the peacekeepers. This did not happen; soon the United Nations was overwhelmed as fighting broke out elsewhere, notably in Bosnia and Herzegovina, and the UN force found itself under pressure to take sides and use force. Not only did this add to the contradictions in a mandate that still largely required the troops to function with the consent and cooperation of the parties; equally troubling, the UN force was not provided with the necessary backing to fulfill its mandate, in terms of properly equipped ground troops in sufficient numbers. The United Nations has suffered somewhat from an unavoidably dysfunctional relationship between the UN-EU negotiating effort and the four main mandates of UNPROFOR: peacekeeping in Croatia; protection of humanitarian convoys in Bosnia and Herzegovina; protection of safe areas in Bosnia and Herzegovina; and preventive deployment in the Former Yugoslav Republic of Macedonia.

Nonetheless, a measure of fragile stability has been achieved in Croatia, and the fury of fighting has shifted to Bosnia and Herzegovina. Negotiations continue in Geneva under the auspices of the UN and European Union co-chairmen of the International Conference on the Former Yugoslavia (ICFY), bolstered by a hands-on effort by the U.S. and Russia in early 1994 and the subsequent efforts of the "Contact Group." Contrary to popular belief, much progress has been achieved in the ICFY framework. Building blocks exist which can rapidly be put in place when the combatants are ready to put down their weapons or at least stop firing them.

Another bright spot in this bleak picture was the deployment of a peacekeeping contingent in the Former Yugoslav Republic of Macedonia, along the border with the rump Yugoslavia. This is the first-ever use of peacekeeping as an instrument of preventive diplomacy to deter a spillover of fighting. This follows a proposal contained in *An Agenda for Peace*. A little-known fact about this operation is that a U.S. military contingent participates in it under Nordic command beneath the UN flag.

It took the Sarajevo market massacre of February 5, 1994, and the secretary-general's catalytic action calling upon NATO to define its position, to galvanize the international community into the firm stance which led to the cease-fire in that city. The first-ever use of NATO close air support requested by UNPROFOR to protect its personnel in the besieged Gorazde was a further sign of determination. While the ethnic cleansing and killing have continued for more than two years in Bosnia and Herzegovina, the number of lives saved by humanitarian action through the UN-administered Sarajevo airlift and UNHCR convoys escorted by UNPROFOR may well be in the hundreds of thousands. Cease-fires in Sarajevo and moves toward federal arrangements between the Bosnian government and Bosnian Croats in March 1994 held out hope at last for the beginning of the end, but, as events in Gorazde in April 1994 demonstrated, false dawns continue to be the rule rather than the exception in the former Yugoslavia.

In Somalia, the United Nations was faced with the wrenching combination of interclan strife, massive famine and migrations, food used as a tool for the achievement of power, the collapse of the institutions of the state, and the disappearance of any internal capacity to cope with the ensuing human catastrophe. To compound the problem, the Horn of Africa epitomizes the regions of the world which, with the passing of the Cold War, seem to have lost strategic interest for the major powers. As in the case of the former Yugoslavia, the complex challenges of Somalia confront the United Nations with varied tasks meant to underpin each other but which are sometimes difficult to harmonize: delivery of humanitarian assistance, promotion of political reconciliation, and restoration of security.

The Security Council agreed, with reluctance and somewhat belatedly, to Secretary-General Boutros Boutros-Ghali's proposal for involvement. This took the form of a peacekeeping operation, which presupposed the cooperation of the belligerents. When it came time to deploy the force, however, consent was withheld by one of the parties. Deployment was thus prevented, and the delivery of humanitarian assistance continued to be severely hampered by the action of armed groups which intercepted and used it for their own purpose and profit.

In late November 1992, the secretary-general concluded that the situation was so grave as to require emergency action. It was clear that it would not be possible to feed the hungry while the armed groups ran rampant, and that the basis for a military operation which assumed the consent of the different sectors did not exist, politically or even legally. There was, in effect, no government in Somalia. If the international community was to save Somalia, it would have to be in a position to use force, as necessary, to neutralize and disarm those who were impeding this goal. There was strong support for such action among Somali leaders. For this, the secretary-general told the council, it was necessary to resort to the means provided under Chapter VII of the UN Charter, allowing for enforcement action.

In the wake of the secretary-general's dramatic recommendation to the Security Council, the U.S. government informed him that it would be prepared to spearhead such an operation. This the secretary-general brought to the attention of the council, along with other options. The Council acted promptly to authorize it. Thus UNOSOM stepped aside and deferred to a U.S.-led coalition known as UNITAF — the United Task Force

— which began to deploy by December 9, 1992. In a few months, the operation succeeded by and large in ending the famine and achieving stability in most of Somalia — Mogadishu, the capital, remaining an island of strife amidst a sea of relative calm. In most of the country, schools began to reopen and a semblance of normality appeared to set in. Local and regional structures of government were set up by the Somalis with UN encouragement. Production and exports resumed. UNITAF did not, however, disarm the irregular groups. When it was withdrawn in the spring of 1993, the United Nations had to assume command, for the first time in its history, of an operation under Chapter VII with considerably reduced means, in the field or at headquarters in New York, to carry out its assigned tasks, and in a far larger area than that to which UNITAF had confined its activities. UNITAF had been *authorized* by the Security Council but conducted, much as Desert Storm in January 1991, without any real UN control. UNOSOM II is a UN-commanded operation under a UN flag.

A major incident in Mogadishu in June 1993, in which a large number of Pakistani troops were killed, spurred the Security Council to issue a mandate to UNOSOM II, the successor of UNITAF, to apprehend those responsible with a view to bringing them to justice. This led to very visible actions which caught the attention of the world media and led to the impression that the UN's role in Somalia had totally changed from restoring security, assisting national reconciliation, and delivering humanitarian aid to a purely partisan manhunt. The success achieved in most of Somalia was totally overshadowed by the images of violence in Mogadishu.

The United States had not entirely removed its military presence when UNITAF was withdrawn. Indeed, a formidable logistical support unit remained as part of UNOSOM II. Substantial combat units also stayed, both within the theatre and offshore. These latter units, though not under UN command, participated in some of the actions in the early autumn of 1993 which resulted in significant loss of life of U.S. servicemen and were quickly followed by a clamor for the withdrawal of its military forces, which it did by the end of March 1994.

The U.S. withdrawal coincided with that of the well-equipped military contingents of several other Western powers. There remain, thankfully, a substantial number of troops from developing countries, though in a still uncertain number and decidedly not as well equipped. The mandate of UNOSOM II has been adjusted as a result of the Security Council's most recent decisions. Notwithstanding notable progress under the aegis of the secretary-general's acting special representative to bring together the main warring parties, the fear remains that fighting will resume, as the rearmament of the clans — whose weapons are certainly not manufactured in Somalia — has continued unabated. The secretary-general's preference did not vary, that UNOSOM II should be enabled to carry out disarmament of irregular groups by coercion if necessary. But this view did not prevail, and UNOSOM is now expected to rely on voluntary handover of weapons and to continue to emphasize political reconciliation and the building of basic structures such as a new police force. Meanwhile around 18,000 UN troops, largely from developing countries, remain in Somalia confined mainly to the Mogadishu and Kismayo areas.

The United Nations was drawn into the Haiti crisis because of the deadlock in the efforts to resolve it at the regional level. It had monitored the 1990 elections, which led to the overwhelming victory of Father Jean-Bertrand Aristide, together with the OAS. Following his overthrow in a military coup in September 1991, barely eight months after he took office, the regional machinery for the preservation of democracy was triggered, the *de facto* military authorities were denied international recognition, and voluntary sanctions were decided by the OAS. There ensued an OAS-led diplomatic effort to draw up a formula which would lead to the restoration of democracy. This proved unsuccessful, however, and late in 1992 the UN General Assembly asked the secretary-general to assist in breaking the stalemate. The secretaries-general of the United Nations and the OAS jointly appointed a special envoy to undertake such a mission. The United Nations and the OAS succeeded in persuading the military authorities to accept the deployment in Haiti of an International Civilian Mission (MICIVIH) whose principal purpose was to monitor respect for human rights.

In July 1993, under the auspices of the special envoy of the two secretaries-general, an agreement was reached at Governors Island, New York, between President Aristide, still in exile, and the commander of the armed forces on a series of steps which would lead to the president's return to Haiti. These included the deployment of a technical mission with the purpose of assisting in military reforms and in the formation of a new police body separate from the army. The commander of the armed forces refused to step down as he was committed to do. A ship carrying U.S. and Canadian military personnel failed to dock at Port-au-Prince in the face of a hostile demonstration onshore which remained unchecked by the authorities. The ship's sailing was interpreted by the demonstrators and other Haitian hardliners as a demonstration of lack of seriousness of purpose.

The Security Council subsequently imposed an oil and weapons embargo to press the armed forces to comply with the agreement. This embargo, however, has yet to break the deadlock. Alarming press reports about the deterioration of the human rights situation, the effects of the sanctions on the most deprived sectors of the population, and the persistence of the deadlock have led to an impassioned debate. This debate pits those who would exert even stronger pressure — some even suggest the use of force — to restore democracy and those who feel that the pressure so far hurts only the poorest while leaving intact those in power and their supporters. In July 1994, the Security Council authorized the use of "all means necessary" to facilitate the departure of the *de facto* military authorities. The agreements reached at Governors Island put Haiti within reach of a process which could give its people the first genuine chance of breaking the sad pattern of its recent history with the strong backing of the international community.

Unfortunately, selective press reporting has created a widespread impression that these three experiences — the former Yugoslavia, Somalia, and Haiti — are total failures and that they somehow reveal an ineffectual United Nations. This is a mistaken impression, as witness the hundreds of thousands of lives which have been saved in both Somalia and Yugoslavia; the progress toward pacification and rebuilding of local and regional institutions in most of Somalia, and the ongoing contacts under UN auspices between the leaders of the two principal opponents in the Somali civil strife; and the containment of the fighting to Bosnia in the former Yugoslavia.

Multidisciplinary Operations

In fact, Somalia, Yugoslavia, and Haiti present a deceptive portrait of today's United Nations and its growing role. More illustrative are the new multidisciplinary operations which have revolutionized peacekeeping and made its name somewhat outdated: Namibia, Cambodia, El Salvador, and Mozambique. These ambitious endeavors epitomize a new breed of challenge for the United Nations and the agencies of the UN system. They embrace a wide variety of tasks, far beyond the purely military, including humanitarian assistance, repatriation of refugees, verification of elections and respect for human rights, monitoring of police activities, reform and building of institutions, and other confidence-building measures.

The United Nations oversaw the coming to independence of Namibia in a large and complex civilian-military operation, the first of its kind. The long war in Cambodia was brought to an end through an accord that provided for a large UN operation which included, in addition to its military component, a broad role in the administration of the country as well as the holding of nationwide elections.

El Salvador and Mozambique are showcases of the UN's engagement in post-conflict peace-building as set out in *An Agenda for Peace*. In El Salvador, the United Nations conducted the negotiations which led to peace after a decade-long civil war (peacemaking), oversaw the cease-fire and disarmament arrangements (peacekeeping), and is currently verifying the continued implementation of the peace accords and lending good offices to promote this implementation (post-conflict peace-building). The United Nations also observed the March elections. The peace accords contemplate a vast array of reforms including the confinement of the armed forces to a role of defense against external enemies and the reduction of the army as well as the purge of the officer corps; the creation of a new nationwide civilian police as the sole body responsible for maintaining internal order; a pluralist electoral authority; and a national ombudsman for human rights. An international panel appointed by the secretary-general, the Commission on the Truth, made a number of binding recommendations, which have yet to be implemented, to ensure the reform of the judiciary. The accords also provided for a number of measures for the reintegration of former combatants, including the transfer of land to them and to squatters in the former conflict zones.

The cease-fire in El Salvador unfolded in an exemplary manner: the guerrilla army has turned into a political party, playing a prominent role in the March 1994 elections (which would have been unthinkable a short time ago); and many of the reforms are well advanced. But the time has not yet come to catalogue El Salvador as a full-fledged success story and file it away. Serious delays and distortions have arisen in the implementation of some of the reforms and reintegration measures. The international community needs to remain vigilant to ensure that the causes that led to the conflict are satisfactorily addressed, to put the process irreversibly back on track, and to ensure that a framework for the respect of human rights is solidly in place — one in which atrocities such as the murder of nuns and priests will never again occur.

The United Nations played only a last-minute role in the design of the peace agreement between the government of Mozambique and the guerrilla group RENAMO, which was brokered primarily by the Rome-based Community of Saint Egidio and a handful of African and European governments. But the United Nations is overseeing the implementation of the agreement, including cease-fire arrangements, disarmament of combatants, merger of armies, formation of a new police, return of refugees and displaced persons, transition of RENAMO into a political grouping, and elections scheduled for October 1994. Persistent delays have bedeviled the unfolding of the process. These included slow — through no fault of the United Nations — deployment of troops contributed by member states as part of ONUMOZ, the UN's operation in Mozambique, which left the parties in effect without a safety net for several months. The fact that the cease-fire has held despite these difficulties is a testimony to the political will of the parties to abide by their agreements, and an encouraging sign that it will be possible to hold elections in October 1994.

There is reason to hope that success will be achieved in Mozambique. But, as in the case of El Salvador, success can only be measured over the longer term, once the sectors of society that remained out of the mainstream of national life are properly integrated, and an institutional framework which will ensure that peaceful means are available to redress grievances without taking up arms is solidly in place. This is the challenge of post-conflict peace-building, which it is not possible to do without the continued backing of the international community. It is a challenge in which it is extremely difficult to succeed unless the United Nations as a whole, including the agencies which are part of the UN system but which have grown somewhat apart over the decades, particularly the International Monetary Fund and the World Bank, are able to work in concert.[*]

Setting the Limits

Although the Cold War is over, there is as yet no consensus on how to handle the post-Cold War, or even on what to call the new period, perhaps because the current phase is still transitional. No one seems to speak of a new world order anymore. Notwithstanding the ringing declaration of the January 1992 Security Council Summit, there is still lacking a consensus regarding how central a role the United Nations should play in formulating global policy regarding the decisive problems of the day, let alone in guiding the implementation of policy.

Yet in the post-Cold War era, there is a newfound atmosphere of collegiality between China, France, Russia, the United Kingdom, and the United States — the permanent members of the Security Council. The council is taking up the challenges before it in a dynamic way, strongly asserting its role under the Charter as the primary organ responsible for the maintenance of peace and security. No longer hamstrung by Cold War confrontation, it often takes the initiative without awaiting the secretary-general's lead, which is as it should be but was not until recently.

The Security Council working collegially, as envisaged in the Charter, is all well and good. But in the months that have elapsed since *An Agenda for Peace* was declared, the challenges have sometimes appeared to overwhelm the United Nations — both the secretary-general and the secretariat which he heads as well as the member states which compose its legislative and governing bodies. We seem to suffer from collective perplexity. The fits and starts in action in the former Yugoslavia and in Somalia described earlier, and more recent hesitations in Rwanda, reveal a continuing uncertainty regarding how far nations are prepared to go to uphold the principles and purposes of the UN Charter. Much rhetoric barely conceals a basic reluctance to cross the threshold in terms of commitment of material and other resources, which would permit the

---

[*] For a discussion of the challenges of coordination within the UN system and the dilemmas arising between economic development and peace consolidation, see A. de Soto and G. del Castillo, "Obstacles to Peace-building," *Foreign Policy* 94 (Spring 1994).

United Nations to carry out its manifold tasks. This is hardly surprising in the absence of a clear definition of what member states want the United Nations to do for them. Yet this lack of definition cannot be repaired by the secretary-general; it falls to the member states of the United Nations.

When decisions are taken to venture forth on new operations, the means to back them up sometimes follow far behind. This is reflected in the increasing difficulty in obtaining troop contributions and ensuring that they are properly equipped with the necessary logistical support. It also appears in the sometimes unacceptable delays in deploying personnel as well as the vehicles and communications gear without which they are quite useless. It is felt as well in slow payments of contributions — the United States, for one, is about $1 billion in debt to the United Nations at this writing, a staggering sum in terms of the total annual peacekeeping bill, some $4 billion. In all these problems, the United Nations, which has no standing army or stock of equipment, let alone financial reserves worthy of the name, is at the mercy of the member states.

Is there anything that can be done to move out of this period of uncertainty? Can we seek inspiration in prior moments of historical transition?

The modern era of international organization was almost a century away when European negotiators gathered in Vienna in 1815 in the aftermath of the Napoleonic wars and drew up a new continental map and a new balance of power. When world leaders met at Versailles in 1919 after the end of World War I, they decided to create the League of Nations, the first real global institution with the mandate of preserving peace. While World War II was still raging — partly due to the failure of the League — efforts were launched to establish what became the United Nations with the signing of the Charter at San Francisco in 1945, a more sophisticated arrangement based on the lessons of the League, good and bad, and the carefully wrought vision of the leaders of that day. Indeed, postwar preparations actually began very soon after war broke out.

Today, notwithstanding the mounting pressure and the gravity of the challenges before us, there is no gathering of world leaders foreseen to consider how to face the future. It can be argued that no such need arises since mechanisms which did not exist in 1815, 1919, or 1945 for such collective soul-searching are in place today at the UN General Assembly and the Security Council. It is also said that there is a certain inexorability about historical transitions; that they cannot be foreshortened or accelerated. But are the mechanisms in place appropriate to undertake this assessment and produce the required definitions? Can the international community run the risk of continued drift? Should something be done to precipitate the movement of tectonic plates which may be needed? Can the problems discussed here be kept at bay, and world leaders remain insulated from them?

There is a school of thought according to which the world is edging toward anarchy, even slipping into a new Middle Ages. In parts of the industrialized West there is a siege mentality reminiscent of the Roman Empire: barbarians at the gate. Whether we share these apocalyptic scenarios or not, we should take up the array of challenges which inspires them in a deadly serious and utterly earnest manner, by tightening up the global institutions which, fortunately, we already have in place. Clear guidelines need to be laid down concerning how far states, who are the policymakers for these institutions, wish them to go. If they want to establish limits to the use they want to make of these global institutions, so be it. But they should do so in full awareness of the dangers involved and assuming the responsibility for the consequences. And once they have set those limits, they cannot thereafter drop out in the midst of endeavors which they have undertaken. They must be prepared to stay the course or not engage in such endeavors, lest expectations are unduly dashed and credibility undermined.

States must also "take the hard decisions" needed to better integrate the approach of the disparate institutions of the UN system to problems which cannot readily be fractionated or compartmentalized between them. The strengthening of global institutions must include updating and adjusting the way these institutions interact so that they can jointly meet the needs of tomorrow. Wherever necessary, and most dramatically in the case of the United Nations, they will have to be rescued from their parlous financial state simply by the payment of assessed contributions to them, punctually and in full, a legal obligation under the UN Charter.

The solution is certainly *not* for member states to crawl back into their national shells hoping that these great problems will be avoided. Not only will they not be avoided: they are already here with us. A like-minded grouping such as the G-7, composed of the most powerful industrialized states of the North, would ignore the South at its peril. Indeed, the South is already within it, among the immigrants and in the inner cities of the North (just as most countries of the South have their islands of North within them). There is a basic wrongheadedness and myopia about trying to beat back the problem by strengthening the ramparts around the North. Have we unlearned everything we learned in the last 20 years about the global nature of the challenge? Are we unable to accept the simple corollary that it must be addressed globally?

This does not mean that certain problems cannot be addressed regionally, so long as this is done within the global context in a manner consistent with the universal goals as set out in the UN Charter. Ways are being devised as part of the current experimentation and innovation for the United Nations and regional organizations to act in cooperation. There remains, however, a reluctance to strengthen regional organizations even greater than the reluctance to strengthen global ones. Most regional organizations remain institutionally or financially weak, some both, and the desire of a hard-pressed United Nations, particularly its secretary-general, to leave to regional bodies the solution of problems which can be regionally contained is severely hampered. In most cases where protagonists to disputes are willing to seek outside help, they tend to knock on the UN door.

In the case of the critical and immediate problems which are the main subject of this paper, however, the solutions do not necessarily involve structural change. They require policy decisions, and decisions of policy priority by member states. There is a tendency to blame "the United Nations" or, since it is always easier to apportion blame if there is a person who is a convenient scapegoat, the secretary-general, for going too far, not going far enough, or trying to grab power. But the United Nations is not some sort of autonomous or alien body placed in our midst by agents from outer space. Nor is the secretary-general endowed with the powers he is sometimes accused of misusing. The United Nations is (or perhaps *are* would be more appropriate) the member states who compose it.

It is the UN's member states rather than the secretary-general which must make the fundamental decisions regarding what it is they wish to take on, how far they are prepared to go, and whether they are going to provide the resources — financial, material, and human — to carry out what they do in fact decide to take on. It is no longer possible to differentiate categorically between problems that can be contained within a nation's borders and those likely to produce incalculable spill-over. The position of the secretary-general, whose authority is in the final analysis largely moral, can only be that the United Nations should not discriminate or establish a hierarchy between the crises and challenges which confront it. To borrow from the realm of medicine, the United Nations should be like a public hospital, one that accepts all cases arriving at the emergency or outpatient entrances — with or without proof of insurance or a major credit card. Accepting or rejecting patients in need involves profound ethical decisions which should not be left to the secretary-general. If a *Schindler's List* of those to be saved is to be drawn up, this should be done by the member states.

It is the member states of the United Nations who are called upon to take the hard, vital decisions regarding the strengthening of global institutions, with the United Nations in the central role. And the peoples of the United Nations, in whose name the Charter was enacted, have a distinct say at this trying time. This is the merit and the timeliness of *A Harvest of Justice Is Sown in Peace*.

Global Institutions

Action for the Future

Edward Joseph Perkins

The modern-day global institution is a conflict resolution activist whether it intends to be or is actively conscious of that role. No global institution can lay claim to the term "global" without embracing conflict resolution. As a concept, conflict resolution has been around for some time, but is only of late being accepted as an institutionalized operational tool for international relations. Woodrow Wilson was one of the leaders in conflict resolution. Drawing on Emmanuel Kant's Perpetual Peace, his experience of the devastation wrought by World War I, and theories of public administration, Wilson developed a theory of conflict resolution for nations that would replace armed conflict as a means of redressing perceived or imagined grievances. He applied this theory in envisioning the method of conflict resolution for the League of Nations:

> [a nation] will never go to war without first having done one or another of two things: without either submitting the matter in dispute to arbitration, in which case it promises absolutely to abide by the verdict, or, if it does not care to submit it to arbitration, without submitting it to discussion by the council of the League of Nations, in which case it promises to lay all the documents and all the pertinent facts before that council; it consents that

Editors' Note: The comments herein represent the views of the writer and not necessarily those of the Department of State or the United States Government.

that council shall publish all the documents and all the pertinent facts, so that all the world shall know them; that it shall be allowed six months in which to consider the matter; and that even at the end of six months, if the decision of the council is not acceptable, it will not go to war for three months following the rendering of the decision.[1]

Unfortunately, Wilson's vision of an effective conflict resolution mechanism was not realized through the League.

The United Nations' Charter, especially its vision for the Security Council, was the most ambitious method of conflict resolution arising out of the ruins of World War II. While the United Nations is the preeminent global institution for conflict resolution, regional organizations, such as the Organization of American States and the Organization of African Unity, and nongovernmental organizations, such as the Martin Luther King Center and private relief agencies, can also play an important role in conflict resolution insofar as they can contribute to resolving some of the many problems that affect populations of the world.

A Broad Agenda for Global Institutions

While its purposes may vary widely, an institution must have a reach that touches the lives of populations of the world in a majoritive sense in order to be considered "global." The United Nations is a global institution affecting international politics, peacemaking, peacekeeping, and peace enforcement. Like all global institutions, armed conflict is a key area of concern to the United Nations. But other matters, such as trade, religion, health-delivery systems, food, and low-cost housing, are of equal importance for global institutions concerned with conflict resolution. Development focused on making nonproductive countries productive and tradeworthy also contributes to the resolution of conflicts.

Another matter of concern to global institutions involved in conflict resolution is unemployment — not just people out of work but a social dysfunction of global importance that demands global responses from global institutions. Unemployment, whether due to layoffs, retrenchment, or temporary shutdowns, is a problem that transcends borders. Massive unemployment contributes to conflict because it exacerbates multicultural as well as interstate tensions. This is especially the case when large

---

1 Woodrow Wilson, *Woodrow Wilson's Case for the League of Nations* (Kennikat Press, Port Washington, N.Y., 1923, 1969).

numbers of people are considered useless to society and their experience and talents are no longer valued. No nation can long afford the luxury of large-scale unemployment, either on a temporary or, as is the case in some countries, on a permanent basis.

There is a tendency to attempt to create more institutions to deal with these problems, but that may be unnecessary as we institutionalize the concept of truly "global institutions." As Australian Foreign Minister Gareth Evans notes:

> There is already in place today a substantial framework of levels and structures permeating every facet of international relations. They operate at the global, regional and bilateral level. . . . They cover virtually every field of interstate activity — including diplomatic relations, maritime affairs, international environmental protection, human rights and international trade and communications."[2]

The task is to build on these existing institutions as they take on, as they must, greater responsibility for conflict resolution.

What changes, reforms, or other adjustments must be made to strengthen global institutions and make them relevant for meeting conflict resolution challenges for the future? The United Nations was not always seen by the United States as a useful institution. The Gulf War was a turning point in U.S. support of the United Nations because the United Nations began to work as it was intended. The Security Council worked because the Permanent Five, with U.S.-Russian cooperation, operated as a team. This smallest and most powerful club in the world, with support from the Non-Aligned Movement and the G-77, ensured the passage of appropriate resolutions authorizing a fighting force composed of soldiers from several nations. "Desert Shield" and "Desert Storm" could have been done only under the aegis of the United Nations and specifically the Security Council. The UN's response to the Gulf War shows how the United Nations can play an important role in addressing conflict between states.

The United Nations is needed now more than ever. But current and future problems and challenges cannot be handled by the United Nations alone. The United Nations was never intended to be "all things to all nations"; it was intended to handle issues that could be solved through conflict resolution.

As I have noted elsewhere,[3] the drafters of the UN Charter faced a world far different from today. Hampered by the Cold War superpower competition, the Security Council never worked as it was intended. While

---

2 Gareth Evans, "Cooperating for Peace: The Global Agenda for the 1990s and Beyond."

3 Edward Perkins, "Should the United Nations Have a Standing Army?" *The Georgetown Compass* (Fall 1993).

the United Nations has managed to be relevant in recent years, such relevance is largely accidental and not planned. Recent UN involvement in several countries has met with mixed success. There are many reasons for this ineffectiveness, but two are particularly important. First, the United Nations is unable psychologically to take on the role of peacemaker and peace enforcer. Second, the UN Secretariat has yet to structure itself so that it can manage peacemaking, peace enforcement, and peacekeeping forces efficiently. For example, the system for supply and maintenance of a large military force — including intelligence gathering, analysis, and deployment — are just now being addressed. As a result, both the Security Council and the secretariat are overloaded.

Improvements in the United Nations, while essential, are by no means sufficient. In addition, other global institutions must be recognized as permanent players in conflict resolution. For example, religious bodies are global organizations that can and do play important roles in conflict resolution broadly understood. The work of religious organizations in addressing such problems as religious conflict, world hunger, refugees, inadequate health care, and other causes of conflict is an indispensable form of conflict resolution. These religious bodies should seek to remove any existing impediments, whether internal or external, that limit their ability to become more effective in conflict resolution.

The work of the Islamic Conference at the United Nations is another example of nontraditional conflict resolution by religious-affiliated institutions. As the Permanent Five of the Security Council sought some way out of the Bosnia situation, it found that increased contact with conference members and the conference chairman made the job of sorting out what would be useful approaches much easier, although no solution was or has been found.

The role of regional organizations is also important in conflict resolution from peacemaking to peacekeeping, as UN Secretary-General Boutros Boutros-Ghali has pointed out.[4] In fact, the secretary-general has suggested that regional organizations should take the first step in solving armed conflicts, with the support of the United Nations. This has not always worked, but the concept fits the purpose of the major regional organizations. The Organization of American States in Haiti; the Organization of African Unity in Angola; and the European Union, NATO, and the Conference on Security and Cooperation in the Balkans, are now being asked to play a decisive role in conflict resolution.

The fact of economic and other forms of interdependence and the broad agenda of regional organizations mean that regional organizations

---

4 Boutros Boutros-Ghali, *Agenda for Peace: Preventive Diplomacy, Peacemaking and Peacekeeping* (Report of the UN Secretary-General, 47th General Assembly, 1992).

cannot help but be drawn together in common pursuits that often extend beyond purely regional concerns. The question is whether they will encourage or hinder global collaboration. That will depend on their view of their collective interests. These organizations should work together more on common interests of a global nature rather than look only to their regional role.

Trade is the regional and global concern that may offer the most important common interest that can bring nations together in peaceful coexistence. Until recently, trade was more or less subordinated to security concerns. As trade comes to play a more prominent role, its beneficial effect on conflict resolution will increase. The means to resolve trade conflicts embodied in the North American Free Trade Agreement (NAFTA), the European Union, APEC, and other regional agreements (not to mention GATT) are especially useful because they codify agreed principles governing trade, they deepen economic cooperation between nations and they allow for more transparent trading patterns. In the future, these regional trading blocs will be the basis for interregional and global economic cooperation.

New Roles of Global Institutions: Integration and Synthesis

Armed conflicts, trade wars, trade development, religious conflicts, refugees, hunger, and lack of even the most rudimentary health delivery systems are the issues that dominate the international agenda. Each has the potential to upset the precarious balance of peaceful coexistence at any time. Global institutions can address these and other sources of conflict and instability only if they are strengthened considerably. The United Nations does well with what it has to work with, but if it is to avoid a disorderly and dysfunctional triage approach to these issues, member states will have to insist on the kinds of changes recommended in the secretary-general's 1992 report, *An Agenda for Peace*. This includes developing an on-call military force, more efficient procedures for allocating resources, changes in personnel practices, and better funding. The UN will also need the support of its member nations not only to meet peacekeeping challenges, but also to address economic, trade, and political issues.

Strengthening global institutions must begin with a new and enlarged vision of the world, which should include the following elements:

- Communications technology will play an influential role in the new institution building. Global institutions must give it the highest priority. It is now possible for blocks of information to reach large populations across borders at lower and lower costs. Similarly, governments are now able to use increasingly simplified and less costly communications to reach — and sometimes manipulate — their populations. Global institutions will be much more effective in conflict resolution if they understand the technological changes which make communications technology an invaluable tool in addressing a host of problems they face.

- Political and public administration theories constitute an essential core of conflict resolution. Global institutions will be strengthened immeasurably by a healthy understanding, acceptance, and development of theories of government that can transcend cultures and borders and reflect changing realities. For starters, one could envision a different paradigm for political arrangements (including governmental structures) that would consider and tolerate religious ethics and would incorporate theories of justice and public welfare that clarify the responsibility of the state in meeting the basic needs of its citizens. New theories also should embrace the tenets of the UN Commission on Sustainable Development, the Framework Convention on Climate Change, and other new approaches arising out of the 1992 Rio Summit. Finally and most important, new theories must have people and their ability to make a difference as their central focus. The range is unlimited, but global institutions rather than theoreticians are probably in the best position to embrace those new concepts that will lead to a considerable shift in paradigms.

- Regional integration is essential in order to improve cooperation among regional organizations themselves, and between regional organizations and the United Nations and other global entities. This kind of cooperation will be enhanced if regional organizations can develop an expanded vision of their role, a vision that would embrace trade, economics, hunger, and agriculture.

- Economics and trade have come to play a useful role in achieving a peaceful world community. Economics, both in theory and practice, will be preeminent in the future. Heretofore laggard economies and weak countries are changing fast. Perhaps the best example is China, which could become an economic giant surpassing the United States in the next few years. As trade becomes more important, it is imperative that global and regional institutions be competent to address trade and economic issues.

- Citizenship. It would be appropriate for global institutions to adopt a theory of citizenship as part of a broader theory of conflict resolution. Citizenship is ordinarily thought of as a state of entitlements and obligations which constitutes an essential part of the strength of a nation. An evolving notion of citizenship could play a similar function for global institutions.

If these elements are taken into account, global institutions may well become the effective means of conflict resolution that they were intended to be.

IV.

The Use of Force after the Cold War

Ethical Dilemmas in the Use of Force in the Post-Cold War World[1]

George A. Lopez

In 1983, amidst an escalation of tensions between the United States and the former Soviet Union and of the nuclear arms race, the U.S. Catholic bishops sought to interject a series of ethical concerns into the public discussion of these trends. History shows that their pastoral letter, *The Challenge of Peace*, made a major contribution to the democratization and humanization of the nuclear debate at that time.[2]

---

1 Many of the ideas contained in this chapter and some of the material used are drawn from George A. Lopez and Michael Stohl, "The Ethical Dimensions of 'the Changing Use of Force,'" and in George A. Lopez and Drew Christiansen, SJ, eds., *Morals and Might: Ethics and the Use of Force in Modern International Affairs* (Boulder, Co.: Westview Press, 1994), 29-42.
2 Of the many sources available to support this claim, the most helpful may be Bruce Russett, *The Prisoners of Insecurity* (New York: W. H. Freeman, 1983); Jim Castelli, *The Bishops and the Bomb: Waging Peace in the Nuclear Age* (Garden City, N.Y.: Doubleday, 1983); Freeman Dyson, *Weapons and Hope* (N.Y.: Harper & Row, 1984); Russell Hardin, et al., eds., *Nuclear Deterrence:*

More than a decade later, the varied patterns and lethality of "the use of force short of war" may warrant a similar and serious ethical scrutiny. Formed as part of Cold War strategy and praxis, mimicked by states at the second and third tiers of power, and now left as "acceptable" uses of force in a post-Cold War environment, the repertoire of state violence has become quite diverse. Ours is a world in which coercive diplomacy, either in the form of direct military intervention by one state into the boundaries and affairs of another, or in the increasingly popular (and some would claim palatable) enforcement of economic sanctions, operates alongside low-intensity war, devastating civil wars within states, *and* conventional war between states. The resulting death and destruction have reached such massive proportions that such a world appears no less in need of a moral voice to comment on such violence than the nuclear era of the previous decade.

In this chapter, I briefly detail the changing character of global violence in a summary fashion and via reference to coercive diplomacy and low-intensity war in their most general forms. Then I will discuss three explanations for why these patterns in the use of force have emerged. In the final section, I will delineate the ethical dilemmas that these new forms of state violence pose for those concerned about placing moral constraints on the use of force by states.

The Changing Character of Global Violence

For most of the post-World War II era, when ruling elites opted to use force against another state, this decision entailed (1) the deploying of the national armed forces in substantial numbers; (2) engaging in direct and often prolonged hostilities; and (3) the preoccupation of much of a government's policy agenda, if not the attention of the greater society, with the confrontation. Although a rather small number of forceful actions of states continue to necessitate one or more of these conditions, as in the Persian Gulf War, the majority of "use of force situations" seldom demands

---

Ethics and Strategy (Chicago, Illinois: University of Chicago Press, 1985); Joseph Nye, et al., *Living With Nuclear Weapons* (Bantam Books, 1983); John E. Keegan, "Freezing the 'Challenge of Peace,'" *Cross Currents* (Summer/Fall 1987), 254-270; Patricia MacNeal, *Harder Than War: Catholic Peacemaking in the Twentieth Century* (New Brunswick, N.J.: Rutgers University Press, 1992), especially 249-258; and David Cortright, *Peace Works: The Citizen's Role in Ending the Cold War* (Boulder, Co.: Westview Press, 1994), especially 40-60.

any one of these to a pronounced degree. Almost never do they involve all three.

Rather, in recent times the use of force by nations has been characterized by a number of distinct and mutually reinforcing behaviors that have altered both the message sent via resort to force and the means of its delivery. Economic, political, and military measures are mixed with varying levels of "war mobilization" to accomplish specific foreign policy goals. Working within the classic tradition of Thomas Schelling and the thinking that guided much of the nuclear diplomacy of the Cold War, states have engaged in an escalation of violence which employs force just short of full-scale war.[3] Such measures have come to include coercive diplomacy, low-intensity war, the use of surrogate forces, covert action, and even forms of state terrorism.[4]

These forms of state violence have developed quite gradually over the past three decades and often were obscured by the dynamics of the Cold War. Now, in the demise of this era, we can recognize them in the historical record of the behavior of the two superpowers, especially in their action in "third areas" where they competed for resources and allegiance.[5] At the same time, other powerful states, such as France and Great Britain, and major second-level states, such as Israel, India, and South Africa, also engaged in these practices.[6] More unpredictable in their use of such violence have been a number of other states, especially Arab states in the Middle East. To illustrate these forms, I briefly describe two, coercive diplomacy and low-intensity war, in general terms.

---

3   The most concise articulation of this approach is presented in Thomas Schelling, *Arms and Influence* (New Haven, Ct.: Yale University Press, 1966), especially 54-67.

4   The linkage among these are discussed in Michael Stohl and George A. Lopez, eds., *Terrible Beyond Endurance? The Foreign Policy of State Terrorism* (Westport, Ct.: Greenwood Press, 1988), 1-12; Michael Stohl, "States, Terrorism and State Terrorism: The Role of the Superpowers" in Robert O. Slater and Michael Stohl, eds., *Current Perspectives on International Terrorism* (London: MacMillan Press, 1988), 155-205; and George A. Lopez and Michael Stohl, "The Ethical Dimensions of 'the Changing Use of Force,'" op. cit.

5   The classic studies of these superpower patterns include Barry Blechman and Stephen Kaplan, *Force Without War* (Washington, D.C.: The Brookings Institution, 1978); Stephen Kaplan, *The Diplomacy of Power* (Washington, D.C.: The Brookings Institution, 1981); Phillip D. Zelikow, "Force Without War, 1975-1982," *Journal of Strategic Studies*, vol. 70 (March 1984); and Charles W. Ostrom and Brian Job, "The President and 'the Political Use of Force,'" *American Political Science Review*, vol. 80, no. 2 (June 1986), 541-566.

6   A useful example is found in Michael L. Castillon, "Low-Intensity Conflict in the 1980s: The French Experience," *Military Review* (January 1986), 68-77.

Coercive Diplomacy

Coercive diplomacy is the use of a variety of diplomatic, military, or economic measures by one or more states against a designated target state with the aim of making the latter's noncompliance with the desired policy outlined by the former particularly painful. The reality of threatened action is openly communicated, while the exact form it will take may be unclear or implicit, and is often left unstated by the conveying state.

As distinct from both diplomacy and traditional military activity, coercive diplomacy has a clearly instrumental character in that it:

> ... emphasizes the use of threats and the exemplary use of limited force ... . using just enough force to demonstrate resolution to protect one's interests and to emphasize the credibility of one's determination to use more force if necessary.[7]

The willingness of the superpowers to employ force and to threaten its use in a variety of ways during the Cold War period now has set a tone within which to understand the strategy of coercive diplomacy of other states. An essential element of the strategy is retaining the use of force as a viable means for settling disputes. But by not relying on military force as the first or only option, coercive diplomacy appears as a more "economical" — and thus some would claim more ethical — approach.

Not all coercive diplomacy, of course, employs or threatens direct violence. For example, states may employ economic sanctions in an avowedly coercive manner, as did the members of the United Nations with respect to ending apartheid in South Africa, without any serious consideration or resorting to violent tactics. But, as has occurred in the last decade in situations as diverse as Panama and the Persian Gulf, the economic and political measures of coercive diplomacy appear to be meant — by design — to precede the use of military force. This stands in contrast to the arguments made by some that the new emphasis on coercive diplomacy should be a welcome phenomenon for it serves as "an alternative to war."[8]

Whether coercive diplomacy is meant to precede war or to serve as an alternative to it often depends on its context. The pattern of military action following coercive diplomacy tends to occur the more unilateral the action, especially when a first order (world) power is coercing a much less (Third World) powerful state with which it has a history of dominance

---

7 Gordon A. Craig and Alexander L. George, *Force and Statecraft: Diplomatic Problems of Our Time*, 2d ed. (New York: Oxford University Press, 1990), 197.

8 The foremost spokesperson for this is Alexander L. George, *Forceful Persuasion: Coercive Diplomacy as an Alternative to War* (Washington, D.C.: United States Institute of Peace, 1991).

and difficulty. This was certainly the case with United States actions against Libya and Panama in the 1980s. If many states engage in a coercive, nonmilitary action, as has recently been the case in various United Nations-imposed economic sanctions, in order to achieve a distinct goal, coercive diplomacy may reach its best "alternative to war" potential.

One may argue that these two contexts illustrate the virtues of coercive diplomacy in that the strategy permits "achieving one's objectives economically, with little bloodshed, for fewer psychological and political costs, and often with much less risk of escalation."[9] Saving lives is indeed a virtue. This virtue, however, does not alter the fact that the strategy is based on the threat of state violence and the power to destroy if "proper" responses are not engendered by the threats and/or the relatively low levels of violence employed. Such coercive strategies, ranging from cutting off a state's access to shared borders to imposing major multilateral economic sanctions, must be judged with some moral criteria in mind, not the least of which might be the probability of success in effecting target state policies and the comparative impact of the coercion on the state decision makers as opposed to defenseless citizens. The latter, of course, represent the case, as in the sanctions situations against Cuba and Iraq in the early 1990s, of coercive diplomacy taken against authoritarian societies.

Low-Intensity War

Low-intensity war, or low-intensity conflict as it is often called, may be described as a form of state violence which combines the elements of guerilla and civil war in a "coherent" strategy that is especially suited for use against states and actors much less powerful than one's own. Low-intensity war represents a new wave of counterinsurgency theory formulated in First World policy circles and executed within and across Third World boundaries.[10]

Two distinct dimensions of this use of force contribute to the label "low-intensity" war. First, except for limited training, advisory, and tactical support roles played by elite units of the First World state, the strategy requires low levels of direct participation by the external patron. In such

---

9 Alexander L. George, "The Development of Doctrine and Strategy," in A. George, D. Hall and W. R. Simons, eds., *The Limits of Coercive Diplomacy* (Boston, Mass.: Little, Brown and Co., Inc., 1971), 19.

10 The definition and description of low-intensity war/conflict used here are drawn from Michael Klare, "The Evolution of U.S. Doctrine for Low-Intensity Conflict," in George Lopez and Drew Christiansen, SJ, eds., *Morals and Might*; and, Michael Klare and Peter Kornbluh, eds., *Low-Intensity Warfare* (New York: Pantheon Books, 1988), especially 49-79.

an arrangement, the dependency of a Third World client on a larger, quasi-interventionist nation serves the needs of both groups. Secondly, in the execution of such tactics, the resident military employs an "economy of force" approach with the goal to control quickly and then defeat, the challenge to the state by hostile forces.

One of the problems with the strategy and practice of low-intensity conflict in the past decade has been that, somewhat contrary to its purpose, it gives new life to the primacy of military solutions to essentially sociopolitical conflicts which have deteriorated into factional violence. Another difficulty, as articulated in detail by U.S. strategists in the celebrated document *Discriminate Deterrence*, lies in the vision of this strategy of the use of force as the appropriate one for strong states in a post-Cold War political climate.[11] In light of two decades of low-intensity tactics and strategy as the guiding style of U.S. involvement in Central America, followed by the style of the U.S. response in Somalia in 1992, special scrutiny should be given to the logic of low-intensity conflict.[12]

A pronounced difficulty with low-intensity strategy as it has unfolded in practice is that such efforts have a high likelihood of being accompanied by dramatic increases in internal repression and gross violations of human rights. In low-intensity war, military operations in the field take on new "politicized" dimensions. They are likely to result in greater numbers of civilian casualties, either "by design" in search of improved kill ratios, or, because the military "unconsciously" created a free-fire zone.

This situation develops because the protracted nature of the conflict forces increased reliance on ill-trained and less-disciplined soldiers. These troops often engage in various "excesses" in discharging their duty, which may very well generate more support for the insurgents whom the population judges may provide more security from state violence than the army. Elements of this complex situation are fueled by the increased economic and political dependence of the Third World society on the military patron. As the situation continues, the political stakes for the patron become higher as well, and the imperative not to lose the conflict pushes elites to

---

11   The U.S. Commission on Integrated Long-Term Strategy, *Discriminate Deterrence* (Washington, D.C.: U.S. Government Printing Office, 1988).

12   Although the discussion has focused on U.S. strategy and behavior, it should be noted that the U.S. has not had exclusive rights to this conflict dynamic. French actions in Africa for over a decade and the behavior of the former Soviet Union during various phases of the Afghan intervention and the Ethiopian conflict clearly fit the low-intensity pattern as well. See Michael L. Castillon, "Low-Intensity Conflict in the 1980s," op. cit., and Douglas M. Hart, "Low-Intensity Conflict in Afghanistan: the Soviet View," *Survival* (March/April 1982), 61-67.

opt for increasing levels of violence.[13] This also raises the moral stakes in the situation for the patron and elite group alike.

Why Have New Patterns in the Use of Force Emerged?

There are a number of explanations why contemporary patterns of resort to force short of war, such as coercive diplomacy and low-intensity war, have emerged and become preferred by states. While not mutually exclusive, each explanation logically reinforces the others to provide a neat intellectual web that sustains a preference for the use of force in post-Cold War foreign affairs. For purposes of brevity, I will discuss only three here.

A first explanation considers *the new force postures as part of the requisite national defense against new and elusive enemies of the state, especially internal insurgents and nonstate terrorists.* This explanation argues that nation-states began to employ coercive techniques, clandestine actions, and low-intensity war, and engage in counterterrorism as active policies only when threatened by nonstate actors or renegade and lawless states, who attacked or threatened attack on the state. Because these enemies operate without standing armies, without identifiable territory, and did not themselves conduct violence according to the traditional laws of war, they pose a special challenge to the state and require special defense strategies. Such strategies must, by necessity, mirror that employed by terrorists and insurgents.[14]

In U.S. defense policy, such an emphasis began in earnest during the confirmation hearings of Secretary of State designate Alexander Haig in 1981 and was reinforced by the "Schultz doctrine" of mid-decade. Under the Clinton administration, it has taken the form of arguments for a commitment to defense expenditures and programs to cope with the

---

13 Examples of these patterns in the past decade have been Peru and El Salvador as detailed in *Americas Watch, Tolerating Abuses: Violations of Human Rights in Peru* (Washington, D.C., 1988), and T. D. Mason and D. A. Krane, "The Political Economy of Death Squads: Toward a Theory of the Impact of State-Sanctioned Terror," *International Studies Quarterly*, vol. 33 (1989), 175-198.

14 One of the best examples of such an argument appears in Neil Livingston and Terrell Arnold, eds., *Fighting Back: Winning the War Against Terrorism* (Lexington, Mass.: Lexington Books, Inc., 1988).

threats of narcotics criminals, nuclear terrorists, and states that assist such criminals.

Thus, states have become more focused, diverse, and determined in the level and purpose of their use of violence in order to cope with unprecedented threats. When thinking about how such a pattern of state violence might develop over the long term, one scholar worried that:

> We may be on the threshold of an era of armed conflict in which conventional warfare, guerrilla warfare, and international terrorism will coexist, with governments and sub-national entities employing them individually, interchangeably, sequentially, or simultaneously — and having to defend against them.[15]

This is the world that some analysts and policymakers believe now exists and which demands new approaches to the use of force.

A second explanation for the emergence of these new types of violence claims that *states have increasingly resorted to the use of force short of war because the gains from so doing far outweigh the costs of resorting to this type of violence or to war in a more traditional sense.* In other words, we have witnessed an increase in these new forms of state violence not because states are defenseless before nonstate terrorists and domestic insurgents and have reluctantly employed such tactics. Rather, state leaders learned well the tactics of these presumed foes. They knew that advances in weapons, technology, communications, and access to the media, when combined with the existing resources of the state, would allow far greater versatility in deploying violence than that available to individual or small groups of terrorists. In short, the effective utility of coercive diplomacy and low-intensity violence has increased dramatically because of changes in the two "cost areas" which contribute to the calculation of this effective utility.[16]

At the first level, the production costs of employing state violence short of war, defined as the costs of taking the action, in terms of weapons, personnel, and other economic factors, have declined. By their very nature, the coercive diplomacy and low-intensity war will almost always cost relatively little to a powerful state as compared to the alternatives of waging open, protracted violent conflict. Further, whereas there may have been a time when a state would pursue a surgical air strike against another state, or fund a group of mercenaries warring against a regime which is unpopular in the powerful state, with guilt and reluctance, that time has

---

15 Brian Jenkins, *International Terrorism: The Other World War* (Santa Monica, California: The Rand Corporation, 1985), 20.

16 Much of the logic of this argument is drawn from Raymond D. Duvall and Michael Stohl, "Governance by Terror" in Michael Stohl, ed., *The Politics of Terrorism* (New York: Marcel Dekker, 1983), 179-219.

surely passed. In fact, rather than speaking of psychological or public opinion costs incurred in the production of such use of force, modern leaders have found ways, including manipulation of their own free press, to architect large-scale public approval for such violence (e.g., Grenada, Libyan air strike, Panama). What once was cost has become a substantial benefit.

At the second level, when nations pursue the new forms of state violence, they face response costs, defined as those which may be imposed on the initiator of the action by the target, its supporters, or other bystanders. Although there certainly has been a recording of protest by various states against particular resort to force, for example, in Europe regarding the April 1986 U.S. air strike on Libya, or the reactions of Latin America to the December 1989 U.S. invasion of Panama, no punitive action that might deter similar U.S. action in the future has emerged.

Thus, this explanation argues that the resort to force short of war by states in recent times lies in a general decline in critiques of such action and a reduction in the production costs of the same. In fact, many states may now consider that the mix of these factors generally predicts to a forceful action being a low-cost, high-gain option.

A third explanation lies in *the changing composition of, and countries involved in, the production and trade of the weapons of state violence*. As a factor influencing state capabilities, the arms production and arms trade nexus warrants substantial attention. For the better part of three decades, the Cold War's primary powers engaged in a conventional arms supply race to surrogates, mostly in the Third World. In addition to arming regional rivals, arms also flowed unabated to regimes engaged in some form of surrogate war in which segments of its own population were considered representing a greater, internationalized enemy in the Cold War.

Although nation-to-nation arms sales showed decline in real dollar volume for the late eighties, they are on the rise again in the early nineties. Already in the late 1980s, the development of what was being termed "black and gray" markets appears to have more than compensated for the "official" market declines. This illegal trafficking delivered a steady flow of weapons and munitions to areas of war violence, such as to the Persian Gulf and also to areas of low-intensity violence, such as Central America, South Africa, and the Middle East. Whether the product be military helicopters, spare missile parts, or grenade launchers, a nearly incalculable and secret supply of weaponry became readily available to states or their surrogates interested in pursuing equally clandestine acts of violence.[17]

Even as illegal arms merchants engaged in international deals, the credo witnessed a dramatic increase in the number of legally operating

---

17 For the best analyses of these trends, see Michael Klare, "The Arms Race Shifts to the Third World," *The Bulletin of the Atomic Scientists* (May 1990).

private arms merchants and the number of nations entering the arms production and sell-for-profit game. In both areas, the power of the available market sustained each supplier group, even as some nations attempted to argue for greater controls on such exchange. However, the voices of restraint were (and are) quite dim. As was demonstrated in the cases of West Germany and Brazil, it is difficult for a policy of restraint in arms production and sales to retain support in a democracy experiencing economic decline. And as in such nations as China and Brazil, the foreign exchange impact of arms sales even for a second-level producer is far greater than any competing growth sector of the nation.[18]

And finally with the breakup of the Warsaw Pact alliance, and most notably with the demise of the former Soviet Union, new arms problems fuel state violence. In addition to large caches of weapons finding new homes outside of Eastern Europe, the recent "brain drain" of weapons producers and engineers poses more difficulty than simply the trade of new arms. Moreover, the lethality of weapons that are now available from willing sales agents of the former republics of the one-time USSR exceeds what has been available in the global arms market in earlier years.

Ethical Concerns with the Use of Force Short of War

What are the moral dilemmas in the use of force in the post-Cold War world that demand ethical comment? Three seem to be most prominent in the current era. The first has been dramatically portrayed in the Yugoslav war but is no less true for the pattern in wars and uses of force for the past decade: *the number of civilian, noncombatant casualties in violent conflicts has increased significantly*. The data for declared and undeclared wars, as well as for military interventions, is clear and striking. Whereas the civilian death toll constituted one-half of the war dead during the early 1950s, by the late 1980s civilians comprised nearly three-fourths of the total of those perishing in war. Of this number, more than half died at the hands of their own countrymen.[19]

---

18 First-rate studies in this problem are available in William Hartung, "Nations Vie for Arms Markets," *The Bulletin of the Atomic Scientists* (December 1987), 27-35; and Michael Brzoska, "The Erosion of Restraint in West German Arms Transfer Policy," *Journal of Peace Research* (May 1989), 165-178.

19 Cf. Ruth Leger Sivard, *World Military and Social Expenditures, 1989* (Washington, D.C.: World Priorities, Inc., 1989), 22-23.

Of course, death is not the only plight facing civilians. As this decade began, more than 14 million people, or about 95 percent of the global refugee total, had fled their living areas due to armed conflict. Both in real numbers, and especially in the percentage of the national population which is displaced, the refugee data for conflicts as different as those raging in Cambodia, Afghanistan, Mozambique, El Salvador, and Ethiopia is staggering. This refugee situation has become so regularized, and so severe, that it is not outlandish to suggest that the number of displaced persons — either within or outside a nation's boundaries — may now be a more accurate indicator of the severity of a contemporary conflict than the battles won and lost or the amount of geography that has changed hands.[20]

If we place this empirical evidence alongside the graphic film footage which plays in American living rooms as a portrait of civil wars, "low-intensity" wars, and coercive diplomacy efforts (including economic sanctions), the phrase "waging war against the innocent" takes on new meaning. What has developed *in practice* is a creeping loss of moral restraint on the killing of noncombatants. With each new instance of large-scale civilian death that fails to mobilize the moral disdain of the international community, we create an illusion of acceptable customary conduct that will be employed by new antagonists in the next conflict.

Thus, local hatreds and military dynamics notwithstanding, the road to atrocities in Bosnia — and the slow reaction of the international community to condemn them — began a decade ago with the bombing of medical clinics and schools in Nicaragua and Angola, and continued through village massacres in Mozambique and El Salvador. It took a further turn for the worse with the attack on civilian life support structures during the Persian Gulf War.[21]

If the first major moral dilemma, in which the changing face of violence presents the post-Cold War order, is the increased lethality of violence for civilians, then the second ethical concern is that this pattern no longer occurs accidentally. Rather, the damage done to civilians has moved from being collateral to premeditated: *there are new normative rationales which justify the use of force in a way that increases civilian deaths.* These rationales are often quite intricate — much like nuclear deterrence theory — and reinforce one another when played out as policy.

---

20 Christer Ahlström, *Casualties of Conflict* (Sweden: University of Uppsala, 1991) provides the best combination of recent data with an analysis of the "logic" of refugee creation in internal wars.

21 For an argument about the morality of various forms of attack on civilian infrastructure in terms of the just-war tradition, see George A. Lopez, "Ethics in the Gulf War: Not so Clean," *The Bulletin of the Atomic Scientists* (September 1991), 30-35.

One rationale that has developed prominently in the actions of states, and even in the impositions of sanctions, involves arguments for the "economy of force." Simply put, elites argue that in a serious confrontation, it is better "to kill one and frighten a thousand" than to engage in long and bloody battles. In such a situation, those who are innocent and vulnerable often become instrumental targets. Drawing from Thomas Schelling's discussions of strategy and tactics in the nuclear age, this diplomacy of violence — even when enacted as sanctions forged with peaceful goals in mind — is meant to inflict pain "terrible beyond endurance."[22] In situations of low-intensity conflict or conventional war, this logic often combines with the long-standing practice of military ethics that the humane conduct of war involves attaining one's objective as quickly as possible and with the least possible loss of life, to make attacks on those "in harm's way" appear both pragmatic in the short term and ethical in the long run.

In light of such arguments in an era of Salvadoran truth commission reports, inhumane actions in Bosnia, and anarchy in Somalia, what is called for is a renewed ethics of the primacy of civilian life, even in situations of indirect coercion as occurs in imposing sanctions. A major part of this task, and one especially appropriate for the Church, involves exposing the lack of moral logic of these rationales and the antiseptic language with which they are articulated.

The third ethical dilemma which warrants our attention involves *the new calls for and justification of international military intervention in large-scale civil violence.* At first glance, it would seem that developing an ethic to protect civilians, as I have suggested in highlighting the first two moral dilemmas, almost necessitates support for more proactive measures, such as military intervention in situations of massive internal violence. Without denying the imperative to protect civilians or to guarantee compliance with important international norms, to argue that the only — or that the preferred — manner of so doing entails military intervention, demands some serious moral reflection.[23] Of the many elements to consider in this area, I highlight two.

One concern, present in the medium-term histories of both the Yugoslav and the Somalian situations, involves where the intervention option

---

22 Thomas Schelling, *Arms and Influence*, 66.
23 The journal which has taken the lead on this issue is *Ethics and International Affairs* which is published by the Carnegie Council on Ethics and International Affairs. For skeptical views on the likelihood that intervention can meet moral criteria of justifiability, see Terry Nardin, "Sovereignty, Self-Determination, and International Intervention," and Russell Hardin, "Popular Sovereignty and International Intervention," in George A. Lopez and Drew Christiansen, SJ, eds., *Morals and Might.*

fits among the range of response options open to the international community *and* when it is discussed. However compelling it may be under circumstances of current civil strife to argue for external military intervention, if such a policy becomes the norm after the internal factions of a divided society have been armed by outsiders and little has been done by the international community to ease the transitional shocks of the collapse of former governing structures, intervention appears a shortsighted approach. If the goal has been to preserve civilian life and support systems, a moral perspective would argue that the lessons of Somalia and Bosnia suggest an ethical imperative of controlling arms flows to any country, but especially with a deeply divided population and a history of authoritarian rule. Success in such preventative measures are likely to present fewer crises where intervention appears the only viable option.

A second moral concern is to ensure that the humanitarian goals of the intervening parties are of the highest order and that those engaged in intervention be truly representative of the international community's interests and standards, not simply furthering their own. As with other harsh realities of the 1990s, the legacy of the 1980s makes this a formidable criterion. Even while acknowledging the manner in which the Cold War encouraged interventionism by the large and powerful states, the Cold War's demise does not mean that the resort to intervention is any less capable of serving rather narrow foreign policy interests of a strong state.

For example, somewhat outside of the Cold War context, both the French and the U.S. have attempted since the early 1980s to dramatically extend the international legal community's definition of the rights of a state to employ a "peacetime unilateral remedy." These remedies were considered primarily, although not exclusively, as necessary tools of action against those who did not comply with existing international norms. Such efforts have taken not only the form of proclamations, such as the Shultz doctrine aimed at justifying preemptive attacks against suspected terrorists harbored in a particular state, but also in the form of legal arguments in the World Court as voiced by the U.S. in defending its right to mine Nicaraguan harbors in order to thwart arms flows to the FMLN of El Salvador. And most importantly, both the French and the U.S. have pushed the principle in practice with respective unilateral forceful actions in Chad, Grenada, Panama, and Libya. More often than not, such actions have not been supported by the international community.[24] Such a legacy makes the call for humanitarian intervention more difficult to uphold at a high moral standard.

Beyond these concerns, calls for collective humanitarian intervention would seem to fall under the scrutiny of just-war categories just as

---

24 The best examination of this trend is provided by Elizabeth Zoller, *Peacetime Unilateral Remedies* (New York: Transactional Publishers, Inc., 1985).

unilateral actions of a single state would. Such interventions would be especially hard-pressed to ensure they will remain respectful of the rules of proportionate response and civilian immunity, and that probability of success is high.

Conclusion

The emerging order of our era suggests that there will be fewer worries about war between "great powers" but no decline in death and destruction due to the use of force within and between nations in other ways. While collective economic measures to punish renegade states or to uphold international norms may emerge from the best of intentions and attempt to be a moral equivalent of war, in some cases they will harm civilians as disproportionately as traditional military collateral damage during a bombing raid. This reality combines with the more general erosion of the moral restraints against attacks on civilians and recent calls for increased intervention within states experiencing large-scale violence to pose new and perplexing ethical dilemmas.

There are a number of "new" forms of international violence and their attractiveness to states is on the rise. But these patterns have their roots in longer-term factors of international relations and thus are more stable forms of behavior than may first appear. These trends pose new ethical challenges to those in the scholarly and practitioner worlds who uphold standards that constrain the use of force by states. Due to the deep-seated doctrines and factors which sustain the changing use of force, it will take more than casual claims about protecting eroding standards of ethics and international law to reassert the primacy of these rules over the self-interest of states in the use of force. But the need to begin articulating those claims and building their strength has never been greater.

Developing the Just-War Tradition in a Multicultural World

John Langan, SJ

During the millennium and a half that has elapsed since the Roman Empire became a Christian state and since St. Augustine provided a decisive and enormously influential formulation of its principles, the just-war tradition has functioned in many different ways. Prominent among these have been: (1) the legitimation within a Christian theological framework of the use of force by the political authorities, (2) the restriction of the use of force by warriors and states, (3) the establishment of a set of norms governing combatants in a religiously and politically divided world, (4) the determination of the moral status and appropriate treatment of peoples subject to the Western Christian empires of the early modern age, (5) the moral criticism of new military technologies, particularly weapons of mass destruction, (6) the legitimation of selective conscientious objection by those who have serious moral objections to particular wars, and (7) the moral assessment of government policies and strategic doctrines. This listing of functions, some of which have developed only in more recent times but which were latent in the tradition from the beginning, should make it clear that just-war theory, like some weapons, cuts in several ways and that it cannot properly be reduced to a mere instrument of power or treated as something to be employed in a partisan or exclusive manner.[1]

Just-war theory is a flexible and developing instrument of analysis, a fact which increases the likelihood of its being misunderstood and misused. Originally developed for a world in which political power was held mainly by autocrats, it now figures prominently in debates in democratic societies. Elaborated in an age of chivalry, it is now invoked to assess nuclear threats to civilian targets. Just-war theorizing has foundations in theology and in ethical theory, and it has applications in an increasingly technical and professional military world; as a result, it is subject to pressures for change and development that are both theoretical and practical.

From the time that Augustine formulated its basic affirmations with an eye to defending the imperial order of Rome against the incursions of the barbarians, it has served on the frontiers between conflicting cultures; but that very fact lays it open to the charge of being conditioned and perhaps corrupted by the culture on whose categories and assumptions it relies. In a world in which Western societies with their distinctive common history frequently come into violent conflict with non-Western societies whose worldviews, religious beliefs, and methods of reflection are often quite different, the question inevitably arises: How can a tradition and a mode of theorizing articulated by Augustine, Aquinas, Victoria, Grotius, and other figures of Western high culture provide an appropriate and fair standard for dealing with Mayans, Maoris, and Muslims, with Blackfeet, Bushmen, and Buddhists? A theory which serves to express the moral judgments of Harvard professors, Protestant theologians, and Catholic bishops may still be dismissed as parochial in a world of multiculturalism, of disintegrating empires and resurgent ethnic demands, and of declining confidence in enlightenment and other projects for shaping a cosmopolitan world order. The fact that *The Challenge of Peace* in 1983 aroused such wide interest and provided a very widely used point of reference, even for many who did not agree with its conclusions, may simply show that it was

---

1 In this essay, I will use the expression, "the just-war tradition" to refer to the historical succession of authors who held both that some wars could be justified by appealing to morally significant values and that the use of force must be limited if it is to be justifiable. Pacifism rejects the first of these claims; holy war or crusade ways of thinking about warfare have been slow to emphasize the second, even when they have not denied it. I shall use the expression "just-war theory" to refer to a formulation of a set of principles specifying these two fundamental claims. I will take the formulation of just-war theory offered in *The Challenge of Peace*, nos. 80-110, as a standard reference point.

well suited to a particular moment in the history of American public life and that it must therefore have shared in the concerns and prejudices of the culture that shapes U.S. public policy. (This, we might observe, is a line of criticism that could be advanced by persons who would think of themselves as embodying a culture of resistance, by those who feel called to follow the Gospel against the dominant culture, and by militant representatives of foreign cultures.)

The difficulties that we are sketching here are very similar to the difficulties that philosophers, anthropologists, lawyers, and others have raised about the universality and immutability of the natural law, with which just-war theory has been closely aligned over the centuries. But they are, if anything, more intense for just-war theory because the history of its transformations and the record of its cultural embeddedness have been detailed at considerable length.[2] At the same time the difficulties here are closely connected with opportunities for developing the theory so that it applies to a new stage in international relations and to new forms of violent conflict. The development of a theory, as contrasted with its repetition or replacement, involves an effort to answer new questions for which older formulations of the theory do not provide determinate answers. Arriving at a satisfactory answer may well mean that terms in the theory need to be redefined; that further distinctions have to be introduced in applying the principles to cases, that cases have to be redescribed, and that the context for applying the principles has to be reconceived. Developing a theory in the face of new questions may well provoke disagreement among experts and dissension among those who previously thought they shared a normative consensus. At the same time, development of a theory implies a substantial measure of continuity with earlier stages in the articulation of the theory; but this continuity does not seem to be something which we can identify with fixed elements in the theory. Rather, it is something which we ascertain by scrutinizing proposed modifications of the theory for their fit with previous formulations of the theory and for their ability to handle the new questions and problems in a way that satisfies most of the proponents of the theory in its standard form over time.

A brief example of what I have in mind in offering this very generic sketch of developing theory can be found in a discussion provoked by the Gulf War. The principle of noncombatant immunity has commonly been interpreted to exclude attacks on persons who are civilians and are not engaged in military activities. In guerrilla warfare, where combatants on

---

2 See, for instance, the extensive writings of James Turner Johnson on this theme, especially *Ideology, Reason, and the Limitation of War: Religious and Secular Concepts, 1200-1740* (Princeton, N.J.: Princeton University Press, 1975) and *Just-War Tradition and the Restraint of War: A Moral and Historical Inquiry* (Princeton, N.J.: Princeton University Press, 1981).

one side do not clearly identify themselves as such, this principle is in practice very difficult to apply; but its general intent seems clear enough. The stress both in the scholarly literature and in the training of U.S. military personnel has been on the prohibition against directly killing innocent civilians. The principle of double effect was commonly understood to allow the indirect killing of some civilians as a consequence of attacks on military targets.[3] But, given this quite reasonable way of interpreting and applying the original principle, what is one to make of allied air attacks on the electrical grid of Iraq?[4]

On the one hand, in modern warfare this counts as a legitimate military target since it is an essential part of the infrastructure which enables the aggressive Iraqi government to function and to prosecute the war which it began with its invasion of Kuwait. On the other hand, that same infrastructure enables the Iraqi civilian population to survive and to go about the business of life in an industrializing society. In particular, it provides power for the water filtration plants, which are needed to ensure safe and pure water for the Iraqi population. Destroying the electrical grid would increase the likelihood of disease and death. It sets in motion a causal chain which has an indeterminate number of deaths as one of its foreseeable outcomes.

Now this is not, either as a matter of fact or in our moral evaluations, the same as directly killing or massacring civilians. The deaths of these civilians are neither one of the goals of military operations nor a means to those goals. Countermeasures can be taken over time to protect civilians and to lessen the impact of the bombing on the civilian population. Nonetheless, a serious thing has been done, which increases the risks to civilians to a significant degree. The action of bombing the electrical grid thus becomes morally problematic. It becomes plausible to hold that not only civilian persons are prohibited targets not to be aimed at directly but also those systems that are necessary for the survival of the civilian population as a whole are prohibited targets. But such a conclusion is not logically required and cannot be shown to be true simply by appealing to the principle of noncombatant immunity. Prohibiting attacks on infrastructure systems that sustain the civilian population will provide more protection for the centrally important value of innocent human life, and so it can be considered a reasonable and appropriate extension of the principle of noncombatant immunity. But it is also clear that just-war theory taken as a whole does not allow us to absolutize this value, giving it priority over all

---

3 See, for example, Michael Walzer, *Just and Unjust Wars: A Moral Argument with Historical Illustrations* (New York: Basic Books, 1977), 152-159.

4 For a critical assessment of some of the early responses to this question, see John Langan, SJ, "Just-War Theory after the Gulf War," *Theological Studies* 53 (1992), 106-110.

competing values in conflict situations; rather, it acknowledges that in certain situations it may be unavoidably necessary to put at risk or to take lives in order to protect other lives and other highly important values.

So there remains room for a counterargument, which would probably emphasize two points: first, a claim that the proposed restriction of military targets would impede effective military strategy and tactics and thus would make considerably more difficult the protection or achievement of those other important values for which the war is being fought; second, that it is very unlikely that a firm and effective consensus in support of the more restrictive norm could be maintained on both sides of a conflict.

The first point involves considerations of professional judgment and expertise, even while the norm being proposed would restrict the options available to those professionals whose judgment is being invoked. Of course, generals would prefer to fight wars with fewer restrictions. At the same time, they recognize that some restrictions (e.g., on torture and killing of prisoners of war) can be mutually beneficial, even if they often prove to be burdensome to implement in practice. Military convenience is in no way an adequate moral justification for military operations that greatly increase the risks to civilians or that actually bring about greater numbers of civilian deaths. Military necessity, which can provide such justification, needs careful and honest scrutiny.[5] More specifically, in the current American political context, care must be shown so that risks are not shifted in a self-protective and self-serving way from American soldiers to foreign civilians. The combined memories of heavy casualties in the Vietnam "quagmire" and of very low allied military casualties in the Gulf War can create in the American public and in its political leadership an unrealistic demand that future wars and interventions be conducted with an extremely low level of U.S. casualties. This is not a bad objective in itself, but it is very likely to lead to strategies that effectively devalue lives on the other side or to the avoidance of serious problems that do not have quick and easy solutions.

The second point, about the unlikelihood of achieving mutual agreement on a more restrictive norm, need not be morally decisive; for it is often the case that moral obligations have to be fulfilled even if competitors or adversaries do not acknowledge or observe them. But it is also true that such a lack of shared recognition of the norm will make it more difficult to resist the political and practical pressures that will build up to overturn proposed restrictions that are seen by many as self-imposed and perhaps optional.

---

5 A discussion of what such scrutiny involves can be found in William V. O'Brien, *The Conduct of Just and Limited War* (New York: Praeger, 1981), 66-67.

The Gulf War is an atypical and probably misleading basis for developing norms for the future, precisely because it was such a lopsided conflict. From this, two points follow:

First, one side (the coalition) was not pressed to anything like the limits of its capabilities and resources. In a more close run contest, the military leadership would presumably have stronger objections to restrictions that might make the difference between winning and losing or between winning at a moderate cost and winning at a heavy cost.

Second, the lopsidedness of the outcome and the clear predominance of the coalition on the land, on the sea, and in the air made it possible for the air war to be conducted with an even higher level of discrimination. The only way that the Iraqis had of inflicting damage on the coalition's military forces (so long as the latter did not launch ground attacks on Iraqi troop concentrations) and on the neighboring civilian populations in Israel and Saudi Arabia was the firing of SCUD missiles. If these had been more effective or if they had had chemical warheads, the pressure on the coalition military leadership to use all available means in response would have been unbearably strong.

In the light of these admittedly inconclusive considerations, I am ready to conclude that the right thing for the coalition in the actual circumstances was to refrain from bombing those parts of the infrastructure needed to sustain civilian society, even though these also constituted legitimate military targets. My basic reason for holding this is that this further level of destruction and of threats to civilian life was unnecessary in fact. On the other hand, I do not think that this case suffices to establish a universal norm prohibiting all such attacks in any future circumstances. But also I believe that such a norm should be adopted and that its adoption would lead to a more humane way of conducting war.

My interest in sketching out this example is certainly not to defend or criticize specific aspects of the U.S. and allied conduct of the war in Iraq or to argue for a specific way of interpreting or applying just-war theory, but to lay out the logical structure of one possibility for the development of just-war theory suggested by current events and needs. For, as a result of changes in the technology of warfare, in the technologies of information and communication, in the awareness of minority and marginal groups, in the variety of groups and organizations that have to be considered as participants in the international areas, just-war theory confronts many new questions for which its traditional or classic formulations do not provide clear-cut answers. Each significantly different conflict puts new questions to the theory. In the American war in Vietnam, there were very difficult questions about permissible and effective ways to respond to guerrilla attacks without attacking civilians directly as well as about how to interpret and apply the norm of proportionality in arriving at judgments that the objectives of the war did or did not justify the great sacrifices of both

American and Vietnamese lives. The PLO's conflict with Israel has raised questions about the applicability of norms designed for nation-states, to a conflict between a state and a movement proposing itself as the representative of a people's claims, drawing extensive international support and sympathy, and using terrorist tactics that often inflicted grievous damage on third parties. So we should not expect that the effort to apply a body of norms to a complex and heterogeneous series of events will yield judgments that are standard products of a straightforward calculus.

At the same time, we should avoid an approach that insists on the heterogeneity and discontinuity of cases in a way that implies that we cannot make reasonable judgments about how to evaluate classes of actions morally. Indeed, it is one of the primary functions of just-war theory to enable us to pick out those features in the war being considered that are truly important for moral evaluation and at the same time to discard those features that in the last resort do not matter. A's being like B in some respects will normally coexist with A's being unlike B in other respects; so that arguments from analogy with prior cases will not be logically conclusive. Nor will they be practically decisive unless they invoke general principles such as we find in the norms of just-war theory which direct us to treat certain similarities as morally crucial. Particular cases may teach us about the incompleteness of the principles that have already been elaborated; but cases that are not scrutinized in the light of principles remain radically unintelligible. Without principles we are in a state of confusion, amazed at the technique and power of modern warfare and grieved by its destructiveness and cruelty.

The principles of just-war theory, articulated in *The Challenge of Peace* and in the distinguished contemporary formulations of Michael Walzer, Paul Ramsey, William O'Brien, James Turner Johnson, and others, are a necessary form of guidance for those who believe that it is legitimate to use force for the protection of the political order and its care values. At the same time, the points made in this paper about the logic of its development and about the prudent application of its principles to cases do not rescue just-war theory from the charge that it is biased and even corrupted by its place in Western culture. Now it is not possible to rebut such charges by denying that just-war theory in both its secular and Christian forms belongs to the Western tradition. So what strategy can we propose for the development and application of just-war theory in a multicultural world in ways that will make it a more universal and more impartial instrument for moral reflection and judgment and that will make it, when protagonists in a conflict come from differing cultures or civilizations, a means for arriving at common judgments and practices rather than for expressing unilateral moral denunciations?

There are five considerations that may enable us to meet the challenge raised by a multicultural world.

First, like every statement or theory which aims to state what is true, just-war theory lives with a tension between the truth intended and never fully or definitively expressed and the particular formulations in which that truth is imperfectly expressed and which are themselves cultural and historical products. This is not a condition found only in just-war theory or in moral theories; but it is common to all our efforts to state the truth of things, though it may be felt more keenly with regard to moral matters. It is also common to similar efforts to state the truth of things that are present in all other cultures.

Second, it is important to recognize that not all elements of just-war theory bear the same relation to the surrounding culture and history. The bearers of legitimate authority, the forms of diplomatic practice, the techniques of warfare, even the notions of combatants and noncombatants are subject to historical change and are dependent on the surrounding culture in ways that are easy to ascertain. At the same time there are elements in the theory that express conditions for rational action in general, conditions that we formulate within our own culture but that we expect to hold good within other cultures, e.g., the norm of proportionality, the requirement of reasonable hope of success. Looked at on one level, just-war theory is a set of specific regulations for the conduct of one social institution, the military. On another level, it is a way of thinking about the conditions under which it can be justified to inflict harm on others. I would not want to hold that the notion of rational action is universally present in all cultures or that it plays the same role as an evaluative touchstone that it does in Western secular culture; but it does constitute a formal effort to transcend cultural particularities, and it can provide a framework in terms of which initially disparate assessments from other cultures can be partially understood.

Third, it is possible and valuable to find significant parallels to just-war theory in other cultural, religious, and intellectual traditions. The parallels will be imperfect, but they can provide evidence that societies other than our own have attempted to protect certain values (justice, innocent lives, and the integrity and moral character of warriors) which are imperiled in a violent world. What we can get from the scholarly collaboration which is needed in order to work out such parallels at a more than superficial level is a sense of the partial convergence of intellectual, cultural, and religious traditions and of the specific historical problems and pressures that caused them to articulate norms protecting their values in different, sometimes contradictory, ways.[6]

---

6 An example of such scholarly collaboration is provided by *Just War and Jihad: Historical and Theoretical Perspectives on War and Peace in Western and Islamic Traditions*, ed. John Kelsay and James Turner Johnson (New York: Greenwood Press, 1991).

Fourth, it is important to recognize that one of the major spurs to the development of just-war theory in the past has been the experience of conflict between cultures in conflict (particularly the Spanish wars with Islam and in the Americas) or within a civilization that has experienced a breakdown in normative consensus (Christendom divided between Catholics and Protestants). Just-war theory does not articulate the higher ideals that distinguish communities from each other, but rather attempts to state and protect a moral minimum in the way that antagonistic societies and cultures deal with each other. This is a project that at least in its general scope and intention, if not necessarily in its particular formulations, is an indispensable task in a multicultural world in which societies often come into conflict with each other.

Fifth, precisely because just-war theory is rooted both in the notion of rational action and in the necessities of a divided and conflictual world, it can be commended on contractarian and utilitarian grounds to societies that are attempting to define themselves in secular terms or that are interested in establishing secular relationships with neighboring societies that do not share a body of religious ideals and norms with them.

In a multicultural world, in which mutual understanding is a difficult task rarely accomplished but in which interests come into frequent conflict, the just-war tradition with its commitments to reason, history, and the values of both individual life and community order, is an intellectual and moral resource that is needed both by those called to exercise power and by those who may be the objects and the victims of power. But to conceive it as a treasure to be preserved is to make a fundamental error; rather, it is an instrument that needs to be sharpened so that it may be used more precisely in difficult situations and hammered out anew so that it may be used more flexibly in unprecedented crises. *The Challenge of Peace* made a distinguished contribution to carrying out these tasks, especially with regard to the moral status of nuclear deterrence and the possibility of nuclear war. It is the responsibility of moralists, commentators, and the shapers of policy to carry on the work of reflection and criticism which will sustain the just-war tradition as a developing reality.

Casuistry, Pacifism, and the Just-War Tradition in the Post-Cold War Era

Richard B. Miller

It is now commonplace to say that the global context for thinking about the ethics of war and peace has changed dramatically with the breakup of the Soviet Union, the reunification of Germany, and the "quiet revolutions" that have occurred in Eastern Europe. But this does not mean that conventional approaches to war and peace in Western ethics have diminished in importance. Quite the contrary: although the Cold War may be behind us, war and coercion are still very much a part of the international scene, and the United States has yet to extricate itself from regional conflicts across the globe. There are no indications that war will disappear with the ending of superpower rivalry and ideological tensions. This means that war as a basic practice in international affairs will continue to pose problems for pacifists and just-war theorists. What has changed are the kinds of cases to which ethicists of war and peace must now pay fuller attention.

I want to discuss two such cases, for they force on pacifists and just-war theorists some fundamental problems: embargoes (or economic sanctions) and humanitarian interventions. What these cases illustrate is that pacifists and just-war theorists must carry out much-needed clarification about basic conceptual issues in the ethics of war and peace and for American public policy. Here I want to engage in the modest task of specifying what that conceptual agenda should be, along with some obstacles that stand in the way of developing that agenda. As recent history has shown in the Gulf War, Bosnia, Somalia, Libya, and Haiti, embargoes and humanitarian interventions have engaged the energies of various policymakers in ways that were unforeseeable five years ago. Yet the extent to which either of these methods of coercion can (or ought to) pass muster from pacifists or just-war theorists remains unclear.

In order to clarify this point, I need to make two sets of preparatory remarks. First, I should indicate what it means to think in terms of cases in ethics, or what is commonly called *casuistry*. Second, I would like to consider how the ethics of war and peace during the Cold War was notably different than the kind of casuistry that is necessary today. Eventually, I want to show that the end of the Cold War also means an end of self-defense as the central rationale for U.S. military activity and the buildup of a vast military arsenal. With self-defense as a less obvious justification for the preparation and use of military force, the question of the legitimacy of war as a political tool becomes especially acute. For this reason, it is natural to expect pacifist voices to become more vocal in public discourse and debate, and just-war theorists to clarify *other* possible causes that might justify recourse to lethal force. By the same token, so long as policy leaders in the United States and the United Nations continue to coordinate embargoes and humanitarian interventions, pacifists and just-war theorists will rightly be called upon to clarify the basis and limits of coercive measures as alternatives to diplomacy.

I. Casuistry: Taxonomies and Maxims

While the term *casuistry* often conjures up pejorative associations (moral laxity, sophistry, and semantic equivocation), it also points to the importance of practical reasoning about particular cases in our everyday moral experience. Thinking about cases has the advantage of casting ethical discourse in pragmatic, concrete terms. As Albert R. Jonsen and Stephen Toulmin demonstrate, problematic cases focus our attention on the practical implications of our more general values, virtues, and duties.[1]

---

1 Albert R. Jonsen and Stephen Toulmin, *The Abuse of Casuistry: A History of*

Indeed, it is often only in terms of cases that the actual meaning of a general obligation can become clear. Among other things, cases arise when the meaning of an obligation is vague, or when we are unsure about which of two important obligations is more pressing when they conflict.[2] Casuistry helps to address these common moral experiences — doubt and conflict — by providing tangible problems on which to focus our attention.

When attempting to provide clarity or resolve conflicts, the casuist's first step involves finding the right classification for the case in question. In many respects, casuists resemble natural scientists: both begin their work by seeking to determine the proper paradigm for the problems that present themselves for analysis. In casuistry, paradigms constitute presumptive starting points for moral reflection, furnishing a way of seeing the problem to be addressed. In effect, casuistry must begin with an interpretive, optical query: How do we envision the problem that lies before us? In much of Catholic moral theology, for example, the act of killing can take on a different moral force, depending on whether the act in question is classified as an act of self-defense or an act of vengeance. How it is interpreted determines in large part how it is judged.

It also happens that taxonomies in casuistry enable us to reason analogically when the problem in question is not entirely clear-cut or familiar. Often we can settle our cases by drawing parallels with stable paradigms, keeping an eye to relevant similarities between the familiar and the new. As Thomas Kuhn observes in the context of scientific research, unfamiliar problems are dealt with analogically. Scientists proceed "by modeling [novel data] to one or another part of the scientific corpus which the community already recognizes as among its established achievements."[3] Similarly, in casuistry we can seek a solution by first seeing how our novel case resembles one that ethicists have already encountered and for which they have developed a clear paradigm.[4] In this way, as Jonsen and Toulmin write, casuistry as paradigm-based research moves "from clear and simple cases to the more complex and obscure ones."[5]

Moral Reasoning (Berkeley: University of California Press, 1988).

2 Cases also arise in instances of what Kenneth E. Kirk calls "error," which I shall not address here. For an illuminating discussion, see Kirk, *Conscience and Its Problems: An Introduction to Casuistry* (London: Longmans, Green and Co., 1948), ch. 5. Moreover, cases arise when we need to determine the extent to which individuals or groups are culpable for their conduct, focusing our attention on degrees of merit or blame.

3 Thomas Kuhn, *The Structure of Scientific Revolutions*, 2d ed. (Chicago: University of Chicago Press, 1970), 45.

4 Ibid., 189.

5 Jonsen and Toulmin, *The Abuse of Casuistry*, 252.

In addition to paradigms (and their analogical application), casuists rely on maxims, or general, aphoristic rules. Maxims are, in effect, formulaic generalizations, which serve "as fulcra and warrants for argument."[6] These aphorisms draw from the tradition of moral theology and human experience in general, e.g., "one good turn deserves another," "force may be repulsed by force," or "war is a symptom of sin in the world." Maxims assist in the process of ethical judgment by articulating distilled bits of practical wisdom about a range of issues in ordinary life.[7]

Within the post-Cold War context, the cases of economic sanctions and humanitarian interventions now generate (or ought to generate) rather conspicuous anxieties about the proper role and methods of military force. This means, among other things, that pacifists and just-war theorists are now confronted with some basic questions about how to classify these cases. It also means that which maxims are appropriate to invoke will likewise prove a daunting question. As a result, the casuistry of war and peace in the post-Cold War era is likely to be highly vexed. But in order for this point to become clear, it is important to consider some of the casuistry of the Cold War, if only to sharpen by way of contrast and comparison the issues that confront us today.

II. The Casuistry of Deterrence

From the early 1950s until 1990, the centerpiece of American foreign policy — and a critical case for ethicists — consisted in deterring Soviet expansion throughout the globe. By *deterrence* I mean the strategy to prevent the outbreak of nuclear and some conventional war by threatening to retaliate against a potential aggressor. Deterrence is a preventive measure that is fundamentally paradoxical: nations threaten to wage war in order to prevent war from being waged.

Deterrence provided the prism through which just-war discourse was often refracted during the Cold War. And, in a less obvious way, it provided an interesting case for pacifists as well. Yet, however difficult the case of deterrence proved to be, it put little stress on the foundational philosophies of either moral vocabulary.

For the just-war theorist, the initial question surrounding deterrence was taxonomic or, more specifically, analogical: Is the paradox of deterrence sufficiently similar to the paradigm of war to allow for the application

---

6 Ibid., 252-53.
7 There are other features of casuistry, e.g., circumstances and probable reasoning, that I shall not discuss here. For a discussion, see ibid., 253-54.

of just-war criteria in evaluating deterrent plans? Deterrence is not, strictly speaking, the use of force to repel aggression; it is, as I have said, the threat of force in order to prevent the outbreak of war. When we think of defending family members from attack, for example, it is rather easy to proceed from the paradigm of individual self-defense to justify defending one's spouse, given the mediating notion that family members constitute an "extended self." But the paradox of deterrence admits of no easy or obvious analogies with familiar paradigms about the use of lethal force.

Nevertheless, the case of deterrence was managed within the framework of just-war tenets insofar as those criteria presuppose the legitimacy of self-defense and the importance of carrying out that defense with discriminate and proportionate methods. These presuppositions respectively shape the *jus ad bellum* and the *jus in bello*, the two main pillars of just-war criteria. For just-war theorists, deterrence found presumptive plausibility insofar as the right of self-defense implied the right not to be vulnerable to outside aggression. The preventive aims of deterrence, in other words, more or less cohered with the *ad bellum* notion of a just cause: states have the right — indeed, the duty — to protect their citizens from unjust uses of force. Insofar as deterrence could be interpreted as a strategy of self-protection, it could be "seen" within standard just-war categories. The general moral simplicity of the Cold War era — arraying Western forces as the children of light against Soviet forces as the children of darkness — provided the main parameters within which deterrence was understood in the strategic literature. This outlook easily hooked up with one of the fundamental tenets of the just-war tradition: the legitimate right of self-defense.[8]

This is not to say that deterrence could (or did) find sanction among just-war theorists. For there is also the question of the proper means of warfare, enshrined in the criteria of limited war. And it is in regard to these concerns that deterrence generated considerable casuistic anxiety: Were the means necessary to deter aggression compatible with the requirements of discriminate and proportionate uses of force? Or was it the case that the only way to institutionalize a successful deterrent was to threaten (and plan) to use nuclear weapons in ways that were intentionally indiscriminate or foreseeably disproportionate?

These queries generated a dilemma between *ad bellum* legitimations of self-protective measures and *in bello* restrictions on the morally available means for institutionalizing those measures. What is important to note here is that this dilemma arose from *a tension internal to the just-war tradition itself*. Deterrence forced just-war theorists to determine which of

---

8 One notable exception to this emphasis on self-defense as a just cause is found in the work of Paul Ramsey, *Just War: Force and Political Responsibility* (New York: Charles Scribner's Sons, 1968), ch. 6.

the two main pillars of the criteria finally had more weight. Did the *ad bellum* warrant for self-defense trump concerns about limited means, allowing us to "look the other way" when it came to the immorality of deterrent threats? Or did *in bello* restrictions hold indefeasibly, requiring vast reductions in the nuclear arsenal and subsequent vulnerability to nuclear blackmail?[9] These questions pit one set of just-war criteria against another. But deterrence did not send just-war theorists to the drawing board to reconceive some basic theoretical assumptions about their political morality; it did not generate what might be called foundational or political-philosophical inquiry. Thus, however tortuous debates about deterrence might have been, they typically operated in a political-strategic horizon in which the importance of self-defense was central, or at least assumed. The case of deterrence in the Cold War era essentially forced just-war theorists to determine how strong (or weak) they understood the imperative of self-protection to be.

Although pacifists rarely if ever said so, deterrence likewise presented an interesting case of conscience for them as well. On the one hand, the preparations for war necessary to sustain a deterrent seemed to typify the kind of reliance upon violence that pacifists so often call to our attention. Yet, as I have said, deterrence is not exactly war, which is the institution that pacifists characteristically wish to abolish. Indeed, at a *prima facie* level, the preventive aims of deterrence would seem to resonate with pacifists' aims of eliminating the outbreak of war.

Once again, however, the case of deterrence provided little reason to engage in foundational or terminological inquiry. Pacifists saw the vast arsenal arrayed on behalf of deterrence as symptomatic of the grave evils associated with war: inordinate national pride, vilification of the enemy, loyalty to the state, militaristic hubris. In other words, pacifists could look

---

9 The former line of reasoning is developed in different ways by, e.g.: Michael Walzer, *Just and Unjust Wars: A Moral Argument with Historical Illustrations* (New York: Basic Books, 1977), ch. 17; William V. O'Brien, "Just-War Doctrine in a Nuclear Context," *Theological Studies* 44 (June 1983), 191-220. The latter line of reasoning is defended by John Finnis, Joseph Boyle, and Germain Grisez, *Nuclear Deterrence, Morality and Realism* (New York: Oxford University Press, 1987).

Paul Ramsey and David Hollenbach tried to finesse this tension by distinguishing between the ends of war and the ends of deterrence; see Ramsey, *The Just War*, ch. 15, and David Hollenbach, *Nuclear Ethics: A Christian Moral Argument* (New York: Paulist Press, 1983). My own view is that these prodigious efforts fail. For a review of these and other discussions of the ethics of deterrence, see Richard B. Miller, *Interpretations of Conflict: Ethics, Pacifism, and the Just-War Tradition* (Chicago: University of Chicago Press, 1991), chs. 6, 7.

beyond the paradoxes of deterrence to find its basic theological core: misplaced loyalties and idolatrous trust in political or military power.[10] As a result, the casuistry that deterrence might have generated for pacifists could be easily abbreviated by invoking the maxim that war (and preparations for war) are symptomatic of sin. If self-defense served as the rationale among nonpacifists for deterrence, then pacifists could invoke the standard trope that self-defense attenuates the demands of neighbor love and love of the enemy. Such critiques are familiar themes in pacifist literature, and could be invoked rather easily to assess the case of deterrence. Deterrence could thus be framed within a relatively simple theological-ethical framework, pitting children of light (pacifists) against children of darkness (militarists and their apologists).

All of this must of necessity change in the post-Cold War era. For, as I have said, the rationale for using force — self-defense — has more or less receded from the moral (and political) landscape. This means that if force is to be used, it must find another clear rationale from just-war theorists. It also means that if pacifists continue to condemn uses of military force, then something other than self-love and national loyalty must set the terms for their critique. Within the current context, some uses of force are likely to receive less opprobrium from pacifists than self-defensive wars. In any event, insofar as the rationale of self-defense recedes in the post-Cold War period, the use of force or coercion will not occur within the political-strategic horizon of the Cold War. The cases of economic sanctions and humanitarian interventions illustrate a different complexity, one which will require just-war theorists and pacifists to develop some basic foundational issues.

III. Humanitarian Interventions

Nothing that I said about deterrence as the centerpiece of Cold War foreign policy was meant to suggest that we should overlook the interventions that occurred throughout the Cold War era. But within the context of Cold War animosities, interventions by the United States had national security, not humanitarianism, as their overriding rationale. As Stephen Van Erva notes, one of the principal claims during the Cold War was that interventions "were required to blunt the Soviet Union's 'imperial thrust'

---

10 See, e.g., James Douglass, *The Non-Violent Cross: A Theology of Revolution and Peace* (New York: Macmillan, 1968), 161-173, 182-214; Stanley Hauerwas, *Against the Nations: War and Survival in a Liberal Society* (Minneapolis: Winston Press, 1985), ch. 8 and passim.

in the Third World, in order to preserve the global balance of power."[11] With the promulgation of NSC-68 in 1950, U.S. foreign policy focused on containing Soviet expansionism, viewing communism as a voracious imperialistic doctrine that was intent on extending its sphere of influence.[12] So, as Richard Falk remarks, "intervention to avoid the influence of values associated with world communism was an implied feature of the U.S. role as guarantor of free world security."[13] The general outlook was a zero-sum mentality, where every advance in the Kremlin's sphere of influence signaled a loss to the West. For all practical purposes, this zero-sum mentality meant that interventions by the United States in Iran, Guatemala, Indochina, Chile, Grenada, Nicaragua, El Salvador, and Angola were directly or indirectly justified in the name of national security — that is, self-defense.

With the thawing of Cold War tensions, this rationale and its corresponding mentality have disappeared (however, much interventions remain with us). The activity of the U.S. military in Somalia, for example, has been justified under the rubric of humanitarian intervention, and appeals for a U.S.-led intervention in Bosnia have likewise invoked the maxim that strong powers have (general) obligations to protect the weak. Whether those appeals are heeded is not my immediate concern here. What is important from an ethical standpoint is that for just-war theorists and pacifists alike, the case of humanitarian intervention requires a somewhat different taxonomy and an inquiry into philosophical-political terms that are fundamental to each moral vocabulary.

For just-war theorists, the case of humanitarian intervention poses the question, What kind of cause beyond that of self-defense can justify the use of military force? Generally, the answer has been that the defense or promotion of human rights can authorize such uses, that protecting people from politically induced famine or various forms of political repression provides a just cause for an outside party to intervene. A theology of peace, centered on the value of human dignity and the respect for individual well-being, generates a strong basis for using force to protect the innocent — be they one's own citizens or members of the human family.[14] The

---

11 Stephen Van Erva, "The Case Against Intervention," *Atlantic Monthly* 266 (July 1990), 76.

12 For a discussion, see Lawrence Freedman, *The Evolution of Nuclear Strategy* (New York: St. Martin's Press, 1983), 51, 69-71, 76-77.

13 Richard Falk, "Recycling Interventionism," *Journal of Peace Research* 29 (1992), 130.

14 This is the center of the moral theory of the U.S. Catholic bishops, *The Challenge of Peace: God's Promise and Our Response* (Washington, D.C.: USCC Office for Publishing and Promotion Services, 1983), developing the implications of Pope John XXIII's vision of the global human family in *Pacem in Terris*.

defense and promotion of human dignity can authorize the use of force as a form of *rescue*, a more altruistic purpose than self-defense.

Two things about this appeal to human rights and the cause of rescue merit our attention. First, the idea that lethal force might be justified to defend human rights by outside parties requires another paradigm for seeing the act in question. Interventions for humanitarian purposes cannot be viewed in terms of self-defense, either in a narrow or "extended" understanding of that rubric. Rather, moral analysis must rely on the maxim that one has the obligation to help others when rescue does not impose excessive costs to the self. For these reasons, the case of humanitarian intervention poses the question: Should the use of military force in places like Somalia be classified as *war*, or is another paradigm more fitting?

One response to this query has come from pacifists, although their response is relevant to just-war theorists as well. The idea is to classify humanitarian intervention in Somalia as a *police action* instead of a war, drawing on the analogy of the (acceptable) use of force in the civic realm. Pacifists believe that war is immoral, but they do not necessarily ban the use of force by civic authorities. Police force can be justified as a way of maintaining a modicum of order in civil society. Thus Stanley Hauerwas remarks: "It is essential to distinguish between a war and a police action. A police action means that there is a specified crime; the police go in to stop it using no more force than needed and they do not serve as the judge and jury."[15] Insofar as humanitarian interventions are described (or redescribed) in such terms, they appear to pose little difficulty for casuistry among pacifists. The paradigm of police action, allowing for the use of violence in order to stop criminal activity, may enable some pacifists to accept military action, even killing, as a means of establishing order.

This is not to suggest that classifying humanitarian interventions in this way is problem-free, however. The analogy becomes problematic for just-war theorists when it is joined to the idea that international police actions are meant to serve human dignity and human rights. But just-war theorists are understandably cautious about what these notions might entail. In just-war theory, foreign nations are not authorized to enter civil wars, to tame a tyrant, or to suppress another nation's security forces every time human rights are violated. This is because a competing duty is relevant: each nation's sovereignty, its right of self-determination, and its corresponding immunity from outside interference. Accordingly, even

---

15 Peter Steinfels, "Reshaping Pacifism to Fight Anguish in Reshaped World," *New York Times*, December 21, 1992, sec. A, 1. See also Kenneth R. Himes, "Just War, Pacifism, and Humanitarian Intervention," *America*, August 14, 1993, 12. Not all pacifist organizations endorsed the intervention into Somalia, as the *New York Times* article makes clear.

nations in which there is widespread oppression or suffering do not provide an open door through which foreign powers may enter. Generally speaking, the case of humanitarian intervention must satisfy two conditions: Only after suffering is clear and long-standing, and only when the intervening power enters into the interests of those who suffer, may intervention be justified.[16] Otherwise the defense of human rights by an outside party violates a people's right to self-determination. It is open to the charge of paternalism or, even worse, imperialism. The defense of human rights must be traded off against the respect for sovereignty, and when the duty to defend those rights trumps, the duty of noninterference is by no means self-evident.[17]

This moral complexity surrounding humanitarian interventions requires a more elaborate set of casuistical considerations in just-war theory than did interventions or deterrence during the Cold War. *Indeed, the case requires just-war theorists to address a tension that stands "outside" their ethical vocabulary.* It is not, in short, a dilemma wrought by a tension internal to the criteria themselves; it is a political-philosophical tension. Depending on how much weight one puts on the value of sovereignty, the defense of human rights will be more (or less) difficult to invoke as a just cause. The strength of the former, in other words, will necessarily weaken the force of the latter in decisions about recourse to lethal force. How to settle the basic tension between the value of sovereignty vis-a-vis the value of human rights is a question that must be answered before just-war criteria are wheeled in to assess the use of military force for altruistic purposes. In the post-Cold War context, it is necessary for just-war theorists to return

---

16 For an important discussion, see Michael Walzer, *Just and Unjust Wars: A Moral Argument with Historical Illustrations* (New York: Basic Books, 1977), ch. 6. Walzer cites with approval the example of India's intervention on behalf of Bengalis against the East Pakistani government in 1971, the force of which I have distilled in the two conditions I state in this paragraph. Walzer's discussion of humanitarian interventions should be read in conjunction with his account of the legalist paradigm on pages 58-63.

17 No doubt the reality of sovereignty has experienced a variety of pressures over the last 40 years, owing largely to the communications revolution, increased economic interdependence, and nations' vulnerability to attack by strategic nuclear weapons. Yet, from these data, it would be hasty to conclude that the value of sovereignty is likely to disappear (or ought to disappear) from international law or from political theory. For instructive discussions, see Stanley Hoffmann, "A New World and Its Troubles" in *Sea Changes: American Foreign Policy in a World Transformed*, ed. Nicholas X. Rizopoulos (New York: Council on Foreign Relations Press, 1990), 274-292; J. Bryan Hehir, "Just-War Theory in a Post-Cold War World," *Journal of Religious Ethics* 20 (Fall 1992), 237-257.

to the drawing board to clarify some fundamental philosophical-political considerations.[18]

At a practical level, the issue of sovereignty is (or ought to be) a concern for pacifists as well. Pacifists tend to downplay, if not ignore, the issue of sovereignty at a theoretical level, but the question of the appropriate time and place to intervene cannot be dismissed. At the very least, it cannot be dismissed unless pacifists wish to allow for police actions to protect innocent people throughout the globe. Without further qualifications, classifying humanitarian interventions in terms of police actions easily generates the idea that powerful nations have the right, or duty, to police the crimes committed in other nations. It would be no small irony if pacifists' casuistry led to such a conclusion, for it would allow for considerably more uses of military force than would a theory which weighs the duty of protecting human rights against the duty to respect sovereignty.

This practical difference in the way just-war theorists and pacifists might handle the case of humanitarian intervention suggests an important point for the casuistry of war and peace: Pacifists might find it easier to accept the kind of lethal force that just-war theorists typically have the most trouble justifying. This is because standard just-war theory considers the case of self-defense the strongest kind of cause, whereas pacifists characteristically consider self-defense insufficient for killing in war.[19] Moreover, just-war theorists have more trouble justifying altruistic wars than wars of self-defense, given (among other things) the importance of another nation's sovereignty in just-war theory. Pacifists typically do not pay much attention to sovereignty, and are quicker to commend altruistic motives. For this reason, pacifists may have less trouble justifying humanitarian interventions than do most just-war theorists.

---

18 *The Harvest of Justice Is Sown in Peace* follows this general line of reasoning, placing relatively greater weight on sovereignty than on the defense of human rights when considering cases of humanitarian intervention. However, those who follow the bishops' line of reasoning should articulate why we should rank sovereignty and human rights in this way, or what it is about sovereignty that allows it to trump considerations of human rights in all but exceptional circumstances. For a brilliant discussion of this tension, see Walzer, *Just and Unjust Wars*, ch. 6.

19 Again, in just-war theory Paul Ramsey's work constitutes a notable exception to this rule (see no. 8).

IV. Sanctions

In recent years, economic sanctions have become more common as a prelude or alternative to the use of lethal force. North Korea, Iraq, the former Yugoslavia, Haiti, South Africa, and Libya have all felt the brunt of economic sanctions. The main goal of import or export embargoes is to coerce recalcitrant leaders into cooperating with the international community by putting pressure on their economic infrastructure or by denying them various technologies that would be useful to their military.

Sanctions seem attractive at first glance because they avoid direct military confrontation. For those who frame moral discourse about war in terms of a presumption against the use of force (as we find, for example, in the U.S. Catholic bishops' theology of peace), sanctions seem to recommend themselves because they institutionalize the mandate to try nonmilitary forms of coercion. Even more important, at the practical level, sanctions put fewer soldiers' lives at risk. This is no small concern in cases where soldiers may have to intervene in a military action that is shaped by altruistic rather than self-defensive purposes. Why should American or British lives be risked in a humanitarian intervention if alternatives haven't been tried first? Nonmilitary forms of coercion may produce change at a significantly less cost to human life, and there is nothing obviously wrong with worrying about the lives of one's own soldiers when calculating the costs of going to war.

Yet whether and to what extent just-war theorists and pacifists should condone sanctions is not entirely obvious. This is because sanctions almost inevitably affect the civilian population of the targeted nation. As G. E. M. Anscombe argued during the Second World War, sanctions resemble bombing missions that "enlarge the target." Such a strategy, Anscombe observed, fails to distinguish between combatants and noncombatants, and finds no warrant according to the rule of double effect.[20] For this reason, it has been suggested that citizens in nations on whom sanctions are imposed should be allowed to exit and find sanctuary elsewhere.[21] Those who consent to stay rather than become refugees assume the burdens that have been imposed upon their leaders.

For just-war theory, this problem produces a profound moral dilemma. This is because sanctions are (sometimes) interpreted as required by the criterion of last resort.[22] During the months preceding the Gulf War,

---

20 G. E. M. Anscombe, "The Justice of the Present War Examined," in *War in the Twentieth Century: Sources in Theological Ethics*, ed. Richard B. Miller (Louisville, Ky.: Westminster/John Knox Press, 1992), 445-48.
21 See Walzer, *Just and Unjust Wars*, ch. 10.
22 Himes, "Just War, Pacifism, and Humanitarian Intervention," 15.

for example, the U.S. Catholic bishops called for the continuation of economic sanctions against Iraq by appealing to this criterion.[23] Those who objected to the use of sanctions did so by arguing either that Iraq's invasion of Kuwait meant that the criterion of last resort was irrelevant, or that last resort had been given too much weight in debates about whether to go to war.[24] Sanctions take time and are often insufficiently coercive. Having to wait to see if sanctions work ties the hands of political leaders who must make decisions within a limited time frame. Presidents and ministers of defense cannot always enjoy the virtues of patience.

For pacifists, the main question posed by sanctions is taxonomic: Can sanctions be classified as "nonviolent"? On the one hand, the answer appears to be in the affirmative: Sanctions do not directly attack bodily integrity and thus differ from the kinds of dangers imposed by soldiers armed with weapons. But individuals suffer nonetheless; if they did not, the sanctions would not be coercive. Sanctions hurt — which is why they are used.[25] Saying that sanctions are nonviolent seems counterintuitive, requiring us to engage in the kind of verbal equivocation that can get casuists into trouble.

This need for conceptual clarification is especially important given the tendency in pacifism to talk about the evils of structural violence.[26] *Structural violence* refers to political and economic arrangements that impoverish significant segments of the population, denying citizens the elementary conditions for human flourishing. Violence occurs "invisibly," as it were, resulting from systems of oppression that are instituted in a nation's legal, cultural, or economic arrangements. Pacifists are well equipped to criticize societies which institutionalize patterns of oppression insofar as pacifists are alert to the multiple causes of suffering and sources of domination. But that would make it difficult for pacifists to condone sanctions as a tool of nonviolence, given the parallels between the kinds of suffering caused by effective sanctions and structural violence. Accordingly, the case of sanctions raises a question that is fundamental to

---

23 Daniel Pilarczyk, "Letter to President Bush: The Persian Gulf Crisis," in *War in the Twentieth Century*, ed. Miller, 445-48.

24 See, e.g., Francis X. Winters, "Freedom to Resist Coercion," *Commonweal* (June 1, 1991): 369-72; Walzer, *Just and Unjust Wars*, 2d ed., xi-xxiii.

25 For a portrait of the effects of sanctions on Iraq, see Alberto Ascherio, et al., "Effect of the Gulf War on Infant and Child Mortality in Iraq," *New England Journal of Medicine* 327 (September 24, 1992), 931-936, which reports that the number of deaths among children after the war (during which time sanctions have been in place) was three times higher than before the war. For a recent account of the effects of sanctions on the citizens of Serbia, see Tom Post, et al., "A Price No One Can Justify," *Newsweek*, December 6, 1993, 30-32.

26 See, e.g., Johan Galtung, "Violence, Peace, and Peace Research," *Journal of Peace Research* 6 (1969), 167-191.

pacifism itself. Depending on the pacifist's definition of violence, sanctions may not pass muster from persons shaped by the virtues of peaceableness.

A second difficulty for pacifists concerns cases in which sanctions might be used as a prelude to humanitarian interventions. It is not clear how sanctions could be justified by pacifists who view those interventions as "police actions." This is because in the domestic sphere, police forces typically do not impose economic sanctions on criminals as a prelude, or alternative, to the use of more aggressive (and potentially dangerous) methods. Police seek out criminals in order to put an immediate end to crime, often removing the criminal from the community. But sanctions take time and are meant to induce cooperation with the wider community. Police actions and sanctions operate within different time frames and pursue quite different aims. For this reason, the paradigm of police actions provides little if any justification for using sanctions in advance of, or as an alternative to, humanitarian interventions. Indeed, that paradigm would render the use of sanctions counterintuitive.

V. Conclusion

With the collapse of the Second World, the United States will undoubtedly find itself involved in the ongoing travails of the Third World. But, for the most part, those involvements will be driven less by considerations of national interest than by the imperative to protect and promote human rights. This shift will make for a different set of complexities in the ethics of coercion and the use of lethal force. The cases of humanitarian intervention and economic sanctions are not new to the ethics of war and peace, and the questions they raise are not unique to the post-Cold War era.[27] But the moral framework of Cold War animosities focused the attention of ethicists and intellectuals on foreign policy driven by the imperatives of containment and self-protection. That framework is gone, and with it the innocence that has often shaped American perceptions of international conflict and the justification to use lethal force. Now, in a different international environment, just-war theorists and pacifists will be called upon to clarify some theoretical and practical issues in political philosophy that emerge from cases and contexts in which self-defense is virtually irrelevant. Those issues arise from familiar occasions of casuistry, the experiences of doubt and conflict.

Just-war theorists have two sets of issues to address, both of which are generated by basic ethical conflicts. First, there is the question of the

---

27 See nos. 16, 21.

grounds for intervention, and the relation between those grounds and the value of sovereignty. Negotiating this conflict will be part and parcel of the desire to carve out a sphere for military action that heeds the demands of human rights and human dignity without allowing for paternalism or imperialism.

Second, just-war theorists must articulate the extent to which economic sanctions are required by the *ad bellum* criterion of last resort. Then there is the subsequent question of how to impose sanctions in ways that abide by the *in bello* mandate not to put innocent lives at risk. With sanctions no less than war, the general ethical consensus of the West is that innocent people have a right not to be instrumentalized. The question facing just-war theorists concerns the extent to which *in bello* restrictions limit the kinds of options available to political leaders to resolve conflicts in the international community.

Pacifists' casuistry will have less to do with conflicting values or duties than with doubts about the meaning of some basic terms. They will have to clarify the outer limits of international police actions, or at least clarify the conditions that must be met in order to justify humanitarian intervention. This clarification will turn on how to specify the meaning and limits of interventions understood as police actions. When it comes to sanctions, pacifists need to rearticulate their understanding(s) of the meaning of *nonviolence* and the relation of pacifism to various forms of coercion. It is by no means obvious that sanctions are "nonviolent," especially given the prominent place that pacifists often give to the harmful effects of structural violence.

The case of sanctions is especially problematic for pacifism in those contexts in which they are imposed as a prelude to the (possible) use of military force for humanitarian purposes. Depending on how pacifists come to classify economic sanctions, new moral and political configurations are likely to appear on the intellectual landscape. In the post-Cold War era, one should not be at all surprised to find some pacifists approving the use of military force (as a police action) more readily than the use of various forms of economic coercion (understood as structural violence). In casuistry now no less than during the Cold War, descriptions can make all the difference.[28]

28 I am grateful to Lucinda Peach for her generous assistance in producing this essay, and to Barbara Klinger and David H. Smith for their comments on an earlier draft.

Catholic Social Thought and Humanitarian Intervention

Kenneth R. Himes, OFM

The late R. J. Vincent, a respected British political theorist, once wrote of diplomats, "given that *sangfroid* is their business, human rights are one more thing for them to be unenthusiastic about."[1] Vincent's remark may be too sarcastic with regard even to diplomats but it is certainly not applicable to the many voices within the Catholic community which have taken the Church's social teaching seriously. The advocacy of human rights and the employment of rights language in the formulation of the Church's social vision have become commonplace. Surveying the evolution of the topic within Catholic circles, one commentator has concluded: "Various groups within the Catholic Church have become highly visible on the global horizon as advocates of respect for the full range of human

---

1 *Human Rights and International Relations* (Cambridge: Cambridge University Press for Royal Institute of International Affairs, 1986), 143, as quoted by Adam Roberts, "Humanitarian War: Military Intervention and Human Rights," *International Affairs* 69 (1993), 429-449 at 432, no. 9.

rights. Also, the central institutional organ of the Catholic Church, the Holy See, has adopted the cause of human rights as a prime focus of its ethical teaching and pastoral strategy in the domain of international justice and peace."[2]

The interest in human rights is rooted in Roman Catholicism's theological anthropology. Twentieth-century theology has had a markedly anthropocentric outlook, and while other perspectives have tempered that bias, it remains true that theology is not simply concerned with God, but God for us, *Deus pro nobis.* It is the message of much of contemporary Catholic theology that one studies the revelation of the Jewish and Christian communities in order to understand the meaning of the human. As the present bishop of Rome stated in his first encyclical, "The man who wishes to understand himself more thoroughly — and not just in accordance with immediate, partial, often superficial, and even illusory standards and measures of his being — he must with his unrest, uncertainty and even his weakness and sinfulness, with his life and death, draw near to Christ."[3] The conviction that in Christian revelation one finds insight into the meaning of human life is a foundational theme of the tradition and has led to the Church's resistance to any movement which would debase the dignity of the person.

At the very heart of Catholic social teaching is a commitment to the dignity of the individual created in the image of God. "In reality, the name for that deep amazement at humanity's worth and dignity is the Gospel, that is to say: the Good News. It is also called Christianity. This amazement determines the Church's mission in the world. . . . "[4] When the Catholic Church reflects upon the present struggles in our troubled world, it begins from the premise that each person is a creature of inestimable dignity and that the policies, structures, and decisions which affect human beings must be shaped by a commitment to the well-being of all. The emergence of human rights as a central element in Catholic social thought is a direct reflection of that commitment, for the ideology of human rights has become one of the primary vehicles for giving expression to the practical meaning of human dignity as a norm of social life. In their statement commemorating the tenth anniversary of *The Challenge of Peace,* the American bishops speak clearly: "An indispensable condition for a just and peaceful world order is the promotion and defense of human rights. In our religious tradition and international law, human rights include the spectrum of civil, political, social, cultural, and economic rights."[5]

---

2   David Hollenbach, *Justice, Peace and Human Rights* (New York: Crossroad Publishing, 1988), 87.

3   John Paul II, "Redemptor Hominis," no. 10.

4   Ibid., no. 10.

5   National Conference of Catholic Bishops, *The Harvest of Justice Is Sown in*

It is in the context of this strong support for human rights that the topic of armed intervention for humanitarian purposes must be considered.[6] For today the argument in favor of humanitarian intervention has relied upon a commitment to the "promotion and defense of human rights" as justification for employment of violent force. Such a forceful intervention, if necessary, is to rectify human rights violations of foreign nationals within the territories of their own state.

But the commitment to human rights is not the sole shaper of the context within which the Catholic community reflects upon the matter of humanitarian intervention. Understanding the other elements shaping the context is crucial to grasping why humanitarian intervention is such a nettlesome question for the Roman Catholic community.

Factors in the Debate

There are four influential themes which ought to be considered in addition to human rights when discussing humanitarian intervention: (1) state sovereignty, (2) the duty of solidarity, (3) the relationship of order to

---

Peace (Washington, D.C.: USCC Office for Publishing and Promotion Services, 1994), 9.

6 It may be useful to clarify the limits of this essay. As I use the term, intervention means "dictatorial interference in the internal affairs of another state involving the use or threat of force, or substantially debilitating economic coercion." Humanitarian intervention is intervention (as previously described) "in order to remedy mass and flagrant violations of the basic human rights of foreign nationals by their government," either through that government's direct actions or inaction due to inability or indifference.

My usage borrows from two sources: for intervention, Jack Donnelly, "Human Rights, Humanitarian Intervention and American Foreign Policy: Law, Morality and Politics," *Journal of International Affairs* 37 (1984), 311-328 at 311. For the further qualifier of intervention as humanitarian, Kelly Kate Pease and David P. Forsythe, "Human Rights, Humanitarian Intervention, and World Politics," *Human Rights Quarterly* 15 (1993), 290-314 at 291.

An important question which is not part of this analysis is whether nongovernmental organizations can be accused of intervention. For example, international relief agencies do not use force to intervene but do operate within a state's territory without always having the clear consent of the government. For this study, I shall restrict my remarks to state(s) activity against another state.

justice in international affairs, and (4) the ongoing conversation between proponents of just-war theory and pacifism.

1. *State sovereignty.* In Catholic teaching sovereignty has never been accorded the pride of place it was granted in the writing of international lawyers and political theorists. As a way of resolving the Thirty Years' War, the principle of *cuius regio eius religio* (the religion of the prince is the religion of the people) was an expression of the idea that states should respect the autonomy of domestic order within other states. Sovereignty was upheld in order to maintain some limitations on the constant provocation for states to meddle in the internal life of other states in an age of religious intolerance. It was also a restraint on the political or economic ambitions lurking beneath the pretext of religious faith.

While the sovereignty of states has been praised as a building block of modern world order, it is not a principle which has been understood in the same way by everyone. What Joseph Nye calls a state moralist position focuses on the "the rights of states as a collective form of their citizens' individual rights to life and liberty. The nation-state may be seen as a pooled expression of individual rights."[7] This approach, therefore, would place great weight on state sovereignty and self-determination by a people since such ideas are really means for upholding the rights of individual persons. Sovereignty would be an absolute principle, or nearly so in such a framework, for the rights of the individual to life and liberty are highly esteemed.

In contrast, there is the cosmopolitan school which "stresses the common nature of humanity. States and boundaries exist, but this does not endow them with moral significance."[8] Human rights, at least certain basic rights, take precedence over territorial boundaries. We ought not grant very much to a presumption in favor of sovereignty but rather uphold the overriding import of human rights whenever and wherever violated. The presumption here is that the state may not in fact serve the rights of individual citizens and thus a state cannot expect that our esteem for the rights of the person carries over to a respect for territorial boundaries or governments.

My reading of the Catholic tradition suggests that the Church expresses a growing preference for the cosmopolitan approach while avoiding too simple a dismissal of the insights found within the state moralist outlook. For example, in Pope John XXIII's *Pacem in Terris*, there is an argument throughout that a state's sovereignty must be restrained by forces both "lower" and "higher" than the state. Catholic social thought begins with a

---

7 Richard Cooper and Joseph Nye, Jr., "Ethics and Foreign Policy" in Samuel Huntington and Joseph Nye, Jr., eds., *Global Affairs* (Lanham, Md.: University Press of America, 1985), 23-41 at 25.

8 Ibid., 25.

society of persons, not a society of states. But it does not end with a society of persons, since the state is a legitimate structure. Within Catholic teaching, persons in society are also citizens of states, and states are members of an international society. The state has a legitimate role in Catholic social thought but one circumscribed by the role of persons making up a society and the place of states in the scheme of international society. Thus, "from below," the state is bound to respect the rights of individual human beings who have basic needs, essential freedoms, and fundamental relationships which are given expression in the language of human rights.[9] "From above," the individual state is limited by the duty to cooperate with other states and institutions in creating a global order which serves the international common good. The state, while important, is neither the beginning nor the end of Catholic political thought. Its value is instrumental. State sovereignty, therefore, cannot be absolute but must be tempered by the importance of the human person and the goal of international community. Human rights and the international common good are important elements in Catholic teaching which serve as restraints upon any state's claim of sovereignty.

Sovereignty, when understood according to Catholic theory, meant that within its legitimate realm of competency the state was the final arbiter. With respect to the purpose of government, the state is supreme, but the purpose of government is not all-encompassing, as there are areas of human existence which are beyond the proper activity of the state. Thus, a state's sovereignty is exercised "only in regard to certain matters and to a certain content."[10] It was the Hobbesian notion of the state as leviathan which distorted sovereignty.

When the principle of *cuius regio, eius religio* was accepted, it reflected the corruption of sovereignty according to Catholic thinking, however practical it may have seemed at the time as a resolution to protracted violence. For a subsequent effect of such an understanding of the authority of the prince was to extend the state's authority into areas where it lacked competency, i.e., religion and worship. Once the Church was made subject to the prince, then there was no possibility of distinguishing between the law of the state and any higher moral law. In effect, the recent emphasis on the normative place of human rights in political theory and the duties of the state to the international common good are modern

---

9 " . . . [T]he very heart of international life is not so much States as man." John Paul II, "Address to the Diplomatic Corps accredited to the Holy See," *L'Osservatore Romano* (Weekly Edition in English) 26 (January 20, 1993), 1-3 at 3.

10 Heinrich Rommen, *The State in Catholic Thought: A Treatise in Political Philosophy* (St. Louis: B. Herder Book Company, 1945), 398. This work remains a classic statement of traditional Catholic political theory.

variations on a traditional theme in Catholic social thought — the limited role of the state and the restriction of its sovereignty to certain areas of social life.

When this outlook is applied to the issue of humanitarian intervention, it suggests that state sovereignty must not be used as an excuse to tolerate grievous abuses of human rights. We can conclude this section by agreeing with George Weigel that "whatever else it might mean, the principle of state sovereignty cannot mean that states are free to engage in the indiscriminate slaughter of religious, racial, or ethnic minorities within their borders.[11]

2. *Solidarity in Catholic teaching.* A variety of church statements during the last decades have highlighted the theme of solidarity. Sometimes spoken of as a virtue, at other times as a duty, the idea has its roots in a vision that is foundational to Catholic social teaching, i.e., we are all members of one human family. This vision has roots in theological convictions about the nature of the Church and the very nature of God. In the pastoral constitution on the Church promulgated at Vatican II, the bishops of the world wrote: "The promotion of unity belongs to the innermost nature of the Church, for she is, 'thanks to her relationship with Christ, a sacramental sign and an instrument of intimate union with God, and of the unity of the whole human race.'"[12] It is of the essence of a sacrament that it embody or incarnate a truth so that reality can be understood. The Church promotes unity because it must embody the truth that we are one family of creatures united with our creator.

Pope John Paul II has further linked the moral call to solidarity with the doctrine of the Trinity. "Beyond human and natural bonds, already so close and strong, there is discerned in the light of faith a new *model* of the *unity* of the human race, which must ultimately inspire our *solidarity.* This supreme *model of unity,* which is a reflection of the intimate life of God, one God in three Persons, is what we Christians mean by the word '*communion.*'"[13] The pope goes on to state that "solidarity therefore must play its part in the realization of this divine plan, both on the level of individuals and on the level of national and international society."[14] Solidarity is an obligation because we are created in the image of God who is

---

11 George Weigel, "The Summer of Our Discontent: II," *American Purpose* 6 (1992), 41-48 at 45.

12 Second Vatican Council, *Pastoral Constitution on the Church in the Modern World (Gaudium et Spes)*, no. 42. Here the Council Fathers quote themselves from *Lumen Gentium*, no. 1.

13 John Paul II, *On Social Concern (Sollicitudo Rei Socialis)*, papal encyclical (Washington, D.C.: Office for Publishing and Promotion Services, 1987), no. 40.

14 Ibid., no. 40.

Trinitarian, not unitarian. If the inner life of God is loving communion, so too must the life of creatures made in the divine image be marked by loving union. Solidarity points us toward that goal.

In his encyclical, *Sollicitudo Rei Socialis*, the pope explained the meaning of solidarity in Catholic social teaching. Interdependence, as awareness of the linkages between people and nations, is a hallmark of our era. When the empirical reality of linkage is transformed into a personal awareness of interdependence, it acquires a moral connotation for it allows persons to "feel personally affected by the injustices and violations of human rights committed in distant countries. . . . " For Pope John Paul, that ability to see interdependence as a moral category and not just a political or economic fact is the breakthrough to an ethic of solidarity. "When interdependence becomes recognized in this way, the correlative response as a moral and social attitude, as a 'virtue,' is *solidarity*." Such an attitude is not "a feeling of vague compassion or shallow distress at the misfortunes of so many people. . . . On the contrary, it is *a firm and persevering determination* to commit oneself to the *common good*; that is to say, to the good of all and of each individual, because we are *all* really responsible *for all*."[15]

The context in which Pope John Paul applied this treatment of solidarity back in 1987 was a discussion of economic development and the need to close the gap between rich and poor nations in the international economy. More recently, the context for developing the idea of solidarity has been international politics. Cardinal Joseph Bernardin put it succinctly: "Peacemaking requires new forms of solidarity in the 1990s. Perhaps the bluntest way to put this message is the immorality of isolationism."[16] The International Policy Committee of the American bishops had issued an earlier statement: "For decades the Catholic Church has championed the unity of the human family, the interdependence of peoples and the need for solidarity across national and regional boundaries." Assessing the present national mood the bishops noted, "Out of an understandable desire and clear need to face neglected problems at home, then, many Americans may be tempted to shut out international problems and to shun global responsibilities. Yet as pastors in a universal church, we appeal to the American people not to turn away from the cries of a still suffering world beyond our shores." Calling upon the underlying vision of Catholic social teaching, the bishops continue, "We urge U.S. Catholics at this pivotal moment to renew their commitment to the good of the whole human family." What this renewed commitment entails is "an ethic of solidarity and a vision of the global common good."[17] In an echo of Pope

15 Ibid., no. 38.
16 Cardinal Joseph Bernardin, "The Post-Cold War Agenda for Peace," *Origins* 23 (1993), 1-7 at 7.

John Paul's dismissal of feelings of "vague compassion or shallow distress," the bishops declare, "The people of far-off lands are not abstract problems, but sisters and brothers. We are called to protect their lives, to preserve their dignity and to defend their rights."[18] Solidarity demands action which reflects and fosters the Catholic commitment to unity in the family of creation.

Solidarity shapes the Catholic perspective on humanitarian intervention by declaring, in the words of Pope John Paul: "States no longer have a 'right to indifference.'" Rather, there is a duty to end injustice since "principles of the sovereignty of states and of noninterference in their internal affairs — which retain all their value — cannot constitute a screen behind which torture and murder may be carried out."[19] In sum, solidarity reminds us that we have duties to others beyond territorial borders.

3. *Justice and International Order.* As Pope John Paul indirectly admits in the previous quote, state sovereignty and noninterference are of value in international politics. Some worry that too much emphasis on human rights and social justice may undercut the values protected by the norm of sovereignty. Supporters of "realism" in foreign policy remind their audience "that justice depends upon a degree of order and community, and that international moral crusades can lead to disorder, injustice, and consequences that are immoral even by the standards of the crusaders."[20]

Often when appeals to order are made, the underlying premise is a world system of states in precarious balance. Destabilization is the great enemy and continuity is the goal. Such an outlook may prize the status quo and resist change, especially if the result is an alteration in the balance of power among nation-states. Yet for adherents to Catholic social teaching, appeals to order can too often silence cries for justice from the weak who suffer under the present balance of power in the international system.

In Catholic thought, the idea of order has a different meaning than that held by proponents of "realism." In encyclicals such as *Pacem in Terris*, *Progressio Populorum*, and *Sollicitudo Rei Socialis*, the papacy has "outlined a moral order of international relations, i.e., how the international community *should* be organized."[21] Order in Catholic social teaching is not so much an argument for the status quo as it is a moral vision of what ought to be in international affairs. Order is not something to be played off

---

17 USCC International Policy Committee, "American Responsibilities in a Changing World," *Origins* 22 (1992), 337-341 at 339.

18 Ibid., 341.

19 John Paul II, "Address to Diplomatic Corps," 3.

20 Cooper and Nye, "Ethics and Foreign Policy," 24.

21 National Conference of Catholic Bishops, *The Challenge of Peace: God's Promise and Our Response* (Washington, D.C.: USCC Office for Publishing and Promotion Services, 1983), no. 239 (emphasis in original).

against justice, since there is a fundamental moral component to any genuine understanding of order. One cannot speak of order in Catholic political theory without acknowledging the import of the international common good, respect for human rights, resistance to aggression, a commitment to economic development, and broad participation in the affairs of the community.

A danger in the Catholic usage is that emphasis on the moral ideal of international order leads to denial or dismissal of how the present world is structured. While this risk is real, I agree with those who hold that, for the most part, the tradition "has been sensitive to the actual pattern of relations prevailing among states."[22] The Church's teaching does not deny the reality of states or the role of national interest in shaping the foreign policies of those states. There is an awareness of the balance of power between different states and recognition of the limits to the transformation which can be attempted without undue risk. The challenge is to achieve the right kind of transformation within the present so as to make the future different but not chaotic.

As any adult understands, a child does not move from crawling to running without first learning the skills involved in standing and walking. Growth and development for the future entail building on the achievements of the present. Those voices calling for change toward a true order in international life do not demand the elimination of states as we know them any more than the parent expects the child to run before achieving the ability to stand and take his or her first steps. Establishing a boundary-free world community is not the immediate task before us. What the Catholic vision of human unity and solidarity does seek is movement within the present system toward genuine world order. As the American bishops wrote, "While not ignoring present geopolitical realities, one of the primary functions of Catholic teaching on world order has been to point the way toward a more integrated international system."[23] For the bishops, the path to world order entails coming to terms with interdependence and developing an ethic of solidarity in international affairs.

When Catholicism promotes the primacy of order, therefore, it must not be read, as some "realists" would have it, as an appeal to stay within the existing framework of foreign policy. Rather, it is a call to transform, through a prudent strategy, the status quo. The aim is that a true world order be achieved. Such an order would not necessarily mean the withering away of the state, but it will demand that a reciprocal relation of rights and duties be created between states and citizens and between states and other states. If just relations are thereby developed, it may be the case that states will be able to claim sovereignty properly understood, but overbear-

22 Ibid., no. 239.
23 Ibid., no. 239.

ing claims of absolute sovereignty cannot be admitted. Stronger than the appeal of sovereignty are the human rights of persons and the obligations of solidarity. As Bryan Hehir has aptly summarized the matter: "If the concept of order is the primary theme in Catholic teaching on international relations, human rights now defines the content of that order."[24] In such a perspective, humanitarian intervention arguably can be part of a sound strategy for achieving international order.

4. *Just War and Pacifism*. If a tradition is really an ongoing conversation over time, then few, if any, conversations have been as long- running as Catholic reflection on the morality of armed force. The subtraditions of just war and pacifism have been present within the tradition of Catholic social thought almost from the beginning. Each of these perspectives has spawned multiple theories of ethical assessment of warfare.[25] Today, support for both outlooks is strong within the Church as pacifists and just-war theorists struggle to apply the insights of both traditions to contemporary issues. In either camp, believers will "continue to face difficult tests in a world marked by so much violence and injustice."[26] Resort to humanitarian intervention is one of those "difficult tests" which both sides in the just-war/pacifist discussion must face.

For pacifists, the issue which looms large is whether a use of military force can be permitted which approximates in its intent and execution domestic police action rather than large-scale war. If the cause is truly "an authentic act of international solidarity and not a cloak for great power dominance,"[27] are pacifist objections to war applicable? Certainly, it must be emphasized that resort to armed violence is a last resort. Here the pacifist position has been strengthened in the eyes of the bishops by various nonviolent revolutions which have occurred in recent years. "National leaders bear a moral obligation to see that nonviolent alternatives are seriously considered for dealing with conflicts. New styles of preventative diplomacy and conflict resolution ought to be explored, tried, improved, and supported."[28] Yet the question remains what is to be done if

---

24 J. Bryan Hehir, "Christians and New World Disorders," in Richard Neuhaus and George Weigel, eds., *Being Christian Today* (Washington, D.C.: Ethics and Public Policy Center, 1992), 223-245 at 236.

25 For a more detailed examination of Roman Catholic teaching as found in official magisterial pronouncements on just war and pacifism, see Kenneth R. Himes, "Pacifism and the Just-War Tradition in Roman Catholic Social Teaching," in John Coleman, ed., *One Hundred Years of Catholic Social Thought: Celebration and Challenge* (Maryknoll: Orbis Books, 1991), 329-344.

26 National Conference of Catholic Bishops, *The Harvest of Justice Is Sown in Peace*, 5.

27 Ibid., 16.

28 Ibid., 5.

nonviolent measures are not judged to be effective in alleviating a gross injustice such as genocide.

Many in the pacifist segment of the Catholic community are struggling with this question. One writer/activist asks whether the crisis of humanitarian intervention will force pacifists to move beyond "a method of protest, to join others in active global problem-solving."[29] A refrain heard in a number of places is that what is needed is a "nonviolent army" which can intervene as a peaceful presence in war zones to separate victims from their tormentors by creating, if necessary, a human shield. Such nonviolent actions admittedly will take a good deal of time and effort in four stages: recruitment, long-range training of personnel, immediate preparation for a specific intervention, and financing of such an army.[30] Meanwhile, however, the tragedies of Bosnia, Somalia, Liberia, Guatemala, Burundi, Haiti, and other places continue. Lacking the present ability to rely on creative enterprises like the nonviolent army, some within the pacifist community have expressed a willingness to consider armed humanitarian intervention.[31]

Just-war theorists also find the question of humanitarian intervention to be difficult. Just-war theory has never provided a "set of mechanical criteria that automatically yields a simple answer," but rather the theory offers "a way of moral reasoning to discern the ethical limits of action."[32] The difficulty is precisely our ability in the present climate to discern the limits to new kinds of military action. Assessment of the present context for moral reflection leads one to agree with the bishops: "The increasing violence of our society, its growing insensitivity to the sacredness of life and the glorification of the technology of destruction in popular culture could inevitably impair our society's ability to apply just-war criteria honestly and effectively in time of crisis."[33]

In one sense, the category of just cause is not as troubling as other elements of the theory when just-war advocates discuss humanitarian intervention. Yet, in another sense, the topic of just cause is highly controversial. As the bishops note, "Force may be used only to correct a grave,

---

29 Shelly Douglass, "Questions for the Heart," *Sojourners* 22 (April 1993), 14-15 at 14.

30 Two reports in *The Wolf* (Fall and Winter 1993), a newsletter of the Pace e Bene Center, a Franciscan nonviolence project, were among the first to suggest such an undertaking in the face of calls for humanitarian intervention.

31 See the remarks of Jack Nelson-Pallmeyer, "Wise as Serpents, Gentle as Doves?" *Sojourners* 22 (April 1993), 10-13 at 13. In the same issue, a number of other authors associated with pacifism express their difficulty in simply dismissing the idea of armed intervention for humanitarian aims.

32 National Conference of Catholic Bishops, *The Harvest of Justice Is Sown in Peace*, 6.

33 Ibid., 6.

public evil, i.e., aggression or massive violation of the basic rights of whole populations."[34] On the face of it, this would seemingly include humanitarian intervention as a just cause. And, at least, for cases of genocide the issue is clear enough that a finding of just cause would not be debated. Most people would hold that an evil of the enormity of genocide merits armed resistance. In that sense, the reality of massive human rights violations will generally satisfy the category of just cause as a "grave public evil." But what human rights violations other than genocide are to count as "grave public evil" remains an open question. Given the lengthy lists of human rights proposed by the United Nations or those rights found in Catholic teaching, how does one determine which human rights are so basic and when are these basic rights so extensively violated that armed intervention is justified? Answers to those questions elicit a wide variety of responses even among just-war theorists.

As to other criteria of just-war theory (right intention, comparative justice, proportionality, last resort, noncombatant immunity), all will raise questions for disputants in the argument over humanitarian intervention. But I shall simply note two criteria around which controversy swirls when applied to the topic under review: legitimate authority and probability of success. Humanitarian intervention has moved to the forefront of discussion because it is now more thinkable with the end of the Cold War. One of the reasons why it is thinkable is that consensus is now possible within the UN Security Council, thus leading to collective endorsement of an intervention. This UN backing would provide a measure of legitimation for an intervening force. Yet optimism may be too high in some circles about the ability of the United Nations to endorse many such actions. This opens up the question of non-UN-sponsored multilateral actions or even unilateral interventions. Interventions of that type, however, will certainly be more controversial than UN-sponsored ones. Determining the legitimacy of any act of intervention will require examination of the danger to international law and order when individual states or a group of allies invade a nation under the mantle of humanitarian concern.[35]

It would be a major error to think of humanitarian intervention as the use of military force untainted by political goals. The use of the word humanitarian to modify intervention ought not lead us to think that we are dealing with an action which is apolitical. There is no such animal as apolitical military action. All military force, if it is to be morally responsible, must serve some legitimate political aim. Humanitarian intervention cannot entail the mere delivery of foodstuffs or medical care by the military

---

34 Ibid., 5.

35 A more extensive analysis of the legitimacy of a right to humanitarian intervention, either by the UN or others, is found in my essay "The Morality of Humanitarian Intervention," *Theological Studies* 55 (March 1994).

which quickly depart the scene like Santa Claus leaving behind a sack of toys. Military intervention must be accompanied by a clear strategy for military withdrawal. But withdrawal cannot occur unless there is some alteration of the situation in the targeted state which necessitated the intervention. Otherwise we will only find ourselves in an endless cycle of crisis and intervention.

Political goals must be considered in humanitarian intervention since that is what is required to rectify, or at least prevent from reoccurrence, the state of affairs which led to the need for intervention. This means some sort of ongoing assistance in reorganizing government, disarming military or paramilitary forces, establishing safe enclaves, reestablishing civic peace, supporting negotiated settlements of grievances, etc. All these activities entail money, personnel, and energy invested over time. Part of the calculus in determining probability of success is consideration of the commitment of the intervenors or additional parties to assist the targeted nation-state in resolving its difficulties. The speed with which domestic support for the Somalian intervention evaporated following the death of American military personnel, and the Congressional posturing over immediate withdrawal, suggests that we as a nation have not seriously grappled with what any successful humanitarian intervention entails.

Conclusion

In his speech to the diplomatic community in January 1993, Pope John Paul II apparently endorsed the idea of humanitarian intervention. Early in the speech, the pope called upon the international community to oppose "territorial conquest by force" and the "aberration of 'ethnic cleansing.'" He denounced "practical indifference" in the face of such aggressive behavior and spoke of it as a "culpable omission." Returning to the theme at the end of his remarks, Pope John Paul spoke positively of the development of humanitarian law as well as humanitarian assistance and noted the idea of humanitarian intervention. He went on, "Once the possibilities afforded by diplomatic negotiations and the procedures provided for by international agreements and organizations have been put into effect, and nevertheless, populations are succumbing to the attacks of an unjust aggressor, states no longer have a 'right to indifference.' It seems clear that their duty is to disarm this aggressor, if all other means have proved ineffective."[36]

---

36 John Paul II, "Address to the Diplomatic Corps," 2-3.

The papal remarks have been interpreted as support for some sort of military intervention in areas like Bosnia. Several months later, however, in an interview with a reporter whom he has known from his days in Krakow, the pope appeared to distance himself from the position ascribed to him. He was asked, "When you spoke about a 'humanitarian intervention' in the Balkans, some interpreted that as a call for military intervention. Was that so?" His response: "No, that's not it. What I meant is that in cases of aggression it is imperative to deny the aggressor the possibility of doing harm." Pope John Paul went on to say, "It is a subtle distinction. . . . "[37] Just what the pope meant by his remark is not terribly clear. Indeed, he may be making a distinction that is so subtle that it is a distinction which makes no difference. How should the international community act on the "imperative" of denying the aggressor if, as was initially postulated in the January speech, we have a case where all diplomatic and other ordinary measures have failed in their desired effects? What is the papal proposal for "disarming the aggressor" in such cases if he is not endorsing military intervention for humanitarian reasons? Unless the pope clarifies his viewpoint, I think it necessary to conclude that the pope endorses the idea of humanitarian intervention even if he is reluctant to call it by that name.

In their argument developed in the tenth anniversary reflection, the American bishops conclude that humanitarian intervention "could be an exceptional means to ensure that governments fulfill the purposes of sovereignty and meet the needs of their people" even as the search continues for alternative nonviolent means to remedy injustice. My personal conviction is that the idea of humanitarian intervention is a sound one, in accord with basic principles of Catholic social thought. Yet great caution is needed in the practice of humanitarian intervention since many factors besides just cause must be weighed before approving military force. As the bishops acknowledge when discussing the principles which make up the just-war tradition, the "application of these principles requires the exercise of the virtue of prudence."[38] While humanitarian intervention is legitimate in theory for the faithful disciple, the decision for intervention is fraught with difficult judgments for the wise policymaker.

---

37 Jas Gawronski, "Pontiff Reveals Opinions on Balkans, Communism," *San Antonio Express-News* (November 4, 1993), 14A-16A at 14A.

38 National Conference of Catholic Bishops, *The Harvest of Justice Is Sown in Peace*, 6.

Humanitarian Intervention

Its Possibilities and Limits

Charles William Maynes

One of the most promising developments in international relations has been the growing acceptance of the view that the United Nations and the international community have a *droit de regard* over the way member states treat their citizens. When Jimmy Carter early in his administration suggested that henceforth no nation could consider the way it treated its citizens a domestic issue about which the international community had no legal right to concern itself, he was ridiculed as being too idealistic or naive. Today, international interference in internal affairs to promote human rights is much more widely accepted.

This change in attitude is revolutionizing statecraft. For centuries, religious figures and philosophers might have concerned themselves with such issues but statesmen did not. The latter took whatever action was necessary to strengthen the state. The religious wars in Europe finally came to an end when exhausted populations agreed with the principle that *cujus est regio, illius est religio* (whoever governs the region, controls the religion). But that compromise, which brought peace to Europe, also prepared the ground for an enormous increase in power to the state. If states could not be challenged on the basis of the way they ordered their citizens to worship, how could they be challenged on other aspects of their rule?

In the centuries that followed, increasingly they were not and the rise of the modern state began as it assumed growing control over the most intimate details of the lives of its citizens. The unfortunate consequence was that, up until the outbreak of World War II, states were assumed to have the right to treat their citizens pretty much as they wished. Appeals to show greater respect to human dignity could be made to conscience but not to law.

It is instructive that although much writing about World War II speculates on whether the allied powers could have stopped Hitler's external aggression by vigorous diplomatic or military actions in the 1930s, there is almost no consideration of the steps that the world might have taken to intervene in Germany's domestic affairs to halt the abusive actions being taken against Gypsies, Jews, and Social Democrats. Perhaps because another path did not seem practical, most authors, even to this day, make the silent assumption that Hitler could have done what he wanted inside Germany as long as he did not invade another country.

Knowledge of the Holocaust did not immediately shake the international consensus favoring the rights of states over the rights of citizens. After all, Article 2, Section 7, of the United Nations Charter states: "Nothing contained in the present Charter shall authorize the United Nations to intervene in matters which are essentially within the domestic jurisdiction of any state. . . . "

But there has always been a certain legal tension within the United Nations Charter between the rights of states and the rights of citizens. The same charter that accords member states protection against outside interference in internal matters also charges the new organizations with the duty to protect the rights and welfare of all the world's citizens. Over time, this tension has tended to tilt the balance a little more in the direction of the rights of citizens and a little further away from the rights of states.

In retrospect, it is clear that this process really began with the UN's early attention to the problem of apartheid in South Africa. Although the South African government could argue that the condition of the races in its territory was an internal affair about which the rest of the world should not concern itself, there was little international support for this position. The increasingly intrusive UN involvement in the internal affairs of South Africa helped legitimate the idea that the UN could be equally concerned with the internal order of other states.

At first, Chile and Israel were the only other countries whose internal practices were regularly criticized by the international community. This fact gave rise to the charge that the international community was adopting a double standard in the implementation of human rights: Certain countries were condemned while others committing similar or worse violations were not studied or criticized. But that period began to come to an end during the Carter administration, when the international community slowly — too slowly — began to enlarge the circle of countries whose human rights records were criticized beyond those normally targeted three — Chile, Israel, and South Africa. Today, although it is still not fair to say that the UN examines the internal record of every country with a single standard, it is fair to say that the scope for official hypocrisy has been dramatically lessened.

The next stage beyond criticism, however, is implementation of international standards. How far should the international community go? It can examine the internal practices of a state and raise any criticism privately. It can decide to go public. Should it go even further and impose economic sanctions? What if the sanctions do not work? Should it use military force?

With the end of the Cold War, the world has hesitantly moved away from a double standard even in the implementation of human rights. Before the Berlin Wall fell, the United States, for example, would never have permitted the UN to sanction Haiti economically. It would have feared a domestic upheaval that would only benefit the Soviet Union. The end of the Cold War, therefore, opened up the possibility of a much more consistent policy of humanitarian intervention.

Unfortunately, a new problem has arisen. It now is possible to argue that in terms of implementing international human rights, the world is following, not a double standard, but a random standard. The world intervenes in Somalia but not in the Sudan. It tries to prosecute war criminals in the former Yugoslavia, but it blesses a general amnesty for those who had committed vicious crimes during the civil war in El Salvador. It intervenes to help the Iraqi Kurds but not the Turkish Kurds.

The world has no easy answer to this problem. Any effort to address all of these crises at the same time would be completely impractical. Massive force would be required and that is inconceivable. It may not even be desirable.

It is not conceivable that young men and women will be willing to die for humanitarian intervention on a significant scale. There is general agreement that young men, and increasingly even young women, have an obligation, if necessary, to lay down their lives in defense of the motherland. They willingly fight to defend institutions and individuals that have protected them and their families. But humanitarian intervention demands a new level of disinterested sacrifice and raises a new order of questioning: Who is to decide that certain interventions are humanitarian? Can we trust UN member states to make that judgment with sufficient discrimination? Will they act with necessary disinterest?

Then there is the issue of desirability. The UN and other international organizations have credibility in large measure because they stand for a higher order of behavior than traditionally practiced by member states. If the international community blesses the widespread use of force, even for highly desirable ends, that legitimacy may be lost. Can the international community really kill to save?

How far states should be willing to go in the practice of international humanitarian intervention is a very difficult question. It probably can only be answered over time and after contributions from many participants — political figures, religious leaders, and international affairs specialists. We are operating on new ground and we have to feel our way intellectually. But suppose we decide that we have the legitimacy to order a forceful humanitarian intervention in which large numbers of innocents may die. What do we do when the cases in need are so many and the international treasury is so small? How do we choose one country over another? How do we organize the international community to carry out such operations?

Today the UN is in Somalia and not the Sudan because the media pay attention to some crises and not to others. There is no other reason. Unrelenting press coverage of Somalia and the famine there finally persuaded George Bush in his final weeks as president to reverse the U.S. position of caution toward international involvement in the Somalia crisis and to authorize the U.S. military to take over the country in order to feed the people. The power of the media was again displayed when in response to televised pictures of the corpses of U.S. servicemen being defiled by Somali mobs, the Clinton administration decided to announce a date certain for the withdrawal of U.S. forces.

In Bosnia, we again see the power of the media to set the international community's moral and political agenda. Can anyone doubt that the much greater attention that that crisis is receiving as compared to the comparable crisis in Nagorno-Karabakh reflects press priorities? Bosnia is a story that the press is prepared to do. Nagorno-Karabakh is not.

In some respects, of course, media priorities simplify the problem of humanitarian intervention. They limit international attention to a handful of countries. But they may not be the right countries and, in any event, governments have shown that they are not prepared to make a major sacrifice in treasury and blood to carry out humanitarian interventions even when success appears likely given some minimum level of determination.

Somalia was almost a test case of the international community's ability to engage in forceful humanitarian intervention. Although the various clans had many arms, they were primarily light arms. They had no tanks, no aircraft, and little sophisticated command and control equipment. In addition, the international force sent in enjoyed unquestioned legitimacy. There was no local governmental authority to protest international interference. The international human rights community was in favor of intervention to end the starvation and suffering. Religious figures around the world applauded the arrival of the U.S. and UN troops. Even the clan leaders initially seemed to accept the respite from conflict that the international intervention brought.

Then the entire enterprise began to unravel. The world looked in disbelief as the UN found itself firing on civilians who were willing shields for clan members attacking the international peacekeepers. At one point, UN soldiers under fire called on a U.S. helicopter gunship to direct cannon shots into a hospital emergency room, in an attempt to hit alleged snipers. Whether they were in fact killed, patients in the hospital were. The UN defense of this action reminded many of the famous line from the Vietnam War that U.S. troops had to destroy a village to save it.

What went wrong? The basic difficulty is that many of us were asking the UN to undertake "Mission Impossible." We were asking it to take on an imperial mission after the age of imperialism.

International organizations have traditionally performed five functions in the field of peace and security: investigation, mediation, observation, defense, and deterrence. They have seldom been able to take over whole countries and when they have tried, difficulties have arisen as in the Congo in the early 1960s or in Somalia today.

The United Nations and various regional organizations have all — rarely publicly, often quietly — defused international crises over the decades by sending out investigators/mediators who try to persuade the parties to compromise before tension erupts into conflict. Most successes never break into the news. Usually, when mediation efforts are successful, the great powers have backed the international organizations involved.

These organizations have also been helpful when a conflict has finally broken out. The Middle East is an example. When Israel and its neighbors reached a point in past wars where they wanted a ceasefire, the UN could legitimate the result, observe compliance with its terms, and then permit the U.S. and others to resume the effort to nudge the parties toward some final accommodation.

In cases of outright aggression, international organizations have traditionally played a more marginal role. They have been able to censure but not compel the aggressor to retreat unless some large power was prepared to assume the role of the international enforcement arm and commit a large number of ground troops to repel the invading forces. The U.S. was willing to assume that role when South Korea in 1951 and Kuwait in 1991 were invaded and with UN blessing was able to repel the aggressor. America was not willing to play a similar role when the Soviet Union invaded Hungary, Indonesia seized East Timor, India invaded East Pakistan, or Israel occupied part of southern Lebanon.

Finally, some international organizations — NATO is the most prominent — have performed the task of deterrence. NATO's capability to defend Western Europe was never tested, but for decades it was assumed that NATO military successfully deterred Soviet troops from moving into West Germany.

Regrettably, none of the current crises that so trouble international peace fit into the traditional categories of action by international organizations. In Angola, Bosnia, Liberia, Nagorno-Karabakh, Tajikistan, Somalia, or Sudan, the only way to ensure a quick end to the violence is through the introduction of a large number of outside forces to compel the parties to cease fighting. What is being asked of the UN, NATO, or other international organizations is then the establishment of what might be called a peace protectorate. The task is of imperial proportion and possibly of endless duration. In many of these areas, troops would have to remain quasi-permanently on station to prevent recurrence of the conflict. The lengthy period of UN involvement in Cyprus or the British presence in Northern Ireland are very different but very instructive examples.

There are several reasons why international organizations find it difficult to carry out the protectorate function many now propose. First, when significant elements of the population will not cooperate, the task involved in trying to establish a peace protectorate is immense. In Northern Ireland, for example, the British enjoy excellent intelligence. They speak the same language, they have agents and sympathizers in both the Catholic and Protestant segments of the population, and they have occupied the area for centuries. Yet the British cannot identify their enemy with sufficient precision to end the civil strife there.

The UN's dilemma in Somalia has been even worse. There, the terrain was strange, the language was unintelligible, and the UN undoubtedly had few if any agents in place. At one point, the U.S. forces were actually using as a translator the son of dissident clan leader Mohammed Farah Aidid, whom they were later trying to capture. Little of the sophisticated eavesdropping equipment that the U.S. or others might bring to bear is terribly useful in such an environment. The international contingent was forced to operate half blind. This is why the UN stumbled into such embarrassments as mistakenly attacking one of its own agencies in the search for Aidid.

But the problems of establishing a protectorate do not end there. In the past, imperial powers could impose their sway on vast sections of the globe because few at home paid much attention to the methods being employed by their imperial agents to bring law and order. Rebels could be suppressed ruthlessly without risk of censure. The international press was largely absent. The international human rights movement had not been born. The religious community often cheered the imperial interventions despite the brutal methods employed. All this has changed.

Prior to Somalia, the UN attempted to establish a peace protectorate only once — namely, in the Congo during the 1960s. How it accomplished its mission has troubling implications for a similar effort today. At a critical moment, the UN commander on the spot cut off telephone contact with New York and proceeded to crush the rebellion in Katanga. Once successful in reestablishing central control over all the country's territory, the UN concentrated on establishing an effective government, not on establishing democracy. The real power in the country was General Mobutu, who formally seized power in 1965 and went on to become one of this century's great tyrants. Notwithstanding this outcome, the UN operation was judged a success. It would not be judged a success today.

Because of the difficulties encountered in Somalia, the Clinton administration has temporarily retreated from its early optimism about forcible humanitarian intervention. In her September speech, United States ambassador to the UN Madeleine Albright stated that in the future, the U.S. would insist that a genuine cease-fire prevail before the U.S. committed its ground troops to UN peacekeeping operations. This, of course, means that the U.S. will not participate in another Somalia.

What then is the future of humanitarian intervention? There seem to be four general conclusions.

Transparency: The most important step the international community can take toward principled humanitarian intervention is transparency. The international community should develop mechanisms for throwing an equally bright light on abuses wherever they take place. The world should not depend on the uncertain result of the interaction between tight media budgets and random media interest. The UN desperately needs a serious fact-finding capability.

Volunteer Force: Much of the media coverage of the UN's difficulties in Somalia seems to assume that the UN soldiers were put in harm's way against their will. The perception was that, for large political reasons, governments put individual soldiers at risk for a cause that had little to do with the survival of the states from which they were drawn.

Another problem with the intervention in Somalia and elsewhere is the unpreparedness of some of the troops used. There have been scandalous reports about misbehavior of some units in UN peacekeeping efforts. Some are too aggressive and cause unnecessary civilian casualties. Others are too undisciplined and engage in illegal or politically vulnerable acts.

There is too little accountability even of the well-disciplined troops. If the U.S. had acted alone in Somalia and one of its helicopters had fired into a hospital emergency room, there would have been an investigation. Perhaps the pilot would have been cleared but at least there would have been an effort at accountability. With UN forces, there is no clear body of law to guide behavior.

Some of the criticism of UN forces is manifestly unfair. When tough decisions have to be made, states fail to back the effort politically, financially, or logistically. There is no one except the secretary-general to act and then he is criticized when he does. The Security Council members shirk their responsibility.

That has happened in the Somalia operation. The United States, in particular, has tried to hide its own shortcomings in policy by blaming the secretary-general and the UN for the number of American soldiers who have died in combat there. But there has never been and probably will never be another UN operation so completely under the control of the United States. The U.S. insisted that its troops in Somalia report through U.S. channels of command up to and including the Joint Chiefs of Staff. The U.S. demanded that a U.S. national with a security background in the Bush administration be named the top civilian in the UN operation. It is demeaning for the United States to contend that the force has suffered setbacks because of UN incompetence.

Yet it is also true that if the U.S. had placed its troops and confidence in the UN and had not attempted to manage the operation behind the scenes, the results might have been worse. The reason is that the UN is not equipped or organized to carry out a sustained combat mission. It lacks the intelligence capability, the clear lines of command and control, and the cohesive political will.

To cope with some of these problems, the UN must establish a small, independent volunteer force, based on the model of the French Foreign Legion. Those individuals who of their own free will decide to join would be declaring their willingness to undertake dangerous duty for the international community. The permanent members of the Security Council should set up appropriate command and control procedures for the equipment, training, and use of this force. That responsibility should not be put on the secretary-general alone.

But there is need to establish parallel volunteer units within the militaries of the major troop contributor countries. In the future, no U.S. troops should be sent to a troubled area like Somalia unless they are drawn out of volunteer units specifically designated for such dangerous duty. There would then be no doubt that U.S. troops had accepted the perilous assignment they were undertaking.

But the UN must also be more discriminating in accepting contributions to peacekeeping than it has been. Military officials from the Permanent Five should establish procedures for certifying units from other member states suitable for service. Today some smaller countries participate in UN peacekeeping as a form of hard-currency gain. There is every incentive to participate and few incentives for proper training. That should change.

More Discrimination: A better instrument for intervention is important. But the UN must also address the issue of overextension. The world has come to a watershed in UN peacekeeping. After casually approving peacekeeping efforts in several conflicts around the globe and driving the cost of UN peacekeeping over $3 billion in 1993, the UN has suddenly shown hesitation. In November 1993, the UN informed the government of Burundi that although the situation required UN peacekeeping, no force would be sent. The UN could not afford it. Only a few weeks after, President Bill Clinton had told the General Assembly that it was important for the UN to know when to say no. Officials of the Security Council seem to have learned.

But this form of solution is no solution at all. The UN, the permanent members of the Security Council, and the international community generally will look ridiculous if they stand aside with arms folded as a crisis in the middle of Africa is ignored while a similar crisis in some other part of the world is addressed. One has to have some criterion for engaging in such international triage.

The answer lies, I believe, in a clear embrace of a more regional approach to international security and humanitarian intervention. Somalia has shown how difficult it is to mobilize an international coalition to intervene selflessly in some troubled country. Efforts should be made to build up regional organizations that can rely on diplomacy, common culture, and bilateral ties to intervene early and more effectively. The outside world may have to provide these organizations, like the Organization of African Unity, financial and logistical support.

New Resources: Many countries contend that their UN financial obligations are becoming too onerous. Although they are a pittance compared to the large military budgets that most of those complaining maintain, the fact is that a large number of countries, and particularly the United States, are in arrears at the UN and this has practical consequences. Long before George Bush decided to send U.S. forces to Somalia, the U.S. had taken a very hard-nosed position on the issue of a UN presence in Somalia. The U.S. wanted a small volunteer force in order to minimize its dues. That penny-wise-pound-foolish approach may have cut off the only possibility for early preventive diplomacy.

The international community needs some autonomous sources of revenue to finance the growing number of international programs designed to help people in need — humanitarian interventions, refugee efforts, and disaster relief. This is particularly urgent now that many member states, faced with fiscal problems, are cutting back on their international expenditures. The United Nations needs to undertake a study of possible sources of autonomous revenues — fees on the use of the airways, fees on international travel, fees on the use of space, and fees on arms transfers. No one should doubt that imposing an international tariff on any of these would be extraordinarily difficult. But if it can be shown that the world is unable to finance with existing resources programs that are vital to the health and survival of the international community, a willingness to consider such radical schemes may increase.

There is a final reality that those who support humanitarian intervention must address. Although the power of television with its sudden images has made us impatient for quick solutions to the world's problems, forcible humanitarian intervention is unlikely to be the answer, except in rare situations. The international community does not have the wisdom or the ability to act with effective military force in most situations. International efforts to compel people to behave are likely to cause more harm than good. The international community lacks the cohesion and the sense of purpose to carry out such a role.

The lesson of the past few years is that the international community cannot use bayonets to make men and women around the globe behave with greater rationality and decency. They must be persuaded to act in that way. Diplomats are more important than generals. Priests and poets are more important than politicians.

The Challenge of Peace and Stability in the New International Order

Catherine M. Kelleher and
Rachel A. Epstein

The end of the Cold War signals a dramatic transformation in the international political system. With the dissolution of the Soviet bloc, we have a new opportunity to restructure and redefine international relations much as we did following World War II. Moreover, we have far fewer constraints today than we did in 1945. No longer is the world plagued by two competing ideologies; no longer is the precarious nuclear standoff that characterized much of the Cold War period the primary security concern. The enormous conventional and nuclear arsenals built up over four decades have lost their justification; the endless supply of arms and aid to client states around the globe to fight proxy wars has diminished.

New opportunities, however, mean myriad new complexities as well. Armed conflict has taken hundreds of thousands of lives in the former Yugoslavia, while civil war and political decay have become a way of life in many parts of the former Soviet Union (FSU) and of Africa. The specter of rogue states led by unconstrained dictators has risen anew, with Iraq under Hussein being only the most obvious example. There are new threats of accelerated proliferation of weapons of mass destruction made easier by the increasing availability of advanced technology, the possibility of diversion from former Soviet nuclear stockpiles, the loose safeguards on many fissile materials, and the pool of highly educated, underemployed FSU nuclear physicists.

The challenge now is to create a new global agenda that best serves the maintenance of long-term global peace and security. Needed will be a new strategy of cooperative security, one that asserts the primacy of cooperative action and restraint on the use of force and the further development of offensive forces, in addition to an end to the secrecy and national exclusivity that were Cold War hallmarks.[1] To implement this, the international community, with the United States in a leadership position, must design new mechanisms and new procedures for joint action at the international and regional levels. The foundation may be older organizations — the United Nations, or a NATO expanded to include the willing nations of the Northern Hemisphere. But they will have to be substantially reconsidered and transformed in light of new political realities.

Perhaps the most fundamental revolution of all must be at the conceptual level. During the Cold War, nuclear deterrence was the primary tool with which the superpowers managed the bipolar security dynamic. Both the United States and the Soviet Union engaged in an arms race that simultaneously threatened world security and enhanced stability. Third World countries were not only left with few defenses but also found their room for political maneuver drastically limited. Central and Eastern Europe were tightly fettered by the Soviet bloc, while NATO, despite frequent internal bickering, generally maintained a united front against a direct Soviet threat and the potential risk of revived German militarism. Throughout the rest of the world, in Africa, Latin America, Asia, and the Middle East, the United States and Soviet Union fueled regional conflicts through political, economic, and military support to warring factions. Only rarely were the superpowers actively involved, and, except in Europe, they were never in direct military confrontation.

---

1 For a comprehensive study on the concept and potential utility of cooperative security arrangements, in addition to analyses of regional case studies, see Janne E. Nolan, ed., *Global Engagement: Cooperative Security in the 21st Century* (Washington, D.C.: Brookings, 1994); John D. Steinbruner, Ashton Carter, and William J. Perry, *A Concept of Cooperative Security*, Brookings Occasional Paper (Washington, D.C.: Brookings, 1992). Also see Paul B. Stares and John D. Steinbruner, "Cooperative Security in the New Europe," in Paul B. Stares, ed., *The New Germany and the New Europe* (Washington, D.C.: Brookings, 1992).

In 1983 when the bishops spoke to these issues, the United States and its key allies believed the ideological gulf between East and West was too wide to allow serious consideration of the elimination of nuclear deterrence as the central organizing principle of national security. Today, the United States and other leading nations may still falter in indecision and isolationism, inadvertently perpetuating the hierarchical status quo and the strategic obsessions of the past. But to limit future conflict and minimize the possibility of a nuclear exchange, the themes of the next era must emphasize new definitions and measurements of security. Transcending traditional military-oriented solutions, the United States must work with like-minded states to promote not only conflict management and conflict resolution but also conflict prevention and conflict termination. The tools are largely at hand — policies regarding the nonproliferation of weapons of mass destruction, security and confidence building through transparency and intensive military dialogue and cooperation, the promotion of economic development and democratization, and the recognition of the primacy of human rights and social justice.

The specific requirements for post-Cold War military establishments are only partially defined. Nuclear disarmament is now not only widely acknowledged as morally desirable but is seen by an increasing number as also within the limits of the politically possible. The benchmarks for conventional forces — advanced and traditional — are to be set far lower and at far less cost. But the size and type of forces that can be justified in moral and political terms are far less clear as are the conditions under which we and other states would use such forces outside our borders. As recent wars and the disturbing successes of irredentist and revanchist leaders demonstrate, however, the challenge of conflict remains. And the crucial element will still be creative, courageous, and proactive leadership, both internationally and at home.

I. Nuclear Deterrence: A Reappraisal

In the present debate in the United States, the primary limits on these goals are seen to be the "lessons" of the past, especially those with regard to nuclear weapons. Realist and neorealist political critics argue not only that it is nuclear weapons and nuclear "superiority" that won the Cold War but that nuclear deterrence remains the principal guarantee of the new peace.[2] Nuclear disarmament or even deep nuclear reductions are ill advised not only because the technology of nuclear weapons cannot be "uninvented," but also because we live in an uncertain world. The reversion of Russia and the rest of the FSU to hard-line and anti-Western regimes, the threat of an expansionist China, and the risk of new rogue states rank among the most frequently discussed dangers. The United States and any other state aspiring to defense against a nuclear-armed adversary must therefore continue to maintain a credible nuclear retaliatory capability — at lower numbers and levels of alert, perhaps, but not at lower capacity or responsiveness.

A. The Conceptual Reappraisal

To counter these arguments, it is important to be clear about what lessons can be derived from the past four decades of nuclear deterrence. During the Cold War, U.S. nuclear deterrence operated on two levels. The central objective was to prevent the Soviet Union or other nuclear states from threatening or actually attacking the United States and its allies. In order to prevent nuclear blackmail and assure immediate retaliation, the superpowers engaged in a quantitative and qualitative arms race to ensure survivability of their respective nuclear arsenals against preemptive attack. Maintaining formidable arsenals also promoted a second objective of minimizing the proliferation of nuclear weapons capability. The superpowers thus preserved a comfortable technological and numerical advantage over nuclear powers that developed subsequently, most notably China, Great Britain, and France. Both the United States and the Soviet Union also tried to deter acquisition by extending security guarantees to their respective allies and by promoting the Nuclear Non-Proliferation Treaty (NPT) as a means of global control over nuclear proliferation.

A critical examination of the operation of nuclear deterrence during the Cold War, however, reveals serious shortfalls in the implementation of both goals. American and Soviet foreign policy predicated on nuclear defense may indeed have stifled proliferation to some degree; the rate of dissemination until the early 1990s was far below the dire predictions of the 1950s and the 1960s. But such policies failed to prevent proliferation to China, India, Pakistan, Israel, South Africa, and perhaps North Korea, and Argentina, Brazil, and Iraq all nearly achieved nuclear weapon capability. With the exception of Iraq and perhaps now North Korea, deterrence of acquisition depended more on cooperative superpower diplomacy and

---

2   See, for example, John J. Mearsheimer, "Back to the Future: Instability in Europe After the Cold War," *International Security*, vol. 15 (Summer 1990). In his newest book, *Out of Control: Global Turmoil on the Eve of the Twenty-First Century* (New York: Scribner's Sons, 1993), Zbigniew Brzezinski also predicts that war and revolution will characterize the post-Cold War era as rapid industrialization and political chaos in the former Communist bloc and developing world cause intensified competition for limited resources.

the extension of American security guarantees in support of antinuclear decisions taken at the national level than on the explicit or implicit threats of retaliation.

In hindsight, the desirability of mutual nuclear deterrence is at best questionable. For more than 40 years, the superpowers and the world at large lived under constant nuclear alert. Even in the event of an accidental launch, the threat of nuclear escalation was substantial.[3] Attempts through arms control to mitigate the worst impacts of the superpower standoff proceeded slowly and often with ambiguous success. Some weapons were dismantled, but new nuclear and delivery technologies replaced them; communication and transparency were increased but then brought forth new measures of secrecy and deception. Only since the superpower standoff has ended have these circumstances changed. Whatever the practical limits, the symbolism of the 1994 Russian-American agreement to begin a program of retargeting the ICBMs away from traditional military, economic, and political sites while they continue to reduce drastically the state of nuclear alert should not be underestimated.

Without question, despite the precarious nuclear deadlock maintained at high levels of readiness, there was unprecedented international stability, broadly defined. Even during periods of heightened political tension as during the successive Berlin crises or the Cuban missile crisis, no near nuclear accidents ever culminated in superpower war.[4] Moreover, political and military stalemate meant armed conflict in Europe essentially ended for the duration of the Cold War. Realists deduce that the Cold War and the attendant nuclear standoff thus fostered peace and stability, if not at all times and the world over, then at least for most of the postwar period and especially on the continent.[5] Moreover, the shadow of nuclear escalation played a contributing role in the dampening of other conflicts — the containment of Korea or Vietnam to a level below direct superpower

---

3 In recent years, there has been increasing speculation about automatic launch systems that might have been enacted during a nuclear exchange, even in the event of an accidental first strike. One such Soviet system is described as the "Doomsday Machine," and was apparently programmed to enable "thousands of nuclear warheads to be launched automatically if the top nuclear commanders were killed or otherwise neutralized." See Bruce Blair, "Russia's Doomsday Machine," *New York Times*, October 8, 1993, A35.

4 For an in-depth study concerning risks of nuclear accidents during the Cold War, see Scott D. Sagan, *The Limits of Safety* (Princeton University Press, 1993); and Paul Bracken, *The Command and Control of Nuclear Forces* (Yale University Press, 1983).

5 See, for example, Benjamin Frankel, "The Brooding Shadow: Systemic Incentives and Nuclear Weapons Proliferation," *Security Studies*, vol. 2 (Spring/Summer 1993).

confrontation, the limitation of the impact of crises in Czechoslovakia or Poland, and the avoidance of a Mideast conflagration aimed at Israel.

Conclusive historical evidence to substantiate these arguments is not at hand; that which is available underlines the possibility of other explanations. Primary is the phenomenon of self-deterrence, the recognition by leaders on both sides at least by the late 1950s of the potential for destruction and for the loss of not only control but of all political life as they had known it.[6] Even in the early 1950s, when the confidence in massive strategic retaliation was solid and the commitment to using battlefield nuclear weapons was still firmly rooted in public rhetoric, American policymakers considered and almost immediately rejected nuclear use in Korea and Indochina, or even preemption against a China beginning to go nuclear. Later, even on the edge of humiliating defeat, neither the United States in Vietnam nor the Soviet Union in Afghanistan invoked nuclear threats. Berlin and Cuba remain special instances, and even there, nuclear use was seen at most as a last resort, after all possible conventional force options had been exhausted.[7] There are even arguments that it was one side's clear conventional superiority that decided the outcome in each case.

The neglected fact that neither superpower ever put exclusive reliance — in hot crisis or cold standoff — on nuclear weapons alone is also critical. Both sides invested in mammoth conventional forces at levels of readiness never before seen in peacetime. These levels were justified because of the perceived weakness of nuclear deterrence. They were to fill in the "gaps"; provide a "pause" for deterrence, constitute a reassuring guarantee to allies, especially in Europe, against imminent nuclear destruction; or raise the nuclear threshold and allow "flexible response." Furthermore, every American attempt to "conventionalize" nuclear weapons foundered, whether it was directly in the form of tactical nuclear weapons that would affect battlefield outcomes without instantaneous escalation to general war; or indirectly, in attempts to allow the replacement of conventional capability with nuclear threats.[8] Reports now available suggest that the Soviet experience ran in parallel.

---

6 See McGeorge Bundy, *Danger and Survival: Choices About the Bomb in the First Fifty Years* (New York: Random House, 1988); and John Lewis Gaddis, *The Long Peace: Inquiries Into the History of the Cold War* (Oxford: Oxford University Press, 1987), 104-146.

7 See Kori Schake, *Contingency Planning for the 1961 Berlin Crisis*, Nuclear History Program Working Paper #1 (University of Maryland, 1989).

8 Although originally introduced to save money and manpower in the defense of Western Europe against a Soviet conventional invasion, it became obvious by the late 1950s that Tactical Nuclear Forces (TNF) would only be useful as a deterrent, not as a defense. More explicit attempts to use nuclear weapons

B. Reassessment of Costs

Missing from the realist calculus is an evaluation of the costs the policy of nuclear deterrence exacted. Before the Berlin Wall fell, there was very little discussion about these issues beyond the moral burdens addressed by the bishops in their 1983 letter. Most basic of all was the lack of debate as to whether the United States would continue to pay the costs of maintaining all aspects of its nuclear posture in order to win the ideological battle with the communist world. The enduring assumption was that we would for as long as we could. It is important now to reevaluate these costs paid both by the superpowers and by third states, even if a direct assessment of the tradeoffs between nuclear stability and these costs is not yet possible.

The most often discussed and easily quantified cost of the nuclear standoff is the very high material cost of building and preserving the military arsenals, conventional as well as nuclear. The American taxpayer committed enormous resources to this policy, the result being a richly endowed, Byzantine military industrial complex predicated on a constant cycle of weapons innovation and production that became an integral part of the U.S. economy. The normal level of the defense budget came to be between 5 to 8 percent of GNP, supporting a military establishment employing between 3 and 4 million people.

The Eastern bloc suffered in far greater measure politically as well as economically from these burdens. The economic onus of defense and the command economy extracted a greater proportion of resources; the ecological and societal damage went almost unremarked for most of the four postwar decades. In the end, as Khrushchev foresaw, the demands of the "metal eaters," the military industrial complex and the rigid system of economic and political privilege that grew up to preserve it, led to the stagnation and finally the collapse of the Soviet Union itself.

The development of such weapons involved enormous environmental costs, not only globally from nuclear fallout as a result of testing,

---

to replace conventional capability were embodied by subsequent war-fighting doctrines such as Eisenhower's massive retaliation or Kennedy's flexible response. Neither enjoyed substantial political acceptance, however. The credibility of the United States' nuclear guarantee against a purely conventional attack in Europe has always been suspect to those outside the war-planning community, notwithstanding the role of TNF. For more information on TNF integration into NATO war plans, see Robert Endicott Osgood, *NATO: The Entangling Alliance* (University of Chicago Press, 1962), especially 118-119; and Catherine M. Kelleher and Ivo H. Daalder, *The United States and Theater Nuclear Modernization Since 1970*, Nuclear History Program at University of Maryland (Oxford, forthcoming).

but also from the production, storage, and now the dismantlement of outdated weapons as well, especially for the United States and former Soviet Union. Only very recently have scientists, scholars, and policymakers begun to draw together the overall costs of the nuclear weapons complex in the United States and to assess the data that is now available on the former Soviet Union. The risks and harm inflicted on life and ecology — in the past, the present, and for the unlimited future — had been unknown, underestimated, or declared secondary to the requirements of national security.

The long-term task for the United States and the republics of the former Soviet Union is to dismantle these complexes along with most, if not all, of the weapons they produced. In particular, they must attempt to undo whatever human and ecological damage that can be remediated, and finally store excess plutonium and other fissile materials in such a way as to protect human health, even into the far distant future. The more immediate danger, however, is the threat of unauthorized seizure of the toxic materials that becomes more likely as central control in the FSU disintegrates, as economic conditions there decline, and as black marketeers become more powerful.[9] Such hazards necessitate a short-term approach to protecting the remains of dismantled nuclear weapons. The Nunn-Lugar program which authorizes $1.2 billion in demilitarization assistance for the former Soviet Union is helpful, but it will barely ameliorate the financial and technical burden posed by weapons dismantlement.

The impact of nuclear primacy on American democracy also needs to be revisited. A legacy that stretches all the way back to the clandestine Manhattan Project is secrecy by those charged with the duty of designing and developing nuclear weapons and plans for their use. To cite only the most obvious examples: the Single Integrated Operations Plan (SIOP) of nuclear targeting, unmanned nuclear command and launch systems,[10] a

---

9   According to a recent study, approximately 100 metric tons of plutonium will remain by the year 2000 after the U.S. and Russia have dismantled obsolete nuclear weapons. This presents a "clear and present danger" to world security because of the potential terrorist and other illicit uses and because of the severe environmental risks posed by plutonium's existence. The problem of where and how to store it is as yet unresolved. See the *Management and Disposition of Excess Weapons Plutonium*, Committee on International Security and Arms Control (Washington, D.C.: National Academy Press, 1994).

10   One such system is the Special Weapons Emergency Separation System (SWESS), a "highly classified program in the 1960s," that was also known as the "Dead Man's Switch by SAC (Strategic Air Command) bomber crews." The system is designed to facilitate the automatic release of nuclear bombs from B-52 bombers in the event that the crew is debilitated during combat. See Sagan, *Limits of Safety*, 187. Sagan also points out that "preventing accidents under all conceivable peacetime circumstances was not the Strategic Air

"Doomsday Project" designed to sustain the nuclear chain of command in the event of a nuclear war,[11] and secret nuclear testing were all developed far from public scrutiny.[12] More recently, there have been revelations about U.S. government radiation and plutonium tests that were conducted on unaware or misinformed citizens.[13]

All of these policies were justified as being in the public interest and accepted by elected officials and civil servants in the belief that they were serving the highest public good. But these remain fully at odds with the ideals and the requirements of democratic oversight and consent. The rigid system of ever-expanding classification restricts debate; the basic assumptions of secrecy quickly become subverted to the lesser end of avoiding dissent and political or personal embarrassment. The impact within the military services themselves is less open to question but there is no doubt that purported requirements of maintaining an ever-ready nuclear retaliatory posture have led to a breach in the underpinnings of U.S. civil-military relations as a democratic nation understands them. With the end of the Cold War and a new environment of openness in government regarding formerly secret activities such as plutonium testing, civilian leaders should reassert whatever control they may have lost over the war-planning process, paying particular attention to formulating a defense policy that corresponds to stated foreign policy objectives and the dictates of democracy.[14]

Command's only objective. SAC also had to ensure that the weapons would go off under all conceivable wartime circumstances." It is also worth noting that the existence of SWESS was not made public until it was declassified at Sagan's request.

11 The Doomsday Project was financed under the so-called "black budget" intended for top-secret projects of government and military officials. The Doomsday Project officially folded October 1, 1994. The program will have reportedly cost $8 billion. See Tim Weiner, "Pentagon Book for Doomsday Is to Be Closed," *New York Times*, April 18, 1994, A1.

12 Regarding previously undisclosed nuclear testing, see *Openness Press Conference: Fact Sheet*, United States Department of Energy, December 7, 1993.

13 See, e.g., Arjun Makhijani, "Energy Enters Guilty Plea," *The Bulletin of Atomic Scientists*, vol. 50 (March/April 1994).

14 Nuclear targeting plans have more often than not failed to accurately reflect stated political goals, and for as long as nuclear weapons have played an integral role in U.S. defense policy, there has been tension between civilian leadership and military war planners over the appropriate policy for nuclear use. While the military has tended to favor a war-winning strategy and hence accommodates escalation in war-fighting strategies, political spokesmen have tended to favor greater flexibility and graduated options in which a political settlement might still be attained even after a limited nuclear

Countries with lesser stakes in the superpower conflict also paid costs, sometimes as they were receiving some of the explicit benefits as participants in the global ideological confrontation. Developing countries were sought-after allies and clients, and assisted in preventing civil conflict or in inciting rebellion favoring a particular side. Yet the levels of military assistance and the form of economic aid they received did little to advance what we now recognize as the requirements of sustainable development. Security guarantees were often partial and always divisive; states outside of the alliance frameworks were left either with negative security assurances (pledges by nuclear powers not to use nuclear weapons against nonnuclear signatories of the NPT) or no guarantee at all. Moreover, third countries always lived with the oblique threat of nuclear war. Although they may not have been in the direct firing line, there is little doubt that a superpower nuclear exchange would have resulted in grave environmental and political consequences for populations even in the farthest reaches of the earth.

The absence of war in Europe reversed the previous four decades of bloodshed, and clearly resulted from the military confrontation frozen in place in the early 1950s and the rigid confines of the bipolar relationship. But even there, the related costs were significant. Stability meant repressive regimes for all of Eastern Europe, not just the bloody putdown of opposition in East Germany and Poland in the 1950s and Czechoslovakia in the 1960s. Even as late as the 1980s, the West feared the emergence of organized dissent in Poland, and counseled restraint when martial law was established lest unrest unleash European war. The emergence of dissident movements challenging civil society in several East European states was not so much a threat to the stable European framework, but for many in the West still did imperil the state systems that, however illegitimate, guaranteed civic order and the stability of borders.

Even in Western Europe, reliance on nuclear deterrence provided by American weapons, in addition to national nuclear forces in Britain and France, meant secrecy and the disregard for democratic oversight. Populations were at best only hazily aware of war plans made in their name; few knew the specific nature of the weapons that might be launched from their territory or stored indefinitely. According to popular belief, deterrence could not fail because the alternative to those who had borne the destruction of World War II was too horrible even to imagine.

---

exchange has already taken place. To the dismay of some scholars and policymakers, changing political objectives have had relatively little impact on war planning. This may be due to complacent civilian leadership as much as it is to recalcitrant military strtegiss, however. For a revealing study of the civil-military relationship surrounding U.S. nuclear planning, see Janne E. Nolan, *Guardians of the Arsenal* (Washington, D.C.: Brookings, 1989).

How these costs compare to the security and stability gained must be left to a later calculus. But the costs cannot be forgotten nor continually assessed through Cold War lenses given the new international conditions.

II. Nuclear Deterrence after the Cold War: Still Credible?

In this new order, is nuclear deterrence, even with vastly lower forces and at lower levels of alert, still a credible military strategy? Does it meet the focused test its proponents always asserted was the one valid policy measure? That is, moral and cost considerations aside, will nuclear weapons deter attack or the threat of attack against the United States and its allies? Against which kinds of attack? From which countries? And will the threat of nuclear retaliation in each case garner the support of the American people?

A resurgent, recidivist Russia is the case that realists and other foreign policy conservatives see as the principal short-term threat. The standard scenario is familiar: the failure of economic reform leads to an authoritarian, nationalist, expansionist regime, anxious to recover the former Soviet empire and to secure its influence over a turbulent periphery.[15] The Russian nuclear arsenal, with approximately 3,500 weapons after START I and II, will be the only one commensurate in both technical sophistication and number to that of the United States. Such a Russia would also need to oppose the United States, the argument runs, as the demonic opponent, the only true adversary.

There is little in this scenario that reflects current reality. Despite resurgent nationalism about which there is legitimate concern, debate now is most often about the best way to aid Russia, internally to ensure democratic reform and externally to elicit Russian cooperation in international problem solving. Russia, even since the turn rightward after the 1993 elections, seems principally to be seeking legitimation of its international status and the centrality of its role — as in Bosnia or in its peacekeeping in the "near abroad." The Russian military establishment is now formulating policy that reflects fears about its rapid decay and the deteriorating control over its conventional and nuclear arsenal, not ambitions to launch an invasion against Europe or to reclaim imperial boundaries.

---

15 Some much more interesting scenarios are developed by Daniel Yergin and Thane Gustafson in *Russia 2010* (New York: Random House, 1993).

The realist scenario thus has a "bolt out of the blue" quality reminiscent of Cold War planning. Russia somehow slips suddenly into this mode and no other efforts — political, economic, diplomatic, or political-military/arms control — can prevent it. In strict geopolitical terms, it is hard to describe the specific competing interests that would generate new nuclear or conventional threats to the United States, its allies, and its interests, and even harder to imagine an American nuclear threat in response. It may be the task of a prudent military planner to imagine such a scenario, but it is hardly sufficient justification either for the retention of a nuclear arsenal of any substantial size or the continuation of an unchallenged nuclear deterrence strategy.

A more realistic worry is the recent Russian doctrine shift to a strategy of flexible response — that is, the use of nuclear weapons to deter or defend against overwhelming conventional attack. As in the earlier NATO case, this abandonment of the Soviet no-first-use rhetoric is presumably prompted by Russian fears about conventional threats from China or from the South, along its own periphery or that of former republics it seeks to dominate. But again, it is hard to delineate how American interests would be directly affected to a degree that nuclear threats would be a logical or necessary response. Perhaps only if there was a direct threat against Japan, or a major sudden toppling of the strategic balance in North Asia, would such a response be considered, but in the post-Cold War framework the question of the credibility of such threats, at home and abroad, would be less than certain.

A somewhat similar scenario is sometimes developed regarding an expansionist China that uses nuclear threats along with other military and economic instruments to expand its hegemony over Southeast Asia and in the North Pacific. Again, the nuclear commitment to Japan and South Korea's defense would be invoked. But the probability of such Chinese action seems low and quite out of character with Chinese diplomacy even under the most authoritarian of regimes. And support in the American public for such threats against all but the most explicit nuclear blackmail would seem to be increasingly problematic.

Within the last three years, there has been some discussion about invoking nuclear deterrence against rogue states, including explicit inclusion in U.S. targeting plans. The plan would be to target actual and aspiring nuclear proliferants and perhaps also states below the nuclear threshold that may instead have chemical or biological capabilities.[16]

---

16 A wide range of possible targets has been discussed, including Libya, Pakistan, China, India, Iran, and Syria. The final decisions will be reflected in the Pentagon's secret strategic nuclear forces review, currently under way. See James Adams, "U.S. Missiles Target Third World," *Sunday Times*, February 9, 1992. For more information on the Pentagon's review, see Theresa Hitchens,

There are a number of problems with this approach, many of them reflecting mistakes made during the Cold War. First, it reinforces the perception that nuclear weapons are a legitimate currency of power and thereby encourages nuclear proliferation. Second, it strengthens the hierarchical arrangement of the current international system, thus undermining fundamental tenets of the NPT, namely, the pledges by nuclear powers to contain vertical proliferation (increases in their stockpiles) and not to use nuclear weapons against nonnuclear signatories. By undermining the NPT, it weakens the legitimacy of other nonproliferation regimes, as well. Moreover, such a policy threatens to bring nuclear deterrence as an organizing principle of international politics into the post-Cold War era, bringing with it all of the attendant destabilizing features, but leaving behind whatever stabilizing benefits the bipolar stalemate actually contained. Just as there was no certainty that the United States and the Soviet Union would indefinitely be able to avoid a nuclear confrontation during the Cold War, there is at least as great or greater a risk in the relatively unpredictable post-Cold War environment of accidental launch, terrorist seizure of weapons, or escalation from conventional to nuclear conflict.

In addition to the costs and risks inherent in a policy of nuclear deterrence, there is very little evidence that U.S. war planners would be able to replicate the successes claimed for nuclear deterrence elsewhere. The United States' dealings with Iraq during the Gulf War, for example, illustrate the limited utility of nuclear deterrence. It may have been a simple political miscalculation in which Saddam Hussein and his advisers underestimated the intensity and scope of international opprobrium that would follow the invasion of Kuwait; they may not have understood the communication of deterrence threats before the invasion. But even after the United States, the world's preeminent nuclear power, became the leader of the coalition's efforts to force Iraq out of Kuwait, the Iraqi military was not deterred.[17] They were compelled to leave Kuwait only when direct military confrontation physically forced them to do so. During the conflict, Iraq was not even deterred from striking Israel, a noncombatant *de facto* nuclear power, and close ally of the United States. Furthermore, following the cease-fire, Iraq repeatedly attempted to thwart the International Atomic Energy Agency (IAEA) in its efforts to expose and dismantle Iraq's weapons programs — nuclear, biological, and chemical. The argument that Hussein and his cohorts were simply irrational and therefore undeterrable is untenable. More convincing, the Iraqi case underlines the

---

"U.S. to Review Nuke Policy," *Defense News*, October 25-31, 3.

17 See Lawrence Freedman and Efraim Karsh, *The Gulf Conflict, 1990-1991: Diplomacy and War in the New World Order* (London, Faber and Faber, 1994); and Rick Atkinson, *Crusade: The Untold Story of the Persian Gulf War* (Boston: Houghton Mifflin, 1993).

point that, in the circumstances, the U.S. nuclear threat was not credible. Moreover, the issue of American self-deterrence reflected in large measure the U.S. public's intolerance of drastic and disproportionate use of force that a nuclear strike during the Gulf War or a similar contingency would imply.

But the greatest problems are with the inappropriateness of a strategy of nuclear deterrence to solve the problems at hand. Again, the implicit assumption is that no other approach can or will work against a determined proliferator; the monitoring programs of a strengthened IAEA are inadequate; the intrusiveness of the new Chemical Weapons Convention or the hoped-for Biological Weapons Regime fails to give timely warning or an opportunity for diplomatic suasion or clear warning. Sanctions, blockades, a resolute international community, or even coalition of cooperating great powers in or outside the UN Security Council are also assumed simply insufficient.

From a strictly military-operational viewpoint, however, it is not clear that the threat of a nuclear strike is the most effective or credible response to intimidation or military aggression. Highly accurate conventional means could be used at least as effectively to destroy military and production facilities, with far less loss of life and collateral damage, and with a far greater chance of garnering national and international approval, all of which is discussed in greater detail below. The Israeli strike against the Iraqi nuclear reactor in Osirak in 1981, for example, was a conventional operation of only moderate technological complexity.

In the event a proliferator achieves full-scale nuclear development, there would seem to be a range of options and instruments other than nuclear threats to secure compliance with the rudimentary standards of international behavior expected of nuclear states, and a cessation of further development efforts. Cooperative efforts on the part of the United States and Russia, if not in the Security Council itself, may lead to compliance by persuasion, agreement not to threaten nonnuclear states, responsible control and storage procedures, and a ban on testing. Positive security assurances from one or both superpowers, or the brokering of cessation arrangements such as the recent tripartite agreement with Ukraine are other possibilities. Indeed, even at the first stage of development, the proliferating state may already have reached its goal — recognition by neighbors or foes of its potential capability.

The transition in international relations has not in fact precipitated an explosion of new nuclear candidates. On the contrary, several states have recently acceded to the NPT as nonnuclear powers. The reversal of proliferation in South Africa is precedent setting, and on January 22, 1994, Argentina and Chile formally enacted the Treaty of Tlatelolco, an important step in maintaining Latin America as a Nuclear-Weapon-Free Zone. These events suggest that the costs of obtaining and maintaining a nuclear arsenal are perceived as being sufficiently high to some potential proliferants so as to outweigh whatever prestige or security benefits that might accrue to a new nuclear state. The case of North Korea remains worrisome, but here, too, there is evidence of increasing commitment on the part of the international community to engage in joint action, to offer incentives and security assurances in exchange for a decision not to seek full-scale capability, and to explore a range of sanctions, mostly nonmilitary and all nonnuclear, if compliance is not forthcoming. Increasing U.S. and Russian leadership, with emphasis on the costs of nuclear weapons coupled with the continuing emphasis on their lack of military or other utility, will reinforce the central message of nonproliferation rhetoric.

III. The Future Security Policy Agenda

What are the policies that the Clinton administration and its successors must follow to move toward a new international order based on prospects for peace and international cooperation? There are three clear priorities, all of which will require both fundamental changes in the way in which security policy is conceptualized and implemented, and new responsiveness to the requirements of democratic consent and oversight of fundamental national security strategy and force posture.

A. A Renewed Commitment to Nonproliferation

The most immediate policy concern for the Clinton administration must be the successful renewal of the nonproliferation approach embedded in the NPT which is scheduled to undergo its 25-year review conference in 1995. The United States must now design a policy that gives the prevention of proliferation first priority, that represents the dedication of new resources and the undertaking of new explicit constraints on national behavior to achieve this end. Thus far, although the Clinton administration has given nuclear nonproliferation priorities new visibility, the emerging policies are relatively limited and somewhat inconsistent. The Defense Counterproliferation Initiative, for example, announced on December 7, 1993, by then Secretary of Defense Les Aspin, emphasizes improvement of U.S. counterproliferation strike and missile defense capabilities in addition to continued reliance on a strategy of robust nuclear deterrence. This immediately fueled charges, especially in the Third World, that the United States was clinging to the myth that the two-tiered system of nuclear haves and have-nots is desirable and sustainable. As the outcome of the last NPT review conference in 1990 dramatically demonstrated, as long as the United States or any other single actor refuses to surrender ultimate control over all nuclear weapons and promotes their value as a means by which to exert power and influence, there will always be a justification, if not a direct incentive, for other states to procure nuclear weapons. In addition, American domestic economic and export concerns have fueled new skepticism of the value of export controls, one of the traditional instruments of preventive control that, if revised and extended, might still help track, if not stem, the potential for proliferation.[18]

Despite these somewhat mixed signals, however, the Clinton administration has vigorously supported the indefinite extension of NPT. There is considerable opposition to indefinite extension, however, among advanced industrial states as among those in the Third World that fear imposed constraints or increasingly intrusive controls. The regime has been strengthened in recent years by Iraq's submission to IAEA enforcement procedures of the Gulf War cease-fire and empowerment mechanisms provided by the CIA and United Nations.[19] In addition, the accession of South Africa, France, China, Belarus, Kazakhstan, Guyana, and Mauritania have lent NPT credibility, bringing the total number of signatories to 162. While this and other proliferation control arrangements such as the Missile Technology Control Regime have greater centrality and legitimacy than previously, some worry that it is indeed this enhanced power to infringe upon sovereignty that drives states like North Korea out of the nonproliferation community.

The United States must consider ways to demonstrate renewed commitment to Article VI of the NPT that requires the superpowers to control vertical proliferation. Certainly, the end of the Cold War, reduced levels of peacetime nuclear alert, START I and II, and the recent agreement between Moscow and Washington to retarget strategic nuclear weapons away from traditional counterforce and countervalue sites do provide tangible proof of progress, and do provide a new level of reassurance to other adherents to the NPT. Out of these developments rise new points of

---

18 For a highly critical appraisal of the Clinton defense team's approach toward export controls and nonproliferation, see Gary Milhollin, "The Perils of Perry and Co.," *The Washington Post*, February 6, 1994, C3.

19 The IAEA has undergone significant structural and operational changes in recent years. Prior to the discovery of Iraq's extensive nuclear weapons program in the wake of the Gulf War, IAEA measured its success in monitoring according to the quantity of material that it was able to place under international safeguards. Now, however, IAEA's goal is to be informed of all nuclear-related activities in member countries and inspectors can verify compliance more effectively now than before through reactivated so-called "challenge" inspections that give the host country little warning time. Also, IAEA intelligence-gathering resources have improved with the addition of the 100-person Non-Proliferation Center at the U.S. Central Intelligence Agency.

tension, however. India, Pakistan, Mexico, and Sweden are sure to raise the question of when and how Russia and the United States will disarm entirely, while others, most notably Japan, Germany, and other beneficiaries of positive security guarantees, may be reluctantly forced into a debate about international security after the U.S. nuclear umbrella is pulled back. Ironically, as the world comes closer to fulfilling some of the central challenges of the NPT, more complex questions about the fundamental components of a secure international order emerge.

The potential differences need not become intractable schisms, however. Unquestionably, the superpowers have more credibility now than at any previous NPT review conference because of the progress they have made toward the pledge of Article VI, and the clear shift towards accepting, if not welcoming, a discussion about security without nuclear weapons. It means, however, that between now and the conference, the United States must be active diplomatically and prepared to offer new resources and constraints to achieve renewed commitment. It must forge a consensus among its closest allies about issues such as a third round of START involving real reductions and new transparency for the smaller nuclear powers such as China, France, and Great Britain. It must reinforce cooperative measures among the major and regional powers on the treatment of North Korea and other potential defectors from the NPT regime. It must help create innovative policy solutions to the problems of constraints and obligations for India, Pakistan, and Israel, the three known undeclared nuclear powers outside the NPT. And, as in many other post-Cold War security endeavors, American policy will be most effective if its leadership and its willingness to commit diplomatic and material resources is in the service of an "assertive multilateralism."

The Clinton administration has given new support to the Comprehensive Test Ban Treaty, whose negotiations opened in Geneva in early 1994. While previous administrations argued that a ban on testing should be a long-term goal and not an immediate policy objective, President Clinton announced in July 1993 that the United States would abide by the temporary ban on testing, despite objections from other sectors within the government, particularly in the military establishment and in the weapons labs, which argued that testing is a necessary prerequisite to the safety of the nuclear weapons stockpile. Even after China broke the informal testing moratorium among the nuclear powers this fall, the United States has abstained from testing and has called for a total ban as soon as possible.[20]

---

20 U.S. Arms Control and Disarmament Agency Director John Holum told the opening session that the United States "will be out front pulling, rather than in the back dragging our heels" in the effort to negotiate a Comprehensive Test Ban Treaty. Quoted in *The Christian Science Monitor*, January 26, 1994, 24.

If the United States is successful in promoting a test ban treaty, it could prove to be a watershed event in the run-up to the 1995 NPT review conference. Testing is the principal means by which a would-be proliferant can verify its nuclear capability; a ban on tests with agreed sanctions for direct infringement and perhaps even for the more sophisticated circumventions that are within the reach of the advanced industrial states would be a significant proliferation barrier. As in other aspects of arms control, an agreement in which the five recognized nuclear powers adhere to internationally established norms enjoys not only credibility but enforceability — the greater the consensus, the easier it is to apply universally observed incentives and disincentives, such as free trade or economic sanctions, to control proliferation globally. This lesson has certainly been drawn from the Iraqi case following the Gulf War in which broad agreement on Iraq's iniquitous behavior has given the IAEA the international support, credibility, and staying power that has been essential in carrying out UN Resolution 687 and, further into the future, Resolutions 707 and 715.[21] A test ban agreement by the beginning of 1995, even if not yet ratified, will provide new momentum for the broader review.

B. A New Force Posture: A Minimum Deterrent, Advanced Conventional Weapons, and New Defensive Options

Despite the monumental political transformation that has changed the international political order in the last four years, the bulk of the debate about strategic forces is still centered around the question of how many nuclear weapons we need. Understandably, it takes time for policy to address these new international realities, but the degree of change indicates that we can look far beyond our current scope, changing the very premise on which we build our national security, deemphasizing the

---

21 U.N. Resolution 687 stipulates the terms of the cease-fire between Iraq and Kuwait, and is bolstered by the credible threat of member states to use force should Iraq abrogate those terms. Many of Resolution 687's provisions call for the elimination of Iraq's weapons of mass destruction and ballistic missile capabilities over 150 kilometers, and will attempt to prevent Iraq from acquiring such capabilities in the future. Resolutions 707 and 715 provide restrictions on movement and destruction of nuclear materials and long-term monitoring of armament activities. See Johan Molander, "The United Nations and the Elimination of Iraq's Weapons of Mass Destruction: The Implementation of a Cease-Fire Condition," in Fred Tanner, ed., *From Versailles to Baghdad: Post-War Armament Control of Defeated States*, ISBN 92-9045-070-3 (New York: United Nations Institute for Disarmament Research, 1992).

importance and utility of nuclear weapons for political, moral, and security reasons. Technological advancements are never a panacea for what are fundamentally political dilemmas, but the substitution of advanced strategic conventional weapons for many of the roles previously assigned to nuclear forces seems achievable over the next decade. Even under the most conservative interpretation of present international conditions, this would reduce the traditional nuclear deterrence requirements to those called for by minimum deterrence, perhaps as few as several hundred nuclear weapons.[22]

1. A Minimum Nuclear Force

A fundamental question the United States should confront is whether it is possible to move ultimately to a Nuclear-Weapon-Free World (NWFW).[23] There is little debate about the moral value and the political desirability of this goal; more often, arguments focus on whether it would open new options for rogue state behavior, whether it should involve initial assignment of nuclear responsibilities to a strengthened United Nations, whether it can be achieved in years or even in decades. In many ways, the goal has been made more conceivable by the clear strategy of how to achieve a global ban on chemical weapons now agreed to in the Chemical Weapons Convention. Although the goals and specific strategies for a NWFW will require further debate, in the short run, the steps to move toward a NWFW and those needed to implement a credible, sustainable strategy of minimum deterrence are the same or nearly the same.

It is clear that most of the defining characteristics of the Cold War nuclear posture are no longer acceptable or needed. A force numbered in the hundreds does not allow for continuation of a strategic triad of land, sea, and air-launched weapons on constant alert. Rather, it requires a secure, stable force that does not need to be fired hastily in order to have any utility. It must also meet new policy priorities — transparency, positive protection against accidental and unauthorized use, increased safety and security standards for all phases of weapons development from inception to dismantling, openness at home and abroad regarding modification or additions to existing forces. New questions must be confronted. What

---

22 For the calculations supporting a level of 1,000 to 2,000 warheads even under hostile conditions, made on clear and relatively conservative assumptions, refer to the report by the Committee on International Security and Arms Control, National Academy of Sciences, *The Future of the U.S.-Soviet Nuclear Relationship* (Washington, D.C.: National Academy Press, 1991).

23 For an interesting collection of essays debating the possibility and the desirability of such an outcome, see the Pugwash volume edited by Joseph Rotblat, Jack Steinberger, and Bhalchandra Udgaonkar, *A Nuclear-Weapon- Free World: Desirable? Feasible?* (Boulder, Colo.: Westview Press, 1993).

form of basing provides for the greatest reassurance of continuous military and civilian control? Why is any status beyond zero alert necessary or desirable? If it is, should the alert rate not be reciprocal with Russia or at least subject to official declaration?

The new minimal strategy and preparations for limited use must encompass all aspects of the nuclear weapons complex.[24] Entailed are new procedures to account for and to secure all fissile materials produced to date, initially focusing on military plutonium and highly enriched uranium, extending later to civilian plutonium. There should be a ban on further production of fissile materials and destruction of nuclear stockpiles, and monitoring of the large excess quantities of plutonium should be regulated with international safeguards. Weapons reduced under successive START agreements, including a START III of cuts to 1,500 weapons by the year 2010, should be dismantled with all deliberate speed and with great care taken to prevent diversion or the quick reuse of warhead pits or other weapons components. The ideal framework would be a reciprocal agreement with the Russians, particularly at this moment of chaos and crisis. But the United States should be prepared — as it has rarely been in the postwar period — to go a substantial distance unilaterally, to set an example, to demonstrate confidence in the changed strategic circumstances, to provide the basis for new cooperative agreement among the nuclear powers about nuclear forces.

The United States must take the lead in determining what the new principles of behavior should be. Can the assurance against nuclear attack against nonnuclear states be strengthened and extended to all offensive practices — alerts, threats, targeting? Is a multilateral agreement on how to operationalize rhetorical commitment to no first use against all states, nuclear and nonnuclear, possible and desirable? Is a no-first-use policy credible in terms of commitments to allies and to domestic publics? What new inspection and verification practices are acceptable? How can reconnaissance information on capabilities and alert rates be shared more equitably, in peacetime and in crisis? Can early-warning systems be linked into a network allowing global coverage and most information exchanged on at least a reciprocal basis?[25]

---

24 National Academy of Sciences, *The Future of the U.S.-Soviet Nuclear Relationship.*

25 For a fully developed argument on alert and warning options, see Bruce Blair, Nuclear Cooperation: Global Zero Alert and Joint Warning, Brookings Occasional Paper (Washington, D.C.: Brookings, forthcoming). Optimal zero alert refers to a posture in which nuclear warheads are kept separate from their delivery systems, thus minimizing the chance of an accidental launch.

2. Advanced Conventional Strategic Forces

The costs and risks involved in implementing such policies are substantial but not overwhelming. International security in the 1990s appears to be escalation from civil and regional conflicts rather than superpower confrontation. For the United States, at least, nuclear weapons are not a politically or militarily viable tool for controlling these conflicts, except in extremes, and perhaps not even then. Conventional munitions offer more flexibility in war planning, inflict far less collateral damage, and do not threaten escalation to the same degree that even small-scale tactical nuclear weapons do. Moreover, with improved intelligence and increasing accuracy in targeting, it may be possible to neutralize the enemy's war-making abilities as effectively and as quickly as it would be with nuclear weapons, causing only a fraction of the death and destruction.[26]

The Gulf War provides observable consequences of the latest military technology revolution. The coalition forces led by the United States carried out an intensive air campaign against Iraq and subsequently forced Iraq, and thus one of the world's largest armies, to withdraw from Kuwait and submit to an unconditional cease-fire in a five-day land war. Unlimited access to Saudi Arabian bases, a lengthy and pacific deployment period, and advanced conventional munitions all contributed to the coalition's success that, incidentally, did not rely on any weapons of mass destruction, or even the explicit threat to use such weapons, to win the war.

Technologies used in the war against Iraq have come to be known as reconnaissance or surveillance strike capability. Communications, command, control, and intelligence (C3I), suppression of enemy air defenses (SEAD),[27] and precision-guided munitions all contributed to a force multiplier effect that greatly enhanced the ability of military commanders to monitor conditions in the battlefield. In addition to applying swift and decisive offensive force against the enemy, these tools, equipped with Stealth technologies, had the added advantage of preserving coalition lives. During the air campaign, for example, the coalition forces on average suffered 1 loss per 3,000 sorties, a significantly more favorable ratio than losses recorded by combatants in the other most recent wars in the region where the average attrition rate ranged from one-third of 1 percent to 2 percent against air defense systems commensurate with or even less capable than Iraq's dense and hardened air defense system.[28] Of the 2,100

---

26 This argument was advanced most recently by Paul H. Nitze in "Is It Time to Junk Our Nukes?" The Washington Post, January 19, 1994, C1.

27 Combat surveillance, formally dominated by satellites, has been immeasurably strengthened by the employment of the Airborne Warning and Control System (AWACS), capable of monitoring a vast air space relative to one system, and the Joint Surveillance and Targeting System (JSTARS), intended for highly accurate ground surveillance.

precision-guided bombs delivered by Stealth bombers, 1,700 are estimated to have landed within 10 feet of the intended target, yielding an 80 percent success rate, which is unusually high.[29]

The most significant characteristic of these technological achievements is that in the short term, they allow the United States, Russia, and only a few other states to construct a powerful and credible conventional deterrent. The risks and costs of war, even conventional war on the scale in the Gulf, should not be underestimated. But conventional munitions do not inflict nearly the same amount of damage in the compressed time frame that nuclear weapons would, and hence do not constrict the decision-making time of leaders that might lead to hasty miscalculations in a nuclear crisis. As intelligence and accuracy improve, advanced conventional weapons will threaten fewer civilian lives than either nuclear weapons or outmoded conventional weapons. Finally, given the high survival rate of coalition troops during the Gulf War, advanced conventional capabilities will enhance the credibility of an American, and perhaps international, reaction to aggression.

In the post-Cold War world, in conflicts where strategic conventional deterrence fails, it is unlikely that nuclear deterrence would succeed. In the postbipolar environment, regional wars will be the most likely form of international conflict. In such situations, nuclear deterrence has a diminishing influence. Unlike the superpowers locked in Cold War ideological confrontation, regional belligerents may well prefer forces that have military utility, rather than sophisticated weapons that provide status but whose practical purpose is limited. The obvious problem associated with continued development of advanced conventional technology is that it, too, will eventually proliferate, and, in this sense, strategic conventional munitions, regardless of how powerful, are little more than a placebo to tide us over until cooperative conflict management can be implemented.

3. New Defensive Options

Changing global security dynamics, technological advances, and a basic reevaluation of probable U.S. military engagements have also prompted a renewed discussion of the possible uses for limited missile defenses. Developing increasingly sophisticated defenses without prior agreement with Russia, as was advocated during the Reagan and Bush administrations, threatened the integrity of the 1972 Anti-Ballistic Missile Treaty. Thus far, however, the Clinton administration has acted cautiously, wisely eliminating the Strategic Defense Initiative from the budget which would have clearly violated the Treaty, replacing it with the Ballistic Missile

---

28 William J. Perry, "Desert Storm and Deterrence," *Foreign Affairs*, vol. 70 (Fall 1991), 73-74.

29 Perry, "Desert Storm," 76.

Defense Organization. In addition, as the administration now explores theater missile defense options, administration officials have approached the Standing Consultative Commission (the implementing body of the ABM) to request a liberalization of treaty requirements concerning the capability of defenses.[30]

The specific weapons system in question, although at least seven years from being operational at this point, is the Theater High Altitude Area Defense program (THAAD), deployable aboard ships or flatbed trucks, providing maximum mobility. In the interest of preventing casualties, limited area defenses for battlefield purposes are advocated in military circles, particularly as regional wars become the most likely contingency and as peacekeeping operations expand. Sharing defense capabilities with our allies coupled with adept diplomacy may also prove to be a prudent use of such technology. This could have the salutary effects of stemming proliferation of weapons of mass destruction in the same way extended security guarantees thwarted proliferation of nuclear weapons to Germany or Japan. Increasingly, as more countries gain access to the technology and materials needed to build destructive weapons, the United States must develop tools that enhance regional security. It would undoubtedly be preferable to preside over the dissemination of defenses rather than the rampant proliferation of nuclear weapons. THAAD, if technically viable and widely available, could lend material support to the notion of fundamentally changing our dependence on nuclear deterrence as a means of preserving security.

Some in the arms control community have argued that advanced area defenses may indeed change nuclear deterrence, namely by inspiring offensive arms races all over the globe. They see the first perhaps materializing between the United States and Russia with the abrogation of START I and II.[31] Such an apocalyptic vision, however, is not the only possible outcome. Opening the ABM debate will confront us with complexities of overlapping technologies. But the changed international environment and emerging military capabilities also necessitate a clarification of the ABM treaty, to be negotiated and agreed upon with the Russians. Not surprisingly, the Russians have welcomed the opportunity to reexamine the ABM

---

30 The United States has suggested that the ABM Treaty should be altered to allow antimissile systems capable of targeting an incoming missile moving as fast as 5 kilometers per second at altitudes over 40 kilometers. Currently, the ABM Treaty allows systems that can target missiles entering at only 2 kilometers per second. For more information on the Clinton administration's request, see Sidney N. Graybeal and Michael Krepon, "It's Not the Son of Star Wars," *The Bulletin of the Atomic Scientists*, vol. 50 (March/April 1994).

31 See Michael R. Gordon, "U.S. Seeking to Loosen Missile-Defense Curbs," *New York Times*, December 3, 1993, A14.

restrictions because they face immediate military threats from warring neighbors but are prohibited from exploiting new technologies that protect limited areas, military forces in combat, or possibly cities. Following clarification, development and deployment need not be provocative, particularly if transparency and mutual monitoring measures are incorporated.

These technologies are still a long way from actual deployment; even when they are, they will have limited applications. Civil wars, in particular, are rarely settled by international intervention, even if that intervention is for humanitarian or peacemaking purposes and marked by the most sophisticated military technology. The present course of conflicts in Somalia, the former Yugoslavia, and the former Soviet Union aptly demonstrates the limits of external influences short of direct military intervention, and even that does not guarantee decisive settlement.

C. New Priority to Cooperative Security

Perhaps the most fundamental transformation, however, must still be at the conceptual level: a new far-reaching consensus on the necessity for and the benefits of a cooperative approach to the central issues of security. At the most obvious level, this means dramatic changes in the domestic politics of security policymaking. It will mean the death of the myth of splendid American isolationism; the notion that American foreign policy can or should primarily serve the advancement of domestic economic prosperity, narrowly defined, should not dominate the foreign policy agenda. Isolationism and protectionism have little relation now either to the real pattern of public opinion on national security issues or to the ideals and hopes that have always marked the American approach to shaping the international order.

It surely will mean a return to past debates about the wisdom of involvement by the United States in collective or cooperative security arrangement. The specter of failed Wilsonianism, the failure of collective security under both the League and the United Nations in the postwar period is easily invoked. But the unprecedented achievements of the United States in crafting just such arrangements with Western Europe in the NATO alliance, in creating not just a joint military control system but an ongoing diplomatic mechanism for the coordination and common adjustment of military policy, are often overlooked. The planning for the new NATO Partnership for Peace initiative in 1993 suggested ways to progressively transform this mechanism to include self-selecting like-minded states in cooperative arrangements.

The critical issue is how to involve Russia in such arrangements. The challenge is more complex but quite analogous to that of bringing a rehabilitating Germany into the international community after World War

II. Then, the strategy that succeeded involved both the clear definition of the standards and expectations of acceptable international behavior and the willingness of others to constrain their own behavior and capabilities, particularly military capabilities, in parallel to the constraints on Germany. It required of the United States public and its counterparts in Western Europe, so recently defeated by the Germans, a long-run commitment, a refusal to dwell on the past or to react to present irritations, and the mobilization of both substantial economic and social resources to accomplish these tasks.

Cooperation with a Russia still in transformation and far less amenable to external influence will be more difficult but equally rewarding in terms of American security interests. A democratizing Russia, a Russia willing to share responsibility for renewed nonproliferation strategies, a Russia willing to assume the burden of realizing a peace settlement with equity in Bosnia, and a Russia able to contribute to global peacekeeping — these are all crucial elements in the new international order the United States wishes to achieve. It is a chance to revisit the possibilities for peace and cooperation that seemed to exist at the end of World War II — but this time with greater popular support in the United States and the new energy released from the end of ideological confrontation.

There are numerous institutional frameworks, originating in the Cold War, that can be transformed and extended — including the United Nations, a recast NATO or pan-European regional structure, and the attendant arms control regimes, both formal and informal. But the basic assumption must be the same — the willingness on the part of the United States to take the lead in giving multilateral approaches first priority and, where necessary, to sacrifice short-run unilateral advantage for the longer-run cooperative opportunities. Insistence on exclusive American command of forces assigned to international peacekeeping missions, on the promotion of domestic economic benefits of unbridled arms sales, on the special protection the United States must be given on transparency measures regarding national weapons stocks and facilities — none serve to advance the cause of building truly cooperative security arrangements or to attract other states to assume new burdens and new responsibilities to secure international peace and stability.

Several practical short-term examples will perhaps illustrate these points.[32] At present, one of the areas of greatest concern to the Russian military is the loss of early-warning systems along the Russian periphery following the breakup of the Soviet Union. Similarly, the air traffic control

---

32 These examples are dealt with in greater detail in the work of several Brookings colleagues, including Bruce Blair, *Nuclear Cooperation*; and John Steinbruner, "Cooperative Security in the New Europe," in Paul B. Stares, *The New Germany and the New Europe*.

system in Central and Eastern Europe has had to be rebuilt entirely, since it too assumed centralized control and distribution of information. Why is it not possible both to help resolve these specific problems through aid and also to use this opportunity to build linked systems that require and reinforce new levels of cooperation? Linked early-warning systems — to levels allowing the automatic sharing of information in near-real time — would do much to alleviate Russian concerns about the "threat from the south," and remove a number of points of contention with the Baltic states. Moreover, it would provide the basis for cooperative action against a rogue proliferator, with a net that ultimately might be extended to a global scope and with access for other signatories to the NPT. A Europe-wide air traffic control system would have much the same operational effect, lowering the cost of construction in the short term and serving as a confidence-building measure of enormous practical utility.

Similar measures could be achieved in the near term with respect to the control of the American and Russian stockpiles. What the United States should be willing to offer the Russian nuclear establishment is a system of reciprocal controls — declarations of all weapons produced and their current locations, monitoring of dismantlement through control of entry/exit points, the accounting of and perhaps destruction of remaining fissile materials. The Nunn-Lugar funds currently authorized would certainly cover some of the costs involved. Creative solutions in the interest of cooperative control abound — a military plutonium purchase plan similar to that negotiated for highly enriched uranium, joint tests and designs for secure, transparent storage, a monitoring scheme for civilian plutonium safety, and reduced levels of fissile material production. Inertia and a failure to reconsider assumptions presently inhibit much of the nuclear weapons bureaucracies — civil and military — to the practices of the Cold War.

Arguments for such a cooperative approach can focus on the direct measurable benefits to the United States in terms of cost and burden sharing, the political benefits, and the diplomatic possibilities. But in the end, it is possible that this approach, hedged with all the necessary cautions and withdrawal options, seems to offer an opportunity to realize the open, free international system based on peace and equity that the United States has always claimed to be its international vision.

IV. Conclusion

A fortuitous synergy of events, some planned and others unforeseen, has brought us to renewed discussions of nuclear deterrence. Ten years ago, when the bishops' letter was originally promulgated, the second Cold

War was under way, the international environment was static, and there seemed to be little room for optimism about ending the nuclear stalemate in the foreseeable future. The political transformation of the last four years may allow us to reconsider the fundamentals of nuclear deterrence and strategic doctrine. But we are not yet able to conceive of a world without war, or even a world without nuclear weapons.

Reliance on nuclear deterrence implied a specific concept about how international politics function, namely, that national self-interest defined in military-security terms is the most powerful enduring principle of international relations. This axiom has translated into a policy of maintaining ascendant military capability, the best that money could buy, with all available technologies. In this era of transition and uncertainty, the challenge is to rethink this concept, to test this abiding assumption against the opportunities and the risks in the present international environment. We should make a conscious break with Cold War paradigms of security and seek out methods of providing stability that are not contingent on nuclear weapons. At the same time, we must remain wary of approaches that might leave the United States and like-minded allies vulnerable to manipulation by rogue nations or anarchic, competitive conditions that led to the first two world wars. It is now time to pose basic questions about the nature of the new international order we wish to create and to assess whether leadership, diplomacy, international cooperation, and institution building can provide alternatives.

V.

Education and Action for Peace

Education for Peacemaking

Theodore M. Hesburgh, CSC

Peacemaking in our day is everyone's concern but it should be a very special concern for the Catholic university, which is educating some of the most talented young men and women for their role in a troublesome and quickly evolving modern world.

It occurred to me very often during my 35 years as president of the University of Notre Dame that we had a special obligation in the area of education for peacemaking and peacekeeping. Our challenge was to find our niche and set up institutes that would enable us to fulfill our special obligation in this evolving field of education. While I write from my personal experience, I must first acknowledge that many of my colleagues shared the experience, provided much leadership and inspiration, and are an integral part of what has been accomplished. This is a story of Notre Dame's five international institutes: three at the university, one in Jerusalem, and one in Land O'Lakes, Wisconsin. The one of central interest in this account is the Kroc Institute for International Peace Studies.

In chronological order of founding, the first was the Ecumenical Institute for Theological Studies which opened in Jerusalem in 1970 on a 35-acre hilltop near Bethlehem known as Tantur. The locality dates back to Roman times. The inspiration for this endeavor was Pope Paul VI who was deeply moved by the peaceful and fruitful collaboration of Protestant, Anglican, Orthodox, and Catholic theologians, observers or *periti* during the four years of Vatican Council II. He wanted that experience to continue and, after considerable reflection, decided it might best be done in Jerusalem. Since

1970, over three thousand scholars have spent from a few weeks to a year at Tantur, living together, studying together, praying together, and together walking in peace through the inspiring places of the Holy Land.

The current rector is Father Thomas Stransky, CSP, who, together with an international ecumenical advisory council, is exploring the many unique opportunities to expand the work of Tantur, to reach out to the Sons of Abraham, to those religions of the book who believe in one God — Jews, Christians, and Moslems. One need not emphasize the importance of better relationships between these three world religions, so often at war with one another. Tantur is a quiet, reflective place, sacred to all of them in a Holy City, where they can discuss peace in the City of Peace, Jerusalem.

The second institute, now the Center for Civil and Human Rights, originally concentrated on human rights in the United States. It is located in the Notre Dame Law School and has a rich archive of all the materials emanating from my 15 years on the U.S. Commission on Civil Rights (1957-1972). It also has a fine collection of books and articles on human rights. After spending a couple of million dollars, mainly on civil rights issues, the Center exhausted its founding funds (mainly from the Ford and CBS Foundations) and was inactive for a few years. About five years ago, Father William Lewers, CSC, a distinguished professor of international law, revived the center with a strong international human rights concern in connection with new master's and doctoral programs in Notre Dame's Law School. Its latest project was the publishing in English of a massive study of human rights during and after the Pinochet regime in Chile (*Report of the Chilean National Commission on Truth and Reconciliation*). This will be helpful in promoting peace through human rights by new democratic governments following repressive dictatorial regimes — a great problem throughout the world today.

The third institute in order of founding (and funding) is the Kellogg Institute for International Studies. It focuses on political, economic, and social development in the former Third World, mainly Latin America at present, but with comparative studies in Asia, Africa, and Eastern Europe. There is no question today about the intimate connection between new economic and democratic developments (read human rights and freedom) and peace. Pope Paul said it best: "The new word for peace is development." The old Latin adage also says it well: *Opus justitiae pax* — peace is the work of justice.

The Kellogg Institute educates many doctoral and postdoctoral students in the ways of peace. It also hosts numerous conferences and has published several hundred studies. Both the Kroc and Kellogg institutes each have over 20 faculty fellows from 16 departments in all of our five colleges, so the fallout is rich throughout the university, with several dozen new undergraduate courses, making possible a concentration in peace studies for both graduates and undergraduates. Every possible connection between classical university studies and peacemaking and peacekeeping is explored, mainly by summer study grants to all interested faculty members from around the university spectrum. Father Ernest Bartell, CSC, an economist and former president of Stonehill College, is the director of Kellogg. His two close collaborators are Guillermo O'Donnell of Argentina and Alejandro Foxley of Chile (former Minister of Finance).

Fourth, the Kroc Institute for International Peace Studies was pioneered and then expanded tenfold by Governor John Gilligan (with substantial endowment help from Joan Kroc). He was ably assisted by Professor George Lopez and Robert Johansen and, of course, many distinguished faculty fellows.

One unique feature of this program is the annual appointment of 15 master's students chosen from more than a hundred candidates from all over the world, especially the most troubled spots and the nuclear powers. These are mature students, men and women, who will likely spend the rest of their adult lives making and keeping peace in their own countries and regions. We have generally had a core (two or more) from the former USSR, China, and the United States, as well as individuals from Japan, India, Indonesia, Israel, Palestine, South Africa, Uganda, Ghana, Chile, Brazil, Panama, Hungary, Poland, Bosnia, and other troubled areas.

These 15 students live together in our "Peace House" and follow a core program that includes every possible academic way of looking at peace and a few others besides. This yearlong experience, given their religious, ethnic, and national heterogeneity, is an automatic daily course in conflict resolution and peacekeeping. This special course has become so popular that it has been expanded to include a second group of 15 very promising students, predominantly from the United States.

Both Kellogg and Kroc were given greater visibility on campus by the additional generous benefaction of Joan Kroc ($12 million) that enabled us to build and endow a new international center at the very entrance of Notre Dame, thus informing all comers of our special interest in international peace studies of every kind.

We have just appointed a new director for the Kroc Institute, Dr. Raimo Vayrynen, former dean of the University of Helsinki and an internationally renowned authority on peace studies and conflict resolution. This bodes well for the future of the Kroc Institute.

Finally, as the nuclear threat wound down a bit, it became evident that another serious threat to eventual peace was strongly emerging in worldwide discussions — destruction of the environment. While this would not cause sudden death for humanity and our world as nuclear destruction would, if left to fester unchecked we would eventually have water we could not drink, air we could not breathe, climate we could not tolerate, and land we could not farm. Another problem, unreasonable population growth, was inexplicably joined to this galloping degradation of all that makes Mother Earth hospitable to human life.

Fortunately, years ago, the university was given a 7,500-acre tract of wilderness land on the border of upper Michigan and northern Wisconsin by Martin Gillen. It was a perfect giant agar dish for study of the environment — every species of flora and fauna in the North Central United States and Canada, 20 lakes, complete isolation. Any pollution of air, water, animal or plant life, and soil has to come from the outside. Thus, we can establish base levels for air, water, soil, and all forms of plant and animal life. Changes in acid rain, even ozone layer conditions, will give us an effective early-warning system. Even more importantly, we are educating our faculty and graduate and undergraduate students in the importance of these studies. Thanks to great and generous benefactors, we now have yearlong living quarters and are completing the Hank state-of-the-art laboratory for plant and animal life and environmental studies. We also collaborate with surrounding state universities and share federal grants in our joint endeavors. Dr. Ron Hellenthal, biology professor at Notre Dame, directs these efforts.

Linking all of these problems and seeking common and mutually sustaining solutions through the work of these five institutes are a pioneering project for Catholic universities, but I end where I began. Peacemaking and peacekeeping are a moral challenge to Catholic higher education, something we must do if we are to fulfil our special potential for spiritual education and are to respond to the recent eloquent appeal from our bishops, *The Harvest of Justice Is Sown in Peace.*

These five institutes contribute to the goals for peace that the bishops enunciate. Ultimately, all of these efforts will coalesce in the formulation of an overarching plan to create a new world order and the education of bright young people who will work creatively to implement this new order worldwide, especially in those areas where justice and peace are sadly lacking and inhumanly betrayed.

I have written about what I know and have experienced. There are peace studies programs in 200 other colleges and universities. Some are Catholic, most are not. All are deeply involved. There are also about 50 centers that are totally dedicated to the task of peacemaking and peacekeeping in our changing world. We are in touch with most of them and learn from them. In addition, I serve on the board of the U.S. Institute of Peace which spends about $12 million a year to study peace on all levels. We collaborate with this single explicit peace effort of our government and applaud its efforts, too.

Education for peace is a new and promising reality in our times. I trust that more U.S. Catholic colleges and universities will get more involved because that is the precise goal that the bishops seek and which all of us must endorse and support. Returning to our own efforts at Notre Dame, it is perhaps a measure of our times that all the current efforts of our five institutes are supported by an endowment of more than $40 million — a small fraction of the cost of *one* Stealth bomber.

The Challenge of Conscience

Gordon C. Zahn

The tenth anniversary of *The Challenge of Peace: God's Promise and Our Response* represents more than the occasion for celebrating the issuance of an important ecclesiastical document. Though the way had been prepared for it by other more significant moral directives — Pope John XXIII's *Pacem in Terris* and the Vatican Council's *Gaudium et Spes*, to mention only the most obvious — that historic action on the part of the American Catholic hierarchy openly addressing and, in effect, challenging the moral quality of the nation's military policies and power represented a breakthrough the full consequences of which cannot even yet be calculated or judged.

Certainly it was a development not easily foreseen. Except in very limited areas (those bearing upon religious education, for example), the American Catholic community has prided itself upon the display of fervent devotion to national symbolism to the degree that is often characterized, with some justice, as "200-percent patriotism." Sociologists have traced these sentiments to a grim history of prejudices suffered and endured leading to a felt need to prove oneself "as American as anyone else" — preferably more so.

Catholic journals and, often enough, parish pulpits proudly boast that Catholics make up a third or more of the armed forces. Given the situation in which the nation faced the Cold War's "diabolical" threat of communist world domination, those armed forces assumed the added role of "defenders of the Faith." Thus it was a somewhat daring step for bishops responsible for the moral formation and guidance of the Catholic faithful to undertake to review and criticize national defense policy. To dare to question, even oppose, the nation's reliance upon nuclear weapons as the ultimate foundation of that policy risked giving scandal as something akin to treason if not heresy.

In its beginnings, the 1983 pastoral did have somewhat "subversive" overtones. On a visit to Washington, I was privileged to have dinner with a dozen or so "peace bishops" as they made plans for the next morning's session of the annual bishops' conference at which they intended to propose that the conference issue a pastoral dealing with issues of war and peace. If they had high expectations of success, I could not say. I did not.

My pessimism was well grounded in a personal history of unedifying experience with ecclesiastical authority's attitudes and actions on these issues. Forty years earlier, the Milwaukee draft board hearing on my request for classification as a conscientious objector to World War II was advised by a local priest that under church teachings a Catholic could not claim or legitimately be granted such status. I was not surprised. My earlier registered letter to the archbishop explaining my position and seeking his blessing and assistance was neither answered nor acknowledged.

After succeeding — with considerable difficulty — in the appeals process, I was assigned to a Civilian Public Service camp administered by the Association of Catholic Conscientious Objectors. The ACCO was, in reality, a Catholic Worker "front" and could claim no official Catholic recognition or approval. In fact, rumor had it that the local bishop had expressed displeasure to Selective Service for having located a "Catholic" camp in his diocese. If true, his problem disappeared within six months when the camp was closed and its personnel transferred elsewhere — not because of his complaint but because, unlike the other camps supported by their religious communities, Catholic Worker funding could not maintain even minimal Selective Service standards for the care and upkeep of men assigned to it.

Some time later, in another diocese, an appeal to that archbishop to intervene on behalf of a Catholic CO was unceremoniously rejected. The young man in question had completed his prison sentence for refusing military service on grounds of conscience only to be served immediately with a new induction order and faced the prospect of another refusal to be followed by another arrest and prison sentence. The vicar general rejected the appeal for episcopal assistance in protesting what amounted to double jeopardy, explaining that, with Catholic men dying on foreign battlefields, the archbishop could not be bothered with problems encountered by a man who refused! Still later, as a professional sociologist, I discovered — not at all to my surprise — the archbishop's sentiments would have been echoed by his German contemporaries in their loyal dedication to providing encouragement and moral support to Catholics in the military forces of the Third Reich.

Anyway, whether due to the persuasive powers of my conspiratorial dinner partners or divine intervention (possibly a combination of both), their proposal was adopted and *The Challenge of Peace* ultimately emerged to the predictable enthusiasm of what had developed into an active and quite effective Catholic peace movement. What had not been anticipated was the document's equally enthusiastic reception by Catholics in foreign nations and by other religious communities at home. Having contributed as a minor consultant to the drafting committee, I received several invitations from Protestant groups and congregations to discuss the pastoral and its implications and, even more exciting, gave a series of lectures in Austria under the sponsorship of a University of Vienna student organization.

This somewhat extended personal preliminary is provided to prepare the reader for what will be an admittedly biased commentary. After all, having been "in at the beginning" of the 1983 pastoral — actually long before that beginning — it could scarcely be otherwise.

Now, ten years later, we have *The Harvest of Justice Is Sown in Peace*, presented not as an assessment or even as a reevaluation but simply an anniversary "reflection" seeking to build upon and strengthen many of the breakthrough contributions of its predecessor. In keeping with that purpose, I will not attempt a detailed review but rather will focus my comments on what I, as a Catholic sociologist, regard as major issues still to be resolved.

In retrospect, perhaps the most striking innovation of the pastoral was its balanced "rediscovery" of the legitimacy of pacifism even as it reaffirmed the validity of traditional "just-war" teachings. In the process it spelled out the conditions to be met for a war to be considered "just." The full significance of this should not be overlooked: perhaps for the first time, what had been largely restricted to the academic discourse of professional theologians was now presented for consideration and, presumably, *application* by ordinary Catholics likely to be called upon to support or participate in actual wars. *The Harvest of Justice* follows that pattern.

Both documents, however, present a somewhat "revisionist" version of the "just cause" condition which seems to depart significantly from the original Augustinian concept of justifiable war and its elaboration in the Thomist/Scholastic definition. In both, the "justice" of the cause was treated as an objective quality, a factor argued over by the contending sides but not split or shared between them. "Comparative justice" carries more openly subjective implications, changing the question from which cause is "just" to which side can claim more "justice" than the other.

Both Adolf Hitler and Saddam Hussein claimed justice for their invasions of neighboring countries: Hitler claimed the Poles attacked first at

Danzig; Saddam proclaimed the restoration of legitimately Iraqi territory. Both claimed provocation on the part of the enemy as further justification. It has always been that, lacking some external power qualified to weigh or judge the contending claims, the "just cause" condition becomes something of a mockery. Changing the terminology to "comparative justice" does not solve the problem. It merely seeks to validate the mockery.

A more significant and certainly less contestable contribution of the pastoral was its acceptance and promotion of nonviolence ("popular defense") as a viable alternative to the slaughter and devastation of modern war, its weapons, and its strategies. *The Harvest of Justice* adds new and confirming emphasis by applying the evidence provided by the successes of large-scale nonviolent revolutions in Eastern Europe and the Philippines. These are presented as proof of the promise in the nonviolent alternative as a preferred solution to other and future threats to world peace.

Most gratifying of all to this observer is *The Harvest of Justice*'s strong endorsement of the pastoral's call for recognition and respect for conscientious objection, in particular, for *selective* conscientious objection. In this, of course, it not only follows the lead of *The Challenge of Peace* but adds to the lengthening series of such appeals tracing all the way back to the 1968 pastoral, *Human Life in Our Day*.

That repetition is needed was demonstrated by problems encountered by would-be objectors to the Gulf War. As will be developed in more detail at a later point, more than periodic repetition is needed; there is a vital weakness in the hierarchy's failure to draw and promote what should be behavioral conclusions to these laudable sentiments. There are still far too many Catholics (including, one is ashamed to admit, priests — in the Gulf War, even chaplains!) who deny that the Catholic Church permits its members to reject military service on grounds of conscience. We can take pride in knowing there were Catholic bishops who, in spite of the enthusiasm for the war, were ready to testify in court on behalf of military personnel unfairly denied recognition of their right *and duty* to obey the dictates of conscience. Unfortunately, those bishops were far too few.

One welcomes, too, the special significance given by *The Harvest of Justice* to the international arms race and the threat it poses to future world peace. The 1983 pastoral gave some attention to this issue, but there its importance was overshadowed by the primary focus upon the problems of nuclear armaments and the threat of proliferation in the Cold War context. Here the dangers of the arms race are treated in the broader perspective of a world torn apart by regional conflicts seemingly beyond limitation or control. To its credit, the reflection defines the special responsibility borne by this nation as the world's largest supplier of weapons and, as such, the major source and promoter of what the Second Vatican Council proclaimed "one of the greatest curses on the human race."

No less important an advance over the 1983 pastoral is the recognition given to the growing evil of nationalism and the particular dangers it presents. If in 1983 the dominance of the East/West struggle obscured the destructive force that lay ready to be unleashed with the collapse of the Soviet Union, the world is forced to contend today with the moral problem of seemingly boundless orgies of killing and destruction as ancient hatreds and suspicions find expression in unrestrained violence. They were always there, of course, waiting to be unleashed. The document's special attention is drawn to the links between the force of nationalism and the role played by religious and ethnic rivalries and hatreds. This is a valid concern, but this should not lead us to ignore the fact that each must be seen as something to be understood and dealt with as separate threats and problems, not only in fatal combination with the other two.

Nationalism, it can be argued, deserves priority of concern in its own right. Unlike religion with its claims to being rooted in supernatural force and power or ethnic claims to genetic descent and generational linkage, nationalism is a phenomenon with no comparable claim to "external" origin and validity. However much it may draw upon territorial mystique and historical traditions, in expression it stands alone and represents, as Pope Pius XI declared in 1931, "an ideology which clearly resolves itself into a true, real pagan worship of the state — a statolatry . . . " However much nationalism may be entwined with the other two, it should be recognized as a separate and distinct threat and, as our own history will reveal, one that is likely to be given precedence over the other two in time of war.

Finally, take the most serious note of disappointment and disapproval. What Catholics of pacifist persuasion opposed in 1983 as a surrender to political expediency — the tortured moral reasoning of the pastoral's "strictly conditioned moral acceptance" of nuclear deterrence — is repeated and upheld in *The Harvest of Justice*. With the disappearance of the perceived Cold War threats that might have seemed to justify that compromise, one could have hoped for a reevaluation of that judgment. After all, convincing as the need for maintaining the policy of nuclear deterrence may have been and probably still may be in the pragmatics of military or diplomatic objectives, religious leaders should be called to go beyond pragmatism.

In *The Harvest of Justice*, they have done so in their commendable call, belated though it is, for a definite and openly declared "no-first-use" policy; for a halt to nuclear testing (though here, unfortunately, the door is left open to the possibility of resumption should an effective global test ban not be achieved); and, finally, for excluding the use of nuclear weapons to deter nonnuclear threats (which should always have been taken for granted). Welcome though these new limits to policy may be, the new document still does not face the ultimate question: If the bishops morally "abhor" any use of nuclear weapons (would not "condemn" be a more appropriate term?), how can they justify mounting and maintaining the *credible* threat to use them? After all, to be credible to a prospective enemy, the threat we make must first be credible to ourselves.

The real moral problem neither the 1983 pastoral nor *The Harvest of Justice* has seen fit to confront remains unasked and unanswered: How does the Christian fit into the structure of deterrence? In 1988, a PBS (WNET-New York) program filmed at the Vandenberg Air Force Base featured the training of service personnel to become the human appendages of the instruments of deterrence. In the first lecture dealing with the "ethics" of the task, the instructor presented the trainees with military issues and examples that might present personal moral challenges (My Lai, for example). After these were discussed in some detail, the instructor turned to the predictable effects of the orders and duty assignments they might expect to be given. The trainees were informed they would be obliged to sign a statement binding them (and, let us not forget, one of every three might be Catholic) to unconditional obedience to such orders when received *regardless of any problems they might present to their private conscience.*

It is here, not in the War Room of the Pentagon, not in the discussions and duplicities of higher diplomacy, not even in the Oval Office where a president may decide to issue the fateful orders, but in the underground silo (or the bombardier's sights) where the moral problem will have to be faced. It is here, in the voluntary sacrifice or abandonment of conscience — that "most sacred core and sanctuary . . . where one is alone with God" — to superior military authority that, whether we admit it or not, we find the bottom line of "strictly conditioned moral acceptance" of nuclear deterrence.

There are other, more fundamental, criticisms reaching beyond simple evaluation of the reflection's contents. For example, one might hope to find a more direct assessment of the pastoral's impact, the extent to which it did or did not achieve its intended results. Few would deny "God's Promise" is still far from being fulfilled, and this should raise the question why this is so and to what extent its failure to accomplish more is traceable to the insufficiency of "Our Response."

Part of the answer could be that neither the pastoral nor *The Harvest of Justice* deals with the real challenge the Church faces with respect to modern war. Certainly the near unanimity with which the former was adopted and the enthusiasm that greeted its publication should have assured more impressive and more lasting results over the intervening ten years. Some effort should be made to learn why the "seeds" sown by the pastoral were so poorly cultivated and why the "harvest" celebrated in this anniversary reflection is so lean. For pastoral teachings to really take hold, all the teaching agencies of the Church must accept their proper share of responsibility for promoting them as effectively as possible. That responsibility is not met until those teachings are fully understood and accepted by the men and women in the pews, fixed in their consciences, and, most important, finally translated into their actual behavior. This did not happen with the 1983 pastoral.

The Harvest of Justice overstates the depth and scope of its impact. Some dioceses and parishes performed heroically; many, perhaps most, did not. The short-lived official effort that was made to monitor and measure the extent to which study groups and other supportive programs were established at the parish level was at best half-hearted and too soon abandoned. Pax Christi USA in cooperation with local lay groups and other voluntary lay organizations, acting on their own initiative, produced and distributed a veritable flood of study guides and informational programs for use in Catholic schools and parishes. After a promising flurry of interest, these too went into the discard. By 1988, five years after the pastoral was greeted with such excitement and applause, it was all too likely that the Catholic serviceman or woman deep in the bowels of a missile silo would have remembered little or nothing of what the U.S. bishops had said. And, if he or she did, it probably would not have troubled the conscience already surrendered.

It could have been different. In a private conversation that took place shortly after *The Challenge of Peace* appeared, two Pentagon employees noted a significant increase in requests from Catholic service personnel not to be assigned to nuclear-related duties, most requests referring to their bishops' opposition to nuclear weapons. A more active and longer-lasting commitment might have produced a more triumphal anniversary reflection.

As already noted, the pastoral spelled out the conditions of the "just war," making that hitherto specialized information available to the ordinary Catholic. Unfortunately, it did not go further to make certain that the possession of this information was linked to the incentive — actually the moral *obligation* — to accept responsibility for applying those conditions and making a personal judgment in conscience before supporting or participating in actual or prospective wars. Or at least reminding priests and, yes, bishops of pastoral responsibilities to provide adequate facilities for counseling and assisting the faithful in their formation of conscience.

When the need for such decision arose, neither responsibility was met and still remains unmet. In these ten years since the issuance of the pastoral, the nation has been engaged in three wars of doubtful morality if one applies the traditional conditions. The first two were small in scale and quickly over. The invasion of Grenada (ostensibly initiated to rescue a number of medical students who, it seems, were not aware of any threat) was really designed to remove a political leader our government deemed unsatisfactory and dangerous. The invasion of Panama took a bit longer and proved more costly (especially to Panamanian civilian victims) but succeeded again in capturing a dictator who, formerly a friend and sometime ally, lost favor because of involvement in international drug traffic. As our superpower bombs fell on virtually defenseless cities and their populations, few of the bishops who had voted for the pastoral with such near unanimity were troubled enough to remind their flocks there was a moral judgment to be made as to the justice of these actions. Ironically, the only official reference to the traditional conditions was made by the military planners who usurped the terminology by naming the Panama adventure "Operation Just Cause."

Of course, both invasions were of such brief duration and so predictable in outcome that there would have been little time for argument or effective opposition. The Gulf War, however, presented a more challenging moral problem. For many, it was simplified by the almost universally accepted *prima facie* injustice of Iraq's aggression against Kuwait and the cleverly constructed facade of United Nations responsibility and authority. Though the intense diplomatic arm-twisting employed by our secretary of state under presidential direction did produce the desired result, it did not completely hide the obvious fact that "Desert Storm" was a project planned, directed, and fought under United States auspices, by armed forces whose members did not wear blue helmets.

Excluding all other factors (Iraq's claim of provocation, for example), one could have accepted a truly international effort to restore Kuwaiti sovereignty as satisfying the "just cause" condition. That would still leave the other conditions to be applied, however, before the justice of the Gulf War *as a war* could be established. The argument can, and has been, made that none were fulfilled to the extent necessary for moral justification of "Desert Storm."[1]

In this case, there was debate. While the majority of the bishops fell in line behind the familiar "obedience to legitimate authority" principle, a surprising number spoke out in opposition. Many Catholics were shocked to witness their bishops engaged in public contention over the issue. Some went so far as to advise Catholics faced with orders for assignment to Saudi Arabia to become conscientious objectors! Since those likely to receive such orders were already in uniform or in the reserves, several bishops went further to personally testify at courts-martial in support of "offenders" facing serious penalties for following that advice.

Most of these dissident bishops were those who are generally termed "peace bishops" or even "mavericks." For their pains, they were taken to task by Avery Dulles, one of our most distinguished theologians, who held that judgments about the nature and conduct of the war were best left to

---

1 For a systematic analysis of one such position, see this author's "Ethics, Morality, and the Gulf War" in *St. John's Law Review* (Fall 1992).

political and military authorities.[2] (In this, Father Dulles was inadvertently echoing the advice of the German theologian who, in World War II, advised Catholics to not even raise the question of the "just war" but to do their duty "with faith in the cause of the people.") The dissenters, however, could take comfort in knowing that their misgivings about the war and its conduct found support in appeals and cautions issued by Pope John Paul II in Rome. Unfortunately, since these were not given the prominence in diocesan press reports usually assured papal statements, the parallels went largely unnoticed until after the war when they were published in book form by the Vatican's Permanent Observer to the United Nations.[3]

By breaking the pattern and making their opposition to the war public despite the customary posture of open support or silence maintained by more prominent members of the hierarchy, these bishops demonstrated the true, but generally unrealized, potential of the 1983 pastoral. Through their efforts, "the challenge of peace" became what it could have been *and should have been* from the very start: a challenge of conscience addressed to every Christian faced with the choice to personally accept or oppose the evils of modern war.

Though *The Harvest of Justice* does not deal with that debate and its implications, its echoes can be heard in the document's references to "contemporary strategies, theories, and practices [which] seem to raise serious questions when seen in the light of strict just-war analysis." Surely the warning that "strategic theories calling for use of overwhelming and decisive force can raise issues of proportionality and discrimination" has direct relevance to the principles expressed then and since in more recent military contexts by the nation's highest-ranking military officer (a Catholic, now retired). So, too, with the reference to "the targeting of civilian infrastructure" still claiming civilian lives in Iraq. Warfare on the scale planned and executed in "Desert Storm" makes a grim parody of the traditional principle of noncombatant immunity. Sociological and moral perspectives become one in *The Harvest of Justice*'s perceptive wisdom in linking what modern war has become to "the increasing violence of our society."

Unfortunately, this anniversary reflection pulls back as did the pastoral it honors. Until the distinguished authors' skepticism that "modern war in all its savagery can meet the hard tests set by the just-war tradition" is finally replaced by the firm conviction that it simply cannot do so, this document's message, like that of its predecessor, will go unheard.

---

2 Michael F. Flach, "Jesuit Theologian Discusses Theology, Faith and Ecumenism," *Arlington Catholic Herald* (March 21, 1991), 12-13.

3 *John Paul II for Peace in the Middle East — War in the Gulf: Gleaning through the Pages of L'Osservatore Romano* (New York: Permanent Observer Mission of the Holy See, 1992).

Those bishops who recommended conscientious objection to the Gulf War were trying to compensate for the pastoral's failure to link principles and teachings to individual moral judgments and behavior — and acceptance of the consequences for doing so. This was no easy demand to make of men and women ordered to active duty in the Gulf War. They were not "draftees" but had volunteered for military service or reservist status. Instead of facing civilian draft boards, they had to deal with generally nonreceptive superiors and the rules and procedures of the military establishment.

All the armed forces make provision for "crystallization of conscience," service-initiated discovery of moral objections to duties they are, or may be, called upon to perform. Such appeals must meet the same definitions set forth under Selective Service law, including the discriminatory limitation which excludes from eligibility Catholics and members of other "mainstream" churches who accept a moral distinction between "just" and "unjust" wars. Only opposition to war *in any form* is recognized as a claim for separation from service on grounds of conscience.

In the Gulf War, a further complication was introduced by a presidential order which circumvented normal procedures for consideration of such claims. Instead of the applicant's claim being dealt with at the place of current assignment (while he or she is relieved of combat-related duties), President Bush decreed that appeals were to be considered *after* reporting to one's new assignment. Since the transfer was to Saudi Arabia, the applicant was denied access to documentary or witness testimony to support the claim.

This suspension of established procedures designed to assure the service person a fair hearing meant that the only option left was to "violate" the orders for transfer and be subject to arrest on charges of disobedience or desertion. What the bishops who urged conscientious objection to the war were asking, in effect, was nothing less than a "sacrificial witness" carrying the certainty of arrest and the grim prospect of severe punishment, not excluding death.

Theologically, perhaps, the bishops were right in doing so; but the problem illustrates the underlying fault in the 1983 pastoral and now in *The Harvest of Justice* as well. Both can be charged with being misdirected in message and addressed to the wrong audience. Again one cannot deny that official spokespersons of a religious community have the right *which can become a duty* to issue institutional critiques of the policies and acts of secular authority. Both documents serve this function well. Nevertheless, viewed in the sociological perspective, neither fulfills what one would expect to be the primary objective of documents designed to provide *pastoral* advice and guidance for the faithful. Indirectly, of course, they deal with issues that should affect the formation of conscience and its translation into personal moral judgments and behavior; but much of this is lost in the concentration upon the broad policy judgments at the expense of what they should mean to the individual believer.

As noted earlier, the enthusiasm with which the 1983 pastoral was received was not limited to Catholics but spread to men and women of all faiths who saw in it the promise of release from the terror of nuclear annihilation. The near unanimity of its acceptance by the bishops was taken as a commitment on the part of the Church to marshall its members to effective action for peace and disarmament. Unfortunately, as we have seen, this did not happen. Instead, the enthusiasm waned and threatened to disappear altogether.

The failure was a failure in commitment. Whatever effort has been devoted in recent years to promoting the pastoral's recommendations has been concentrated in minor dioceses headed by those "peace bishops" or by individual pastors and teachers acting on their own, often enough without the knowledge of — thereby avoiding interference from — the chancery.

That recurring pattern of unquestioning loyalty and patriotic support for the nation and its military policies still reigns. Diocesan commissions for justice and peace, one of the more promising responses to the pastoral's reaffirmation of the peace objectives promoted by Popes John XXIII and Paul VI and given formal validation in Vatican II, flourished for a time but have since diminished in importance — and in some cases have been redefined if not abandoned. One such commission had a change in name because the word "peace" made some people uneasy and suggested pacifist activism. In that particular case, the explanation may have been offered with tongue in cheek, but the overall change reveals some discomfort with groups or individuals whose attitudes might challenge or undermine the traditional pattern in which the dice are always loaded in favor of the "legitimate authority" of political and military leadership in matters relating to war and peace.

It is not unreasonable to suggest that many of the votes cast for the pastoral — and now for *The Harvest of Justice* as well — did not represent full commitment to their criticisms of government policy or all the changes they propose. In both documents, the criticisms are valid and the recommendations sound, but this is not enough. What is missing is the clear link between them and the instruction of "the faithful." Once that is achieved, there is the need to marshall the Catholic community to organized action to put those recommended changes in policy and program into effect.

Where approval is routine and divorced from commitment, that all-important process by which teachings are incorporated into the conscience and behavior of the individual believer is in jeopardy and pastorals risk becoming dead letters. Episcopal opposition, even mere disinterest, will be reflected in parish operations and, even more tragic, in diocesan schools charged with the formation of the Catholic community of the future.

Several years after the issuance of *The Challenge of Peace*, the Center on Conscience and War conducted a survey of Catholic high schools focused on the adequacy of instruction being provided on questions relating to the Church's teachings on war and peace. The results were disappointing in several respects. Almost two-thirds of the religious studies teachers in the diocesan and private Catholic high schools sampled failed to respond to the questionnaire and its follow-up reminder. The results from those who did made it clear that students are not being prepared to made a serious personal decision about the morality of wars they may be called upon to support. Many schools used texts giving no or very inadequate coverage to the "just-war" conditions and omitting all mention of conscientious objection as an option. Thus, even those privileged to receive a Catholic high school education, presumably a minority, are likely to graduate (and go on to military service?) knowing little or nothing about the Church's teachings on war and peace.

Nor are the teaching personnel entirely to blame. One respondent wrote (after reminding us of our pledge of confidentiality), "The system fails: mainly most adults are uninformed and prefer it that way. Most do not yet see this as having anything to do with the Church. . . . Theirs is a church of law, not a church of love. Whatever they learned in childhood is all there is to know and anything beyond or else is suspect and rejected. The situation in our area is pitiful, lacks leadership and the 'right wing' exercises a strong influence on the local church. If my bishop knew I said this, I'd be fired without so much as a hearing."

Another wrote of "great frustration" that the curriculum does not provide enough time to cover "the value and importance of peace [which] outweighs all other considerations" and continued, "We also are working with youth already convinced of their *duty* to kill all enemies of our flag and country. The recent actions by our country — Grenada, Panama, Iran-Contra, etc. (the list goes on) — validate a violent solution to all actions. It's a 'tough crowd to play to.'"[4]

Obviously, the pastoral message of *The Challenge of Peace* failed to register to the extent its authors intended. But that document, again, was a policy statement addressed most directly to an unresponsive government confident that it need not worry that those pious criticisms and

---

4 Michael W. Hovey and Gordon C. Zahn, *Catholic Education and The Challenge of Peace: High Schools and the Formation of Conscience* (prepared for the Center on Conscience and War and privately distributed). The Center was founded primarily for counseling prospective Catholic objectors when President Carter reinstituted draft registration. After the Gulf War, it closed and consolidated its activities with those of Pax Christi USA.

recommendations would be converted into specific political demands or opposition. And the intervening years have shown that the government was right. Perhaps it was too much to expect, but if anywhere near the effort that is devoted to abortion as a political issue had been put into promoting peace as a matter of personal moral challenge and responsibility, the "response" might have brought "God's promise" closer to fulfillment.

The Harvest of Justice offers the opportunity to recapture the momentum that marked the period following the issuance of the 1983 pastoral and, one hopes, bring forth a better and more lasting response to its own call to conversion and hope. That "conversion" must begin with Catholics themselves if the hope is to be fulfilled. Only through Catholics' exercise of their power and privilege as citizens *and voters* will the bishops' messages of peace be taken seriously enough to have their desired effect upon public policy.

It will not be easy, and part of the difficulty lies in the fact that not all of those objectives can count on the support of the religious leadership in whose name they have been proposed. Consider, for example, the provision in *The Harvest of Justice*'s excellent "agenda for action, which will guide the Conference's future advocacy" promising to work for "legal protection for selective conscientious objectors and improved protection for conscientious objectors."

Most, if not all, of those would-be Gulf War objectors were "selective" and denied recognition by the military on precisely that ground. As already noted, the bishops have been recommending this since 1968 and in 1983 declared (again, almost unanimously), "We continue to insist upon respect for and legislative protection of the rights of both classes of conscientious objectors."

In 1993, some members of Congress proposed amendments to the Selective Service laws which would do precisely that. In a private effort to support those efforts, I wrote personal letters to several of our most prominent Catholic religious leaders reminding them of the repeated recommendations made under USCC auspices and in pastoral letters issued at the annual meetings of the hierarchy. I suggested that their endorsement of such legislative action would carry considerable weight. Only one — the Archbishop for the Military Services! — was willing to do so and actually invited me to draft a letter he might send. Others answered graciously but gave no indication that my suggestion would be considered. There was one response, however, that was something of a shock given the virtual unanimity of episcopal approval for the 1983 pastoral: a three-page letter in which the author expressed a rejection *in principle* of selective conscientious objection to a specific war. As he saw it, since only the president and his advisors possessed the relevant data regarding the background causes of the war (being privy to the benefits of classified reconnaissance and highly secret diplomacy), the ordinary citizen was incapable of determining whether the war was justified or not. Like Father Dulles (and his Third Reich theological counterpart), he was confident that government authorities could be relied upon to do all in their power to avoid war unless that war is a just war "in the normally accepted use of that word."

The letter gave no consideration to, and made no allowance for, the probable sincerity of the individual involved and his or her moral obligation to obey even the erroneous conscience or, even more surprising, of the secular power's obligation to respect and honor — not penalize — the fulfillment of that personal moral obligation. Most disturbing of all was the unwillingness, even in the light of the writer's private reservations, to support a policy the bishops' conference was "on record" as demanding for more than 24 years.

The Harvest of Justice Is Sown in Peace, like the predecessor it honors, performs a service in reminding political and military leaders of the moral principles that must be taken into account in determining public policy relating to war and international justice. Both documents fit into the "rediscovery" of the Church's peace-oriented traditions by Pope John XXIII confirmed in the council he called into being. However, as seems most likely, if the position of the letter mentioned above is more representative of prevailing Catholic opinion, that problem must be addressed and resolved at the pastoral level. Policy critiques addressed to Washington will still be needed, but unless the Catholic community "gets the message" and willingly accepts its share of the responsibility for bringing *The Harvest of Justice*'s "agenda for action" to fruition, there is no reason to expect the White House or the Pentagon to give serious attention to such critiques. And ten years from now, God's promise of peace will be no closer to being fulfilled.

Pastoral Response to the Ongoing Challenge of Peace

Dr. Mary L. Heidkamp and
James R. Lund

Given the sweeping, global agenda established by *The Challenge of Peace* and reiterated by the tenth anniversary statement, *The Harvest of Justice Is Sown in Peace*, what can a diocese or parish do? The timeworn aphorism, "Think globally, but act locally," fits here. In this chapter, we will describe what dioceses and parishes have done and are doing in response to the 1983 pastoral letter. These efforts strive to be faithful to the closing words of the U.S. bishops in *The Harvest of Justice*: "To be a Christian is to be a peacemaker and to pursue peace is to work for justice."

Through *The Challenge of Peace*, the Church's peace and justice ministry received a tremendous boost. Yet the momentum for social action came from more than the 1983 pastoral letter alone. It rode on the shoulders of a decade in which the National Conference of Catholic Bishops concentrated significant attention on the Church's social mission. The process of drafting and implementing the two pastoral letters, *The Challenge of Peace* and *Economic Justice for All*, began in 1980 and ended in 1989. Moreover, the bishops' efforts received widespread media coverage. In the spring of 1983, for example, the substitution of the word "halt" with "curb" in the third draft of *The Challenge of Peace* made front-page headlines.

The high profile of the pastoral sparked a flurry of implementation activities in dioceses and parishes throughout the country that attracted a broader and deeper base of people than previous efforts. In the diocese where we worked at the time, an interdepartmental steering committee, the first of its kind, was organized to plan and execute a comprehensive follow-up effort. As a result, the diocese organized its most extensive adult education program ever on peace and convened a two-day conference that involved more than three times as many people as had ever gathered for a peace and justice program. The energy and action that we experienced were replicated in many dioceses across the country.

Because *The Challenge of Peace* fits into a larger context, and because this context has led to the transformation and consolidation of peace and justice ministries in parishes and dioceses, our article explores not only the response to *The Challenge of Peace* but also broader responses to the Church's social mission of the past decade. *The Harvest of Justice* mentions many of these explicitly. In addition, this article examines ongoing social action efforts that work hand in hand with the agenda explicit in both the pastoral letter and the anniversary statement. Finally, it points to work that has yet to be done, namely, the challenge of peace the Church must face in the years to come.

The wide-ranging pastoral response to peace and justice concerns generated by Catholic dioceses and parishes may be grouped into five categories: convening, international relationship building, peace ministry, public policy advocacy, and prayer and liturgy. All relate to *The Challenge of Peace*'s call for the Church to "create a community of conscience." While the manifestations differ widely, all include education components, some implicit, others explicit. To carry out this work, dioceses throughout the country have either used existing structures or created new ones. In 1990, 127 of the 174 dioceses in the United States had social action offices. Sixty-two were established between 1980 and 1989, doubling the previous total. These offices generally play a central role in carrying out the initiatives cited here, both within the diocesan structure and as a resource to parishes.

The most direct outgrowth of *The Challenge of Peace* is convening, that is, gathering people together for the purpose of dialogue. The partners in the discussion usually come from divergent perspectives, including the Church, academia, the military, and the nuclear arms industry.

The Diocese of Oakland has continued such a dialogue for ten years. Under the leadership of Bishop John Cummins, the diocese has sponsored, with the University of California-Berkeley, the Graduate Theological Union, and the Lawrence Livermore National Laboratories, a dozen colloquia that have examined the ethical, political, and technical aspects of nuclear weapons policy. The driving force behind this dialogue was a pastoral problem that arose with the publication of *The Challenge of*

Peace. The pastoral threatened to alienate the institutional Church from Catholics who worked in the defense industry. The Oakland diocese, with no assurance of success, began the process amidst a climate of deep distrust. These colloquia drew upon experts in related fields to deal with the dynamic dimensions of the ever-changing international reality. Involving between 50 and 150 participants each time, the colloquia engaged the leadership of the respective institutions in a unique assembly of scientists, educators, and ethicists. As a result, unexpected convergence has occurred and consensus on a variety of points has emerged over the decade.

Pastoral concerns also arose with regard to Catholics in the military. The Diocese of Richmond, home of the largest collection of military installations in the country, has responded with dialogue sessions in that part of the diocese where military bases predominate. The discussion of controversial issues has taken place in a context of mutual respect, characterized by the civility and charity prescribed in *The Challenge of Peace*. Richmond Bishop Walter Sullivan emphasized that the focus is on policy not personality. Respect for the integrity of the participants, who all see themselves as peacemakers, forms the backdrop for the dialogue.

International relationship building, the second category, has the specific connotation of linking people in the United States with people in other parts of the world. The relationship building between the U.S. Church and the Latin American Church had begun in 1960, when Pope John XXIII challenged the U.S. Church to take up the mission to Latin America. Throughout the 1980s, Central America was a focus of international concern for Catholic peace and justice groups, and long-standing, deeply personal relationships had a great deal to do with it. The region was close to home in many ways. The murders of four American churchwomen in 1980 captured its proximity very dramatically. Two were missioners from the Diocese of Cleveland who had been sent to El Salvador by James Cardinal Hickey of Washington, D.C., when he was bishop of Cleveland. A third, Maryknoll sister Maura Clarke, had spent much of the previous three years doing mission education in dioceses and parishes in the Northeast.

Twinning relationships between parishes and dioceses has been one means for international relationship building. In some cases, a direct link with a U.S. parish is made with missionaries who come from the local area. In other cases, organizations like the SHARE Foundation, which does development work in El Salvador, and other groups, which link parishes here with ones in Haiti, Latin America, and Africa, provide the connection. Recently, the United States Catholic Conference Office for Central and Eastern Europe has begun to establish relationships between U.S. and Central and Eastern European parishes. Financial support is part of these relationships, but the creation of personal ties is fundamentally important. In the best of circumstances, a certain reciprocity exists between these partners. Most particularly, however, the U.S. visitors to Third World countries gain dramatic insights into global realities, insights that have the effect of mobilizing people for action back home.

Building relationships also is taking place through a variety of other means, which generally involve personal experience of global situations. Some dioceses have programs that routinely send people to international sites. Catholic Relief Services plays an important role in making these opportunities accessible. It has involved diocesan CRS directors in tours of overseas field operations, and it has developed a program for seminarians to gain exposure to the global Church. The relief and development agency also sends international representatives on speaking tours throughout the United States. The USCC has also done this, jointly sponsoring ecumenical teams from Northern Ireland that have visited numerous U.S. cities over the past five years. In short, international relationship building has the effect of creating a domestic constituency that cares about global issues. When this constituency is mobilized, it can be a political force that can impact public policy.

The third category, peace ministry, refers to local responses to local needs that have a fairly direct link to *The Challenge of Peace*. These include refugee resettlement, conflict resolution or peacemaking initiatives, and justice education and advocacy. They are an inevitable outgrowth of the pastoral letter, although the pastoral letter certainly is not responsible for all of them.

The USCC's Office of Migration and Refugee Services (MRS) has worked together with dioceses throughout the country even before the decade of the pastorals. However, refugee resettlement offers a particularly poignant example of the Church facing the consequences of war. The dramatic influx of Indochinese refugees that came in a series of waves after the fall of Saigon in 1975, through today's assistance to Iraqi and Bosnian refugees personify grievous effects of war. Like other forms of international relationship building, refugee resettlement provides an intensely intimate experience of global conflicts to parishioners who assist in this process.

The depth and breadth of this involvement suggest the reach of its effect. Since the end of the Vietnam War, the USCC has helped resettle over 1.5 million refugees. The 130 participating dioceses virtually blanket the country. The parishes and people who have sponsored refugees have made extraordinary commitments that have made this ministry possible.

Conflict resolution or peacemaking initiatives also emanate fairly directly from the pastoral letter. Violence has surged in the United States, and with it the teaching of skills to resolve conflict nonviolently has begun to grow in importance. Catholic schools around the country have been involved over the years in teaching conflict resolution, and there is a great deal of growth potential. One diocese has recently sent leaders for training who, in turn, will be training teachers in all the diocesan schools. This has pertinence to inner-city schools that are surrounded by violent neighbor-hoods, as well as to schools that are largely removed from such routine strife. The call to peacemaking that *The Challenge of Peace* issued thus becomes manifest in day-to-day life, in classrooms, schoolyards, and homes.

Social justice education and advocacy take a variety of forms in parishes and dioceses. Some perceive all that is done in this regard through the lens of peacemaking. Pope Paul VI's frequently quoted state-ment, "If you want peace, work for justice," captures the interlocking relationship between the two. However, social justice education and advocacy have been a hallmark of Catholic social action throughout this century, from labor activism through community organizing. *The Chal-lenge of Peace*, inasmuch as it animated the U.S. Catholic Church's social ministry, made justice-seeking more integral to church life just as it made peacemaking so. The contemporary situation in the U.S., in which Catho-lics have attained considerable socioeconomic prominence, creates a circumstance where Catholic involvement in the struggle for social justice in the U.S. parallels its role vis-à-vis global issues. The virtue of solidarity, as defined by Pope John Paul II, calls upon affluent Catholics to substantial giving. To exercise solidarity, he writes, "Those who are more influential, because they have a greater share of goods and common services, should feel responsible for the weaker and be ready to share with them all they possess."[1] The U.S. bishops' Campaign for Human Development (CHD), which funds low-income groups working to overcome the root causes of poverty and which educates non-poor Catholics about poverty, is an example of a national response to solidarity that is carried out diocese by diocese, parish by parish.[2]

Catholic Relief Services also intersects with dioceses and parishes in a similar way as CHD. The American Bishops' Overseas Appeal is an annual collection whose proceeds go substantially toward CRS develop-ment projects. In addition, CRS has a Lenten prayer, fasting, and almsgiv-ing program called "Operation Rice Bowl." Both of these efforts raise funds and educate American Catholics about global poverty. In 1991, around 9,500 parishes took part in Operation Rice Bowl, and raised over $4 million.

The fourth category, public policy advocacy, has taken hold among grass-roots church groups over the last ten years. Legislative networks, which are the principal vehicles for this work, have become prevalent throughout the country. Organizations like Bread for the World and NET-

---

1 John Paul II, *On Social Concern (Sollicitudo Rei Socialis)*, papal encyclical (Washington, D.C.: USCC Office for Publishing and Promotion Services, 1987), no. 39.

2 Mary L. Heidkamp and James R. Lund, "A Campaign, Not a Collection," *Church* (Fall 1993).

WORK have enrolled significant numbers of Catholics into their membership. State Catholic conferences and diocesan social action offices have been providing the impetus for their formation and development of parish-based networks that enlist Catholics for legislative advocacy.

The United States Catholic Conference's Department of Social Development and World Peace has been instrumental in resourcing diocesan offices on international and domestic issues. For a legislative network to operate effectively, it requires the establishment of a clear agenda, sophisticated understanding of the legislative priorities, knowledge of the inner workings of the legislative process, and the ability to respond promptly. Few diocesan offices possess this kind of capacity for international issues, and therefore most rely on USCC for support. Current international priorities include the reform of foreign aid, defense of human rights, and support for U.S. reconstruction assistance to various regions.

Statewide and diocesan legislative networks have had their most measurable impact on the state level. Networks in Maryland, Minnesota, and Arizona have all enjoyed notable success. Constituents are generally more responsive and thus easier to mobilize for issues that are close to home. Accordingly, a challenge for legislative advocacy on international issues arises from the need to make it "close to home." Whether the vehicle be an institutionally organized legislative network or not, public policy advocacy points to an important way for the vocation of citizenship to be lived out.

Prayer and liturgy, the fifth category, occupy the center of church life, and prayer for peace is the most frequent pastoral response that the Church makes to war and injustice. For those seeking empirical measures of effectiveness, this is a classification that defies analysis. Even so, the Church's prayer and worship embody the hope-filled belief in God's promise of peace.

The Church gathers for liturgy at times of crisis as well as on ritual occasions. Preceding and during the Persian Gulf War, church attendance swelled. In Chicago, a special Mass celebrated for peace in Croatia filled the cathedral with 1,400 people for a noon weekday service. New Year's Day is also the World Day of Prayer for Peace, which despite obvious scheduling problems receives significant attention in many parishes. The feast of St. Francis of Assisi in October is also becoming a more widely celebrated annual event, linking peace with concern for the environment. Besides these formal observances, other dates have found a way onto the liturgical calendars of peace groups, most notably the anniversaries of the assassination of Archbishop Oscar Romero of San Salvador and the murder of the four churchwomen in 1980. Without ever preordaining specific actions, prayer that focuses on peace connects the act of praying with working for peace. The sanctuary provides a separate space in which the fullness of God's promise can be revealed. It is, however, linked inextricably with the world where individuals and communities respond to the promise.

The isolation of prayer and liturgy from everyday life is a temptation too often taken. It is seldom easy and less often clear how one is to make appropriate connections. One innovative program that is serving the Church to integrate liturgy and the Church's social mission better is the "Preaching the Just Word Institute," founded by Father Walter Burg-hardt, SJ, and run by Woodstock Theological Center. Burghardt and his colleagues travel around the country offering five-day retreats for preachers to assist them in making these connections. The Institute's formula for preaching on justice presents an approach that respects the liturgical texts, the complexity of social issues, and the appropriate role of the preacher.

The ground-breaking initiative in the area of preaching provides a lead-in to this article's concluding section. What do dioceses and parishes need to do to vitalize further their peace and justice ministry? The first step necessarily involves preaching the Gospel in a manner that invigorates the Church's mission to work for peace and justice. Many pastors are understandably wary of wading into an area that can provoke disagreement and even controversy. Few have been trained to maintain the delicate balance that "Preaching the Just Word" preserves, a fact that suggests that the institute has a vast market to tap. Unless the preaching in a diocese and a parish reverberate the themes of the pastorals and the vast body of Catholic social teaching in a meaningful and sustained way, the social mission will not be able to move to the center of the local Church's mission.

Preaching is one component of a parish's ministry that serves to form the community of faith. In-depth formation of church members that adequately reflects the Church's mission to work for peace and justice needs to occur more widely. *The Challenge of Peace* declares that peace-making is essential to our faith. In *The Harvest of Justice*, the U.S. bishops cite Pope John Paul II in setting forth the task that lies before us. "Our nation," they write, "needs to offer hope for a better future for millions here at home, but, in the face of the world's enormous needs, Pope John Paul II reminds us that a turn to 'selfish isolation' would not only be 'a betrayal of humanity's legitimate expectations . . . but also a real desertion of a moral obligation.'"[3] To take up the vocation to be peacemakers and to be advocates for social justice and peace in the United States and abroad will only be possible if suitable priority is given to forming members of the Church in the tradition that gives rise to this aspect of the Church's mission.

---

3 National Conference of Catholic Bishops, *The Harvest of Justice Is Sown in Peace: A Reflection of the National Conference of Catholic Bishops on the Tenth Anniversary of* The Challenge of Peace (Washington, D.C.: USCC Office for Publishing and Promotion Services, 1994), 18.

Parishes differ markedly, from the inner city where people experience privation and violence like that experienced in poor nations, to affluent suburban communities that have become more normative to a growing number, and to vast rural territories where some parishes cover more territory than some states. How parishes manifest this mission and how they form members to carry it out will consequently vary widely. The goal will be the same, however. That is, the mission of peacemaking and justice-seeking will be integral to the life of the parish. One suburban, upper-middle-class parish with which the writers are acquainted has done this with great success.

Graduates of the justice formation process provide a strong nucleus for the parish's social action ministry. Over 120 of the parish's 1,200 families have active involvement in the parish's social justice and peace ministry. This parish has incorporated many of the responses to the pastorals reflected in this article. It twins with four parishes, three in the U.S. and one in El Salvador. It participates dependably in diocesan efforts like legislative advocacy and relationship building between whites and African-Americans. It donates funds to a wide range of organizations. It has also dedicated financial resources for a parish staff person with primary responsibility for this area of mission. Each year for the last five years, 15 adults have enrolled in a 32-week formation process that steeps participants in contemplative spirituality and theology of justice and peace. Over the nine-month period, they meet weekly, participate in six days of retreat, and several days of workshops. This adult formation process has had dramatic effects on the individuals who have taken part, and it has provided tremendous impetus to the parish's peace and justice ministry. In short, peace and justice have secured a central role in the life of this parish.

This parish's success also points out other parishes' failings. The dominant paradigm for parish formation for justice is minimalist at best. A unit in the religious education program, one session in the Rite of Christian Initiation for Adults formation process, or a once-a-decade lecture on the anniversary of Pope Leo XIII's encyclical, seems to be the best that most parishes can do. Central to meeting the ongoing challenge of peace will be the replacement of this model with one that brings formation for justice and peace into a more central place in the life of the parish.

Important lessons can also be learned from dioceses that took the risk of initiating dialogue with people and institutions that seemed inimical to the Church's peacemaking mission. The convenings that have occurred represent determined efforts that grew out of pastoral concerns. Church leaders believed there was no compromising the Church's mission to work for peace, and this conviction compelled them to engage in dialogue despite limited expectations of success.

The vocation to peacemaking has relevance now that is very different from what it was ten years ago. While many felt captive by the fear of nuclear war then, today a growing number worry about the random gunshot. With the perceived explosion of violence at home, the local and the global realities have grown closer. The domestic agenda, therefore, will continue to include the need for conflict resolution skills, and it will engage the Church in efforts to halt the shootings that terrorize a widening span of neighborhoods. It will require work to stop the proliferation of semiautomatic weapons on the nation's streets along with laboring to stop the proliferation of nuclear, chemical, and biological weapons across national boundaries. One danger, with which we are well acquainted, is that the pressing domestic concerns will dispatch international issues to the margins of the agenda, even among the people who would most likely be sympathetic to the plight of the world's poor and would be most committed to international peacemaking and peacekeeping ventures.

This hazard grows when people in the United States question whether they can have any impact abroad. The soured public mood regarding the United Nations operation in Somalia and the international paralysis in the face of Bosnia's plight both exemplify the post-Cold War dilemma that faces peace and justice advocates. *The Harvest of Justice* points to another disturbing piece of the current reality. The bishops state, "One of the disturbing signs of the times is a reduced priority given, and growing indifference to, the world's poor."[4] With this as a backdrop, finding handles on the various problems facing the global community that can energize and activate people in the U.S. becomes a critical challenge.

The Harvest of Justice presents a compelling agenda from which these issues may come. It suggests, for example, that "the growing awareness of the planet-wide ecological crisis" may provide a focus that can mobilize people to action. Current USCC legislative priorities such as the reform of foreign aid and support for U.S. reconstruction efforts could provide the basis for Catholics around the country to advocate for government policies that would move us in the right direction. The essential step of defining issues, however, must be coupled with the creation or sustenance of vehicles that can carry out the agenda. "We are still called to build a peacemaking church that constantly prays and teaches, speaks and acts for peace,"[5] the bishops declare in the tenth anniversary reflection's concluding section. A great deal has been done over the past ten years to move in this direction. Continued progress will require a renewed commitment to this aspect of the Church's mission, and dedication of resources at the national, diocesan, and parish levels that can bring the mission to life.

4 Ibid., 10.
5 Ibid., 19.

Conclusion

The Power of Virtue, the Virtue of Belief in Foreign Policy

Gerard F. Powers

This collection of essays reflects the fact that international affairs and U.S. foreign policy are in a state of tremendous flux and uncertainty. It is a time when many people are searching for new paradigms and new overarching strategies that can make sense of and provide direction to a world that is increasingly "out of control," to borrow Zbigniew Brzezinski's term. Proposed paradigms range from universalizable models, such as Bruce Russett's moral imperative of democracy, to Samuel Huntington's clashing civilizations or traditional balance of power concepts. Others, such as Brzezinski and George Weigel, resist these efforts to shape policy according to a master concept, so as to retain the freedom and flexibility to reflect and respond creatively to a world not susceptible to general formulations.

While some authors in this book would propose new paradigms, this book as a whole reflects the latter, more open-ended approach to the new world order. It examines a broad range of questions facing today's world from a variety of moral and policy perspectives. It does not represent a search for new paradigms as much as a conviction that religion and morality will — and, more importantly, should — play a critical role in shaping a post-Cold War world, a controversial and by no means widely shared view.

In this concluding essay, I will first pull together the many issues discussed in this volume and sketch, in broad terms, the signs of these turbulent times. I will then consider the relevance of religion as a force for peace in contemporary world affairs. Finally, I will propose four theses about the contribution of social ethics to foreign policy in the coming years.

The Signs of the Times

The host of issues examined in this book may be categorized under four signs of the times, namely, simultaneous processes of (1) integration, (2) disintegration,[1] (3) increasing marginalization of large parts of the world's population, and (4) growing isolationist sentiments in the United States and other countries.

The first sign of the times highlighted in these essays is a largely hopeful move toward greater unity or integration. Long-term trends of greater economic, social, and cultural interdependence coincide with new prospects for creating a more integrated international order. The international community is more aware of the fact of interdependence and the need for greater cooperation to address transnational issues, such as the environment and the global economy. The international community also has a new capacity to work through multilateral institutions, especially the United Nations, now that the political shackles of the Cold War have been removed. Nevertheless, the halting and ineffectual attempts by the international community to bring peace to the Balkans, to rebuild Somalia, and to restore democracy in Haiti contribute to what Alvaro de Soto sees as "a surprising degree of uncertainty, even bafflement, regarding how and whether to enhance international cooperation by using global institutions."

These unsteady steps toward greater integration and unity are challenged by a second sign of the times: fragmentation. Haiti and Bosnia-Herzegovina are two examples — Rwanda, Burundi, Somalia, Angola, Liberia, and Afghanistan are others — of a disturbing trend toward disintegration and anarchy, fueled by chauvinistic nationalism, ethnic and religious conflict, injustice, economic deprivation, and an abundant supply of arms. This fragmentation is closely connected to the interrelated phenomena of new claims of self-determination and the growing number of failed states. The suffering and violence from Yugoslavia to Haiti reflect a deep crisis of political legitimacy, whether of existing political arrangements or existing states themselves.

---

1 See John Lewis Gaddis, "Toward the Post-Cold War World," in Charles W. Kegley, Jr., and Eugene R. Wittkopf, eds., *The Future of American Foreign Policy* (New York: St. Martin's Press, 1992), 16-32.

If ways are not found to better deal with the dissolution of states from the Balkans to Haiti, a third sign of the times will be greatly aggravated: marginalization. Intolerable misery and deprivation are the daily lot of a fifth of the world's population. These people are marginalized in that they are increasingly isolated from the economic and political developments in the rest of the world and their misery is met with a growing indifference on the part of the more developed countries. As the bishops note in *The Harvest of Justice*, the story of the modern world is increasingly the story of the rich man and Lazarus, with an ever-widening gulf between the haves and the have-nots.

Marginalization is not only a problem of the developing world. In Eastern Europe and the newly independent states of the former Soviet Union as well, hundreds of millions are at risk of having the isolationism imposed by communism replaced with a post-Cold War marginalization from the rest of Europe. Most of these countries long to be integrated into the West but find many obstacles placed in their way.

The anxiety inherent in a time of transition from Cold War certainties to an uncertain and unstable aftermath, the difficulties of achieving integration, the intractable problems associated with disintegration, and indifference to and fear of the world's marginalized, each contribute, in their own way, to a final sign of the times examined in these essays: a new form of isolationism. This is not an ideological but a practical isolationism. The positive side of this new inward focus is the recognition that a nation's contribution to the international community is dependent, first of all, on its own internal strength and stability. This inward focus, as several authors fear, threatens, however, to become an excuse to avoid responsible engagement in addressing the inherently difficult challenges of contemporary international affairs.

Religion and Morality: Sources of Peace or Conflict in Today's World?

How do religion and morality intersect with these signs of the times? Can we expect religion and morality to be positive or negative factors in integration, disintegration, marginalization, and isolationism?

Most foreign policy specialists tend to ignore religion and morality as mostly irrelevant to world affairs. This tendency is reinforced by three prevailing modes of analysis. First, a Western secularist worldview equates Western notions of secularization with that which is "modern," "democratic," and "pluralistic." The cultural and political arrangements in which religion is much more visible and salient — the arrangements that prevail in much of the world — are equated with that which is "premodern," "undemocratic," and "intolerant." As Brzezinski points out in his essay, "[t]he prevailing orthodoxy among intellectuals in the West is that religion is a waning, irrational, and dysfunctional aberration." Second, this secularist worldview leads naturally to an amoral realism that assumes that religion and morality do not — and certainly should not — be major factors in foreign policy. Finally, foreign policy tends to focus on the structure of the international system, notably political, economic, and military power relationships. Therefore, relatively little attention is paid to "people power" or citizens' movements of the kind that brought down the Marcos regime in the Philippines, the Berlin Wall in Germany, and the communists in Poland and Czechoslovakia.[2] Given this lack of attention to movements from below, the religious influences — which are strongest at this level — often are missed or underestimated.

The end of the Cold War has brought a new and welcome interest in religion on the part of foreign policy specialists and practitioners. The most obvious example is Samuel Huntington's widely discussed thesis that intercivilizational conflicts have replaced the Cold War paradigm. His thesis is based in part on his contention that "[i]n the modern world, religion is a central, perhaps *the* central, force that motivates and mobilizes people."[3] It follows, he argues, that the West must develop "a more profound understanding of the basic religious and philosophical assumptions underlying other civilizations."[4]

While this new interest in religion rightly focuses on the long-ignored movements from below and the values which shape them, it does not represent a departure from the prevailing orthodoxies of the secularist and realist worldviews. Religion, these analysts are willing to acknowledge, might not be "waning," but it remains, in their eyes, mostly "irrational and dysfunctional." Religion is of concern mainly as a threat; it is a source of fragmentation, disintegration, and marginalization because it is "fundamentalist" and because its tendency to discriminate among people fuels sectarian strife and chauvinistic forms of nationalism. From Bosnia-Herzegovina and the West Bank to Sri Lanka and Sudan, according to this

---

2 Stanley Hoffmann, "The Case for Leadership," *Foreign Policy* (Winter 1990-1991), 25-30; Henry A. Grunwald, "The Post-Cold War Press: A New World Needs a New Journalism," *Foreign Affairs* 72:3 (Summer 1993), 12.

3 Samuel Huntington, "If Not Civilization, What?" *Foreign Affairs* 72:5 (November/December 1993), 192.

4 Samuel Huntington, "The Clash of Civilizations?" *Foreign Affairs* 72:3 (Summer 1993), 49.

view, religion is implicated as a significant cause of conflict in the post-Cold War world.

This view that religion is part of the problem undoubtedly has some merit. As David Little points out, "religion is frequently not incidental as a contributing factor to communal conflict" because it can legitimize chauvinistic nationalisms and ethnic divisions. Little is correct in identifying a "recurring affinity between religion and nationalism" but the role of religion in nationalist and ethnic conflicts is frequently exaggerated. Ted Gurr's recent study of communal conflicts around the world found that "religious cleavages are at best a contributing factor in communal conflict and seldom the root cause."[5] Since 1960, according to Gurr, there has been a dramatic increase in rebellions by militant sects (mostly Islamic), but ethnonationalist conflict remains a much greater factor than religious extremism in communal violence.

The tendency to focus on religion as a source of conflict must be balanced with a more serious examination of the positive role of religion in promoting justice and peace. If we learn anything from the revolutions of 1989 in Eastern Europe, the peace process in Central America, the fight for human rights in South Africa, and the downfall of the Marcos regime in the Philippines, it is that religious faith remains a powerful force for nonviolence, human rights, and freedom. Moreover, in cases like Poland and Lithuania, religion has been a positive force for freedom because of, not despite, its link with national identity. Even where this link is not strong, religion is a vital part of healthy democracies, stable economies, and strong civil societies.

The standard analysis seeks a solution to religious extremism and religious nationalism in a secularized society that privatizes or marginalizes religion. Such an approach can have the unintended effect of feeding religious extremism by further threatening traditional sources of personal and cultural identity. Worse, it ignores the fact that the best way to counter extremist religion is with authentic religion, not weakened religion.

Most, if not all, religious traditions contain within them rich resources for countering disintegration and marginalization and fostering integration and human development. As Jean Elshtain argues in her essay, Christianity (and other religions), no less than civic liberalism, rejects exclusivist forms of nationalism, as well as absolutist conceptions of sovereignty in which loyalty to the nation-state is paramount. The moral norms and fundamental beliefs of most religions — e.g., transcendence, charity, justice, reconciliation, and human dignity — are consistent with and reinforce the

---

5   Only 8 of 49 militant sects (out of 233 communal groups) are defined solely or mainly by their religious beliefs. Ted Robert Gurr, *Minorities at Risk: A Global View of Ethnopolitical Conflicts* (Washington, D.C.: U.S. Institute of Peace, 1993), 317.

pluralist goal of engendering unity while respecting diversity. The fact that most religious bodies are transnational actors, closely aligned with core-ligionists around the world, also serves as a brake on any tendencies to become too nationalistic and to see the world exclusively from the prism of their own particular culture or nation.

It should not be surprising, then, that in places like Mozambique, Guatemala, and Northern Ireland, it has been religious leaders who have led the way in promoting national reconciliation and in modeling cross-community cooperation. The most effective response to religious extrem-ism is not to press an even more uncompromising Western secularism, for that only fuels the extremism, but to strengthen these more moderate — and more authentic — understandings of religion.[6]

The Contribution of Social Ethics to Foreign Policy

In rebutting claims that religion is mainly a negative force in world affairs, I have focused on the sociological aspects of religion, that is, its impact on social and political developments. But what of the substantive contribution of religion and morality in defining an ethic suitable for a new world order? I will answer this question in the form of four theses.

Thesis 1. Both the nature of the issues and the nature of the times require that we reject amoral forms of realism and insist that religious and moral perspectives be an integral part of foreign policy considerations. As Charles Kegley points out, "the relevance of morality to statecraft is not as widely accepted as we might presume, and resistance to moral thinking remains entrenched."[7] The nihilist or might-makes-right version of real-ism, which considers power politics or the amoral pursuit of national interest as determinative in international relations, remains influential, if not dominant. This version of realism is not averse to using morality and religion for instrumental purposes — to rationalize decisions made on other grounds or as propaganda against other nations — but it does not consider religion and morality as relevant in their own right. Moreover,

---

6   R. Scott Appleby argues that the best safeguard against the "Islamic threat" is to support policies that strengthen Islam as a vital world religion and "erode the radical fundamentalists' corner on the market of religious orthodoxy." Letter to the Editor, *Foreign Affairs* 72:3 (Summer 1993), 218.

7   Charles W. Kegley, Jr., "The New Global Order: The Power of Principle in a Pluralistic World," *Ethics & International Affairs*, vol. 6 (1992), 22.

turning Brzezinski's thesis on its head, these realists continue to argue that it is not the absence but the very presence of religion and morality that will result in a post-Cold War world that is "out of control."

An amoral realism falters foremost because it ignores or considers irrelevant the fact that many of today's most pressing international issues are laden with moral content. Some realists might regret that humanitarian impulses, as opposed to a cold calculus of national interests, justify interventions in Somalia or Bosnia-Herzegovina. It is hard to deny, however, that a decision about intervention is replete with moral implications of the kind described by Kenneth Himes, Richard Miller, and George Lopez in their essays. One contribution of moral analysis is to provide a framework that can avoid what William Maynes sees as an increasingly "random standard" for such humanitarian decisions.

Looking beyond particular issues, the current reassessment of the first principles of the international system raises fundamental questions about the nature of political order, the existence and adequacy of universal values, the elements of a peaceful international system, and the relationship of the individual and the community — all questions with a high moral, philosophical, and religious content. Unless one holds a highly individualistic view of morality, it is difficult to avoid the conclusion that a comprehensive evaluation of most major foreign policy issues requires appropriate attention to their moral and religious dimensions.

Thesis 2. A morally responsible foreign policy should have as an overarching objective a more united international community based on mutual cooperation and justice among and within states. An ethic that can serve a more just global order begins with a conception of a genuine international community based on cooperation rather than competition and a set of shared principles that can serve as an alternative to a strictly power politics or national interests approach to international affairs.

Two developments suggest that this statement is not as utopian as it might seem. First, there is a growing acceptance that national interests are not a zero-sum game but are interdependent and mutually reinforcing. As Kegley points out in arguing for an international ethic of reciprocity based on the Golden Rule:

> Reciprocity is at the root of *common security*, which proceeds from the conviction that disputants have an interest in reducing their adversary's insecurity. Second, reciprocity is also built into Japanese advocacy of *comprehensive security* that stresses how the economic, political, and military dimensions of security intersect with one another. And third, reciprocity underlies the call to revive *collective security* by fostering community responsibility to mount a collective response to the aggression of any actor against another.[8]

Second, as James Bishop, Bruce Russett, and John Langan argue, respectively, there is a growing, though still partial, consensus on human rights, democracy, and the just-war tradition as normative bases for international order. This nascent consensus is important because it suggests that problems of moral pluralism, serious though they may be, are not insurmountable. These or similar norms could provide a substantive basis for defining the universal common good, a condition for a genuine international community. Without going through the admittedly difficult process of achieving some agreement on the substantive elements of a just society and a just international order, peaceful cooperation between states will remain fragile and elusive.

Thesis 3. Just as no single paradigm is adequate for a complex and messy post-Cold War world, no single ethic can provide the basis for a just and peaceful world. A multifaceted ethic of peace building must replace an ethic of the use of force as the central concern in foreign policy. During the Cold War, the ethics of the use of force were at the center of discussions of international peace, the goal being maintenance of a "peace of a sort" (i.e., a state of nonwar) between the superpowers. Ironically, the use of force ethic is being pushed to the edge of the debate about international peace at the very time that violence is on the rise in many parts of the world. That is because the violence in Somalia, Rwanda, Liberia, Bosnia-Herzegovina, the Punjab, and elsewhere involves a threat to human life and human rights arising out of a breakdown in internal order rather than traditional conflicts between states. Consequently, according to Richard Miller, in many of today's conflicts, it is necessary to clarify fundamental philosophical-political questions about the nature of sovereignty, its relationship to human rights, and the preconditions for a viable political order before one reaches more discrete issues of the morality of the use of force.

Post-Cold War conflicts remind us, therefore, that an ethic of peace is not reducible to an ethic of the use of force. If the substance of peace is what Marilyn McMorrow describes as "a project of social justice and authentic development," then building peace after the Cold War requires a multifaceted social ethic oriented toward a broad and positive conception of peace.

A political ethic is needed to address questions about the nature of self-determination, resurgent nationalism, the legitimacy of democracy as a norm, the role of the United Nations, and the status of sovereignty. An economic ethic, along the lines outlined by Charles Wilber, is needed to address the fact that economic factors increasingly define the relations between states; it is also needed to overcome the marginalization of an

---

8 Ibid., 31.

economically unstable Eastern Europe and the parts of the developing world mired in persistent underdevelopment.

Also needed is an ethic of culture to address questions of individual responsibility, group identity, individualism, materialism, and the requirements of a civil society at the national and international levels. Dianne Bergant argues persuasively for an environmental ethic that defines our responsibilities for upholding the integrity of creation. Finally, an ethic of institutions is needed if we are to construct fair and effective structures and processes to translate our philosophical and moral values into political realities.

This multifaceted, building block approach to peace recognizes both the complexity of the task as well as the richness that must be part of any moral framework used to address today's international order. Some aspects of this multifaceted ethic need further development, especially an environmental ethic, an ethic for economic sanctions, and an ethic of structures. Other areas, such as culture and humanitarian intervention, need renewed attention.

Thesis 4. The moral fabric and moral influence of nations will become increasingly important factors in international affairs. Discussions of the relationship between domestic and foreign policy in recent years have focused on the impact of domestic political systems on international peace, e.g., the "democratic peace" thesis; the relationship between economic health and international leadership, a pillar of the Clinton administration's foreign policy; and the role of public opinion in shaping foreign policy, the CNN effect. These are all important questions that raise interesting moral issues. But another aspect of the relationship between domestic and foreign policy noted in *The Harvest of Justice* and some of the essays in this book deserves much greater attention.

The demise of communism, as Pope John Paul, Vaclav Havel, and others have argued, was ultimately due to its moral bankruptcy. While the West might have confidence in its economic, political, and military superiority, it would do well to heed the warnings of many of these same people about the moral malaise of the West and the implications for international order. America's democratic ideals and economic values have much to offer the world, but, as the bishops warn, "[o]ur society's excessive individualism and materialism, pervasive violence, and tendency to denigrate moral and religious values" can undermine the very values we wish to promote around the world.[9] A recent study found that the values that are most important in the West are least important worldwide.[10] This

---

9 National Conference of Catholic Bishops, *The Harvest of Justice Is Sown in Peace* (Washington, D.C.: USCC Office for Publishing and Promotion Services, 1994), 18.

finding should give us pause, not mainly because it might support a "clash of civilizations" thesis, but because of what it suggests about the credibility of some of our own values. The current predilection of Americans to look inward could be a benefit if it leads us, as Cardinal Joseph Bernardin and Zbigniew Brzezinski urge, to reflect seriously on the moral health of our nation, including the negative, as well as the positive, ways our values affect the rest of the world.

Conclusion

One of the great challenges for religion and morality has not changed with the end of the Cold War. There is still as great a need as ever to counter those secularists and realists who believe religion and morality have no place in the public square, and especially not the foreign ministry. In so doing, those of us who advocate a robust role for religion and morality must acknowledge the legitimacy of some of the realist concerns without accepting their conclusions.

The task for us is not to ignore the fact of religious extremism and the way religion can contribute to ethnic and nationalist conflicts, but to ensure that these religious influences are countered by more authentic religious beliefs and practices, not by marginalizing religion. Rather than reject the realist claim that national interest should be the dominant concern of foreign policy, we should insist on the inextricable link between national interest and morality and national interest and the universal common good. We can acknowledge that a "peace of a sort" is threatened by imbalances in power relationships, yet also insist that a realistic and more comprehensive approach to peace requires a multifaceted social ethic of peacebuilding. We can accept the reality of moral pluralism without resigning ourselves to the impossibility of achieving any international consensus on substantive norms upon which to base a just international order. And, accepting the proposition that our nation's internal strength is a prerequisite for engagement in the world, we must clarify how our own moral weakness can undermine the possibility of a responsible and effective foreign policy.

Finally, the religious/moral agenda for the post-Cold War world is not about moralism or idealism, which offers simplistic or utopian solutions to difficult problems. It is about recognizing that an ethic of peacebuilding

---

10 Huntington, "The Clash of Civilizations?", 41, citing "Cross-Cultural Studies of Individualism and Collectivism," Nebraska Symposium on Motivation, vol. 37 (1989), 41-133.

adequate for addressing the disparate and complex forces of integration, disintegration, marginalization, and isolationism must respect the relative automony of politics, economics, and strategy. That is what this book is about: religion and morality taking seriously the complexities of foreign policy and foreign policy taking seriously the contributions of religion and morality.

The Harvest of Justice Is Sown in Peace

A Reflection of the National
Conference of Catholic Bishops on the
Tenth Anniversary of
The Challenge of Peace

National Conference of Catholic Bishops
November 17, 1993

> The harvest of justice is sown in peace for those who cultivate peace.
> *James 3:18*

Introduction
The Call to Peacemaking in a New World

A decade ago, with our pastoral letter *The Challenge of Peace: God's Promise and Our Response,* our conference of bishops sought to offer a word of hope in a time of fear, a call to peacemaking in the midst of "cold war," a **No** to a nuclear arms race that threatened the human family.

The response to *The Challenge of Peace* was far greater than any of us could have anticipated. While not everyone received this letter with the same enthusiasm and some criticisms were heard from various parts of the Church and of society, the pastoral letter strengthened our Church, engaged our people, and contributed to a renewed focus on the moral dimension of nuclear arms and on broader issues of war and peace. Among us bishops, the pastoral helped unite our efforts to preach the Gospel message of justice and peace. The process of writing the pastoral was also an example of how church teaching can be enhanced by consultation and discussion. The letter led to spirited debate and constructive dialogue in our dioceses and parishes and has been widely used in schools, colleges and universities, the armed forces, and research institutes.

Now, ten years after *The Challenge of Peace,* we renew our call to peacemaking in a dramatically different world. The "challenge of peace" today is different, but no less urgent. Although the nuclear threat is not as imminent, international injustice, bloody regional wars, and a lethal conventional arms trade are continuing signs that the world is still marked by pervasive violence and conflict.

In these anniversary reflections, we seek

- to build on the foundations of our 1983 pastoral,

- to reflect on its continuing lessons and unfinished agenda,

- to explore the new challenges of peacemaking and solidarity, and

- to call the community of faith to the continuing task of peacemaking in this new situation.

Thus, we do not offer a new pastoral letter that revisits the choices of the past, but a reflection on the challenges of the present and future, especially what peacemaking and solidarity require of believers and citizens today.

Some major tasks identified ten years ago need to be addressed, including a comprehensive test-ban treaty, effective action to halt nuclear proliferation, and greater progress toward nuclear disarmament. In 1993, however, the challenges of peace also involve renewing and reshaping our national commitment to the world community, building effective institutions of peace, and alleviating the injustice and oppression that contribute to conflict.

As with the peace pastoral, in these reflections we restate universally binding moral and religious principles. We also seek conscientiously to apply these principles to what, in our judgment, are crucial issues facing our nation and world. Given the nature of these issues, many people who share our values may and will disagree with our specific applications and judgments. We hope that our effort to apply our principles to specific problems will contribute to the public debate on the moral dimensions of U.S. foreign policy and will support the many people in our country who are working to build a more peaceful world.

Among the major challenges peacemakers face in this new era are:

The Human Toll of Violence. At home and abroad, we see the terrible human and moral costs of violence. In regional wars, in crime and terrorism, in ecological devastation and economic injustice, in abortion and renewed dependence on capital punishment, we see the tragic consequences of a growing lack of respect for human life. We cannot really be peacemakers around the world unless we seek to protect the lives and dignity of the vulnerable in our midst. We must stand up for human life wherever it is threatened. This is the essence of our consistent life ethic and the starting point for genuine peacemaking.

The Illusion and Moral Danger of Isolationism. After the Cold War, there has emerged an understandable but dangerous temptation to turn inward, to focus only on domestic needs, and to ignore global responsibilities. This is not an option for believers in a universal church or for citizens in a powerful nation. In a world where 40,000 children die every day from hunger and its consequences; where ethnic cleansing and systematic rape are used as weapons of war; and where people are still denied life, dignity and fundamental rights, we cannot remain silent or indifferent. Nor can we simply turn to military force to solve the world's problems or to right every wrong.

This new era calls for engaged and creative U.S. leadership in foreign affairs that can resist the dangers of both isolationism and unwise intervention. We seek a U.S. foreign policy which reflects our best traditions and which seeks effective collaboration with the community of nations to resist violence and achieve justice in peace.

Structures of Solidarity. Wherever freedom, opportunity, truth and hope are denied, the seeds of conflict will grow. Our country, in this ever shrinking world, should reformulate its policies and programs to address the still widening gap between the rich and the desperately poor. Generous and targeted assistance, sustainable development, economic empowerment of the poor, and support for human rights and democracy are essential works of peace. We cannot abandon our programs of foreign aid; rather, we must reshape them, shifting from a focus on security assistance to a priority of development aid for the poor. "[A] leadership role among nations," Pope John Paul II tells us, "can only be justified by the possibility and willingness to contribute widely and generously to the common good."[1]

---

1 John Paul II, *On Social Concern (Sollicitudo Rei Socialis)*, papal encyclical (Washington, D.C.: Office for Publishing and Promotion Services, 1987), no. 23.

Peacemaking Institutions. The world must find the will and the ways to pursue justice, contain conflict, and replace violence and war with peaceful and effective means to address injustices and resolve disputes. Through the United Nations and regional organizations, our nation must be positively engaged in devising new tools for preserving the peace, finding ways to prevent and police conflicts, to protect basic rights, to promote integral human development and to preserve the environment.

The Vocation of Peacemaking. Part of the legacy of *The Challenge of Peace* is the call to strengthen peacemaking as an essential dimension of our faith, reminding us that Jesus called us to be peacemakers. Our biblical heritage and our body of tradition make the vocation of peacemaking mandatory. Authentic prayer, worship, and sacramental life challenge us to conversion of our hearts and summon us to works of peace. These concerns are obviously not ours alone, but are the work of the entire community of faith and of all people of good will. A decade ago, our letter sought to be a catalyst and resource for the larger national debate on the moral dimensions of war and peace. Today, we hope these reflections may serve as a call to consider the challenges of peacemaking and solidarity in a very different, but still dangerous, world.

I. Theology, Spirituality, and Ethics for Peacemaking

An often neglected aspect of *The Challenge of Peace* is the spirituality and ethics of peacemaking. At the heart of our faith lies "the God of peace" (Rom 15:33), who desires peace for all people far and near (Ps 85; Is 57:19). That desire has been fulfilled in Christ in whom humanity has been redeemed and reconciled. In our day, the Holy Spirit continues to call us to seek peace with one another, so that in our peacemaking we may prepare for the coming of the reign of God, a kingdom of true justice, love and peace. God created the human family as one and calls it to unity. The renewed unity we experience in Christ is to be lived out in every possible way. We are to do all we can to live at peace with everyone (Rom 12:18). Given the effects of sin, our efforts to live in peace with one another depend on our openness to God's healing grace and the unifying power of Christ's redemption.

Change of mind and heart, of word and action are essential to those who would work for peace (Rom 12:2). This conversion to the God of peace has two dimensions. On the one hand, in imitation of Christ we must be humble, gentle, and patient. On the other, we are called to be strong and active in our peacemaking, loving our enemies and doing good generously as God does (Lk 6:35-36, 38), and filled with eagerness to spread the gospel of peace (Eph 6:15).

Likewise, discovering God's peace, which exceeds all understanding, in prayer is essential to peacemaking (Phil 4:7). The peace given in prayer draws us into God, quieting our anxieties, challenging our old values, and deepening wells of new energy. It arouses in us a compassionate love for all humanity and gives us heart to persevere beyond frustration, suffering, and defeat. We should never forget that peace is not merely something that we ourselves as creatures do and can accomplish, but it is, in the ultimate analysis, a gift and a grace from God.

By its nature, the gift of peace is not restricted to moments of prayer. It seeks to penetrate the corners of everyday life and to transform the world. But, to do so, it needs to be complemented in other ways. It requires other peaceable virtues, a practical vision of a peaceful world and an ethics to guide peacemakers in times of conflict.

A. Virtues and a Vision for Peacemakers

1. *Peaceable Virtues.* True peacemaking can be a matter of policy only if it is first a matter of the heart. In the absence of repentance and forgiveness, no peace can endure; without a spirit of courageous charity, justice cannot be won. We can take inspiration from the early Christian communities. Paul called on the Corinthians, even in the most trying circumstances, to pursue peace and bless their persecutors, never repaying evil for evil, but overcoming evil with good (Rom 12:14, 17, 21).

Amid the violence of contemporary culture and in response to the growing contempt for human life, the Church must seek to foster communities where peaceable virtues can take root and be nourished. We need to nurture among ourselves *faith and hope* to strengthen our spirits by placing our trust in God, rather than in ourselves; *courage and compassion* that move us to action; *humility and kindness* so that we can put the needs and interests of others ahead of our own; *patience and perseverance* to endure the long struggle for justice; and *civility and charity* so that we can treat others with respect and love.

"The goal of peace, so desired by everyone," as Pope John Paul has written, "will certainly be achieved through the putting into effect of social and international justice, but also through the practice of the virtues which favor togetherness and which teach us to live in unity."[2]

2. *A Vision of Peace.* A practical complement to the virtues of peacemaking is a clear vision of a peaceful world. Thirty years ago, Pope John XXIII laid out before us a visionary framework for peace in his encyclical letter *Pacem in Terris (Peace on Earth)*, which retains its freshness today. *Pacem in Terris* proposed a political order in service of the common good, defined in terms of the defense and promotion of human rights. In a prophetic insight, anticipating the globalization of our problems, Pope John called for new forms of political authority adequate to satisfy the needs of the universal common good.

Peace does not consist merely in the absence of war, but rather in sharing the goodness of life together. In keeping with Pope John's teaching, the Church's positive vision of a peaceful world includes:

a) the primacy of the global common good for political life,

b) the role of social and economic development in securing the conditions for a just and lasting peace, and

c) the moral imperative of solidarity between affluent, industrial nations and poor, developing ones.

---

2 Ibid., no. 39.

a. The Universal Common Good. A key element in Pope John's conception of a peaceful world is a global order oriented to the full development of all peoples, with governments committed to the rights of citizens, and a framework of authority which enables the world community to address fundamental problems that individual governments fail to resolve. In this framework, sovereignty is in the service of people. All political authority has as its end the promotion of the common good, particularly the defense of human rights. When a government clearly fails in this task or itself becomes a central impediment to the realization of those rights, the world community has a right and a duty to act where the lives and the fundamental rights of large numbers of people are at serious risk.

b. The Responsibility for Development. A second element consists of the right to and the duty of development for all peoples. In the words of Pope John Paul II, "[J]ust as there is a collective responsibility for avoiding war, so too there is a collective responsibility for promoting development." Development, the Holy Father reasoned, will contribute to a more just world in which the occasions for resorting to arms will be greatly reduced:

> [It] must not be forgotten that at the root of war there are usually real and serious grievances: injustices suffered, legitimate aspirations frustrated, poverty and the exploitation of multitudes of desperate people who see no real possibility of improving their lot by peaceful means.[3]

Development not only serves the interest of justice, but also contributes greatly to a lasting peace.

c. Human Solidarity. A third imperative is to further the unity of the human family. Solidarity requires that we think and act in terms of our obligations as members of a global community, despite differences of race, religion, or nationality. We are responsible for actively promoting the dignity of the world's poor through global economic reform, development assistance, and institutions designed to meet the needs of the hungry, refugees, and the victims of war. Solidarity, Pope John Paul II reminds us, contributes to peace by providing "a firm and persevering determination" to seek the good of all. "Peace," he declares, will be "the fruit of solidarity."[4]

B. Two Traditions: Nonviolence and Just War

An essential component of a spirituality for peacemaking is an ethic for dealing with conflict in a sinful world. The Christian tradition possesses two ways to address conflict: nonviolence and just war. They both share the common goal: to diminish violence in this world. For as we wrote in *The Challenge of Peace,* "The Christian has no choice but to defend peace. . . . This is an inalienable obligation. It is the *how* of defending peace which offers moral options."[5] We take up this dual

---

3 John Paul II, *On the Hundredth Anniversary of* Rerum Novarum *(Centesimus Annus),* papal encyclical (Washington, D.C.: USCC Office for Publishing and Promotion Services, 1991), no. 52.

4 *On Social Concern,* nos. 38, 39.

tradition again, recognizing, on the one hand, the success of nonviolent methods in recent history, and, on the other, the increasing disorder of the post-Cold War world with its pressures for limited military engagement and humanitarian intervention.

Throughout history there has been a shifting relation between the two streams of the tradition which always remain in tension. Like Christians before us who have sought to read the signs of the times in light of this dual tradition, we today struggle to assess the lessons of the nonviolent revolutions in Eastern Europe in 1989 and the former Soviet Union in 1991, on the one hand, and of the conflicts in Central America, the Persian Gulf, Bosnia, Somalia, Lebanon, Cambodia, and Northern Ireland, on the other.

The devastation wrought by these recent wars reinforces and strengthens for us the strong presumption against the use of force, which is shared by both traditions. Overall, the wars fought in the last 50 years show a dramatic rise in the proportion of noncombatant casualties. This fact points to the need for clear moral restraints both in avoiding war and in limiting its consequences. The high level of civilian deaths raises serious moral questions about the political choices and military doctrines which have had such tragic results over the last half century. The presumption against the use of force has also been strengthened by the examples of the effectiveness of nonviolence in some places in Eastern Europe and elsewhere.

Our conference's approach, as outlined in *The Challenge of Peace,* can be summarized in this way:

1) In situations of conflict, our constant commitment ought to be, as far as possible, to strive for justice through nonviolent means.

2) But, when sustained attempts at nonviolent action fail to protect the innocent against fundamental injustice, then legitimate political authorities are permitted as a last resort to employ limited force to rescue the innocent and establish justice.

Despite areas of convergence between a nonviolent ethic and a just-war ethic, however, we acknowledge the diverse perspectives within our Church on the validity of the use of force. Many believe just-war thinking remains valid because it recognizes that force may be necessary in a sinful world, even as it restrains war by placing strict moral limits on when, why, and how this force may be used. Others object in principle to the use of force, and these principled objections to the just-war tradition are sometimes joined with other criticisms that just-war criteria have been ineffective in preventing unjust acts of war in recent decades and that these criteria cannot be satisfied under the conditions of modern warfare.

Likewise, there are diverse points of view within the Catholic community on the moral meaning and efficacy of a total commitment to nonviolence in an unjust world. Clearly some believe that a full commitment to nonviolence best reflects the Gospel commitment to peace. Others argue that such an approach ignores the

---

5 National Conference of Catholic Bishops, *The Challenge of Peace,* (Washington, D.C.: USCC Office for Publishing and Promotion Services, 1983), no. 73.

reality of grave evil in the world and avoids the moral responsibility to actively resist and confront injustice with military force if other means fail. Both the just-war and nonviolent traditions offer significant moral insight, but continue to face difficult tests in a world marked by so much violence and injustice. Acknowledging this diversity of opinion, we reaffirm the Church's traditional teaching on the ethical conditions for the use of force by public authority.

Ten years after our pastoral letter, recent events raise new questions and concerns which need to be addressed:

1. *Nonviolence: New Importance.* As *The Challenge of Peace* observed, "The vision of Christian nonviolence is not passive about injustice and the defense of the rights of others."[6] It ought not be confused with popular notions of nonresisting pacifism. For it consists of a commitment to resist manifest injustice and public evil with means other than force. These include dialogue, negotiations, protests, strikes, boycotts, civil disobedience, and civilian resistance. Although nonviolence has often been regarded as simply a personal option or vocation, recent history suggests that in some circumstances it can be an effective public undertaking as well. Dramatic political transitions in places as diverse as the Philippines and Eastern Europe demonstrate the power of nonviolent action, even against dictatorial and totalitarian regimes. Writing about the events of 1989, Pope John Paul II said,

> It seemed that the European order resulting from the Second World War . . . could only be overturned by another war. Instead, it has been overcome by the nonviolent commitment of people who, while always refusing to yield to the force of power, succeeded time after time in finding effective ways of bearing witness to the truth.[7]

These nonviolent revolutions challenge us to find ways to take into full account the power of organized, active nonviolence. What is the real potential power of serious nonviolent strategies and tactics — and their limits? What are the ethical requirements when organized nonviolence fails to overcome evil and when totalitarian powers inflict massive injustice on an entire people? What are the responsibilities of and limits on the international community?

One must ask, in light of recent history, whether nonviolence should be restricted to personal commitments or whether it also should have a place in the public order with the tradition of justified and limited war. National leaders bear a moral obligation to see that nonviolent alternatives are seriously considered for dealing with conflicts. New styles of preventative diplomacy and conflict resolution ought to be explored, tried, improved, and supported. As a nation, we should promote research, education, and training in nonviolent means of resisting evil. Nonviolent strategies need greater attention in international affairs.

Such obligations do not detract from a state's right and duty to defend against aggression as a last resort. They do, however, raise the threshold for the recourse to force by establishing institutions which promote nonviolent solutions of disputes and nurturing political commitment to such efforts. In some future conflicts, strikes and people power could be more effective than guns and bullets.

---

6 Ibid., no. 116.
7 *On the Hundredth Anniversary of* Rerum Novarum, no. 23.

2. *Just War: New Questions.* The just-war tradition consists of a body of ethical reflection on the justifiable use of force. In the interest of overcoming injustice, reducing violence, and preventing its expansion, the tradition aims at:

(a) clarifying when force may be used,

(b) limiting the resort to force, and

(c) restraining damage done by military forces during war.

The just-war tradition begins with a strong presumption against the use of force and then establishes the conditions when this presumption may be overridden for the sake of preserving the kind of peace which protects human dignity and human rights.

In a disordered world, where peaceful resolution of conflicts sometimes fails, the just-war tradition provides an important moral framework for restraining and regulating the limited use of force by governments and international organizations. Since the just-war tradition is often misunderstood or selectively applied, we summarize its major components, which are drawn from traditional Catholic teaching.

First, whether lethal force may be used is governed by the following criteria:

- *Just Cause:* force may be used only to correct a grave, public evil, i.e., aggression or massive violation of the basic rights of whole populations;

- *Comparative Justice:* while there may be rights and wrongs on all sides of a conflict, to override the presumption against the use of force the injustice suffered by one party must significantly outweigh that suffered by the other;

- *Legitimate Authority:* only duly constituted public authorities may use deadly force or wage war;

- *Right Intention:* force may be used only in a truly just cause and solely for that purpose;

- *Probability of Success:* arms may not be used in a futile cause or in a case where disproportionate measures are required to achieve success;

- *Proportionality:* the overall destruction expected from the use of force must be outweighed by the good to be achieved;

- *Last Resort:* force may be used only after all peaceful alternatives have been seriously tried and exhausted.

These criteria (*jus ad bellum*), taken as a whole, must be satisfied in order to override the strong presumption against the use of force.

Second, the just-war tradition seeks also to curb the violence of war through restraint on armed combat between the contending parties by imposing the following moral standards (*jus in bello*) for the conduct of armed conflict:

- *Noncombatant Immunity:* civilians may not be the object of direct attack, and military personnel must take due care to avoid and minimize indirect harm to civilians;

- *Proportionality:* in the conduct of hostilities, efforts must be made to attain military objectives with no more force than is militarily necessary and to avoid disproportionate collateral damage to civilian life and property;

- *Right Intention:* even in the midst of conflict, the aim of political and military leaders must be peace with justice, so that acts of vengeance and indiscriminate violence, whether by individuals, military units or governments, are forbidden.

During the last decade, there has been increasing focus on the moral questions raised by the just-war tradition and its application to specific uses of force. We welcome this renewed attention and hope our own efforts have contributed to this dialogue. We also recognize that the application of these principles requires the exercise of the virtue of prudence; people of good will may differ on specific conclusions. The just-war tradition is not a weapon to be used to justify a political conclusion or a set of mechanical criteria that automatically yields a simple answer, but a way of moral reasoning to discern the ethical limits of action. Policy makers, advocates, and opponents of the use of force need to be careful not to apply the tradition selectively, simply to justify their own positions. Likewise, any application of just-war principles depends on the availability of accurate information not easily obtained in the pressured political context in which such choices must be made.

The just-war tradition has attained growing influence on political deliberations on the use of force and in some forms of military training. Just-war norms helped shape public debate prior to the Gulf War. In addition, the military's call for civilian leaders to define carefully objectives for the use of force is in keeping with the spirit of the tradition. At the same time, some contemporary strategies and practices seem to raise serious questions when seen in the light of strict just-war analysis.

For example, strategies calling for use of overwhelming and decisive force can raise issues of proportionality and discrimination. Strategies and tactics that lead to avoidable casualties are inconsistent with the underlying intention of the just-war tradition of limiting the destructiveness of armed conflict. Efforts to reduce the risk to a nation's own forces must be limited by careful judgments of military necessity so as not to neglect the rights of civilians and armed adversaries.

In light of the preeminent place of air power in today's military doctrine, more reflection is needed on how traditional ethical restraints should be applied to the use of air forces. For example, the targeting of civilian infrastructure, which afflicts ordinary citizens long after hostilities have ceased, can amount to making war on noncombatants rather than against opposing armies. Fifty years after Coventry, Dresden, Hamburg, Hiroshima, and Nagasaki, ways must be found to apply standards of proportionality and noncombatant immunity in a meaningful way to air warfare.

Moral reflection on the use of force calls for a spirit of moderation rare in contemporary political culture. The increasing violence of our society, its growing insensitivity to the sacredness of life, and the glorification of the technology of destruction in popular culture could inevitably impair our society's ability to apply just-war criteria honestly and effectively in time of crisis.

In the absence of a commitment of respect for life and a culture of restraint, it will not be easy to apply the just-war tradition, not just as a set of ideas, but as a system of effective social constraints on the use of force. There is need for greater public understanding of just-war criteria and greater efforts to apply just-war restraints in political decision making and military planning, training and command systems, and public debate.

Ten years after *The Challenge of Peace,* given the neglect of peaceable virtues and the destructiveness of today's weaponry, serious questions still remain about whether modern war in all its savagery can meet the hard tests set by the just-war tradition. Important work needs to be done in refining, clarifying, and applying the just-war tradition to the choices facing our decision makers in this still violent and dangerous world.

C. The Centrality of Conscience

The task of peacemaking requires both just structures and a properly formed conscience. Our policies and structures of peace will reflect the integrity of the individuals who design and participate in them.

For people of faith, this commitment involves a lifelong task of reflecting on Sacred Scripture, cultivating virtues, understanding and applying wisely the Church's teaching on peace, and praying for guidance. We are grateful for all that has been done in the past decade by so many to help form consciences, and we are aware of how much more we can and must do to better translate our moral reflections on war and peace into informed commitments of conscience.

In this statement, just as in our pastoral letter of ten years ago, we state some universally applicable moral principles that are binding on all persons. For example, it is immoral for a commander to issue or for a soldier to obey a command to intentionally kill noncombatants in war. Concrete applications of universal principles — such as our call to reject the first use of nuclear weapons and the targeting of nonnuclear states, and our call for nuclear disarmament — are judgments about which Catholics may disagree. As we said in the peace pastoral, we "do not presume or pretend that clear answers exist to many of the personal, professional and financial choices" facing those in the military and defense industries. "We seek as moral teachers and pastors to be available to all who confront these questions of personal and vocational choice."[8] We hope that they will evaluate seriously the moral basis for our specific judgments and the implications for their work. And we will continue to improve our own efforts to offer our support and guidance to these and others who struggle on a daily basis to integrate their faith and their work.

There is also a need to define further the proper relationship between the authority of the state and the conscience of the individual on matters of war and peace. In 1983, we restated our long-standing position on military service:

> A citizen may not casually disregard his country's conscientious decision to call its citizens to acts of "legitimate defense." Moreover, the role of Christian

---

8 *The Challenge of Peace,* no. 318.

citizens in the armed forces is a service to the common good and an exercise of the virtue of patriotism, so long as they fulfill this role within defined moral norms.[9]

"At the same time," we noted, "no state may demand blind obedience." We repeat our support both for legal protection for those who conscientiously refuse to participate in any war (conscientious objectors) and for those who cannot, in good conscience, serve in specific conflicts they consider unjust or in branches of the service (e.g., the strategic nuclear forces) which would require them to perform actions contrary to deeply held moral convictions about indiscriminate killing (selective conscientious objection).[10]

> As we hold individuals in high esteem who conscientiously serve in the armed forces, so also we should regard conscientious objection and selective conscientious objection as positive indicators within the Church of a sound moral awareness and respect for human life.[11]

There is a need to improve the legal and practical protection which this country rightly affords conscientious objectors and, in accord with the just-war tradition, to provide similar legal protection for selective conscientious objectors.[12] Selective conscientious objection poses complex, substantive, and procedural problems, which must be worked out by moralists, lawyers, and civil servants in a way that respects the rights of conscience without undermining the military's ability to defend the common good.[13] Given the particular problems that arise in the context of an all-volunteer military, individual objectors must exercise their rights in a responsible way, and there must be reliable procedures to verify the validity of their claims. Especially in cases where military service is compulsory, it is appropriate for the government to require alternative service to the community; this may be in or outside a military setting, depending on the abilities and conscience of the particular individual.[14]

---

9 Ibid., no. 232.

10 National Conference of Catholic Bishops, *Human Life in Our Day* (Washington, D.C.: USCC Office for Publishing and Promotion Services, 1968), nos. 143-153.

11 United States Catholic Conference, *Declaration on Conscientious Objection and Selective Conscientious Objection* (Washington, D.C.: USCC Office for Publishing and Promotion Services, 1971).

12 Archbishop John Roach, "Letter to Secretary of Defense Richard Cheney," October 23, 1991, *Origins* 21:22 (November 7, 1991), 352.

13 *Declaration on Conscientious Objection and Selective Conscientious Objection.*

14 Cf. Second Vatican Council, *Pastoral Constitution on the Church in the Modern World (Gaudium et Spes)*, nos. 79, 80.

II. The Challenges of Peace in a New World An Agenda for Peacemaking

Peacemaking is both a personal and a social and political challenge: How do we live lives of love, truth, justice, and freedom, and how do we advance these values through structures that shape our world? International peace is not achieved simply by proclaiming peaceful ideals; it also requires building the structures of peace.

The Cold War subjected the world to "structures of sin."[15] It divided the world into blocs sustained by rigid ideologies. Its hallmarks included a massive denial of human rights by dictatorial regimes, an insane arms race, and proxy wars fought mainly in the developing world.[16] The challenge today is to build a new international order that will be more just and more peaceful than the one it replaces.

The millions and millions of people killed just in this century in war or by repressive regimes are ample proof that we must chart a new path to peace and justice. Pope John Paul II outlined this challenge this year in Denver,

> [T]he international community ought to establish more effective structures for maintaining and promoting justice and peace. This implies that a concept of strategic interest should evolve which is based on the full development of peoples — out of poverty and toward a more dignified existence, out of injustice and exploitation toward fuller respect for the human person and the defense of universal human rights.[17]

As we consider a new vision of the international community, five areas deserve special attention:

(1) strengthening global institutions,

(2) securing human rights,

(3) assuring sustainable and equitable development,

(4) restraining nationalism and eliminating religious violence, and

(5) building cooperative security.

A. Strengthening Global Institutions

Catholic social teaching has long advocated a more integrated international system to serve the cause of human rights, to reduce war between and within states, and to help transform political and economic interdependence into moral solidarity that reflects the common good. At this moment in history, we wish to affirm the positive duty of political leaders and citizens to support the development,

---

15 *On Social Concern*, no. 36.

16 Ibid., nos. 20-22, 36; *On the Hundredth Anniversary of* Rerum Novarum, no.18.

17 John Paul II, "Remarks at Welcoming Ceremonies and at Regis College," *Origins* 23:11 (August 26, 1993), 188.

reform, and restructuring of regional and global political and legal institutions, especially the United Nations.

The United Nations should be at the center of the new international order. As Pope John XXIII observed in *Pacem in Terris,* a worldwide public authority is necessary, not to limit or replace the authority of states, but rather to address fundamental problems that nations alone, no matter how powerful, cannot be expected to solve.[18] Just as the United Nations should not be asked to solve problems it has neither the competence nor the resources to solve, neither should it be prevented from taking the bold steps necessary to fulfill the promise of its charter to save "succeeding generations from the scourge of war." Perhaps no challenge is more urgent or more complex than that of improving the United Nations' ability to reduce conflict in the world. Preventative diplomacy; peace-building after war, as in Cambodia and El Salvador; and peacekeeping all deserve special support and attention.[19]

The United States should play a constructive role in making the United Nations and other international institutions more effective, responsible, and responsive. Effective multilateral institutions can relieve the United States of the burden, or the temptation, of becoming by itself the world's police force. Effective institutions, however, require the United States and other countries to make a sustained commitment of significant financial, material and political resources and to nurture a spirit of shared sacrifice and collaboration. At a minimum, the United States must pay in full its UN assessments. All nations, including the United States, will have to accept the legitimate authority of these institutions; decision-making processes will have to be more truly democratic; decisions will have to be applied more consistently; and these institutions will have to have the capacity to enforce international law. For example, the international system could be strengthened if the United States and other nations could move toward accepting the compulsory jurisdiction of the International Court of Justice.

The United Nations system has its own responsibility and obligation to bring to an end the waste of material and human resources that seems to afflict the system today. It has a task of reforming its own structures, to see to it that the end of its activities is not the continuation of bureaucracy but a service to the building up of peace and the common good.

It is not enough, however, to pursue the common good of humanity through multilateral governmental institutions. If a healthy nation-state requires a strong civic society, so also a healthy international system requires strong nongovernmental groups. These transnational actors — human rights groups, humanitarian aid organizations, businesses, labor unions, the media, religious bodies, and many others

---

18 John XXIII, *Peace on Earth (Pacem in Terris),* papal encyclical, (Washington, D.C.: USCC Office for Publishing and Promotion Services, 1963), no. 140.

19 Of the many proposals being considered, special attention should be given the UN Secretary General's wide-ranging blueprint for strengthening the United Nation's ability to keep and build peace through collective security: *An Agenda for Peace* (New York: United Nations, 1992). See also UN Association of the USA Global Policy Project, *Partners for Peace: Strengthening Collective Security for the 21st Century* (New York: UNA-USA Publications, 1992).

326 — The Harvest of Justice Is Sown in Peace

— can build bridges of understanding and respect between cultures and can contribute to positive social change and a sense of global community.

We have no illusions about the daunting task of constructing a more viable international order, nor do we have any doubts that it must go forward if the twenty-first century is to be less violent and more humane than the twentieth.

B. Securing Human Rights

The future of international peace hinges more than ever on the initiatives we are willing to take and the sacrifices we are willing to make for justice both within and among nations. An indispensable condition for a just and peaceful world order is the promotion and defense of human rights. In our religious tradition and international law, human rights include the spectrum of civil, political, social, cultural, and economic rights. Promotion of the full complement of human rights and religious liberty has been and remains a central priority for our conference. Explicit recognition of these rights, as Pope John Paul II has reminded us, provides "an authentic and solid foundation" for the reforms of emerging democracies.[20]

Over the past four decades, some progress has been made by the international community and nongovernmental organizations in advancing the rights of oppressed peoples on every continent. In the years ahead, the maintenance of peace and the progress of authentic democracy in the world will require enhancing the priority in U.S. foreign policy of human rights, especially of the poor, women, and vulnerable children, and improving international arrangements for their enforcement.

We continue to be concerned about violations of human rights in many parts of the world. Religious liberty is too often denied or threatened in many countries, including China, some former Soviet Republics, Vietnam, Sudan, Cuba, and parts of the former Yugoslavia. In several African countries, especially Zaire, Angola and Nigeria, political leaders have impeded progress toward democracy. The people of East Timor are denied human rights and self-determination. Even as the Middle East struggles toward a just peace, human rights continue to be a serious problem there. In Latin America, most notably in Brazil, death squads murder children, and in East Asia, the tourist trade makes young people victims of sexual exploitation. And on every continent, indigenous peoples have suffered egregious violations of their basic rights. There can be no true peace where governments, insurgencies, or criminal elements deny people of any age their rights and dignity as human beings.

Finally, we strongly condemn once again the horrible evil of ethnic cleansing in the Balkans.[21] We are dismayed that the world community has been so

---

20 *On the Hundredth Anniversary of* Rerum Novarum, no. 47.

21 See, e.g., Archbishop John R. Roach, "Letter to Secretary of State Warren Christopher," May 11, 1993, *Origins* 23:2 (May 27, 1993), 22; USCC Administrative Board, "War in the Balkans: Moral Challenges, Policy Choices," March 25, 1993, *Origins* 22:43 (April 8, 1993), 733; Archbishop Daniel Pilarcyzk, "Statement on War in Croatia," November 11, 1991; USCC Administrative Board, "Statement on the Soviet Union and Yugoslavia," September 12, 1991,

ineffective in preventing this scourge and that it shows such reluctance to assist the victims in a sustained and resourceful way. Every effort must be taken to prevent the spread or repetition of this injustice in the months and years ahead. The destruction of people because of their religion, race, ethnicity, or nationality is a crime against humanity which must be banished forever.

A world marked by true respect for the life, dignity, and rights of the human person will be a world at peace. The defense of human rights must be a consistent and persistent priority for the United States and for a world seeking peace.

C. Assuring Sustainable and Equitable Development

Recent years have witnessed a continual deterioration of the economies of many developing nations, "reaching intolerable extremes of misery."[22] Virtually all authorities agree that the disparity of income and wealth between North and South, as well as within countries, including our own, has grown. The goal established by the United Nations in 1960 (the "Decade of Development") to lessen the gap between the poor nations and the rich nations has never been achieved. In fact, the gap has widened in each of the decades since 1960. In 1960, the richest fifth of the world's population held more than two-thirds of the world's wealth. Today, less than one-fifth of the world's people have more than four-fifths of global wealth, but the poorest billion have less than one-fiftieth. The most affluent fifth controls 80 percent of world trade, savings, and investment. In a world where almost one billion people exist barely on the margins of human life in absolute poverty, more than half of the earth's food is consumed by the rich nations.

Every day, a half billion people go hungry; three times that number are chronically ill. Half the world's population does not have safe water. A third is unemployed or underemployed and at least that many lack shelter. Almost twenty million, mainly women and children, are refugees, and twenty-four million more are displaced within their own countries. A quarter of a million children die every week from hunger, disease, violence, or neglect.

As Pope John Paul II has pointed out, "The collapse of the communist system in so many countries certainly removes an obstacle to facing these problems [in the Third World] in an appropriate and realistic way, but it is not enough to bring about their solution."[23] These problems grew while the West spent billions of dollars to defend against communism, but, ironically, they seem harder to address without their Cold War connection. For example, it has become increasingly difficult to secure funds to support many foreign assistance programs.

One of the disturbing signs of the times is a reduced priority given and growing indifference to the world's poor. From the perspective of faith, the modern world is more and more illustrative of the story of the rich man and Lazarus, with an

---

Origins 21:16 (September 26, 1991), 258.

22 Fourth General Conference of Latin American Bishops, October 12-28, 1992, *Santo Domingo Conclusions: New Evangelization, Human Development, Christian Culture* (Washington, D.C.: USCC Office for Publishing and Promotion Services, 1993), no. 179.

23 *On the Hundredth Anniversary of* Rerum Novarum, no. 42.

ever-widening gap between the world's haves and have-nots.[24]"When the West gives the impression of abandoning itself to forms of growing and selfish isolation," Pope John Paul II warns, "then we are up against not only a betrayal of humanity's legitimate expectations—a betrayal that is a harbinger of unforeseeable consequences—but also a real desertion of a moral obligation.[25]

Perhaps the growing awareness of the planet-wide ecological crisis may offer a new opportunity to overcome "the temptation to close in upon [ourselves]" and to neglect "the responsibilities following from [a] superior position in the community of nations."[26] For as the leaders of the world recognized at the Earth Summit in 1992, our common future on Earth requires a new covenant between North and South, between rich nations and poor for sustainable global development.

Sustainable development goes beyond "economic growth," which has been synonymous with the concept of development since the early 1960s. Rather, sustainable development is concerned with preserving the planet's ecological heritage, addressing the rampant poverty in the poorest nations, redirecting development in terms of quality rather than quantity in the industrial world, creating environmentally sensitive technologies, and keeping population growth at sustainable levels through programs of development and education that respect cultural, religious, and family values.

Such a sustainable future demands heightened commitment by the United States and others to Third World development. Authentic development by poorer nations will not only help safeguard the Earth's resources for all peoples and reduce pollution and environmental degradation, but will also lessen the impact of population growth or decline on the environment and the overall development process.

Only major changes in the international economic order will stop the flow of wealth from the poor to the rich. Arrangements of trade should ensure that poor countries obtain fair prices for their products and access to our markets. Foreign aid should focus more on empowering the poor to improve the quality of their lives than in shoring up the international economic system or pursuing national interest or competitive advantage. The financial system should try to mitigate the human consequences of the massive external debt of the developing countries. Both foreign and domestic investment in the developing countries should increase in ways that neither create nor perpetuate dependency; and environmentally designed technology needs to be shared with Third World countries and developed in ways appropriate to newly emerging economies.

Even with these changes, foreign assistance must remain an important component of a just international economic order. Development assistance has been a shrinking part of U.S. foreign aid in recent years. Compared to other industrialized nations, we continue to rank near the bottom in terms of the share of our economy devoted to development assistance. Rather than abandon foreign aid at a time of growing isolationist sentiments, we need to redirect U.S. foreign assistance toward a more effective effort to help poor people improve the quality of their lives. In this effort, "it will be necessary above all," as Pope John Paul II has written, "to abandon

---

24 *On Social Concern,* nos. 14-17.

25 Ibid., no. 23.

26 Ibid., no. 23.

a mentality in which the poor — as individuals and as peoples — are considered a burden, as irksome intruders trying to consume what others have produced."[27] Rather, we must find new ways to empower the world's poor, especially women, to take control of their own lives so as to lead lives of dignity, not deprivation and dependency.

The redesign of U.S. foreign aid and of aid by the international lending institutions ought to focus primarily on eliminating poverty. As we said in our pastoral letter, *Economic Justice for All,* a major test of all policies is their impact on the poor. Currently over half of all U.S. foreign aid is given for military and security purposes. Funding for development, especially for the poorest nations, can and should be realized through transfers from such economic security assistance and military aid to genuine development assistance. Foreign aid is more than an optional form of largesse. It is a fundamental obligation of solidarity on the part of those who enjoy a plentiful share of the earth's riches to promote the rightful development of those who have barely enough to survive.

In addition, the movement toward peace in the Middle East and Central America and efforts to promote democracy in Haiti will require programs of concerted economic assistance to succeed. If the gains of recent months are to be lasting, these areas, which have drawn so much U.S. attention in times of conflict, must receive high priority, along with the nations of Eastern Europe and the former Soviet Union, as recipients of U.S. foreign aid. As we responded to violent conflict, now let us support the development which can help secure the fragile works of peace.

D. Restraining Nationalism and Eliminating Religious Violence

One of the most disturbing threats to peace in the post-Cold War world has been the spread of conflicts rooted in national, ethnic, racial, and religious differences. While the end of the Cold War may bring new hope for ending some of these conflicts, others continue their bloody logic largely unaffected by recent events and still others, frozen by the Cold War, have erupted with a new and deadly fury, fueled by the dangerous virus of extreme nationalism.

We are especially concerned about the religious dimension of some of these conflicts. Every child murdered, every woman raped, every town "cleansed," every hatred uttered in the name of religion is a crime against God and a scandal for religious believers. Religious violence and nationalism deny what we profess in faith: We are all created in the image of the same God and destined for the same eternal salvation. "[N]o Christian can knowingly foster or support structures and attitudes that unjustly divide individuals or groups."[28]

Some would respond to conflicts with a religious dimension by marginalizing religion in society; by destroying the link between religion, culture, and national identity; and even by repressing so-called fundamentalist movements, especially

---

27 *On the Hundredth Anniversary of* Rerum Novarum, no. 28.

28 John Paul II, "To Build Peace, Respect Minorities," 1989 World Day of Peace Message, *Origins* 18:29 (December 29, 1988), 469.

in the Islamic world. This would be to misinterpret the nature of these conflicts and devalue the positive role of religion in society. In most so-called religious conflicts, political, economic, and ideological factors, rather than religious antagonisms, are the predominant causes of tension and violence. Instances of religion being the principal cause of conflict are extremely rare.

From Central America and Eastern Europe to South Africa and the Philippines, authentic religious belief, rather than being a cause of conflict, has been a powerful moral force for nonviolent human liberation. This moral power is often rooted in the close identification of religious belief with a particular history, culture, language, and nationality. Religious nationalism and religious conflict, while potentially serious problems, are best confronted by an increase, not a disparagement of, authentic religious behavior.

In conflicts in which ethnic, religious, and nationalist factors are present, certain values take on special importance:

1. *Self-determination.* Ethnic conflicts often center on competing claims of self-determination which have enormous appeal because they express a yearning for freedom, usually in the face of injustice and political turmoil. Nevertheless, movements for self-determination can also fuel an aggressive nationalism that can lead to division and civil war. Our own experience exemplifies this ambivalent nature of self-determination. Our nation was founded in the name of self-determination, yet many Americans are understandably uneasy about the disintegration and bloody conflicts sometimes associated with secessionist movements.

Self-determination, understood as full political independence, should neither be dismissed as always harmful or unworkable nor embraced as an absolute right or a panacea in the face of injustice. Rather, efforts to find more creative ways to uphold the fundamental values embodied in self-determination claims are called for; peoples have a right to participate in shaping their cultural, religious, economic, and political identities. Self-determination does not necessarily entail secession or full political independence; it can be realized through effective protection of basic human rights, especially minority rights, a degree of political and cultural autonomy and other arrangements, such as a federal or confederal system of government. While full political independence may be morally right and politically appropriate in some cases, it is essential that any new state meet the fundamental purpose of sovereignty: the commitment and capacity to create a just and stable political order and to contribute to the international common good. As claims to self-determination grow, the international community needs to devise more detailed moral, legal, and political norms for evaluating such claims and for protecting the legitimate right of peoples to self-governance.

2. *Respect for Minority Rights.* Nationalist conflicts often arise out of injustice and, in turn, can create new forms of injustice. Militant nationalism is less likely to flourish where there is a commitment to fundamental human rights — civil, political, economic, social, and cultural. Full respect for freedom of religion and minority rights is especially crucial. Governments have an affirmative obligation to protect the right of minorities to preserve and develop their religious and cultural identities. At the same time, minorities must respect the rights of others and show a firm willingness to contribute to the common good of the nation in which they live.

3. *Unity out of Diversity.* Self-determination and human rights must be firmly linked to a commitment to tolerance and solidarity. Today, when few nations have truly homogeneous populations, increasing diversity can strain the integrity of both majority and minority cultures. Insistence on ethnic purity or efforts to eliminate cultural and ethnic diversity through aggressive assimilation into an overwhelming, homogeneous culture are not solutions to a difficult problem. Rather, the solution lies in striving toward unity while maintaining diversity. Ways must be found to celebrate religious, cultural, and national identities at the same time that diverse peoples participate more fully in promoting the national and international common good.

4. *Dialogue and Reconciliation.* Precisely because of their intractable and explosive nature, ethnic conflicts can be resolved only through political dialogue and negotiation. War and violence are unacceptable means for resolving ethnic conflicts; they serve only to exacerbate them. Nor are political solutions alone sufficient. Also needed is the commitment to reconciliation that is at the heart of the Christian and other religious traditions. For religious believers can imagine what some would dismiss as unrealistic: that even the most intense hatreds can be overcome by love, that free human beings can break historic cycles of violence and injustice, and that deeply divided peoples can learn to live together in peace.

We address these questions of religious, ethnic, and national strife aware of our own failings as a church and as a nation in fully respecting the rights of minorities, in embracing diversity, and in avoiding excessive nationalism. No nation, including ours, has solved all racial, religious, and ethnic conflicts, or is free of nationalist excesses. We, like others around the world, struggle to distinguish between love of country, which is patriotism, and idolatry of one's nation, which is a form of blasphemy.

Finally, since the liberation of Eastern Europe and the former Soviet Union ended the Cold War, it is both just and wise that Americans work with the people of this region to overcome the disillusionment, hardship, and instability that fuel the ethnic and nationalist conflicts there. We applaud and encourage the contributions and sacrifices many are making to help these nations succeed in their transition to democracy. We encourage far greater attention to the positive and essential role that religion has played and continues to play in building just and peaceful societies there and elsewhere in the world.

E. Building Cooperative Security: Special Problems

Earlier, we addressed the need to strengthen our international institutions, especially the United Nations, in order to end the scourge of war. There are a number of special problems of international security that also must be addressed as part of any cooperative security framework, including

(1) the urgency of stopping nuclear proliferation and of promoting further progress toward nuclear disarmament,

(2) the need for general global demilitarization,

(3) the legitimacy and scope of economic sanctions,

(4) the requirements and risks of humanitarian intervention, and

(5) the issue of global responses to regional conflicts.

1. *Unfinished Business: Nuclear Disarmament and Proliferation.* Our 1983 pastoral letter focused special attention on the morality of nuclear weapons at a time of widespread fear of nuclear war. Only ten years later, the threat of global nuclear war may seem more remote than at any time in the nuclear age, but we may be facing a different but still dangerous period in which the use of nuclear weapons remains a significant threat. We cannot address questions of war and peace today, therefore, without acknowledging that the nuclear question remains of vital political and moral significance.

The end of the Cold War has changed the nuclear question in three ways. First, nuclear weapons are still an integral component of U.S. security policies, but they are no longer at the center of these policies or of international relations. In 1983, a dominant concern was the ethics of nuclear weapons. Today, this concern, while still critically important, must be considered in the context of a more fundamental question of the ethical foundations of political order: How do we achieve *Pacem in Terris'* vision of a just and stable political order, so that nations will no longer rely on nuclear weapons for their security? Second, we have new opportunities to take steps toward progressive nuclear disarmament. In 1983, the first task was to stop the growth of already bloated nuclear arsenals; today, the moral task is to proceed with deep cuts and ultimately to abolish these weapons entirely. Third, the threat of global nuclear war has been replaced by a threat of global nuclear proliferation. In addition to the declared nuclear powers, a number of other countries have or could very quickly deploy nuclear weapons, and still other nations, or even terrorist groups, might seek to obtain or develop nuclear weapons. Just as the nuclear powers must prevent nuclear war, so also, they, with the rest of the international community, bear a heavy moral responsibility to stop the spread of nuclear, biological, and chemical weapons.

a. The Moral Judgment on Deterrence. In 1983, we judged that nuclear deterrence may be morally acceptable as long as it is limited to deterring nuclear use by others; sufficiency, not nuclear superiority, is its goal; and it is used as a step on the way toward progressive disarmament.[29]

Some believe that this judgment remains valid, since significant progress has been made in reducing nuclear weapons, including the most destabilizing ones, while at least some of those that remain are still necessary to deter existing nuclear threats. Others point to the end of the Soviet threat and the apparent unwillingness of the nuclear powers to accept the need to eliminate nuclear weapons as reasons for abandoning our strictly conditioned moral acceptance of nuclear deterrence. They also cite the double standard inherent in nonproliferation efforts: What is the moral basis for asking other nations to forego nuclear weapons if we continue to judge our own deterrent to be morally necessary?

We believe our judgment of 1983 that nuclear deterrence is morally acceptable only under certain strict conditions remains a useful guide for evaluating the continued moral status of nuclear weapons in a post-Cold War world. It is useful because it acknowledges the fundamental moral dilemmas still posed by nuclear weapons, and it reflects the progress toward fulfilling the conditions we elaborated in 1983. At the same time, it highlights the new prospects — and thus the added

---

29 *The Challenge of Peace*, nos. 186-188.

moral urgency — of making even more dramatic progress in arms control and disarmament as the only basis for the continued moral legitimacy of deterrence.

b. A Post-Cold War Agenda for Nuclear Disarmament. While significant progress has been made in recent years, we believe additional steps are needed if nuclear policies and priorities are to keep up with the dramatic changes in world politics and if our nation is to move away from relying on nuclear deterrence as a basis for its security. Present challenges include the following:

- *The Role of Nuclear Weapons:* We must continue to say **No** to the very idea of nuclear war. A minimal nuclear deterrent may be justified only to deter the use of nuclear weapons. The United States should commit itself never to use nuclear weapons first, should unequivocally reject proposals to use nuclear weapons to deter any nonnuclear threats, and should reinforce the fragile barrier against the use of these weapons. Indeed, we abhor any use of nuclear weapons.

- *Arms Control and Disarmament:* Nuclear deterrence may be justified only as a step on the way toward progressive disarmament. The end of the Cold War, according to the Holy See, "challenge[s] the world community to adopt a post-nuclear form of security. That security lies in the abolition of nuclear weapons and the strengthening of international law."[30] A first step toward this goal would be prompt ratification and implementation of the START I and START II treaties. Even once these treaties are fully implemented, there will still be more than 10,000 nuclear weapons in the world, containing explosive power hundreds of thousands times greater than the bombs dropped on Hiroshima and Nagasaki. Therefore, much deeper cuts are both possible and necessary. The eventual elimination of nuclear weapons is more than a moral ideal; it should be a policy goal.

  The negotiation of a verifiable comprehensive test-ban treaty would not only demonstrate our commitment to this goal, but would improve our moral credibility in urging nonnuclear nations to forego the development of nuclear weapons. We, therefore, support a halt to nuclear testing as our nation pursues an effective global test ban and renewal of the Non-Proliferation Treaty. Also, steps must be taken to reduce the threat of nuclear terrorism. We must reverse the spread of nuclear technologies and materials. We welcome, therefore, U.S. efforts to achieve a global ban on the production of fissionable materials for use in nuclear weapons. Finally, one should not underestimate the role of the International Atomic Energy Agency as a forum for the discussion of these issues and as a force encouraging nations to take the steps necessary in this area.

- *Cooperative Security and a Just International Order:* The nuclear powers may justify, and then only temporarily, their nuclear deterrents only if they use their power and resources to lead in the construction of a more just

---

30 Archbishop Renato Martino, "Address to the United Nations Committee on Disarmament," *Origins* 23:21 (November 4, 1993), 382.

and stable international order. An essential part of this international order must be a collective security framework that reverses the proliferation of nuclear weapons, guarantees the security of nonnuclear states, and ultimately seeks to make nuclear weapons and war itself obsolete. The United States and other nations should also make the investments necessary to help ensure the development of stable, democratic governments in nations which have nuclear weapons or might seek to obtain them.

An active commitment by the United States to nuclear disarmament and the strengthening of collective security is the only moral basis for temporarily retaining our deterrent and our insistence that other nations forego these weapons. We advocate disarmament by example: careful but clear steps to reduce and end our dependence on weapons of mass destruction.

In our five-year report on *The Challenge of Peace,* we said: "To contain the nuclear danger of our time is itself an awesome undertaking. To reshape the political fabric of an increasingly interdependent world is an even larger and more complicated challenge."[31] Now, on this tenth anniversary, we must be engaged in the difficult task of envisioning a future rooted in peace, with new institutions for resolving differences between nations, new global structures of mediation and conflict resolution, and a world order that has moved beyond nuclear weapons once and for all. We are committed to join in this struggle, to bring the Gospel message of justice and peace to this vital work.

2. Demilitarization. Each year, our nation spends about $275 billion on the military; the entire world spends nearly $1 trillion. The end of the Cold War has led to a welcome decline in U.S. and world military expenditures, but still excessive levels of such spending remain, in the words of Pope John Paul II, a "serious disorder" in a world where millions of people lack even the necessities of life.[32]

According to the Holy Father, the moral judgment about the arms trade "is even more severe."[33] At present, there are more than 40 regional conflicts, almost all of these fueled by a seemingly limitless arms trade. Recent wars in Central America, Iraq, Somalia, Angola, and Afghanistan provide ample evidence that weapons not only exacerbate conflicts and fuel regional arms races, but, as with Iraq, are often turned against those who supply them. Moreover, the recipients are often irresponsible or repressive regimes whose military ambitions rob their people of their right to human development and sentence them to increasing misery. Our experience over the past decade reinforces the judgment of the Second Vatican Council: ". . . [T]he arms race is one of the greatest curses on the human race and the harm it inflicts on the poor is more than can be endured."[34]

---

31 United States Catholic Conference, *A Report on The Challenge of Peace and Policy Developments 1983-1988* (Washington D.C.: USCC Office for Publishing and Promotion Services, 1988), no. 129.

32 *On Social Concern,* no. 24.

33 Ibid., no. 24.

34 Second Vatican Council, *Pastoral Constitution on the Church in the Modern World (Gaudium et Spes),* no. 81.

What is especially discouraging is that our country, as well as other permanent members of the UN Security Council, each of which have accepted a special responsibility for international peace, are the major participants — some would say, profiteers — in this lethal trade. We are faced with a paradoxical situation in which modest defense reductions at home seem to encourage the export of militarism abroad. Defense spending is cut while weapons continue to be supplied to others without effective restraints. It is a matter of concern when the desire to protect jobs in the defense industry overshadows the interests of international peace and stability.

As the world's largest supplier of weapons, the United States bears great responsibility for curbing the arms trade by taking concrete actions to reduce its own predominant role in this trade.[35] The human consequences of unemployment and economic disruption caused by defense cuts must be addressed concretely through economic development and conversion programs, a stronger nonmilitary economy, and other programs to assist those who lose their jobs. Jobs at home cannot justify exporting the means of war abroad.

Neither jobs nor profits justify military spending beyond the minimum necessary for legitimate national security and international peacekeeping obligations. The end of the Cold War still provides an opportunity to reduce substantially military spending. Prudence requires that this reduction take into account emerging threats to world peace. Prudence also dictates that we use the unparalleled opportunities at hand to find alternative ways to respond to new dangers as we redirect resources to meet nonmilitary threats to international security. Diverting scarce resources from military to human development is not only a just and compassionate policy, but it is also a wise long-term investment in global peace and national security.

3. *Economic Sanctions.* In the aftermath of the Cold War, comprehensive economic sanctions have become a more common form of international pressure. In the case of Iraq and the former Yugoslavia, our bishops' conference has supported sanctions as a means of combating aggression short of military intervention; in the case of South Africa, we have supported less onerous sanctions to encourage the dismantling of apartheid and adopted a policy of divestment to renounce complicity in this immoral regime and to stand in solidarity with those who were seeking to end it. In other cases, we have not been convinced that comprehensive sanctions were helpful, and in still others, we have not taken a position. In each case, we have consulted closely with the Church in the country affected and have been guided by its judgment.

Our record on sanctions reflects an inherent dilemma involved in this form of pressure. We hear the cries of innocent people in Serbia, Haiti, Iraq, Cuba, and elsewhere who have lost their jobs, who can no longer afford what food is available, whose health is deteriorating, and whose political leaders remain recalcitrant and as strong as ever. We take very seriously the charge that sanctions can

---

35 According to the Congressional Research Service, the United States has been "the predominant arms supplier. . . since the Cold War's end," responsible for close to 57 percent of the arms trade in 1992. Congressional Research Service, *Conventional Arms Transfers to the Third World, 1985-1992* (Washington, D.C.: Congressional Research Service, 1993).

be counterproductive and sometimes unjustifiably harm the innocent. Yet, sanctions can offer a nonmilitary alternative to the terrible options of war or indifference when confronted with aggression or injustice.

While much more study, reflection and public debate over the moral dimension of comprehensive sanctions is needed, we offer the following tentative criteria as a contribution to this discussion.

First, concerns about the limited effectiveness of sanctions and the harms caused to civilian populations require that comprehensive sanctions be considered only in response to aggression or grave and ongoing injustice, after less coercive measures have been tried, and with clear and reasonable conditions set for their removal.

Second, the harm caused by sanctions should be proportionate to the good likely to be achieved; sanctions should avoid grave and irreversible harm to the civilian population. Therefore, sanctions should be targeted as much as possible against those directly responsible for the injustice, distinguishing between the government and the people. Selective sanctions which target offending individuals and institutions are usually preferable, therefore, to complete embargoes. Embargoes, when employed, must make provision for the fundamental human needs of the civilian population. The denial of basic needs may not be used as a weapon.

Third, the consent to sanctions by substantial portions of the affected population is morally relevant. While this consent may mitigate concerns about suffering caused by sanctions, however, it does not eliminate the need for humanitarian exemptions.

Finally, sanctions should always be part of a broader process of diplomacy aimed at finding an effective political solution to the injustice.

The troubling moral problems posed by the suffering caused by sanctions and the limits to their effectiveness counsel that this blunt instrument be used sparingly and with restraint. Economic sanctions may be acceptable, but only if less coercive means fail, as an alternative to war and as a means of upholding fundamental international norms.

4. Humanitarian Intervention. In recent years, we hear increasing calls for humanitarian intervention, that is, the forceful, direct intervention by one or more states or international organizations in the internal affairs of other states for essentially humanitarian purposes. The internal chaos, repression, and widespread loss of life in countries such as Haiti, Bosnia, Liberia, Iraq, Somalia, Sudan, and now Burundi, have all raised the difficult moral, political, and legal questions that surround these calls to intervene in the affairs of sovereign states to protect human life and basic human rights.

Pope John Paul II, citing the "conscience of humanity and international humanitarian law," has been outspoken in urging that "humanitarian intervention be obligatory where the survival of populations and entire ethnic groups is seriously compromised. This is a duty for nations and the international community."[36] He elaborated on this right and duty of humanitarian intervention in his 1993 annual address to the diplomatic corps:

---

36 John Paul II, "Address to the International Conference on Nutrition," *Origins* 22:28 (December 24, 1992), 475.

Once the possibilities afforded by diplomatic negotiations and the procedures provided for by international agreements and organizations have been put into effect, and that [sic], nevertheless, populations are succumbing to the attacks of an unjust aggressor, states no longer have a "right to indifference." It seems clear that their duty is to disarm this aggressor, if all other means have proved ineffective. The principles of the sovereignty of states and of non-interference in their internal affairs — which retain all their value — cannot constitute a screen behind which torture and murder may be carried out.[37]

The Holy Father's appeal for humanitarian intervention reflects several concerns. First, human life, human rights, and the welfare of the human community are at the center of Catholic moral reflection on the social and political order. Geography and political divisions do not alter the fact that we are all one human family, and indifference to the suffering of members of that family is not a moral option.

Second, sovereignty and nonintervention into the life of another state have long been sanctioned by Catholic social principles, but have never been seen as absolutes. Therefore, the principles of sovereignty and nonintervention may be overridden by forceful means in exceptional circumstances, notably in the cases of genocide or when whole populations are threatened by aggression or anarchy.

Third, nonmilitary forms of intervention should take priority over those requiring the use of force. Humanitarian aid programs, combined with political and economic sanctions, arms embargoes, and diplomatic initiatives may save lives without requiring military intervention. In this context, we affirm the responsibility, which must be respected, of humanitarian relief organizations to aid civilians in war zones and their right of access to vulnerable populations. In the longer run, the international community's first commitment must be to address the root causes of these conflicts, to support the spread of democratic and just political and economic orders, to develop the capacity to prevent conflicts and to settle them promptly and peacefully when they erupt.

Fourth, military intervention may sometimes be justified to ensure that starving children can be fed or that whole populations will not be slaughtered. They represent St. Augustine's classic case: love may require force to protect the innocent. The just-war tradition reminds us, however, that military force, even when there is just cause, must remain an exceptional option that conforms strictly to just-war norms and norms of international policing. The particular difficulties involved in meeting criteria of success and proportionality in cases of humanitarian intervention deserve careful scrutiny and further examination. Intervention should also remain limited to achieving clearly defined humanitarian objectives and to establishing conditions necessary for a just and stable peace. We must be wary that the outstretched hand of peace is not turned into an iron fist of war.

Finally, a right to intervene must be judged in relation to the broader effort to strengthen international law and the international community. Principles of sovereignty and nonintervention remain crucial to maintaining international peace and

---

37   John Paul II, "Address to the Diplomatic Corps," January 16, 1993, *Origins* 22:34 (February 4, 1993), 587.

the integrity of nations, especially the weaker ones. The exceptional cases when humanitarian concerns may justify overriding these principles must be more clearly defined in international law, political philosophy, and ethics. Moreover, effective mechanisms must be developed to ensure that humanitarian intervention is an authentic act of international solidarity and not a cloak for great power dominance, as it sometimes has been in the past. Multilateral interventions, under the auspices of the United Nations, are preferable because they enhance the legitimacy of these actions and can protect against abuse.

If these considerations are taken into account, humanitarian intervention need not open the door to new forms of imperialism or endless wars of altruism, but could be an exceptional means to ensure that governments fulfill the purposes of sovereignty and meet the needs of their people, as the world urgently searches for effective nonviolent means to confront injustice and political disorder.

5. *Global Responses to Regional Conflicts.* Today's threats to peace tend to be more regional than global, more rooted in geographic, tribal, national, and ethnic conflict than in ideological disputes. Though regional, however, they call for a continuing response from the United States and the international community. Without attempting to reiterate our concerns about pressing problems in countries as diverse as Bosnia, East Timor, China, Peru, and Northern Ireland, the following reflections on Africa, Asia, Central America and the Caribbean, and the Middle East highlight the importance of resolving regional and internal conflicts and developing mechanisms for peace building at the local and regional levels.

Africa

The African continent continues to be wracked by conflict and neglected by U.S. foreign policy. While progress has been made toward reconciliation in some Cold War conflicts, like that in Mozambique, elsewhere fighting continues. Since 1960, not a day has passed without armed conflict. In Sudan, no end is in sight to a lengthy civil war in which government troops have massacred Christians, starved them by siege, forced some into slavery, and coerced many into religious conversion. In Somalia, United Nations forces have not yet succeeded in establishing the peaceful conditions which will permit relief work to continue unimpeded and civil life to be restored. In South Africa, a long-awaited transition to nonracial democracy is marred by intergroup violence. In Zaire, troops still loyal to the old dictatorship hamper progress toward a renewal of democratic government, while in Burundi age-old tribal animosities have again brought bloodshed and dislocations.

Asia

In some parts of this important region, the Church is struggling, frequently against official opposition, to win the freedom to openly proclaim the Gospel. We especially support the persistent efforts of our brother bishops in China and Vietnam to demonstrate that genuine religious liberty can improve national harmony, reduce international tensions, and contribute to the common good.

We renew our commitments in our pastoral reflection of 1989, *A Time for Dialogue and Healing*, including "our wish to work with our brother bishops in Vietnam toward a better understanding between our two peoples" and our call for "full and genuine respect for the role of the Church by the Vietnamese government," and for the United States and the broader international community to assist Vietnam "to enter the world trading and diplomatic community."

Central America and the Caribbean

For much of the last decade, Central America preoccupied our nation and this conference. Thankfully, the guns of war have mostly fallen silent as a result of dialogue, negotiation, and a return to democratic decision making. Sadly, the United States, which invested so much in the armed conflict in the region, seems almost indifferent now to the need for significant investment in its development and reconstruction. If the countries of the region are not to return to cycles of violence and repression, continued U.S. involvement and aid will be needed for some time to come. Greater sensitivity on the part of the World Bank and the International Monetary Fund to the impact of their decisions on the abilities of countries to rebuild is also much needed.

We stand with our brother bishops in Cuba in their courageous declaration *Love Hopes All Things.*[38] We support their call for greater religious and political freedom and direct humanitarian assistance, especially food and medicine, from our nation and others at this time of deprivation for their long-suffering people. We hope with them that substantial, improved performance by the Cuban authorities with regard to human rights and religious liberty could lead to progressively greater opportunities for trade and dialogue between our two nations and within Cuban society. We stand in solidarity with the Church and people of Cuba in their hopes for greater freedom and opportunity.

For all too long, the people of Haiti have suffered from grinding poverty, denial of human rights, predatory government, indiscriminate violence, and the indifference of outsiders. Today we must accompany the Haitian people as they travel the long road toward democracy and civil peace. To enjoy the fruits of peace, all parties will have to respect basic human rights and commit themselves to restraint and reconciliation. Once the rule of law is established, the Haitian people will need the support of the United States and of the international community for years to come in the development of their island. Much needs to be done in order to institutionalize democratic political processes that will lead to justice for all Haitians.

Middle East

We give thanks to God for the interim agreement between Israel and the Palestine Liberation Organization. It is an historic opening to a new era for which the whole world has been longing for many years. We applaud the courage, the imagination, and the spirit of compromise that have been shown in negotiating this major advance toward peace in the Holy Land. The agreement is an historic beginning, which must be carried out fully, supported actively, and expanded upon quickly. We support full autonomy for the West Bank and a true homeland for the Palestinians, and look forward to a final settlement that will protect the rights and security of all people, including Israelis and Palestinians.

To succeed, the interim Israeli-Palestinian accord on Gaza and Jericho as well as eventual Palestinian self-rule on the West Bank will require serious support from the international community, especially from the United States. Aid and technical

38 Statement of the Cuban Bishops, "Love Hopes All Things," September 8, 1993, *Origins* 23:16 (September 30, 1993), 273.

support are needed for building up the autonomous Palestinian territories and for reconstruction of Lebanon. As the U.S. has been generous in supporting Israel's security, so now it should be unstinting in helping to build peace for the region.

A lasting settlement in the region must include a resolution of the status of Jerusalem that reflects its unique role as a city holy to Jews, Muslims, and Christians alike. Any settlement must include full recognition of the rights of all believers in the Holy Land and their unimpeded access to the Holy Places.[39]

We hope that a resolution of the Israeli-Palestinian issue will be the impetus for tangible progress toward development and disarmament, peace and security in regional negotiations. Lebanon, which has suffered so much until now and which still needs to reacquire its full sovereignty from all its neighbors, is in special need of peace and reconstruction. The people of Iraq also deserve relief from their present oppressive situation. The new era must bring comprehensive steps toward a just peace for the whole region.

These and other conflicts show the need for early and vigorous responses by the international community to support reconciliation processes whether they are supervised by domestic leaders or outside mediators. During the Cold War, the United States gave substantial support to rebel groups and client governments to prevent the spread of communism. Therefore, it bears a special responsibility in this new era to provide assistance to overcome the legacy of apartheid, civil war, and autocratic rule and to bolster civilian groups eager for peace and the rebirth of democracy.

In these regions and throughout the world, violence and repression have led to a refugee crisis of tragic proportions. The United States and other nations cannot close their eyes or their doors to the tide of suffering humanity. Our laws and policies should reflect our historic openness to victims of war and oppression. Welcoming refugees is an essential part of peacemaking.

F. Shaping Responsible U.S. Leadership in the World

The preeminence of U.S. influence and power in the world is an undisputed fact. This fact is of great moral significance, first, because American values and actions can bring tremendous good or much suffering to people around the world; and second, because with power and influence comes a responsibility to contribute to the universal common good.

Our nation needs to offer hope for a better future for millions here at home, but, in the face of the world's enormous needs, Pope John Paul II reminds us that a turn to "selfish isolation" would not only be "a betrayal of humanity's legitimate expectations . . . but also a real desertion of a moral obligation."[40]

Building peace, combating poverty and despair, and protecting freedom and human rights are not only moral imperatives, but also wise national priorities. They can

---

39 United States Catholic Conference, *Toward Peace in the Middle East: Perspectives, Principles, and Hopes* (Washington, D.C.: USCC Office for Publishing and Promotion Services, 1989).

40 *On Social Concern,* no. 23.

shape a world that will be a safer, more secure, and more just home for all of us. Responsible international engagement is based on the conviction that our national interests and the interests of the international community, our common good, and the global common good are intertwined.

For these reasons, the leaders and people of the United States are called to take up the vocation to peacemaking with new urgency and commitment. Accepting, though not exaggerating, the lessons of recent history, acknowledging the limits of U.S. influence and humbly confessing past excesses and failures, we are called to commit ourselves firmly to joining with other nations in building a new kind of world, one that is more peaceful, just, and respectful of the life and dignity of the human person. Having paid such a price in the lives of their young and spent so much of their national treasure on the wars of this century, it is both wise and understandable that Americans are reluctant to commit themselves also to serve as the world's police force. As a permanent member of the UN Security Council and the strongest military power in the world, however, the U.S. has a special responsibility to work with other nations to find cooperative ways to promote international peace. As Pope John Paul II said this year in Denver, "Together with millions of people around the globe I share the profound hope that in the present international situation the United States will spare no effort in advancing authentic freedom and in fostering human rights and solidarity."[41]

As our nation helps shape a new world, we must be aware of the values we are contributing to this new order. The best of America's values and actions continue to inspire other peoples' struggles for justice and freedom and contribute to building a more just and peaceful world. Of special significance have been our democratic ideals, which have inspired the spread of democracy and political transformations in many parts of the world. Our society's excessive individualism and materialism, pervasive violence and tendency to denigrate moral and religious values, however, can be harmful. A practical materialism and a militant secular mentality undermine cultural and moral values here and abroad, generate expectations that cannot and should not necessarily be fulfilled, and inhibit efforts to strengthen international order.

What the United States can offer the world — and what the world desperately needs — is creative engagement, a willingness to collaborate and a commitment to values that can build up the global community. "Liberty and justice for all" is not only a profound national pledge; it is also a worthy goal for a world leader.

III. Concluding Commitments: Blessed Are the Peacemakers

A. A Renewed Commitment

Ten years after *The Challenge of Peace,* we renew our commitment to peacemaking. We are still at a beginning, not an end. On the fifth anniversary of our

---

41 "Remarks at Welcoming Ceremonies and at Regis College," 188.

pastoral letter, we said we must work "to broaden, strengthen and deepen the Church's work for peace." We are still called to build a peacemaking church that constantly prays and teaches, speaks and acts for peace. Once again, we ask our parishes and people to join with us in:

- *Regular prayer for peace.* Every liturgy is a call to and celebration of peace. The cause of peace should be constantly reflected in our prayers of petition. The scriptural call to peacemaking should be a constant source for prayer and preaching.

- *Sharing the Gospel call to peace and the Church's teaching on peace.* In our schools and seminaries, our religious education and formation efforts, and our colleges and universities, we need to continue and intensify our efforts to integrate Catholic teaching on justice, nonviolence, and peace into the curriculum and broader life of our educational endeavors. Education is a work of peace.

- *Speaking and acting for peace.* In our advocacy and citizenship efforts, we are called to use the resources of our faith and the opportunities of our democracy to help shape a U.S. foreign policy clearly committed to human life and human rights. Through legislative networks and broader participation in the political process, Catholics can take our principles of peacemaking into the public arena, where they can help shape an active and constructive U.S. role in the world.

In these reflections, we outline an agenda for action, which will guide the conference's future advocacy. We will work for:

- Creative, engaged, and responsible U.S. leadership that rejects the illusion of isolationism and avoids the dangers of unwise intervention;

- A reshaped foreign aid program designed to combat poverty with sustainable development and the economic development of the poor, especially women;

- Substantive changes in the international economic order to stop the movement of wealth from the poor to the rich;

- A commitment to strengthening and improving the capacity of the United Nations and other multilateral institutions to promote human development, democracy, human rights, and peace;

- Accelerated progress toward a nuclear test ban, eliminating nuclear weapons, preventing nuclear proliferation, restraining the arms trade, and encouraging worldwide demilitarization;

- Legal protection for selective conscientious objectors and improved protection for conscientious objectors;

- Prudent use of economic sanctions as an alternative to war and means to enforce fundamental international norms; and

- Clarification of the right and duty of humanitarian intervention in exceptional cases, by means consistent with Catholic teaching on nonviolence and just war, when the survival of whole populations is threatened.

The Catholic community in the United States is already a very active and involved part of both the Universal Church and a nation with clear global responsibilities. Day by day, we seek to build a more just and peaceful world through the work of Catholic Relief Services, our migration and refugee programs, missionary efforts, advocacy on international issues, and existing aid programs to the churches in Eastern Europe, Latin America, and the Middle East. In these anniversary reflections, we call on the leaders of these impressive programs to explore together ways of building upon and strengthening our community's efforts to help those in need and to work for justice around the world. Our international education, outreach, and advocacy efforts need to continue to help shape a Church and nation more clearly committed to solidarity and global responsibility.

B. A Call to Conversion and Hope

In our pastoral of ten years ago, we outlined a call to conversion, reflection, and peacemaking: "Peacemaking is not an optional commitment. It is a requirement of our faith. We are called to be peacemakers, not by some movement of the moment, but by our Lord Jesus."[42]

Now ten years later, Jesus calls us to be peacemakers in a very different world. In these anniversary reflections, we have focused less on particular weapons and wars and more on a broader context of violence which still pervades our communities, our country, and our world. This violence is one of the saddest "signs of our times." We see the violence of abortion accepted as normal by too many Americans. We fear our society is becoming accustomed to children dying in our streets and in villages half a world away. We may be growing indifferent to entertainment saturated with blood and death, to nightly television images of deadly warfare, racial hatred, and ethnic cleansing. The pervasiveness of violence deadens our response to the human suffering and the moral damage it causes.

Our age seems to seek quick and decisive solutions to difficult problems, to turn to violence rather than to embark on the painful and complicated search for less deadly, more lasting solutions that require sacrifice, patience, and time. We observe signs of this tragic trend in our domestic life where abortion is seen as a solution to difficult pregnancies, where capital punishment is embraced as a response to rising crime and where euthanasia is advocated in the face of the burdens of age and illness.

In global affairs, we see similar temptations. Age-old antagonisms are fought out in bloody warfare; terrorism is seen as a means of revenge and advancing a

---

42 *The Challenge of Peace,* no. 333.

cause; and military force is too often employed as the principal means to redress injustice or to safeguard interests.

It is time to clearly recognize that in the end violence is not a solution, but more often the problem. As we reaffirm the Church's teachings on war and peace, we insist that the world community must urgently search for effective ways to move beyond the violence of war and terrorism to settle scores or to defend what is precious. We need new policies, new structures, new attitudes to resolve disputes and address injustice.

As our Holy Father has said:

> No, never again war, which destroys the lives of innocent people, teaches how to kill, throws into upheaval even the lives of those who do the killing and leaves behind a trail of resentment and hatred, thus making it all the more difficult to find a just solution of the very problems which provoked the war. Just as the time has finally come when in individual states a system of private vendetta and reprisal has given way to the rule of law, so too a similar step forward is now urgently needed in the international community.[43]

Some will find this goal a pious hope or utopian dream. No doubt, finding ways to move the world beyond war will be a complex, demanding and difficult struggle. But it is a task that must be pursued by all who take faith seriously, and honestly assess the human, social and moral costs of continuing conflict and bloodshed. As history's bloodiest century ends, there should be no question that, in the words of Pope John Paul II, we must "proceed resolutely toward outlawing war completely and come to cultivate peace as a supreme good to which all programs and all strategies must be subordinated."[44]

At its heart, today's call to peacemaking is a call to conversion, to change our hearts, to reject violence, to love our enemies. We will not fashion new policies until we repudiate old thinking. Ten years ago, in addressing the seemingly intractable dynamic of the Cold War, our pastoral letter suggested:

> To believe we are condemned in the future only to what has been the past of United States-Soviet relations is to underestimate both our human potential for creative diplomacy and God's action in our midst which can open the way to changes we could barely imagine.[45]

Changes we could barely imagine ten years ago have taken place before our eyes. Without violence, the hope, courage, and power of ordinary people have brought down walls, restored freedoms, toppled governments, and changed the world.

For believers, hope is not a matter of optimism but a resource for action, a source of strength in demanding causes. For peacemakers, hope is the indispensable virtue. This hope, together with our response to the call to conversion, must be rooted in God's promises and nourished by prayer and penance, including fasting and Friday abstinence.[46]

---

43 *On the Hundredth Anniversary of* Rerum Novarum, no. 52; fn. 104.
44 "Address to the Diplomatic Corps," 531.
45 *The Challenge of Peace*, no. 258.

C. Witnesses to Peacemaking

In our faith, we find the reason for hope and witnesses for genuine peacemaking. In the Scriptures, in the life of Jesus, and in the teaching of his Church are the principles we need to follow as peacemakers.

We also find examples in the witness of peacemakers across the globe. Pope John Paul II has been a consistent voice for peace and justice in a world lacking both. We watched with awe the courage and faithfulness of Solidarity and other movements for freedom in Eastern Europe. We have seen the leadership and sacrifice of church leaders in Central America who stand with the poor and suffering, who call for dialogue and reconciliation to replace repression and war. We cannot forget the scenes of people in the Philippines confronting guns and tanks with rosaries and flowers. Our call to peacemaking does not have the drama and dangers these peacemakers and so many others have faced. But each of us is called in our own way to work for peace with justice in our own families and communities, our nation and world.

As pastors, we especially seek to support lay men and women who are called to serve the cause of peace by breaking down barriers of alienation and creating bonds of friendship and love in their personal and family lives, in their daily commitments as members of our armed forces, diplomats, researchers, advocates, workers, scientists, and public officials. We also seek to encourage preachers, teachers, chaplains, and all believers to share the scriptural call to peace, the teachings of the Church, and the message of our pastoral. We urge all Catholics to join with us in finding ways to be true peacemakers as citizens of a powerful nation and shrinking world.

D. Concluding Word

In this anniversary statement, we have shared more challenges than answers, offered more pastoral reflections than policy prescriptions. This approach reflects our conviction that the most fundamental task is for our community of faith to understand and act on two fundamental ideas. The first is drawn from the beatitudes: "Blessed are the peacemakers, they will be called children of God." The second is the familiar call of Pope Paul VI: "If you want peace, work for justice." These two deceptively simple statements outline the key elements of our mission: To be a Christian is to be a peacemaker and to pursue peace is to work for justice.

The Challenge of Peace contributed to greater prayer, reflection, discussion, and action for peace on the part of many. We hope these anniversary reflections will help renew and revitalize discussion in the Catholic community and contribute to the dialogue in the broader community on the moral dimensions of foreign affairs. Our peacemaking vocation is not a passing priority, a cause for one decade, but an essential part of our mission to proclaim the Gospel and renew the earth. As followers of the Prince of Peace, we work for a world where the promise of the Apostle James is realized for all God's children:

---

46 Ibid., nos. 297-299; *Toward Peace in the Middle East*, p. 43.

The harvest of justice is sown in peace for those who cultivate peace.
James 3:18

About
the Authors

Dianne Bergant, CSA, is professor of Old Testament studies at Catholic Theological Union in Chicago. Having completed five years as the editor of *The Bible Today*, she continues to serve on its editorial board as well as that of *The Catholic Biblical Quarterly* and *Biblical Theology Bulletin*. She is currently working in the areas of biblical interpretation and biblical theology, particularly issues of peace, ecology, and feminism.

Cardinal Joseph Bernardin has been Archbishop of Chicago since 1982. He served as chairman of the bishops' committees that drafted the 1983 pastoral letter, *The Challenge of Peace: God's Promise and Our Response*, as well as the follow-up document, *A Report on The Challenge of Peace and Policy Developments 1983-1988*. He was a member of the subcommittee which drafted the bishops' 1993 statement on international affairs, *The Harvest of Justice Is Sown in Peace*.

James K. Bishop is currently vice president of the Congressional Human Rights Foundation. A foreign policy consultant and retired foreign service officer, he has served as ambassador to Niger (1979-1981), deputy assistant secretary of state for African affairs (1981-1987), ambassador to Liberia (1987-1990), and ambassador to Somalia (1990-1991). For two-and-a-half years preceding his July 1993, retirement he was principal deputy assistant secretary of state for human rights and humanitarian affairs. He has degrees from the College of the Holy Cross and Johns Hopkins University.

Zbigniew Brzezinski, former National Security advisor to President Jimmy Carter, is a counselor at the Center for Strategic and International Studies and professor of American foreign policy at the Paul Nitze School of Advanced International Studies, Johns Hopkins University, Washington, D.C.

Alvaro de Soto has been the senior political advisor to Mr. Boutros Boutros-Ghali, secretary-general of the United Nations, since February 1992. He has held the rank of assistant secretary-general since 1988 and has been a member of the secretary-general's executive office since 1982. His responsibilities at the United Nations have included representing the secretary-general at the Central American Peace Process and conducting the negotiations which culminated in the peace agreement in El Salvador in 1992. He is a career ambassador in the Peruvian diplomatic service.

Jean Bethke Elshtain is Centennial professor of political science and professor of philosophy at Vanderbilt University. She is the author of many books, including *Women and War*. She edited *Just War Theory* and coauthored, *But Was It Just? Reflections on the Morality of the Persian Gulf War*.

Rachel A. Epstein is a research assistant at the Brookings Institution's Foreign Policy Studies Program in Washington, D.C. She specializes in European security studies, German foreign and defense policy, nuclear security, and arms control. Ms. Epstein received her bachelor's degree in international relations at Stanford University in 1992.

Dr. Mary L. Heidkamp is director of the Campaign for Human Development for the Roman Catholic Archdiocese of Chicago. She has worked with her husband, Jim Lund, in diocesan social action offices since 1977. They have published *Moving Faith Into Action* (Paulist Press, 1990) and numerous articles on church-based social action. They have two children.

Theodore M. Hesburgh, CSC, president emeritus of the University of Notre Dame, served as president from 1952-1987. In addition to his career as an educator, his public service has included serving as chairman of the U.S. Commission on Civil Rights, the Select Commission on Immigration and Refugee Policy, the Rockefeller Foundation, and the Overseas Development Council. He also was ambassador to the 1979 UN Conference on Science and Technology for Development. His awards include the Medal of Freedom and more than 130 honorary degrees.

Kenneth R. Himes, OFM, is associate professor of moral theology at the Washington Theological Union. He holds a Ph.D. in religion and public policy from Duke University. One of the founding editors of *New Theology Review*, he is coauthor with his brother Michael of *Fullness of Faith, the Public Significance of Theology* (Paulist Press, 1993).

Catherine M. Kelleher is a senior fellow in foreign policy studies at the Brookings Institution. She formerly directed the Center for International Studies at the University of Maryland, taught at the National War College and the Graduate School of International Studies at the University of Denver. In addition, she was a staff member on the National Security Council in the Carter administration.

John Langan, SJ, is Rose Kennedy professor of Christian ethics at Georgetown University. He is the co-chair of the U.S. section of the Council on Christian Approaches to Defense and Disarmament. He co-edited *The Nuclear Dilemma and the Just-War Tradition* (1986) and *The American Search for Peace* (1991). His articles on the ethics of war and peace have appeared in *Commonweal, America, The Journal of Religious Ethics*, and *The Naval War College Review*.

David Little is a senior scholar in the Religion, Ethics, and Human Rights Program at the United States Institute of Peace. Formerly a professor of religious studies at the University of Virginia, Dr. Little has taught at Harvard and Yale Divinity Schools as well as a number of other colleges and universities. His most recent publications are *Human Rights and Conflict of Cultures: Freedom of Religion and Conscience in the West and Islam* (with John Kelsay and Abdulaziz Sachedina), *Ukraine: The Legacy of Intolerance*, and *Sri Lanka: Invention of Enmity*.

George A. Lopez is director of the undergraduate concentration in peace studies at the Joan B. Kroc Institute of International Peace Studies at the University of Notre Dame. He has written extensively on human rights and peace issues, most recently editing (with Drew Christiansen, SJ) and contributing to *Morals and Might: Ethics and the Use of Force in Modern International Affairs* (Westview, 1994).

James R. Lund is director of the Office for the Ministry of Peace and Justice, Roman Catholic Archdiocese of Chicago. He has worked with his wife, Mary Heidkamp, in diocesan social action offices since 1977. They have published *Moving Faith Into Action* (Paulist Press, 1990) and numerous articles on church-based social action. They have two children.

Charles William Maynes is editor of *Foreign Policy*. He was assistant secretary of state for international organization affairs during the Carter administration. He has written widely on international affairs.

Marilyn McMorrow, RSCJ, is a religious of the Sacred Heart of Jesus and assistant professor of political science at Georgetown University. Her work focuses on normative theory of international relations and ethical issues in world politics. She is author of *Not by Bread Alone: Deprivation, Subsistence Rights, and Obligation in International Society* (Princeton University Press, forthcoming).

Richard B. Miller is associate professor in the department of religious studies at Indiana University. He has written *Interpretations of Conflict: Ethics, Pacifism, and the Just-War Tradition* and edited *War in the Twentieth Century: Sources in Theological Ethics*. He has also written several essays in social ethics and is presently completing a book on casuistry.

Edward Joseph Perkins is U.S. ambassador to Australia. In public service since 1962, he has been U.S. ambassador to the United Nations (1992-1993), director general of the foreign service and director of personnel (1989-1992), and U.S. ambassador to South Africa (1986-1989) and Liberia (1985-1986). He is a recipient of the Presidential Meritorious Service Award and the Presidential Distinguished Service Award.

Most Reverend Daniel P. Reilly has been the Roman Catholic Bishop of Norwich, Connecticut, since 1975 and is chairman of the International Policy Committee of the U.S. Catholic Conference. He chaired the subcommittee which drafted the bishops' 1993 statement on international affairs, *The Harvest of Justice Is Sown in Peace*. He served as chairman of Catholic Relief Services, the bishops' overseas aid and development agency, from 1978 to 1986.

Bruce Russett is Dean Acheson professor of international relations and chair of the political science department at Yale University. He has been editor of the *Journal of Conflict Resolution* since 1972, is past president of the International Studies Association and the Peace Science Society (International), and served as principal consultant to the USCC in writing *The Challenge of Peace*. Currently he and Paul Kennedy are staffing an independent international commission on the future of the United Nations.

George Weigel is president of the Ethics and Public Policy Center in Washington, D.C., and the author or editor of 14 books on religion and public life, including *Tranquillitas Ordinis: The Present Failure and Future Promise of American Catholic Thought on War and Peace* (Oxford, 1987), *Catholicism and the Renewal of American Democracy* (Paulist, 1989), and *The Final Revolution: The Resistance Church and the Collapse of Communism* (Oxford, 1992).

Charles K. Wilber is professor of economics at the University of Notre Dame, where he is also a fellow of the Joan B. Kroc Institute for International Peace Studies and the Kellogg Institute for International Studies. He has published over 50 articles and a number of books, including (with Kenneth Jameson) *Beyond Reaganomics: A Further Inquiry Into the Poverty of Economics* (University of Notre Dame Press, 1990). He has coedited, also with Jameson, *The Political Economy of Development and Underdevelopment*, 5th ed. (McGraw-Hill, 1992). He was a consultant to the Catholic bishops' committee which drafted the pastoral letter, *Economic Justice for All*.

Gordon C. Zahn is professor emeritus of sociology, University of Massachusetts. A Catholic conscientious objector during World War II, Dr. Zahn is a cofounder of Pax Christi, USA and the Center on Conscience and War, for which he served as national director. He has written nine books that include: *German Catholics and Hitler's Wars* (1962) and *In Solitary Witness: The Life and Death of Franz Jagerstatter* (1964).

About
the Editors

Drew Christiansen, SJ, is director of the Office of International Justice and Peace at the U.S. Catholic Conference. In addition to directing the office, he is responsible for the Middle East and staffed the subcommittee that drafted the bishops' statement, *The Harvest of Justice Is Sown in Peace*. He has written widely on issues of Christian social ethics and Catholic social teaching. Recent articles have addressed the moral dimensions of the environment, civil disobedience, and economic sanctions. He edited (with George Lopez) *Morals and Might: Ethics and the Use of Force in Modern International Affairs* (Westview, 1994). He has taught social ethics at the Jesuit School of Theology at Berkeley, the University of Notre Dame, and Santa Clara University.

Robert T. Hennemeyer, a retired foreign service officer, is a consultant to the State Department and the U.S. Catholic Conference (USCC). Ambassador Hennemeyer was director and a foreign policy advisor of the Office of International Justice and Peace of the USCC from 1986 to 1991. During his 34 years in the foreign service, he served as ambassador to The Gambia, consul general at Munich and Duesseldorf, and deputy assistant secretary of state for consular affairs.

Gerard F. Powers has been a foreign policy advisor for the U.S. Catholic Conference since 1987. He has worked on European affairs, arms control and disarmament, and the ethical dimensions of the use of force. Recent articles have examined the use of force in Central America and Iraq, the right to self-determination, and the ethics of economic sanctions. He staffed the subcommittee that drafted the bishops' statement, *The Harvest of Justice Is Sown in Peace*.

Index

Church approach to politics, 6. *See also Pacem in Terris*

John Paul II, 68; balancing act during visit to Lithuania, 102; demise of communism and, 5, 18, 307; on development and peace, 133-134, 145-146; on free economy, 67; on Gulf War, 283; on humanitarian intervention, 23, 227-228; on moral call to solidarity, 220; on peace, 24, 295; on reordering of values, relationships, and structures, 18; on role of Church and its bishops, 58; on sovereignty, 104; on universalism, 103; transformation in Church approach to politics, 5. *See also Centesimus Annus; Redemptor Hominis; Sollicitudo Rei Socialis*

Johnson, Albert R., 200, 201

Johnson, James Turner, 195

Just-war theory: casuistry of deterrence during Cold War, 202-204; casuistry of economic sanctions, 210-211, 213; casuistry of humanitarian intervention, 206-209, 212-213; challenges of multicultural world and, 195-197; development and application of, 189-191; functions of, 189; Gulf War and, 191-192, 194; *Harvest of Justice* and, 277-278; humanitarian intervention and, 225-226; principle of double effect, 192; principle of noncombatant immunity, 191-192; proportionality and, 118-121; refinement in post-Cold War era, 67-68; Vietnam War and, 194-195

Kant, Immanuel, 32, 106, 165

Keane, John, 100

Kegley, Charles W., Jr. 304

Kellogg Institute for International Studies, 270-271

Kennedy, John F., 88

Kenya, use of economic sanctions against, 81

Khrushchev, Nikita, 245

Kirkpatrick, Jeane J., 58

Kroc Institute of International Peace Studies, 269, 270, 271-273

Kroc, Joan, 271

Kuhn, Thomas, 201

Latin America: Church relationship with U.S. Church, 291; gap between rich and poor, 152; role of religion in peace process, 303

League of Nations: conflict resolution theory of Wilson, 165-166; establishment of, 162

Legislative advocacy, as pastoral response to *Challenge of Peace*, 294

Legitimate authority principle, 113, 282, 285; humanitarian intervention and, 22, 231-232

Less developed countries. *See* Third World

Lewers, Rev. William, 270

Lithuania, John Paul II visit to, 102

Lopez, George, 271

Low-intensity war, strategy and practice of, 179-181

Malawi, use of economic sanctions against, 81

Marginalization of world's population, 301; economic development and, 306-307; role of religion in countering, 303, 308-309

Martin Luther King Center, 166

Materialism, 138; balance with spiritual dimensions of life, 32-33; international moral authority and, 28, 35

Mauritania, use of economic sanctions against, 81

Media and setting of international agenda, 232

Moral values: foreign policy and, 21, 63; pluralism of, 308; political need for consensus on, 38-39; relevance to new world order, 21

Morgenthau, Hans, 62, 63, 115

Multiculturalism, just-war theory and, 195-197

Murray, Rev. John Courtney, 63-64

National Catholic Welfare Conference. *See* U.S. Catholic Conference

National Conference of Catholic Bishops (NCCB): global institutions and, 65-70; role of, 58, 68. *See also Challenge of Peace; Harvest of Justice;* U.S. Catholic bishops

National Endowment for Democracy, 64

"National interest," concept of, 62-64

Nationalism, 306; civic identity versus, 99; religion and, 88-89; destructive features of, 100-101; *Harvest of Justice* and, 279; modern notion and examples of, 86; renewal of, following suppression, 97-98, 101. *See also* Religious nationalism

Nation-state, 86, 98, 115; role in fostering global cooperation, 33-34; role of religion in, 88-89

NATO, 155, 168, 233, 250, 262

Nature. *See* Environment; Integrity of creation

NETWORK, 293-294